A
VertVolta Press
Rediscovery
Facsimile

CAPTAIN GEORGE VANCOUVER.
From the painting by Lemuel F. Abbott, in the National Portrait Gallery, London. Engraving made in England for this work.

VANCOUVER'S DISCOVERY OF PUGET SOUND

PORTRAITS AND BIOGRAPHIES OF THE MEN HONORED IN THE NAMING OF GEOGRAPHIC FEATURES OF NORTHWESTERN AMERICA

BY

EDMOND S. MEANY

PROFESSOR OF HISTORY, UNIVERSITY OF WASHINGTON
SECRETARY OF THE WASHINGTON UNIVERSITY
STATE HISTORICAL SOCIETY

Reprint Copyright © 2018 by VertVolta Press

All rights reserved. Published in the United States by VertVolta Press.

No part of this book's design may be reproduced in any manner whatsoever without prior written permission.

Cover design/facsimile formatting:
Vladimir Verano, VertVolta Design

First VertVolta Press reprint 2010
Revised edition, 2013, 2018

978-1-60944-126-5

'Vancouver's Discovery of Puget Sound' by Edmund S. Meany was originally published in New York, 1907.

VERTVOLTA PRESS
Seattle, Washington
www.vertvoltapress.com

To

MY ALMA MATER

THE UNIVERSITY OF WASHINGTON

THIS BOOK IS DEDICATED

PREFACE

THE sources for a work of this kind are not easily accessible. Part of them have been printed in journals and voyages, the books being long since out of print and rare; but by far the greater portion of the sources are in the public and private archives in England and Spain. To search these and to glean from them the information needed, to gather the portraits wanted from public and private collections, to verify obscure or disputed items, — these have been the hardest tasks. The kindest encouragement and the most faithful assistance have been received from far and near. The names of most of these helpers are mentioned here with this expression of sincere gratitude.

The late Mr. Frank George of Bristol freely volunteered to supervise the researches in England. Under his direction, Mr. Frederick V. James of 24 Belgrave Road, South Norwood, S.E., proved a most valuable and painstaking worker.

The Lords Commissioners of the Admiralty were exceedingly gracious in making available the vast store of documents in the Public Records Office and in other departments under their control. Equally kind were the Elder Brethren and the officers of Trinity House during the search for information about old Dungeness. The Director of Greenwich Hospital gave special permission to obtain a photograph of the monument to Lord Hood and others in the old cemetery. The officers of the Linnean Society in London gave their consent for a special photograph to be made of Archibald Menzies, the naturalist of Vancouver's expedition. Officers of the National Portrait Gallery also granted favors.

PREFACE

Many of the photographs used are copyrighted, the right being secured to use them in this work for England and America. These excellent photographs were made by Augustin Rischgitz, Linden Gardens, Bayswater, W.; Walker & Cockrell, 16 Clifford's Inn, London, E.C.; F. W. Reader, Aldenham Road, Watford; W. Heath & Co., 24 George Street, Plymouth; and H. Goulton-May, 11 Hill Rise, Richmond, S.W.

Professor J. K. Laughton, 9 Pepys Road, Wimbledon, the historian, whose fine work on the lives of naval men in the "Dictionary of National Biography" has been of immense help, gave some special attention to the effort to find information about Admiral Peter Puget. Rev. W. H. Oxley, Vicar of Petersham Parish, gleaned all that was possible to find about the burial place of Vancouver. W. H. K. Wright, Borough Librarian at Plymouth, assisted in tracing up the facts about Lieutenant Zachary Mudge. Stillwell & Sons, 42 Pall Mall, London, searched the old ledger accounts of Puget for some possible sidelight on his life.

In Spain the greatest help was rendered by Mr. Cesareo Fernandez Duro, Secretary of the Royal Academy of History, who responded nobly to the request for information about Bodega y Quadra.

In British Columbia Sir Henri Joly G. de Lotbiniere, former Lieutenant-Governor of the Province, encouraged the work and personally paid the Canadian customs duty on the monument at Nootka. R. E. Gosnell, former Secretary of the Bureau of Provincial Information, gave useful hints about the location and meaning of geographic names. Rev. Father A. J. Brabant of Hesquiat, Vancouver Island, freely contributed from his knowledge acquired during thirty years of missionary work among the Indians.

Professor George Davidson, the veteran geographer of the Pacific Coast, President of the Geographical Society of the Pacific, Professor of Geography in the University of California, and a member of many learned societies throughout the world, has been of great help through his book—

PREFACE

"Pacific Coast Pilot"—and through correspondence extending over many years.

Mr. Greene Kendrick of West Haven, Connecticut, while at work on the genealogy of the Kendrick family, found much of the forgotten or unknown history of Captain John Kendrick and his companion, Robert Gray. From this store he gave suggestions helpful in the general researches.

Mr. Orion O. Denny of Seattle defrayed the cost of the Nootka monument, and Mr. H. C. Coffman of Chehalis, Washington, formerly Librarian of the University of Washington, and Miss Mary Banks, of the Seattle Public Library, assisted in collecting and searching old records.

The officers and members of the Washington University State Historical Society have furthered the work by a manifestation of interest and encouragement.

Vancouver's journal was published in London in 1798, in three folio volumes and an atlas. The second edition appeared in 1801, in six octavo volumes and without the atlas. For convenience in handling, the second edition is used in this work. It is designed to follow the explorer from the time he strikes the shore of the present State of Washington, below Point Grenville, on into Puget Sound, and around Vancouver Island, and, finally, through the negotiations at Nootka. This requires the reproduction of Volume II from page 33 to page 385. The page numbering and dating will be retained in brackets to facilitate future citations or comparisons. The interpolation of the biographies and portraits will be arranged so as to quicken rather than to retard interest in the explorer's own narrative. The biographical interpolations are also set in smaller type to permit the original journal to be followed more readily than if the same type were used throughout. Three of the six steel engravings reproduced from the original journal were engraved by John Landseer, father of the famous artist, Sir Edwin Henry Landseer. All six of the engravings were drawn by W. Alexander from sketches made on the spot by members of the expedition.

PREFACE

In conclusion, I wish to thank the following citizens of Seattle whose friendly and generous aid has made possible this first edition: Thomas Burke, Will H. Parry, John H. McGraw, Edward C. Cheasty, J. M. Colman, J. E. Chilberg, Samuel Hill, Hervey Lindley, J. M. Frink, and H. E. Holmes.

EDMOND S. MEANY.

University of Washington, Seattle, U.S.A.,
January, 1907.

CONTENTS

CHAPTER I
Introduction 1

CHAPTER II
Biography of Captain George Vancouver, R.N. 7

CHAPTER III
Historic Nootka Sound 22

CHAPTER IV
Life of Don Juan Francisco de la Bodega y Quadra . . . 50

CHAPTER V
That part of Book II, Chapter III, of the Journal described as "See the Land of New Albion — Proceed along the Coast — Fall in with an American Vessel — Enter the supposed Straits of De Fuca — Anchored there" 61

CHAPTER VI
Chapter IV of the Journal: "Proceed up the Straits — Anchor under New Dungeness — Remarks on the Coast of New Albion — Arrive in Port Discovery — Transactions there — Boat Excursion — Quit Port Discovery — Astronomical and Nautical Observations" 77

CONTENTS

CHAPTER VII

Chapter V of the Journal: "Description of Port Discovery and the adjacent Country — Its Inhabitants — Method of depositing the Dead — Conjectures relative to the apparent Depopulation of the Country". 117

CHAPTER VIII

Chapter VI of the Journal: "Enter Admiralty Inlet — Visit an Indian Village — Account of several Boat Excursions — Proceed to another part of the Inlet — Take Possession of the Country" . 127

CHAPTER IX

Chapter VII of the Journal: "Quit Admiralty Inlet, and proceed to the Northward — Anchor in Birch Bay — Prosecute the Survey in the Boats — Meet two Spanish Vessels — Astronomical and Nautical Observations" 172

CHAPTER X

Chapter VIII of the Journal: "The Vessels continue their Route to the Northward — Anchor in Desolation Sound — The Boats dispatched on Surveying Parties — Discover a Passage to Sea — Quit Desolation Sound — Pass through Johnstone's Straits" . 212

CHAPTER XI

Chapter IX of the Journal: "Pass through Broughton's Archipelago, to pursue the Continental Shore — The Vessels get aground — Enter Fitzhugh's Sound — Reasons for quitting the Coast, and proceeding to Nootka" 259

CHAPTER XII

Chapter X of the Journal: "Passage from Fitzhugh's Sound to Nootka — Arrival in Friendly Cove — Transactions there, particularly those respecting the Cession of Nootka — Remarks on the Commerce of North-west America — Astronomical Observations" . 300

CONTENTS

APPENDIX

	PAGE
Muster Tables of the Sloop *Discovery* and the Armed Tender *Chatham*	335
INDEX	341

ILLUSTRATIONS

	FACING PAGE
Captain George Vancouver, from a painting by Lemuel F. Abbott, now in the National Portrait Gallery, London	*Frontispiece*
George Washington, from the painting by Gilbert Stuart	2
Vancouver's Grave at Petersham Churchyard	8
Monumental Tablet to Vancouver in Petersham Church, Surrey, England	14
Friendly Cove, reproduced from the steel engraving in Vancouver's journal	22
Nootka Monument at Meeting Place of Quadra and Vancouver, erected by the Washington University State Historical Society	55
Lord Grenville, from a painting by J. Hoppner, now in the National Portrait Gallery, London	64
Old Lighthouse at Dungeness, from a water-color drawing now in Trinity House	81
Remarkable Poles at Port Townsend, from the steel engraving in Vancouver's journal	85
The Marquis of Townshend, from a painting by Sir Joshua Reynolds, engraved by C. Turner	95
Peter Rainier, Admiral of the Blue	99
Lord Hood, from a painting by Lemuel F. Abbott, now in the National Portrait Gallery, London	109
Monument to Lord Hood and Other Naval Heroes in the Old Cemetery of Greenwich Hospital	113
Mount Rainier, from the steel engraving in Vancouver's journal	138
Admiral James Vashon, painted by George Watson and engraved in mezzotint by John Young	145
King George III, from a painting by Allan Ramsay, now in the National Portrait Gallery, London	167
Admiral Sir Alan Gardner, engraved by Fenner from a painting by Sir William Beechey	169

ILLUSTRATIONS

	FACING PAGE
Sir Harry Burrard Neale, from a mezzotint by C. Turner, after the painting by Matthew Brown	188
Admiral Earl Howe, from the painting by Henry Singleton, now in the National Portrait Gallery, London	193
Admiral Sir John Jervis, Earl of St. Vincent, from a painting by Sir William Beechey	202
John, Earl of Bute, from an engraving by Richard Purcell, after the painting by Allan Ramsay	223
Village of Friendly Indians, from the steel engraving in Vancouver's journal	224
Admiral Zachary Mudge, from the painting by John Opie, now owned by Arthur Mudge, Esq. Sidney, Plympton, Devon	226
Mudge Window in St. Andrew's Church, Plymouth, England	228
Baron Loughborough, from a painting by William Owen, now in the National Portrait Gallery, London	230
Earl of Hardwicke, from an engraving by W. Giller, after the painting by Sir Thomas Lawrence	238
Second Earl of Chatham, from a mezzotint by C. Turner, after the painting by John Hoppner	245
Lord Thurlow, from the painting by T. Phillips, now in the National Portrait Gallery, London	247
Cheslakee's Village, from the steel engraving in Vancouver's journal	252
Admiral John Knight, from an engraving by Ridley, after the painting by Smart	262
Grave of Captain William Robert Broughton, in the English Burial Ground at Leghorn, Italy	266
Sir Philip Stephens, from an engraving by J. Collyer, after the painting by Sir William Beechey	270
Sloop *Discovery* on the Rocks, from the steel engraving in Vancouver's journal	276
Queen Charlotte, from the painting by Allan Ramsay, now in the National Portrait Gallery, London	282
Penelope Pitt, Lady Rivers, from the portrait by R. Houston	292
Archibald Menzies, from the painting by Eddis, now in possession of the Linnean Society, London	295

MAPS AND CHARTS

FACING PAGE

Part of Meares's famous map, showing the supposed track of the sloop *Lady Washington* in 1789. From his "Voyages," published in London, 1790 32

Map of Quadra's Voyage of 1775, from "Miscellanies," by Daines Barrington, London, 1781 50

Vancouver's Chart of Puget Sound, from the original atlas, London, 1798 61

Chart of Dungeness, England, from the original, published in London, 1794 79

CHAPTER I

INTRODUCTION

THE white settlers first made their homes on the shores of Puget Sound, and these homes, in multiplying, spread along the shores northward and northwestward, carrying with them the name of Puget Sound. The same inclusive notion of the term is used in the title and scope of this book. In this expanded region of Puget Sound we find an abundance of English names scattered along the shores of the great inland sea. The reason for this is easily comprehended after a little reflection. The geographic names on the Atlantic seaboard were in use for more than a century before the war of the American Revolution was fought. Just as that war was beginning the first Spanish caravels crept northward from New Spain toward the fabled Straits of Anian. After the war was ended the wild coasts along the Pacific were a lure for the explorer and the fur trader. Voyages of this kind increased, breeding disputes over sovereignty, which culminated in Great Britain's geographic and diplomatic expedition of 1792. The commanding officer, Captain George Vancouver of the Royal Navy, was the friend and acquaintance of many men who had taken part for their country in the disputes and the war with the American colonies. It was perfectly natural that he should compliment those men as he discovered or rediscovered places that needed naming. An explorer of the same nationality, but of an earlier or a later period, would, of course, have given us a different set of names famous in British history.

The American who loves the history of his country is usually broad enough to love also the great achievements of his kin beyond the seas. He therefore not only tolerates but actually grows fond of such names as Hood, Howe, Rainier, Puget, and Vancouver, as applied to the geography of the northwest. With all this broad and liberal spirit there is another feeling that would cause the American to rejoice over the fact that the unconscious trend of history has erased from the map the name of the British King of 1792 and placed in its stead that of the American President of the same year. At the same time there is probably not one intelligent British subject of the present day who would complain over the geographic fact that Vancouver's New Georgia has become the American State of Washington. In fact, the British have themselves substituted for the name of Hanover, another compliment for George III, a name that is also one of the loved and much-used terms in American geography. They have changed New Hanover into British Columbia.

The geography of the Puget Sound region was probably not very familiar to the members of Congress in 1853, when the bill was up for creating the Territory of Columbia. A motion was warmly welcomed to change the name to the Territory of Washington, and thus was the name of the commander-in-chief of the Continental Army placed over a host of names of those who had been pitted against him on land and sea.

Besides honoring his King by calling the land New Georgia, Vancouver sought to further honor him by calling the whole inland sea he had explored by the name of the Gulf of Georgia. Part of that name still remains to designate the waterway between the southeastern end of Vancouver Island and the mainland. This curtailment is recognized by all mapmakers, British as well as American. In the process of restricting the geographic scope of the name of Gulf or Strait of Georgia the name of Washington again appeared, as is recorded in the "Pacific Coast Pilot," page 556, as follows, "The Canal de Haro and Rosario Strait were surveyed by the United States Coast Survey in 1853 and 1854, when the name of Washington Sound was applied to the whole archipelago between the mainland and Vancouver

GEORGE WASHINGTON.
From the painting by Gilbert Stuart.

Island." That name of Washington Sound appears on all United States government charts, but on ordinary American maps the region is designated as San Juan County of the State of Washington.

On the other hand, the United States Coast Survey added another English name to the chart in 1855. While surveying Port Discovery, which Vancouver had named after his ship, the Coast Survey discovered a mountain south of the bay, having an elevation of 2110 feet. It was named Mount Chatham, in honor of the armed tender accompanying the sloop *Discovery*.

In studying the biographies of the naval heroes honored by Vancouver, a landsman would be puzzled by the degrees and grades of admirals. Of the rank of admiral there are three degrees,—admiral, vice-admiral, and rear-admiral. Of these degrees, each formerly had three grades distinguished by red, white, and blue flags, the red being the highest. On the union of England and Scotland, the red flag was put aside and the union flag took its place. The red flag was revived in the general promotions and jollifications in November, 1805, after the victory off Trafalgar. By an order in council dated August 5, 1864, the three grades of red, white, and blue flag officers were abolished and the white flag was chosen as the sole emblem for a flag officer of the Royal Navy.

It is not necessary to discuss here the quality of Vancouver's work. That will appear in all its excellence during the perusal of the portion of his journal reproduced. However, it will not prove out of the way to say a few words about the general features of observation. The expedition was designed for the dual object of exploring and of transacting diplomatic work with the Spaniards at Nootka. For this reason the work in and around Puget Sound was hurried. Notwithstanding this haste the work was remarkably well done, and the maps are marvels for accuracy under all the circumstances. The observations of the soil, the climate, the trees, flowers, and birds are surprising when one remembers the newness of all to members of the party. Especially valuable and interesting are the recorded observations of the natives. Their houses, canoes, weapons, clothing, food, and language, all were commented upon in a way that will always prove of help to the student of these aboriginal peoples.

In pursuing this investigation a curious comment was discovered in the "Miscellanies" of Daines Barrington, published in London, 1781, where the author discusses the experience of Bodega y Quadra in 1775 with the natives in the vicinity of the present city of Sitka as follows: —

"This contempt for bugles, and other trifles, offered by the Spaniards is a further proof of the civilization of these Indians, whose progenitors, it should seem, must be rather looked for on the Asiatic, than Labradore coast, as I am informed that they have beards, which the Indians of the central and Eastern coast of N. America have not. It is said indeed by some, that these Indians eradicate their beard from its earliest appearance; but I can as little believe that this can be effected by any industry, as that they could by any art or pains make hair grow upon the palms of their hands."

This suggestion was made in the latter part of the eighteenth century, and in the dawn of the twentieth century we see the Jesup expedition of the American Museum of Natural History of New York carrying on an extensive investigation among the survivors of these very Indians to see if a possible Asiatic origin could be traced.

Although Vancouver did not generalize his observations among the Indians, he did generalize on the mountains he saw, and suggested that possibly the peaks he had seen were parts of a chain "in one barrier along the coast." He was exceedingly accurate as to the waterways, capes, and mountains, but he was not quick at detecting rivers. He denied the existence of both the Columbia and the Fraser rivers, though he passed near the mouth of each one of them. On the other hand, he had a clear appreciation of the timber resources of the region, and readers of his journal will find that, while anchored off Restoration Point, opposite the present city of Seattle, he uttered a remarkable prophecy about the future greatness of the country.

It has been erroneously asserted that Vancouver honored only English nabobs and British admirals in compiling his chart of the Puget Sound country. In the region covered by this work he bestowed a total of seventy-five names. Of these, forty-three were for people at home in England, but out of those forty-three, twenty were humble friends who have since disappeared from the records of the time. Nine of the names were for members of his own crews, who were participating in the work of discovery and exploration. The two ships account for two of the names, and one name— New Dungeness — was given because of its resemblance to Dungeness on the English Channel. Because he celebrated Restoration Day gave rise to Restoration Point, and because he took possession of the land for his King caused the christening of Possession Sound. This accounts for all but eighteen of the names, and these we find were given for natural objects or conditions like Protection Island, Birch Bay, Deception Pass, Strawberry Bay, Hazel Point, Foulweather Bluff, Cypress Island, and so on.

There is another false impression calling for a word of comment. It is often claimed that the Spaniards were browbeaten out of their northern possessions and, in the process, Vancouver was but a tool in the hands of the British government. To discuss the original dispute would be out of place here. It is enough to say that up to 1788 honors were about even between the two powers. Drake, Cook, Barclay, and others for England, had certainly equalled the work of Ferrelo, Perez, and Quadra for Spain. In 1788 Meares built a fort to protect his shipbuilders. The next year the Spaniards started a fort and were hasty enough to seize English ships and men, which led to their undoing as a power north of California. In the negotiations at Nootka, Vancouver proved himself a gentleman of tact, dignity, and refinement. No one was quicker to recognize and to warmly appreciate these qualities than Señor Quadra, the representative of Spain. Vancouver was evidently one of that intelligent, alert, well-disciplined class of men who would have succeeded in any walk of life.

VANCOUVER'S DISCOVERY

No effort has been made to gather statistics about the present condition of Puget Sound and its environs. Some such facts might prove entertaining to show the progress made since the times of these beginnings of recorded history, but the purpose of this work is to tell the story of the discoveries and to explain the meaning of the geographic names in use. Other works will record the deeds of the pioneers, who came to the wilderness and made their rude log-cabin homes, who toiled, suffered, triumphed and rejoiced, who saw the forests fall and the cities rise.

CHAPTER II

BIOGRAPHY OF VANCOUVER

GEORGE VANCOUVER is one of those characters whose lives are crowded with achievements, the record of which receives passing approval at the time, but the fame of which assumes enormous proportions in the years that follow death. His was a brief life, and yet his twoscore years rounded out one of the most honorable and useful careers in the annals of the sea.

To one who has lived on the shore of lands discovered and made known to the world by Vancouver, it is a matter of surprise, on beginning a research into his life and work, to find how very little is known of the man himself. His official record is scheduled with others in the archives at London; the rare volumes of his magnificent "Voyage" preserve the account of his greatest service to humanity; brief biographies in the encyclopædias keep his name from total oblivion. Through all these nothing is said of his family or his personality, the place of his birth is not mentioned, and even the exact date is unknown.

We know he had a brother, John Vancouver. This information is not gathered from the published histories, but from the dedication of Vancouver's "Voyage." The discoverer lived to complete his work and to read the proofs on all but the last few pages, when he died, and the dedication was written by the brother. That dedication is of sufficient importance to be reproduced here: —

"TO THE KING

"Sir,

"Your Majesty having been graciously pleased to permit my late brother Captain George Vancouver, to present to your Majesty the Narrative of his labours during the execution of your commands in the Pacific Ocean, I presume to hope, that, since it has pleased the Divine Providence to withdraw him from your Majesty's service, and from the society of his friends, before he could avail himself of that condescension, your Majesty will, with the same benignity, vouchsafe to accept it from my hands, in discharge of the melancholy duty which has devolved upon me by that unfortunate event.

"I cannot but indulge the hope that the following pages will prove to Your Majesty, that Captain Vancouver was not undeserving the honour of the trust reposed in him; and that he has fulfilled the object of his commission from your Majesty with diligence and fidelity.

"Under the auspices of your Majesty, the late indefatigable Captain Cook had already shewn that a southern continent did not exist, and had ascertained the important fact of the near approximation of the northern shores of Asia to those of America. To those great discoveries the exertions of Captain Vancouver will, I trust, be found to have added the complete certainty, that, within the limits of his researches on the continental shore of North-west America, no internal sea, or other navigable communication whatever exists, uniting the Pacific and Atlantic oceans.

"I have the honor to be
"Sir,
"With the most profound respect,
"Your Majesty's
"Most faithful and devoted
"Subject and servant,
"JOHN VANCOUVER."

Besides showing that the discoverer had a brother, the above document shows that the explorations in the Pacific were counted of considerable importance in 1798.

George Vancouver was born about 1758. All the encyclopædias, apparently following the "Encyclopædia Britannica," make that assertion. His tombstone in Petersham Church-

VANCOUVER'S GRAVE.
From a photograph taken in Petersham churchyard.   Engraving made in England for this work.

yard says he died in the year 1798, aged forty. In a little pamphlet called St. Peters, Petersham, Parish Notes, printed at Richmond, Surrey, in 1886, appears a short sketch of Vancouver, giving his birth as in 1750. All biographies say he entered the navy at the age of thirteen and accompanied Cook on his second voyage (1772-1774), as well as the third voyage (1776-1779). If he was thirteen in 1772, his birth year would, of course, be 1759. In the Admiralty Registers, Public Record Office, London, is found the passing certificate of George Vancouver, "who by certificate appears to be more than twenty-three years of age, and find that he has gone to sea more than eight years." The date of this document is October 19, 1780, making the birth year 1757. This same document gives the "quality" of his first service on the sloop *Resolution* under Captain Cook as that of "able seaman." Granting that he was thirteen when he joined the crew of the *Resolution*, it was certainly a young age to be rated as an able seaman. However, youth prevailed on the sea in those days. Of the crews that sailed with Vancouver in 1791 but one had reached the age of forty and many were under twenty. The youngest was Thomas Heddington, a midshipman on the *Chatham*, aged fifteen. On the *Discovery* were Honorable Thomas Pitt and Honorable C. Stuart, each sixteen years of age and each rated as able seaman. So, all things considered, we must be content for the present with the statement that George Vancouver was born about the year 1758.

At what would now be considered the tender age of thirteen we find him launched upon his career as a sailor under the best master of that day, Captain James Cook. After that master's death, at the hands of the natives of the Sandwich Islands, Vancouver returned to London in October, 1780, passed his examination, and on December 9 of that year he received his commission as a lieutenant, serving first in the *Martin* sloop. From this sloop he was moved into the *Fame*, one of the sloops that sailed with Rodney for the West Indies in December, 1781. There Vancouver took part in the battle of April 12, 1782. The *Fame* returned to England in the summer of 1783, and in 1784 Vancouver was appointed to the *Europa*.

In 1786 the *Europa* went to Jamaica with Commodore Alan Gardner, on whom Vancouver later conferred a great honor. In September, 1789, Vancouver was paid off the *Europa*, and at Gardner's suggestion he was appointed to go out with Captain Henry Roberts as second in command of an expedition into the southern Pacific where Cook had gained so much fame. This arrangement pleased Vancouver greatly, who at once plunged into the work of fitting out a sloop just bought by the government and named the *Discovery*. This work was nearly completed when all England was startled by the famous memorial filed with Parliament by Captain John Meares. The English flag had been violated, English territory seized, English ships made prizes and their crews prisoners by Spaniards at Nootka on the northwest coast of America. This was no time for a peaceful voyage of exploration into the South Sea. Great Britain gathered the greatest fleet of war vessels known in history up to that date. It was known as "the Spanish Armament." The men and officers intended for the *Discovery* were distributed to other vessels. Captain Henry Roberts was sent to the West Indies. Vancouver was assigned to the *Courageux*, commanded by Sir Alan Gardner. George Washington had just been inducted into office as the first President of the United States when this trouble began, and it looked for a time as if the new Republic would be forced to take sides in the impending war between Spain and Great Britain. Spain insisted that she was entitled to aid from America because of the assistance she rendered during the American War for Independence. Great Britain asserted the right to march armed troops through her former colonies in order to strike Spain in Louisiana. President Washington took his stand upon a position of neutrality, which is now counted the real beginning of the later Monroe Doctrine in American history.

On the show of such warlike force by Great Britain, Spain yielded, and on October 28, 1790, signed at Madrid what is known as the Nootka Convention. Captain Roberts was still in the West Indies, but when the *Courageux* was paid off, Vancouver was promoted on December 15, 1790, to the rank of Commander, and was selected to command the *Discovery* on her peaceful expedition to the Pacific. There was now an added reason for this voyage.

How Vancouver succeeded Captain Roberts as chief of the expedition is best told in his own words: "Toward the end of April the *Discovery* was, in most respects, in a condition to proceed down the river, when intelligence was received that the Spaniards had committed depredations on different branches of the British Commerce on the coast of Northwest America, and that they had seized on the English vessels and factories in Nootka Sound. This intelligence gave rise to disputes between the courts of London and Madrid, which wore the threatening appearance of being terminated by no other means than those of reprisal. In consequence of this an armament took place, and the further pacific equipment of the *Discovery* was suspended; her stores and provisions were returned to the respective offices, and her officers and men were engaged in more active service. On this occasion I resumed my profession under my highly esteemed friend, Sir Alan Gardner [for whom he subsequently named Port Gardner, on whose shores stands the city of Everett], then captain of the *Courageux*, where I remained until the 17th of November following, when I was ordered to repair to town for the purpose of attending to the commands of the board of admiralty.

"The uncommon celerity and unparalleled dispatch which attended the equipment of one of the noblest fleets that Great Britain ever saw, had probably its due influence upon the court at Madrid, for, in the Spanish convention, which was consequent on that armament, restitution was offered to this country for the captures and aggressions made by the subjects of his Catholic Majesty; together with an acknowledgment of an equal right with Spain to the exercise and prosecution of all commercial undertakings in those seas, reputed before to belong only to the Spanish crown. The extensive branches of the fisheries, and the fur trade to China, being considered as objects of very material importance to this country, it was deemed expedient that an officer should be sent to Nootka to receive back in form a restitution of the territories on which the Spaniards had seized, and also to make an accurate survey of the coast, from the 30th degree of north latitude northwestward toward Cook's river; and further, to obtain every possible information that could be collected respecting the natural and political state of that country.

"The outline of this intended expedition was communicated to me, and I had the honor of being appointed to the command of it."

Vancouver's instructions from the "Commissioners for executing the office of Lord High Admiral of Great Britain and Ireland" are dated March 8, 1791. They are signed by Chatham, Hopkins, Hood, and Townshend, and countersigned by Ph. Stephens, evidently as secretary. By this document he was ordered to proceed to Nootka and receive from a representative Spain would send there "the buildings and tracts of land, situated on the north-west coast above mentioned, or on islands adjacent thereto, of which the subjects of his Britannic Majesty were dispossessed about the month of April, 1789, by a Spanish officer." Besides the *Discovery* with a complement of one hundred men, Vancouver was to have the armed tender *Chatham* with a complement of forty-five men. The latter was to be commanded by Lieutenant William Robert Broughton.

Being allowed to choose his own route, Vancouver decided on first visiting the places partly known to him through his voyages with Cook. He therefore rounded the Cape of Good Hope and began his explorations on the southwest coast of Australia, then known as New Holland. He discovered and named King George the Third's Sound, Cape Hood, Mount Gardner, and other points, and then steered for New Zealand. He had visited Dusky Bay with Cook, and remembered that that captain had left part of it unexplored and called it "No Body Knows What." Vancouver made for this place at once, and on Monday, November 14,

1791, he makes this entry, "The heads of these arms, in conformity with Captain Cook's name of their entrance, I have called 'Some Body Knows What.'"

On leaving New Zealand, Lieutenant Broughton took a different course, and in doing so he discovered Chatham Island, which he named after his vessel. The two commanders met at the Sandwich Islands, where they wintered. Here they left the native Towereroo, who had been carried to England and was being sent home by this expedition.

The instructions of March 8, 1791, included, besides the proposed transactions at Nootka, orders to survey the western coast of America from 30° northward. On Friday, March 16, 1792, Vancouver left the Sandwich Islands for the coast of America, and on Tuesday, April 17, he saw the coast of what was then known to British sailors as New Albion. Proceeding along the coast from 39° toward the north, they approached the entrance of the strait of Juan de Fuca. This part of the story is told by the explorer himself in the reproduced portion of his journal.

Failing to arrive at a satisfactory agreement with the representative of Spain at Nootka, Vancouver sent home for further instructions. He then devoted himself to the work of exploration, going as far north along the Alaskan coast as Cook Inlet, which he carefully examined. He was scrupulously magnanimous and generous and always recognized the geographic names bestowed by his predecessors of any nation whatsoever. It is undoubtedly true that he would have preserved many Indian names of places if he could have learned them. Besides the difficulty of the language, subsequent investigators have found that Indians rarely have fixed or permanent names for places.

After spending the summers of 1793 and 1794 in this valuable work, making charts that were successfully used by navigators for nearly a century afterward, Vancouver sailed for home, rounding Cape Horn, and passing St. Helena. Off the Cape Verde Islands he fell in with the *Sceptre* and the St. Helena convoy and was by them conducted home in safety. This was fortunate, because Great Britain and France were

VANCOUVER'S DISCOVERY

at war, and the French Directory had not issued the usual orders to respect ships engaged in scientific work. The *Discovery* arrived home on October 20, 1795.

Vancouver had spent his winters at the Sandwich Islands. He was greatly interested in those people and received from them a cession of the sovereignty of the islands for Great Britain, but this cession was never followed up by the British government. Rev. Herbert H. Gowen, now of Seattle, was a missionary in those islands about twenty years ago. He learned that the natives loathed the memory of Cook, claiming that he and his sailors brought a disease there which developed into leprosy. On the other hand, those natives loved the memory of Vancouver.

While at work on the coast of Alaska, Vancouver had been advanced to post rank on August 28, 1794. Upon his arrival home he gave himself wholly to the work of preparing his journal for publication, but before this was done, on May 10, 1798, he died. His life was evidently shortened by the hardships endured on his great expedition. He never spared himself, and was frequently exposed to rough weather in open boats, short of food, and roughing it like the hardiest of his men.

Some of the geographic names that he bestowed, like Point Mary and Point Sarah, would possibly hint at a sweetheart at home in England. Still, Vancouver died unmarried.

While Vancouver thus died early with the rank of captain, several of his lieutenants lived to be promoted to the high rank of admiral. It is probably quite true, however, that such names as Admiral Rainier, Admiral Hood, Admiral Gardner, Admiral Peter Puget, and others would be much less known to the world at large to-day if it had not been for the honors generously conferred upon them by Captain Vancouver.

Among the colorless biographies of Vancouver heretofore published there is found one relieving flash in that of the "Dictionary of National Biography" as follows: "It has been said, and recorded by Sir Joseph Banks, on what he considered sufficient evidence, that Vancouver's discipline during

MONUMENTAL TABLET TO VANCOUVER.
Photographed in Petersham Church, Surrey, and engraving made in England for this work.

his voyage was harsh in the extreme; and Lord Camelford — whom he flogged three times, put in the bilboes, and finally discharged to the shore — bitterly resented the treatment."

Here is a little of warm human interest that is wholly absent from the other sketches. It is interesting and important to follow up the clew. In the first place the published account of the "Voyage" reveals the fact that splendid discipline was maintained. All of the principal officers and even some of the petty officers were signally honored by the Captain. Promotions were made on every suitable occasion, and the whole work went on with but very few mentions of any punishments dealt out to the men. They often landed and brewed "excellent spruce beer." They were given double allowances on special days. They answered Spanish cheers with stout British ones. The account is a daily chronicle, and yet all evidence of harshness in discipline is avoided in those pages.

However, evidence of severe discipline is not entirely wanting. In the Public Record Office at London, among the Admiralty Records, are present the logs of both vessels. These were kept by different officers and make a bulky record in unpublished manuscripts.

From the log kept by John Stewart, who shipped as an able seaman, are taken the following entries: —

"March 10, 1791, Punished John Laithwood and Sam Manning (S) for drunkenness.

"April 14. Upon opening a cask of cheese found one to be rotten and unwholesome, threw it overboard.

"April 18. This day we began to serve sourgrout and portable soup to the ship's company.

"April 29. Punished Francis Griffin with 1 doz. lashes for neglect of duty.

"May 19. Punished John Simpson (M) with 2 dozen lashes for quarreling and insolence to his superior officer.

"May 22. Punished Thomas Spears (S) with 1 dozen lashes for contempt to his superior officer.

"May 26. Punished Thos. Glaspole (M) with 24 lashes for theft.

"June 24. Punished Walter Dillon with 3 dozen lashes for drunkenness.

"June 25. Punished Walter Dillon with 2 dozen lashes for being accessory to breaking into hold and stealing liquor, the rest not being found out.

"June 27. Punished Wm. Bailey and Jno. Carter same for similar theft.

"June 21, 1795. At 5 Richard Jones (S) fell overboard from ye main chains, hove the ship to and threw a grating to his assistance but finding it impracticable to send a boat to his assistance, bore up again and made sail."

These random quotations from a document written during the voyage would seem to justify the position taken by Sir Joseph Banks as to the harshness of discipline. It should be held in mind, however, that the flogging of seamen was the rule of discipline in that day, the captain was thrown wholly upon his own responsibility so far from headquarters, and the offences of theft, drunkenness, and insubordination called for severity.

The case of Lord Camelford deserves more extended notice. Any one who will study the life of that pampered child and quick-tempered man will come to the conclusion that he surely deserved any punishment that Vancouver may have authorized or caused to be inflicted. We have already seen that the Honorable Thomas Pitt was shipped on the *Discovery* as an able seaman at the age of sixteen. The fact that he was thus favorably shipped and the prefix "Honorable" put upon the muster book shows that he had been accustomed to some pampering. He was the son of Thomas Pitt, the first Lord Camelford, and was born at Boconnoc, Cornwall, on February 19, 1775. His early years were spent in Switzerland and later at the Charterhouse. In the autumn of 1781, while he was under seven years of age, his name was borne on the books of the *Tobago*, but he probably entered the navy regularly in September, 1789, when he was fourteen. The lad was certainly not without bravery. He was on the old ship *Guardian*, carrying stores to New South Wales, when she struck an ice field near the Cape of Good Hope. She was deserted by most of the crew, but young Pitt was one of the few who staid by the ship and brought her into Table Bay. In March, 1791, he joined Vancouver in the *Discovery*. Of course Commander Vancouver knew of Pitt's family standing, but he had no way of learning on the wild coast of Alaska that Lord Camelford had died on June 19, 1793, and that his troublesome seaman was from that date a member of the British House of Lords. Troubles evidently culminated on shipboard, for on February 7, 1794, his Lordship was discharged on the shore of Hawaii. He found his way to Malacca, entered the *Resistance* as an able seaman on December 8, 1794, three weeks later he was appointed acting lieutenant, but on November 24, 1795, was summarily discharged and left to find his own way home. He took passage in the *Union*, which was cast away on the coast of Ceylon. In September, 1796, he joined the *Tisiphone* in the North Sea, was moved to the *London* of the Channel Fleet, and on April 5, 1797, he passed his examination.

He remembered his troubles with Vancouver, and both being in London he challenged the Captain to fight a duel. Vancouver expressed his willingness to go out if any flag officer to whom the case should be submitted would decide that he owed Camelford satisfaction. Camelford refused this arrangement and meeting Vancouver on the street started to cane him, when he was prevented by onlookers.

Camelford was promoted to the rank of lieutenant on April 7, 1797, and saw service under Captain Russell on the Leeward Island station. He was appointed acting commander of the *Favorite* over the head of First Lieutenant Charles Peterson, who was his senior by two years. Peterson got himself transferred to the *Perdrix*, and these two ships were one day alone in the same port when the young commanders quarrelled over rank. Peterson drew up his men to resist, but Camelford walked up to him, snatched a pistol from an officer, and on Peterson's thrice refusing to obey his orders shot him dead in front of his own men. Camelford was acquitted by a court-martial trial probably because of the panic over mutinies at that time, and it was construed that

Peterson was in mutiny instead of Camelford, though that was certainly not true under strict military law.

Camelford was promoted by the Admiralty and in October, 1798, he was appointed to the *Charon* and resolved to obtain a set of French charts. From a prisoner of war he got a letter to Barras, but was suspected in France and arrested. He got his liberty, but the Admiralty disapproved his conduct and suspended him, when he indignantly demanded his name to be stricken from the list of commanders, which was done.

While living in London he became notorious. On May 17, 1799, he was fined £500 for knocking a man downstairs in a quarrel in a theatre. He refused to illuminate his house in Bond Street to celebrate the peace. He fought the mob with a bludgeon until he was injured, and the angry mob smashed the darkened windows.

His last quarrel was with his friend Best, who was reported to have made uncomplimentary remarks about Camelford to a lady. In the duel Camelford missed, but Best was a fine shot. Lord Camelford fell and died March 10, 1804.

Lord Camelford was unmarried. The title became extinct. In his will he desired that his body should be buried in Switzerland at a place dear to his childhood. War prevented the immediate compliance. The body was temporarily stored and afterward lost sight of entirely. One of the literary quips of that day was, "What has become of Lord Camelford's body?"

So, taking all things into account, it seems unfair to charge Vancouver with unjust or excessively harsh treatment of his men. The worst item found is in the Stewart log, where Richard Jones was allowed to drown with little effort made to save him. On this point, however, the Captain tells a different story in his published journal as follows: "About half past five o'clock on Sunday morning, Richard Jones, one of the seamen, unfortunately fell overboard from the main chains and was drowned. The accident had no sooner happened than a grating was thrown overboard, and the ship was instantly hove to, for the purpose of affording him every assistance; but this was to no effect, for the poor fellow sunk immediately, and was never more seen. By this melancholy event the service lost a very able seaman, and his comrades a good member of their society."

No description of Vancouver's personal appearance has been found, but the National Portrait Gallery at London has a fine painting of the Captain. The description in the catalogue, under No. 503, gives at least an idea of how Vancouver appeared to the artist. It is as follows: "Painted probably by Lemuel F. Abbott (1760–1803). A half length figure wearing dark blue suit with gilt buttons and a plain white neck cloth, seated towards the right. On a table to the right lies a volume inscribed 'Holy Bible.' In the background, arranged on 3 shelves, are books of voyages, inscribed Cook's, Anson's, Magellan and Drake. A red curtain is behind to the left. The terrestrial globe beside him shows the North Pacific Ocean, and a line across it is inscribed 'Cook's track.' Eyes dark yellow grey, fair complexion, smooth cheeks, red lips, double chin. Eyebrows broad, very dark, arched and remarkably short. Countenance rather youthful."

This portrait in dimensions is three feet, eight inches by two feet, nine inches. It was purchased by the Trustees of the National Portrait Gallery of Messrs. Christie, Manson & Woods, 8 King Street, St. James Square, London, on June 29, 1878. The price paid was £31 10s. The owner who sold it was Mr. T. Ford. The sale catalogue called it "Unknown Portrait of Vancouver the Navigator." After its purchase it was assigned to the artist Abbott. The portrait was evidently made soon after Vancouver's return from his famous voyage, for it was made the subject of a caricature that bears the date of October 1, 1796.

In the Register of Petersham Parish, Surrey, is the following entry: "Captain George Vancouver of the Royal Navy, Aged 40, of this parish, was buried May 18, 1798. Registered May 18, 1798, by Jas. Messenger, Clerk."

On the side of the Register, under date of December 17, 1892, W. H. Oxley, M.A., Vicar, makes this addition: "In a bricked grave, S.E. corner, head and foot stones. N.B.

VANCOUVER'S DISCOVERY

The head and foot stone over the brick grave in which the remains of Capt. George Vancouver lie were in my presence lifted, raised six inches and drawn six inches aside to the south. The consent of the Agent General of British Columbia and two church-wardens of this parish having been previously obtained in order to effect an improvement to the churchyard and to place a rail to the Tollemache tomb."

Later the railing to the Tollemache tomb was removed on the death of Mina, Marchioness of Aylesbury, and was replaced by a low curb.

Vicar Oxley has been greatly interested in the history of Vancouver. He has gleaned every possible shred of information at the place of the explorer's burial. He says: "Vancouver came as a traveller to the Star and Garter, Richmond, which is in Petersham parish, stayed a fortnight there and died. On entering the Brewer Room in the old Star and Garter, Richmond Hill, in 1798, Vancouver declared: 'In all my travels I never clept eyes on a more beautiful spot than this! Here would I live and here would I die.' There are of course no records about here which in any way relate to Vancouver. His words were given to me by the daughter of the landlady and landlord of Star and Garter who heard them, and I took them down at her mouth."

The Vicar continues, "Some British Columbians had an idea of erecting a suitable monument a few years since, but it fell through and I tried hard for a new church and wrote the brochure to create interest."

The little brochure mentioned is a loving tribute in verse by Mr. Oxley to the beauties of Petersham Hill. The following stanza deserves a place here:—

> " Here Courtiers, Statesmen, Cavaliers,
> The Penns, Vancouver, Berrys, Peers,
> And peasants, long since dead —
> With Indians from some far-off shore,
> Proud Lauderdale, and many more,
> Rest in their quiet bed."

The Public Librarian of Richmond sends the following quotation from E. B. Chancellor's "History and Antiquities of Richmond": "... beneath it is the most interesting memorial in the Church, that of Captain Vancouver, who lived at Petersham in the latter years of his adventurous life. The plain marble slab has this inscription on it:—

"'In the cemetery adjoining this Church were interred in the year 1798 the mortal remains of Captain George Vancouver, R.N., whose valuable and enterprising voyage of discovery to the North Pacific Ocean, and round the world, during twenty-five years of laborious survey, added greatly to the Geographical knowledge of his countrymen. To the memory of that celebrated Navigator, this monumental tablet is erected by the Hudson's Bay Company, March, 1841.'"

Besides these interesting memorials at his place of burial it is well known that his memory is preserved by his name being bestowed upon the large island around which he sailed in 1792 and also upon the metropolis of the Province of British Columbia and upon the oldest city in the State of Washington. Vancouver is a name that is sure to be remembered and honored along the western coast of America as long as the English language endures.

Professor George Davidson, now of the University of California, was for more than forty years engaged with the United States Coast and Geodetic Survey on the Pacific Coast. A few years ago, in a letter to the present writer, he said, "I have gone over every foot of the work done by Vancouver on this coast and I wish to say that he was a great big man."

This is a monument greater than the naming of an island, more enduring than an engraved slab of marble. The whole world will always honor Vancouver for his brilliant achievements in the science of geography.

CHAPTER III

HISTORIC NOOTKA SOUND

For a period of thirty-seven years, from 1774 to 1811, Nootka Sound was the best-known and most-frequented harbor on the Northwest Coast of America. The first date given is that of the harbor's discovery by the Spaniard, Juan Perez, and the second that of the founding of Astoria at the mouth of the Columbia River. During those years Nootka was filled with the romance of the sea, of the Spanish conquistador, of the explorer, and the British and American traders in furs. Savage life was dominant. Some white men were massacred and others enslaved. Nootka was certainly famous then; but, after the white slaves were rescued in 1806, the place dropped into practical oblivion, where it remained for just one complete century. In 1906 the Provincial government of British Columbia granted licenses and privileges to timbermen who are about to erect a steam sawmill in the famous harbor. Nootka will again begin to figure in the reports of commerce, not as the source of valuable sea-otter skins, but as the shipping point of the more serviceable cedar lumber.

In 1578 Drake sailed along the coasts of what he called Nova Albion, claiming to have reached as high as 48° north latitude. In 1741 Bering, at Mount St. Elias, discovered Alaska for the Russians. On the coast, between these points mentioned, Juan Perez was the pioneer. He was instructed to make no settlements, but to pick out good places for them. He was to sail as far north as 60° if possible, to take possession of the lands for Spain, and to plant bottles containing the evidence. He sailed from Monterey in the *Santiago* on June 11, 1774, and reached 51° 42' by July 15, when a junta

FRIENDLY COVE, NOOTKA SOUND.

From a steel engraving by Heath in Vancouver's Journal. Drawn by W. Alexander from a sketch on the spot by H. Humphries. The little cove on the right marked A, B, C, includes the territory offered by Spain to Great Britain in September, 1792.

decided to make port for water. In that vain search they reached 55°, gave to islands and capes some names that have since been supplanted by others, and then turned toward the south. On August 7 he made a landfall at 49° 35' and called the indication of a harbor there by the name of San Lorenzo. Later it was called San Lorenzo de Nutka, and in 1789 Estavano Martinez changed it to Santa Cruz de Nutka, but common usage made it simple Nootka. On proceeding south, on August 10, 1774, Perez saw in latitude 48° 10' a beautiful snow-white mountain, which he named Santa Rosalia. Fourteen years later it was rechristened by John Meares, the English captain, and from that time it has been known as Mount Olympus. Thus did Nootka enter the realm of recorded history.

In 1778 Captain Cook called the place King George's Sound, but the name did not hold, and in 1791 Vancouver gave the same King's name to a sound on the southwest coast of Australia.

In contemplating the history of Nootka it is somewhat difficult to understand why the Spaniards were so slow in exploring and occupying the lands north of Mexico. Their brilliant achievements fill the sixteenth century with a marvellous record of exploration, conquest, occupation, and national expansion. So far as the northern shores of America are concerned, the Spanish record is almost a blank for the seventeenth and the first three-quarters of the eighteenth century. Then there came a sudden awakening in the voyage of Perez and those that followed. Perhaps one explanation may be found in the curious notion that then prevailed to the effect that gold did not exist except in the tropics and adjacent lands. Vancouver grapples with this singular supineness of the Spaniards in the introduction to his journals. He overlooks the voyage of Perez and starts with the 1775 voyage of Quadra. His comment is as follows: —

"This apparent indifference in exploring new countries, ought not, however, to be attributed to a deficiency in skill, or to a want of spirit for enterprize, in the commander (Señor Quadra) of that expedition; because there is great reason to believe, that the extreme caution which has so long and so rigidly governed the court of Madrid, to prevent, as much as possible, not only their American, but likewise their Indian, establishments from being visited by any Europeans (unless they were subjects of the crown of Spain, and liable to a military tribunal), had greatly conspired, with other considerations of a political nature, to repress that desire of adding to the fund of geographical knowledge, which has so eminently distinguished this country. And hence it is not extraordinary, that the discovery of a north-western navigable communication between the Atlantic and the Pacific Oceans should not have been considered as an object much to be desired by the Spanish court. Since that expedition, however, the Spaniards seem to have considered their former national character as in some measure at stake; and they have certainly become more acquainted than they were with the extensive countries immediately adjoining to their immense empire in the new world; yet the measures that they adopted, in order to obtain that information, were executed in so defective a manner, that all the important questions to geography still remained undecided, and in the same state of uncertainty."

The western and northern shores were visited in 1775 and in 1779 by Spanish expeditions of which Bodega y Quadra was one of the officers in command. The work of exploration was then suspended on account of the American War for Independence into which Spain had been drawn as one of the enemies of Great Britain. During this lull, Russia began to occupy ports from which the Spaniards succeeded in dislodging them through diplomacy. In 1789 they proceeded to occupy and fortify the harbor of Nootka.

In the meantime British explorers and traders had visited Nootka. First and greatest of these was the famous Captain James Cook, during his third and last voyage in the Pacific. His secret instructions on this voyage cautioned him to be friendly with the natives, but with their consent to take possession of the soil in the name of England, and he was to receive a reward of £20,000 if he found the Northwest Passage. On March 7, 1778, he sighted the shores of Nova Albion and began to name the principal points. On March 22 he discovered and named Cape Flattery and then made this entry in his journal: —

"It is in this very latitude where we now were that geographers have placed the pretended Strait of Juan de Fuca. But we saw nothing like it; nor is there the least probability that ever any such thing existed."

The reason for this singular entry is quite clear. He was driven from his newly found cape by a gale and could not approach land for a week. When he did so, on March 29, he found himself in Hope Bay, Nootka Sound, and he concluded that there could be no extensive strait between the two points touched, a rather violent conclusion, to be sure, since there is a difference of more than one whole degree in the latitude of the two points.

Cook remained at Nootka for a month. One of the midshipmen in his crew was George Vancouver, who then got his first glimpse of the land where he was destined to achieve for himself undying fame. Among other things accomplished here was to gather as many as possible of the native words to be used in efforts to talk with other natives of the coast.

On April 26 Cook sailed for the north and made more discoveries, one of the greatest of which bears the name of Cook Inlet. He was a fair man and honest explorer, respecting the names given and work done by Spaniards, Russians, and others. He returned to winter at the islands he had discovered and named after the Earl of Sandwich. Some natives stole a boat. At the head of a few men, Cook sought to recover it, but was killed by the natives on February 14, 1779.

Cook's work pointed the way for the fur hunters. The first of these arrived at Nootka in August, 1785. This was James Hanna, an Englishman, who sailed from China in a brig of sixty tons. On this first voyage he got 560 sea-otter skins, which he sold in China for $20,500. His second voyage in 1786 was not nearly so successful. He named

Sea Otter Harbor, St. Patrick's Bay, Smith Inlet, and Fitzhugh Sound.

In 1786 John Meares made a voyage from China to Alaska, but little is known beyond the fact that the voyage was made and that his ship was called the *Nootka*. In June of this same year James Strange arrived at Nootka with two vessels: the *Captain Cook*, Lowrie, master; and the *Experiment*, Guise, master. He got six hundred otter skins and named Queen Charlotte Sound.

Nathaniel Portlock and George Dixon made their famous voyages along the coasts in 1786 and 1787, spending the winter at the Sandwich Islands. They had been companions of Cook and mingled science and commerce in their enterprise. They named many geographic features along the shores of Alaska and collected 2552 sea-otter skins, which they sold in China for $54,857.

Captain Barclay sailed in November, 1786, in the ship *Imperial Eagle*, from the Belgian port of Ostend, under the flag of the Austrian East India Company. He arrived in Nootka in June, 1787, and though he went no farther north, he secured eight hundred sea-otter skins during his voyage. At Nootka he found McKey, who had been left there the year before by Captain Strange. McKey, who had lived during the year with the natives, said he had learned from them that Nootka was really on a big island around which a boat could be sailed. This is the first intimation of the existence of what later became known as Vancouver Island. In July Barclay sailed southward and discovered Barclay Sound, which, with its long arm called Alberni Canal, is one of the best-known harbors of Vancouver Island. From Bamfield, at the mouth of this harbor, starts the Pacific Cable. Barclay also noted the Strait of Juan de Fuca, but did not attempt to enter or to name it. This captain was accompanied by his wife, who was the first civilized woman to see the Northwest Coast.

From fragments in other journals it is learned that Captain Duncan, in the ship *Princess Royal*, and Captain Colnett, in the ship *Prince of Wales*, were outfitted by the King

George's Sound Company, sailed from England in September, 1786, and arrived at Nootka in July, 1787. They traded along the Queen Charlotte Islands, and Duncan was the first to sail through the water separating those islands from the mainland. He wintered on the coast, returning to Nootka the next year.

John Meares is one of the most picturesque characters in the history of Nootka. A retired lieutenant of the British Navy, he sought his fortune in the fur trade of the Pacific. His first trip in 1786 has been mentioned. In 1787 a company of English merchants in India fitted out two ships: the *Felice Adventurer* of two hundred and thirty tons, in command of John Meares, and the *Iphigenia Nubiana* of two hundred tons, commanded by William Douglas. The latter was to coast southward from Alaska, while Meares was to go direct to Nootka. To avoid excessive port charges in China, and to evade the necessity of a license from the South Sea or the East India monopolies, Cavalho, a Portuguese, was made a nominal partner and through him the Governor of Macao was induced to furnish the ships with Portuguese flags, papers, and captains. If it should become necessary to use these, the real captains would appear as mere supercargoes. Only one occasion called for the use of those Portuguese colors at Nootka, which will be referred to later. Travelling under false or double colors is despised on land, but it is counted close kin to piracy on the sea. In the light of these conditions the following instructions to the captains of this expedition sound almost facetious:—

"Should you meet with any Russian, English or Spanish vessels, you will treat them with civility and friendship; and allow them, if authorized, to examine your papers, which will shew the object of your voyage:— But you must at the same time guard against surprize. Should they attempt to seize you, or even carry you out of your way, you will prevent it by every means in your power, and repel force by force. You will, on your arrival in the first port, protest before a proper officer such illegal procedure. Should you in such conflict have the superiority — you will then take possession of the vessel that attacked you, as also her cargo; and bring both, with the officers and crew, to China, that they may be condemned as legal prizes, and their crews punished as pirates."

Meares took as a passenger, Comekela, a sub-chief of Nootka, who was returning home, and likewise Tiana, a Hawaiian chieftain, took passage with Douglas. The *Felice* had a force of fifty men,—crew and artisans,—some of which were Chinese. This may be called the very first introduction of Chinese labor on the Pacific Coast of America, for Meares had come prepared to use these artisans in the construction of a sloop to be built for the fur trade. The great chief of the natives at Nootka was Maquinna, who is prominent through all the early history of the place and whose name is still revered by his people.

Meares arrived at Nootka on May 13, 1788. He at once bought from Chief Maquinna a small tract of land in what the English called Friendly Cove, at the mouth of Nootka Sound. The price he paid for the land was two pistols. On this ground he built a house for the workmen and stores, and promised, when through with it, to give the house to Maquinna. In front of the house he raised some breastworks on which was planted a small cannon. This was the first act of occupation on the Northwest Coast, but nothing appears in any of the transactions or records up to that time to indicate that it was intended for anything more than temporary protection. Just outside the fort the keel was laid and work was begun on the first vessel built on the Pacific Coast of America north of the Spanish ports in California and Mexico.

Leaving a crew to work on the schooner, Meares sailed southward on June 11. He spent two weeks at Clayoquot Sound, which he named Port Cox. He was very successful in the fur trade and was lavishly entertained by Chief Wicananish. He left Clayoquot on Saturday, June 28, and the next day in latitude 48° 39′ he found a great entrance and declared that he named it after the "original discoverer of Juan de Fuca." Ten years before Cook had denied the existence of this strait, and one year before Barclay had seen it but did not deign to give it a name.

Sailing across the mouth of the strait he was warmly welcomed by Chief "Tatootch." Exploring a little island there in a small boat he gave it the chief's name, and to this day it is called Tatoosh Island. Proceeding southward, on July 4, he saw a beautiful mountain in latitude 48° 10'. He either did not know that the Spanish Captain Perez had named it Santa Rosalia in 1774, or, knowing it, he did not care. He remembered his days at school, and declaring that the mountain was fit to be the home of the gods he called it Mount Olympus.

On July 5 he found a harbor which he called Shoalwater Bay, but which has since been renamed Willapa Harbor. On Sunday, July 6, he rounded a promontory at latitude 46° 10', hoping to find a river hinted at by the Spaniards. He was met by dashing breakers and rough weather. He called the bay Deception and the cape Disappointment. Sailing away he wrote in his journal, "We can now with safety assert that no such river as that of Saint Roc exists as laid down in the Spanish chart."

Arriving at Barclay Sound on July 11, he started into trading operations, while he sent Mr. Duffin with thirteen men in the long boat to explore the strait. At "Hostility Bay," Duffin and several of his men were wounded in a conflict with the natives; yet Meares later claimed in his famous memorial to Parliament that he had taken possession of the "Straits of John de Fuca" and had obtained from the native chiefs permission to erect houses and to carry on exclusive trade.

When Meares returned to Nootka on July 26 he found that his shipbuilders were prospering well and he started again for Clayoquot when the crew, headed by the boatswain, mutinied. Later all submitted but eight who refused to be ironed. They were turned loose among the natives, who promptly made slaves of them. Meares then sailed away on August 8, adding more values to his harvest of furs. On August 24 he returned to Nootka and was joined on August 27 by Captain Douglas with the *Iphigenia*. He had not been successful along the Alaskan coast, but now all hands bent every energy to finish the new schooner and to fit the *Felice* for her return to China. The exiled mutineers were received back except the boatswain who was confined to the house but later escaped.

On September 17 Meares received a peculiar shock. A vessel was approaching under a flag he did not recognize. He hastily called for the Portuguese colors and papers, and made ready to appear other than English. He sent a boat to meet the approaching stranger. His messenger returned with the reassuring news that all was well.

"That flag of white and red stripes, with the blue field and white stars, is the flag of the United States, the new nation on the Atlantic coast of America. The vessel is the *Lady Washington* and her master is Captain Robert Gray."

The Portuguese colors were hauled down and Captain Meares made ready to welcome the *Lady Washington* to Friendly Cove. Two days later Nootka witnessed a big event. The English and American captains and crews and the Chinese artisans joined in the cheering, while the wonder-struck natives looked on in amazement. The new schooner was successfully launched. She was christened the *Northwest America*, and was put in command of Robert Funter.

All the furs had been loaded into the *Felice*, and she now proceeded to take on a deck-load of spars, probably the first lumber shipped from this region. The spars were intended for the market in China. Meares sailed at once for China by way of the Sandwich Islands. Soon after he had gone Captain John Kendrick arrived in the *Columbia*. The two American captains decided to winter at Nootka, and so they gave aid to Douglas and Funter, who proposed to winter at the Sandwich Islands. They left on October 26 and by agreement with Meares they returned to Nootka on April 24, 1789, to begin the traffic in furs north of that harbor.

This was the crucial year of 1789. We have seen Estavano Martinez establishing his fort at Nookta to hold the place for Spain. Meares had abandoned his little fort after the schooner was launched. He had intended to come back in the *Felice* and join with his two companions in the fur trade. Instead of that he entered into a much larger scheme.

He formed a joint stock company with Mr. Etches, representing the King George's Sound Company. The *Felice* was sold, and the *Argonaut* was bought and put in command of Captain Colnett, and the *Princess Royal* was put in command of Captain Thomas Hudson. These captains were instructed to establish a permanent trading post to be called Fort Pitt. They were to carry materials for a small vessel of thirty tons, which they were to construct and launch as had been done with the *Northwest America*. Seventy Chinese were embarked as laborers and it later developed that the plan included a scheme to secure a Kanaka wife for each Chinese settler and thus would Nootka be populated. There was no need now for the double colors, for the King George's Sound Company had a license from the East India Company. The two ships sailed from China in April and May, 1789.

On April 29 Funter sailed from Nootka and obtained over two hundred sea-otter skins on Queen Charlotte Island, but in the meantime Douglas was having trouble. Martinez arrived at Nootka on May 6 and began to build his fort. He did not like the attitude of the English captain and at the end of the first week he seized his ship as a prize. Changing his mind he released the *Iphigenia* and sold Douglas needed supplies on the promise that he would go to the Sandwich Islands. Douglas gave an order on Cavalho for payment of the supplies received from Martinez and then sailed on June 2. Instead of going south he made a successful trip to the north and reached Macao in October with his furs. Martinez learned that Cavalho was bankrupt and so when Funter arrived at Nootka on June 9 the Spaniard seized the schooner to make good that draft from Douglas.

Captain Hudson arrived at Nootka on June 14 and took the company's furs from the seized schooner. He was treated well by the Spaniards and sailed on a trading cruise July 2. The next day Captain Colnett arrived in the *Argonaut*. He seems to have been a peppery individual. At any rate, he rubbed the Spanish fur the wrong way by declaring that he was going to take possession of the region and establish a permanent post. On July 4, the day after his arrival, his ship was seized and he and his crew were prisoners to the Spaniards. He not only brought trouble on himself, but he made it hot for Hudson who had been so nicely treated. When the latter arrived at Nootka on July 14, his vessel was promptly seized.

The ships as prizes and the crews as prisoners were sent to Mexico, or New Spain, arriving at San Blas on August 15 and 27. The Spanish authorities at San Blas appreciated the gravity of the situation much more keenly than had Martinez. They released the vessels after refitting them in good shape, and they released the men, paying each one wages for the time of detention at the rates prevailing for relative rank in the Spanish navy.

While this attempt at reparation seemed ample and fair to the Spaniards, it was far from sufficient in the eyes of the offended Englishmen. Captain Meares posted off to London in haste and filed with Parliament his famous memorial, dated April 30, 1790. He placed his damages at more than $653,433. He claimed the territory about Nootka by right of discovery and purchase from the natives. He also published a journal, which is one of the interesting and valuable documents of that period. In that journal he publishes a map showing Nootka was not on the mainland, but on a large island, and that the *Lady Washington* had sailed around it. Captain Robert Gray was known to have sailed out to Nootka in the *Lady Washington*. So Vancouver, having read the record given by Meares in London in 1790, was delighted to meet Gray off Cape Flattery in 1792, and was more delighted still to learn that he (Gray) had not sailed around the supposed island. When Vancouver later did sail around the island that now bears his name, he did so by cautiously feeling his way in small boats. It was to him a real discovery.

There is an unfortunate confusion in the history at this interesting point. It is true that Gray did not sail around the island, but it is also undoubtedly just as true that the *Lady Washington* may have made that important cruise. The confusion arises from the scant record of authentic nature preserved of the work done by the two pioneer American cap-

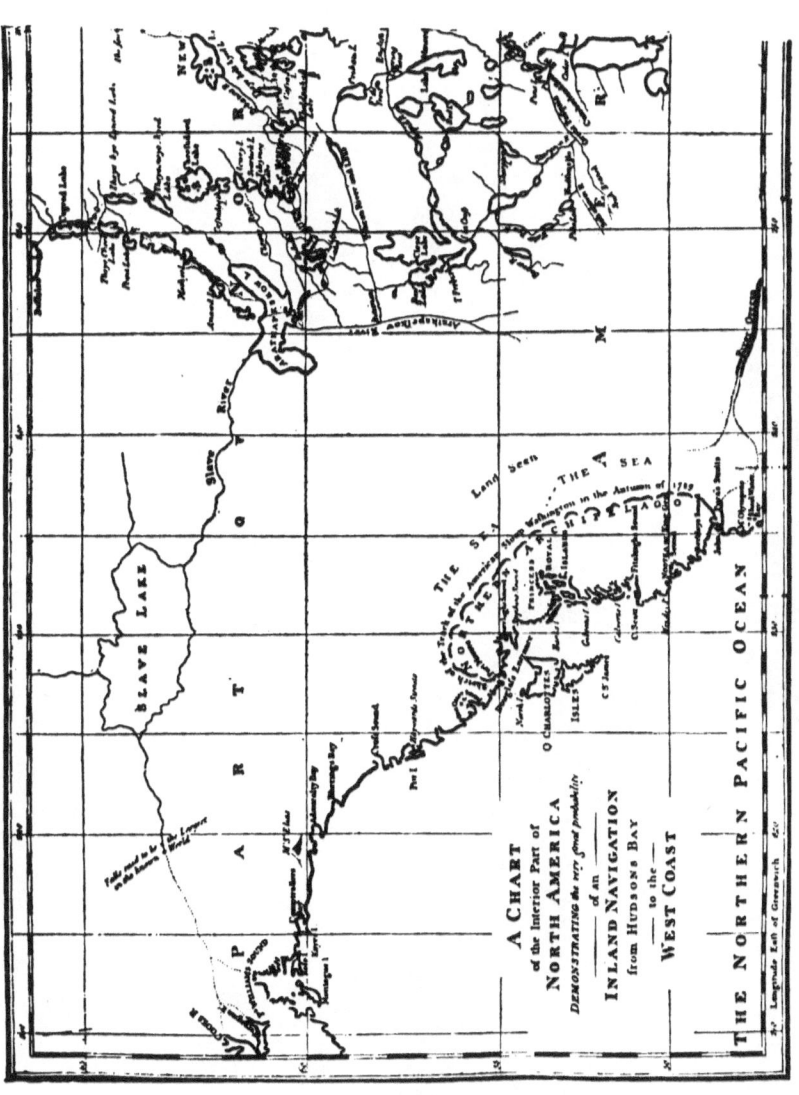

PART OF MEARES'S FAMOUS MAP.

From his "Voyages" published in London in 1790. Here is shown the supposed track of the sloop *Lady Washington* in 1789.

tains, — John Kendrick and Robert Gray. There are masses of documents and records during subsequent boundary disputes. Among these is a Congressional Report in the first session of the Thirty-second Congress of the United States. The heirs of Kendrick and Gray had memorialized Congress for relief on account of the public services rendered by those explorers. It is not the purpose or desire to exploit this phase of the history at this time. One item does need attention, however. All accounts lay great stress on the map and journal published by Meares in London in 1790. George Dixon criticised that map at the time, and Meares published an answer in which he claims that he got his information from a man who had talked with Captain Kendrick upon his arrival in China late in 1789. This shows that the map was constructed on information obtained by word of mouth from a second party, and probably accounts for the great inaccuracies of the map, if Kendrick actually did sail around the land. Kendrick was heard from on other points after this, but he laid no claim to this discovery, which, if true, would have been of far greater importance than the items he did report on.

While there may thus be some doubt about the American having made this discovery, there is none about the participation of these and other Americans in the early history of Nootka. We have seen their arrival in the harbor and their determination to winter there. On October 1, 1788, they celebrated the anniversary of their departure from Boston. The four captains — Douglas, Funter, Kendrick, and Gray — all dined on board the *Columbia*. Five days later the Englishmen departed for the Sandwich Islands, and the Americans were alone at Nootka. They had been outfitted by the Boston Company and had come to trade in furs. It is quite likely that it was hoped that the expedition would do some geographic work and would make for the new Republic some friends among the natives and thus give the United States a substantial footing in the new lands. At any rate, a medal was prepared for the Indians. On one side are the pictures of two ships and around the edge this legend: "*Columbia* and *Washington*. Commanded by J. Kendrick." Around the edge on the other side are the words: "Fitted at Boston N. America for the Pacific Ocean," and in the centre: "By J. Barrel, S. Brown, C. Bulfinch, J. Darby, C. Hatch, J. M. Pintard, 1787."

About the middle of March the fur trade was begun. Gray sailed southward, going into the Strait of Juan de Fuca probably as far as had been explored by Meares's boat the year before. He returned to Nootka on April 22 and sailed again, this time toward the north on May 3. He struck a new spot for trade on the shore of Queen Charlotte Island, where he obtained two hundred sea-otter skins, worth about $8000, for one old iron chisel. Captain Kendrick had also been successful in trade. This is the year in which Martinez brought matters to a crisis by seizing the English ships. The Americans were witnesses and later gave evidence in favor of the Spanish side in the dispute.

Captain Kendrick decided to exchange ships with Captain Gray and to send him home by way of China, where the catch of furs could be sold and a new cargo bought of teas, spices, and silks. The *Columbia* sailed about the middle of July, 1789, and arrived in Boston in August, 1790. In this way Captain Robert Gray was the first one to carry the Stars and Stripes around the globe. Governor Hancock gave a fine reception to the owners and officers of the *Columbia*. A procession marched up State Street, and in it marched Captain Gray arm in arm with Atloo, a Hawaiian chieftain who had taken passage with the *Columbia* to see the outside world.

The voyage was not a financial success, but the Boston Company reorganized a little and sent Gray back to Nootka. On this voyage he left Boston on September 28, 1790, and arrived at Clayoquot Sound, near Nootka, on June 5, 1791. He traded and explored to the northward, and in August he started south for winter quarters. Meeting storms he put back into Clayoquot, decided to winter there, built a house, and fortified it. On October 3, 1791, he laid the keel of a schooner, which was named the *Adventurer* and successfully launched on February 23, 1792. Gray promoted his mate, Robert Haswell, to be captain of the new boat.

In the meantime Captain Kendrick finished the year 1789, bringing up in China. He did not return to the American coast until 1791. On entering Nootka he was treated well by the Spaniards, but he was suspicious and sailed northward, where he experienced successful trade. He bought for himself and for the company large tracts of land, going to the trouble of making out deeds which the native chiefs signed with their marks. These deeds were saved and published during the later disputes. He sailed away for China and then practically disappears from our record.

Captain Gray reached the climax of his life during the year 1792. Haswell went north in the *Adventurer* when Gray went south. On April 29 he met Vancouver and told him he had found a river at 46° 10', but could not enter because of the breakers. He would try again. As he approached his river, on May 7, he found a fine bay which he named Bulfinch Harbor, after one of the owners of the *Columbia*. Later the name was changed to that of the discoverer and it is still known as Gray's Harbor. Four days after that important discovery he succeeded in passing over the bar and called the great river after the name of his ship. This discovery had most of all to do with giving the Americans a standing among the powers contending for sovereignty on the Pacific Coast.

During his trips into Gray's Harbor and the Columbia River, Gray had obtained seven hundred sea-otter skins and fifteen thousand other furs. Haswell had not been so successful, but between them they had made a good season's harvest. They sold the new schooner to the Spaniards and sailed for home.

Among the other Americans at Nootka was Captain Joseph Ingraham, who had been mate of the *Columbia* on her first voyage and was on the coast in 1791 and 1792 as master of the brig *Hope*. Captain James McGee was there in 1792. He also came from Boston. Captain R. D. Coolidge in the *Grace* had come from New York. He was an exception, as most of the Americans came from Boston — a fact that impressed the Indians in a way that will be referred to later.

After the rough experiences in 1789, Englishmen seem to

have avoided Nootka. Not so the Spaniards. While the government of old Spain was being menaced with a serious war by Great Britain, the government of New Spain was making strenuous efforts to rivet more securely its hold upon Nootka and the adjacent regions. Lieutenant Francisco Elisa, Lieutenant Salvador Fidalgo, and Ensign Manuel Quimper sailed from San Blas on February 3, 1790, in the ship *Concepcion*, the snow *San Carlos*, and the sloop *Princesa Real*. By April 7 all three had arrived at Nootka. They had brought supplies for a year and soldiers for the garrison. The mention of these soldiers brings to mind the discovery of the Alberni document. In 1899 Dr. J. P. Sweeney of Seattle obtained from one of his patients, David Ferguson, now of San Diego, California, a bundle of Spanish documents he had collected during a residence of thirty years in Mexico. Among them was one signed by Pedro de Alberni, in which he gives many strong reasons why he should be excused from going to Nootka, and incidentally mentions that his company has a branch garrison at Nootka, composed of two first corporals and eighteen soldiers. This document was dated January 1, 1793. It is quite likely, therefore, that the branch garrison was maintained at Nootka for at least three years. The fact that the Spaniards had a garrison at Nootka has never been disputed. If it had been, this old Alberni document would dispel all doubts. A translation of the first page of the document is as follows: —

"Free Company of Volunteers of Catalonia

"Relation of the force that constitutes the above-mentioned company on this day, at the present writing, the number short of completion, and the additions and diminutions that occurred during the expedition:

"Note

"That the number of officers is complete; sergeants, short, two seconds; corporals, short, one first and one second; according to the last regulations of the 17th of May, 1792.

"OTHER (NOTE)

"This company has a branch garrison in the establishment at Nootka (Nuca), composed of two first corporals and eighteen soldiers; others in the frigate *Aranzazu*, composed of one second corporal and eight soldiers; others in the brig *Activa*, composed of one corporal and eight soldiers; and two soldiers in Mexico in pursuit of their vacation.

"OTHER (NOTE)

"The one who was discharged is the second sergeant, Peter Guiterrez, who, upon the order of your excellency, passed into the department of San Blas.

"SICK IN THE COMPANY

"Officers, 1; sergeants, 1; drummers, 1; corporals, 1; soldiers, 5; and of these one is in Guadalajara, crippled; and four are in this garrison sick with fever; and the drummer is injured in the hand.

"Tepic, 1st of January, 1793.

"PEDRO DE ALBERNI."

Two years before the discovery and publication of this Alberni document, R. E. Gosnell published this paragraph in the Year Book of British Columbia for 1897: —

"Alberni Canal was named after a Spanish officer, Don Pedro Alberni, who was in command of a company of volunteer soldiers in the expedition to Nootka, under command of Lieutenant Elisa sailing from San Blas February 5, arriving at Nootka April 5, 1790."

If this statement be true, then it is evident from the document that Alberni did not remain with what he calls the branch garrison at Nootka.

Three days after the entire Elisa expedition reached Nootka, April 10, 1790, the Spaniards went through a formal act of taking possession. Fidalgo made a trip to the north and returned to San Blas. Quimper explored the Strait of

Juan de Fuca, giving many Spanish names to places which were later supplanted by English or Indian names. His Porto de la Bodega y Quadra became Port Discovery, his Santa Cruz became Dungeness, and his Nuñez Goana became Neah Bay. He sailed away to Monterey without returning to Nootka.

Elisa wintered at Nootka and in March the *San Carlos* arrived in command of Alfarez Ramon Antonio Saavedra y Guyraldo, with Juan Pantojo y Arriago as his piloto. They brought Elisa instructions to survey from Mount St. Elias to the Port of Trinidad. He took the *San Carlos*, and instead of starting north he surveyed Clayoquot Sound and then went around to what is now known as the Strait of Georgia. He gave that waterway this name, "Gran Canal de Nuestra Señora del Rosario la Marinera." Of this passage he wrote to the Viceroy as follows, "It appears that the oceanic passage so zealously sought by foreigners, if there is one, cannot be elsewhere than by this great channel." As a memento of his work we still have with us the name of Rosario Strait, though at a place removed on the map from its original location.

In the year 1792 Lieutenant Jacinto Caamano arrived at Nootka and explored around Queen Charlotte Island. Fidalgo also arrived and proceeded to build at Neah Bay a little fort which was never completed and was abandoned the same year. Dionisio Galliano and Cayetano Valdes were two men whom the scientist and explorer Malaspina loaned to Viceroy Gigedo. They arrived at Nootka in May and proceeded to explore the Gulf of Georgia. There they met Vancouver, who tells the story of mutual courtesies in the journal that follows.

The negotiations between Vancouver and Quadra at Nootka in the same year of 1792 is fully discussed in subsequent chapters.

On September 3, 1794, Vancouver visited Governor Alava, who retained his residence on board of the *Princesa*, which shows that the post at Nootka was not at all looked upon as a permanent settlement, especially as the governor continued his official residence on shipboard. Alava had not been given sufficient credentials to cede Nootka according to the demands of Vancouver, but such instructions were expected to arrive at any hour. They agreed to wait for such papers until October 15. They were disappointed in regard to the arrival of these papers, so both departed for Monterey. Vancouver arrived at the latter port on November 6. There were no despatches there for him. Possibly some might be at San Diego. Governor Arguello sent a courier for the letters, if there should be any there. This journey was fruitless, but Señor Alava stated to Vancouver that his government had notified him that Spain would not longer resist the British demands, but would settle the dispute practically on the same lines as those offered by Vancouver to Quadra in 1792. The Spaniard also stated that another English officer would receive the cession from the Spaniards. Vancouver construed this to mean that he was at liberty to quit the coast, and he lost no time in starting for home by way of Cape Horn, arriving in the Shannon on Sunday, September 13, 1795, the great expedition having consumed four and one-half years.

Vancouver had gone home, but his place was taken by Lieutenant Thomas Pierce of the marines. He and Alava sailed from Monterey on March 1, 1795, for the north. They arrived at Nootka on March 23. The ceremonies attending this meeting have been locked almost wholly in silence or mystery. Historians differ. One states that the Spanish flag and the British flag were hauled down simultaneously. Another claims that the British flag remained as the emblem of sovereignty in conformity with Vancouver's interpretation of the 1790 treaty. It is well established, however, that the Spanish fort was dismantled and the settlement was abandoned, and never again was a Spanish attempt made at settlement north of California.

The element of horrible tragedy entered into the history of Nootka in the year 1803. The Indians had known about white men for nearly thirty years at that time. Chief Maquinna had grow wise, as he thought, with his advancing years. He had been honored and flattered so often by the visiting strangers, and partly in consequence of that fact, and partly because of his own prowess the neighboring tribes of Indians held him in such high repute that he began to expect and demand the deference due a king. This was his attitude on March 12, 1803, when he clad himself in his royal robe, consisting of magnificent sea-otter skins, sprinkled his hair with swan's down, and stalked out on to the deck of the ship *Boston*. This was the finest and largest ship that had ever visited the Northwest Coast. She was owned by the Amorys of Boston and had gone to Hull, England, for a cargo of iron and copper implements suitable for the Indian trade. At that English port a blacksmith by the name of Jewitt persuaded Captain John Salter to take along his boy, John R. Jewitt, and give him a chance at the new business. The old blacksmith had figured out a beautiful dream of wealth for the family. They would convert all their worldly possessions into trinkets, send them with John out into the Pacific, where they would trade for furs, sell the furs in China, buy silks and teas which they would sell in England. A large profit at each turn would put the whole Jewitt family beyond want.

All this did not influence Captain Salter, but another thing did. Young Jewitt had been his father's helper and was himself a clever worker of iron. This quality would be useful and as it turned out this quality was also the means of saving this interesting history for the world. Young Jewitt was shipped on the *Boston* as armorer. A forge was rigged up for him between decks, and after he got over his attack of seasickness he busied himself making axes, knives, and spears for the Indian trade. This forge and this work were marvels to the Indians as they watched the young man making the things they prized so highly.

Captain Salter knew Maquinna was a great chief. If he had not known it, he could have guessed it from his manner. So he treated him well and gave him a beautiful fowling piece. The next day the chief returned, saying the gun was no good. The captain spoke gruffly and probably swore at the Indian's clumsiness. He then threw the gun to Jewitt the armorer for repairs. The rudeness was new to Maquinna. He grabbed his own throat with his hands and left the ship in haste. He planned a frightful revenge. On March 22 he asked the captain when he would sail. The captain said he would leave the next day, and then he accepted the chief's suggestion to send part of the crew to the Indian fishing grounds for salmon. This was Maquinna's hour. He and some of his men loitered listlessly about the deck. Others were paddling near in canoes.

Suddenly the chief gave his signal. He himself grappled with Captain Salter, whom he threw overboard. There in the water he was promptly killed by the Indians in the canoes. The other white men were overpowered and killed. Those at the fishing grounds were killed by Indians there. The head of each was severed from the body, and these twenty-five heads were then ranged in a ghastly row on the deck of the fine ship *Boston*, which had thus suddenly fallen into savage hands. While contemplating their awful work the Indians were startled by a cry from below. A prowler had found another white man still alive, and soon armorer Jewitt, wounded and scarcely able to stand, was dragged to the upper deck. Maquinna held up his hand. He took Jewitt, whom he knew as the maker of knives, and by signs made him understand that if he would be the chief's slave, he could live; if not, his head would be put over there with the others.

He chose slavery.

Then began the plundering of that rich cargo. Each Indian had guns, many guns, and blankets and cloth and beads and iron. They were rich and, of course, the chief's share made him richest of them all. The news spread. Other tribes visited Nootka, and they went away enriched with lavish presents. Four days after the tragedy two vessels, the *Mary* and the *Juno* of Boston, approached Nootka, but the Indians fired upon them and made such signs of hostility that they left.

Jewitt found that Maquinna had a son of whom he was passionately fond. The white man soon became the companion of this boy. Then there was an uproar in camp.

Another white man had been found in the *Boston*. Jewitt managed to save the fellow's life by claiming to be his son. He asked Maquinna if he loved his son. Then he declared he could make no knives if his father were killed. In this way John Thompson of Philadelphia, the sail maker, was saved. A few days afterward, while seeking more plunder in the hold of the ship with the aid of a pine torch, one of the Indians started a fire, and the *Boston* was destroyed. Jewitt and Thompson were in savage slavery, and now even their ship was gone. Jewitt got along very well. He was a prime favorite, but old Thompson was dreaded. He was a rough old tar, who was ready at any moment to quit and to sell his life as dearly as possible in a struggle with his owners. Jewitt's counsel prevailed.

Their lives at Nootka for nearly three years were filled with wonderful adventures. After their rescue Jewitt published the experiences in a frail little volume full to overflowing with valuable information about the Indians and their home. Maquinna became suspicious of the diary and put a stop to it. Then Jewitt kept notes on birch bark, using berry juices for ink. He had saved a portion of a Book of Common Prayer and, though Thompson was far from religious, he accompanied Jewitt each Sabbath in a little service on the banks of the small lake back of Friendly Cove. On other days they went to this pond to bathe and wash their blankets. Maquinna saw them and made them wash his blankets. While doing this they were taunted by young Indians. Old Thompson was furious. He drove them off. They returned and trampled the drying blankets with dirty feet. Thompson caught one, cut his head off, and carrying the head in one hand and the soiled blanket in the other reported to the chief, who approved the execution because the bad boy had walked on the chief's blanket. War with a neighboring tribe added to their excitement.

Maquinna had accumulated some furs. He desired more trade with white men. He had told Jewitt that when Salter talked bad to him his heart started to jump out of his mouth. Now he did not feel mad and would trade with the white men.

But he had no idea of giving up Jewitt. So as the *Lydia*, Captain Hill, of Boston, approached Nootka in July of 1805, Maquinna got Jewitt to write him a letter to the captain. This letter was dated at Nootka, July 19, 1805, and read as follows: —

"The bearer of this letter is the Indian king by the name of Maquinna. He was the instigator of the capture the ship *Boston*, of Boston, in North America, John Salter captain, and of the murder of twenty-five men of her crew, the two only survivors being now on shore — Wherefore I hope you will take care to confine him according to his merits, putting in your dead lights, and keeping so good a watch over him, that he cannot escape from you. By so doing we shall be able to obtain our release in the course of a few hours."

This was a serious matter for a slave to write such a letter about his master. Jewitt in his rare little book comments on it as follows: "I have been asked how I dared to write in this manner: my answer is, that from my long residence among these people, I knew that I had little to apprehend from their anger on hearing of their king being confined, while they knew his life depended upon my release, and that they would sooner have given up five hundred white men, than have had him injured." Jewitt translated the letter in a way that satisfied Maquinna, who went on board and was promptly put in chains. Then there was a terrific clamor on shore, but it all ended in the safe release of the white men, and the chief was given his liberty by Jewitt.

It has been seen that Maquinna was loved and obeyed by his people. He was undoubtedly the greatest chief on that coast. His descendants and successors in the chieftainship, while exercising much less power, have gloried in the name of Maquinna. Probably the one to approach him nearest in power was the chief who died at Nootka about five years ago. He was the great-grandson of the old and famous Maquinna. His body was secreted and then the people erected a gorgeous monument to his memory. It is a huge thunder bird in conflict with a whale. At the base are two sewing-machines, contributed by the squaws who shared in the great grief of the tribe. This figure is emblematic of the tradition that when it storms the thunder bird is in battle with the whale. At such times the Indians make great noise with drums to help the thunder bird, for when the whale is allowed to triumph the world will be destroyed in a great flood. This monument faces the sea from a point of rocks. Near this singular example of primitive art there had fallen to the ground a large white cross, on the arms of which had been painted this legend, "He made potlatch nine different times." To Coast Indians this is a superlative of greatness. Potlatch is a custom held in high esteem. A man accumulates property and then invites friends and relatives from far and near. To these he gives away his property. This makes him a great man, a sort of tyee. The late Maquinna was thus nine times as great as one of these ordinary great men. The potlatch is also a sort of economic institution, a sort of Indian savings bank, for when a man has made a potlatch he has an undisputed right to participate as a beneficiary in all other potlatches of that neighborhood.

Nootka is the birthplace of the Chinook jargon, that strange and unique "Esperanto" of the western Indians. The range of this jargon is from California to Mount St. Elias and from the Rocky Mountains to the Pacific. Take, for example, the name of Nootka itself. The harbor was named San Lorenzo by Perez in 1774. To this was soon added "de Nutka." Whence came this "de Nutka" remained a mystery until Rev. Father A. J. Brabant, a Belgian priest who has been a missionary among those people for more than thirty years, began to study the intricacies of the native language. He says that "Noot-ka-eh" is a native verb meaning "go around." It is now supposed that the first ship paused on the lee of an island, and when the Spaniards followed the motions of the friendly Indians, when they did "go around," they saw the little village in what was later called Friendly Cove and, jumping to the conclusion that "Nootka-eh" was the name of that village, they adopted it as the name of the harbor. As Nootka it has been known from that day to this.

The name by which these Indians themselves know their

village is "Mowitch-at," meaning "people of the deer." The reason is clear to one who visits their home. The forests literally abound in deer. That one village ships out thousands of deerskins every year. It is not possible to trace the origin of all the words in the jargon, but "Mowitch" means "deer," and it is shown that this came from the Nootka language. It is also found that many others came from the same tongue, such as "Klootchman," meaning "woman"; "tanass," little; "cam-mass," fruit; "klat-a-wah," go away; "makook," sell; "clah-how-yah," how do you do; "sie-yah," sky or far away; "wik," no. And one of the best examples of all is the word "tyee," meaning chief. Jewitt uses this word in addressing Chief Maquinna, and of course, Jewitt got his Indian words wholly from Nootka. Vancouver also uses the word in speaking of chiefs, and Vancouver relied upon his Nootkan words wherever he met Indians. Cook made a list of Indian words at Nootka in 1778. This list, with whatever additions he could have collected, is the one that Vancouver used in 1792. So "tyee" as a Chinook jargon word is clearly traced back to Nootka. When the Hudson Bay Company came, they added to and developed the jargon. In fact, they are usually credited with having invented it. The Canadian voyageurs added many French words. The jargon was really an evolution and began at Nootka through the necessities of the explorers and fur traders. It is not difficult to see how this happened. Nootka was the first harbor visited, and for many years was the only one known on the whole coast north of Monterey. The captains listed as many of the native words as they could, and these fell into the hands of other discoverers and fur traders, who repeated them far and wide in an effort to talk with other tribes and, of course, helped out with signs. Pointing to a deer they would say "mowitch," and thus many tribes learned what that word meant to the white men.

Nearly every vessel that came to Nootka under the Stars and Stripes came from Boston. The officers and men spoke the name of Boston frequently and with pride. Then came the destruction of the ship *Boston*, and Americans as they approached the coast asked far and near for news of the *Boston*. This taught the Indians to associate the Stars and Stripes with the name of Boston. That, also, was planted into the Chinook jargon in which language "Boston-man" means "American." In a similar way the Englishmen of that day were always talking about King George and what he could do for his friends, the Indians, and the Chinook jargon was enriched with the phrase "King George-man," meaning Englishman."

While pointing out the origin of the Chinook jargon at Nootka it may also be well to call attention to the fact that the name frequently occurs in disguised forms in scientific literature. The early explorers always collected specimens of the plants, birds, and animals. There are many fine evergreen trees in the botanical gardens of Europe grown from seeds collected on these shores by those first visitors. When the botanists or zoölogists found that the specimens were new to science, they would proceed to describe them as from Nootka, and so we find such Latinized names as Nutkana, Nutkanus, and Nutkaensis bestowed upon a large number of species.

Nootka, wild, romantic Nootka, deserted and neglected by white men for more than a century, though once the most frequented harbor on the Pacific Coast of America, what a lure is this Nootka to one who has searched for truths among the rare and scattered records! With a heart filled with enthusiasm the present writer visited the famous little harbor of Friendly Cove in the summer of 1903. Being secretary, he undertook, on behalf of the Washington University State Historical Society, to erect a monument of granite to mark the place where Vancouver and Quadra met in August of 1792. The cost of the monument was borne for the Society by the pioneer, Orion O. Denny, the first white boy born in Seattle. Canadian law offered an obstacle in the way of customs charges. This condition annoyed the genial and dignified governor, Sir Henri Joly G. de Lotbiniere, who asked the privilege of bearing the charges himself. Thomas Stockham was about to construct a little trading post at Friendly Cove and volunteered to help with his crew of three white men and one Indian to hoist the heavy granite to its place on the summit of a rocky islet in the mouth of the harbor. Here we placed the monument, with its inscription facing the sea, on August 23, 1903.

Vancouver was fortunate in having with him some artists of real merit. One was John Sykes, who was mustered in at the age of nineteen as a midshipman, though he was promoted to master's mate on February 1, 1791. The beautiful pictures engraved on steel for the illustrations of Vancouver's "Voyage" were drawn by Sykes, Mudge, and Humphries. The view of Friendly Cove was very useful during this visit over a century afterward. By it could be picked out the famous acre in dispute where Meares had built his schooner. On that spot was found a small Catholic chapel and Mission home, where Father Brabant lived when he visited the village of Indians once a year. On this same acre we camped while erecting the monument. With the same picture could be located the little Spanish fort, and exploration in that vicinity was rewarded by the finding of a number of the flat tile-like Spanish brick known to have been used in the foundations.

The scenes of Jewitt's experiences as one of Maquinna's slaves were visited, more especially the little lake where he and Thompson stole away for their rude religious services. The little Indian village had undergone many changes during the last century, but the lake shows that it has remained the same. The shores are clothed with forest and undergrowth. The path that leads from the village to the lake is worn deep in the gravel, evidence, probably, of several centuries of use. Herring spawn in this harbor by the millions. The Indians gather hemlock boughs and weight them down in the water with stones. When covered with eggs they are dried on specially built racks, and then the eggs are stored for winter use. Jewitt described the process accurately in 1803, and the same kind of racks were found there in 1903.

It would seem appropriate to add one more item of research. Washington Irving's charming book "Astoria" reaches a climax on this same west coast of Vancouver Island, when the ship *Tonquin* was blown up and Captain

Jonathan Thorn and his entire crew were lost. There has never been any doubt as to the loss of the ship and her crew; the how and the where have baffled all searchers up to the present time. Irving in his beautiful diction causes James Lewis the clerk to become prophetic on leaving the newly planted log fort at Astoria. Lewis tells his friends that he will meet a strange fate. The ship sailed away to trade with the Indians. Off Gray's Harbor an Indian called Lamanse was picked up and made a member of the party as guide and interpreter. Irving then causes the ship to anchor at Nootka in a harbor he calls Newetee. Captain Thorn neglected the strict orders of John Jacob Astor against allowing more than a very few Indians on deck at a time. In parting with his captain, Astor reiterated this caution by saying, "All accidents which have as yet happened there arose in too much confidence in the Indians."

Captain Thorn, reared in the old-fashioned navy, was a strict disciplinarian and had abundant confidence in his men and guns. The Indian chief was a haggler, and Thorn snatched his roll of furs and rubbed the chief's nose with it. He felt triumphant the next day when the Indians seemed ardent for trade. Each brave chose a knife for his pay, and as the captain finally listened to the warning of his men and gave orders to clear away, the Indian signal was given and the crew was promptly slaughtered. Five fell through an open hatch, and these put the Indians to flight by shooting through the hatchway. Four of the men sought safety by flight in an open boat during the night. Clerk Lewis remained on the ship. The next day the Indians, seeing but one man who made friendly signs, cautiously approached and before long the deck was crowded. Then Lewis fired the magazine, and a terrific explosion followed. Many Indians were killed, and the remnant of the village was in a ferment of rage. The four sailors, held in the harbor's edge by storms, were found, and the author says it would have been well for them had they shared the tragic fate of Lewis.

All having been destroyed, how did Irving learn these tragic details? It is known that Irving collected all of Astor's papers and many books, and that he got the rich fur trader so deeply interested that the fine Astor Library of New York is one of the results. One of the books most useful to Irving was that by Gabriel Franchere, one of the clerks at Astoria. This author secured his story of the *Tonquin* from Lamanse on his return to Gray's Harbor. This Indian guide was spared in the slaughter by his becoming a voluntary slave and later escaped to his own people. His scant record was amplified in "Astoria."

Since then the harbor of Newetee has been searched for by no less an authority than Professor George Davidson, of the United States Coast and Geodetic Survey, and now of the University of California. He could not locate it, nor has any one else been able to do so with certainty. Since the other details have depended upon the story of Lamanse, so now the location of the tragedy will depend upon the story of Teetska, or "Smiling Tom."

This Indian is a native of Clayoquot and later lived at Hesquiat, just south of Nootka Sound. He was still living there in 1903 and was then counted about sixty-five years of age. Hesquiat is the home of Father Brabant, the missionary already referred to, who settled there in the spring of 1874. Teetska's father was a slave at Clayoquot. About twenty years ago, this slave, after attaining the age of about eighty years, died and was buried by Father Brabant. Teetska became the friend of the missionary and moved to Hesquiat. Among other information Father Brabant received from Teetska was the tradition obtained from his father of the blowing up of a ship and the place was located at "Clayoquot-Tskwe." The tradition helps to locate the place by the floating of blankets to the shore from the wreck. Father Brabant thus locates the scene of the *Tonquin* tragedy at a place called "Itsape," or on the lee of Lennard Island, at the entrance of Clayoquot Sound.

In relating this tradition to the present writer in 1903, Father Brabant stated that Captain Walbran, formerly of the steamer *Quadra*, had also obtained the same account from an old Indian doctor.

CHAPTER IV

LIFE OF BODEGA Y QUADRA

On Tuesday, August 28, 1792, Vancouver says that he anchored in Friendly Cove, "where we found riding his Catholic Majesty's brig the *Active*, bearing the broad pendant of Señor Don Juan Francisco de la Bodega y Quadra, commandant of the marine establishment of St. Blas and California."

This is the greatest Spaniard of them all. It is extremely aggravating to find him wholly ignored in almost every one of the encyclopædias and other collections of biographies. The exact year of his birth is unknown, but is usually put at about 1740. He was born in Lima, Peru, and, though his parents were of noble blood, his birthplace was a handicap. It needs only to be remembered that offices and commands in the new world were given to those of Castilian birth to know how difficult it was for a native of Lima to climb to high station. That is likely the reason that Bruno Heceta was given chief command of the famous expedition of 1775. Quadra was second then, but he achieved so much in the sloop *Sonora*, a little boat only thirty-six feet long, twelve feet wide, and eight feet deep, that he was quickly honored and rapidly advanced. He proved his courage and ability on this and other occasions until 1792 he was selected for the unpleasant duty of going to Nootka, where he was to fulfil the terms of the Nootka Convention between Spain and Great Britain of October 28, 1790. He was to represent Spain, and at Nootka he would be met by a man authorized to represent Great Britain.

Vancouver and Quadra at once became strong personal friends, and enjoyed many visits with each other, but they

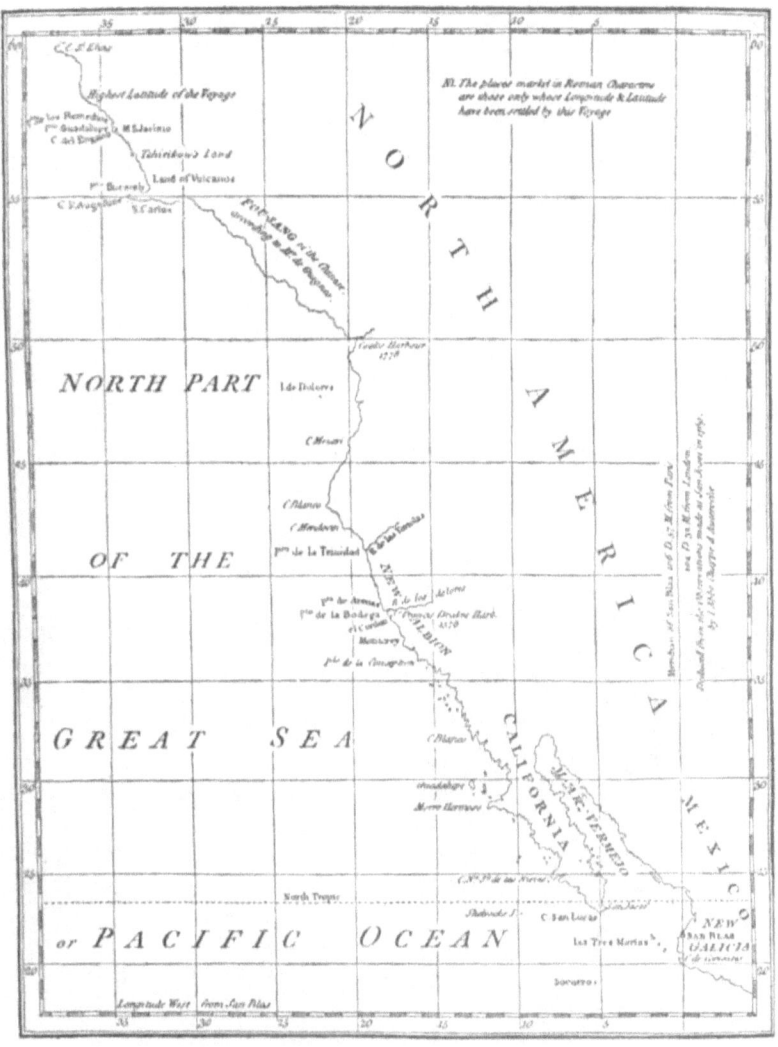

MAP OF QUADRA'S VOYAGE OF 1775.
From "Miscellanies" by Daines Barrington, London, 1781, page 469.

OF PUGET SOUND

could not possibly agree on the points at issue. Quadra insisted that all he was to deliver up was the little piece of ground on which Meares had erected his hut and fort in 1788. Vancouver insisted that he should receive possession of Nootka and Clayoquot, and that the settlement of Neah Bay should be considered a free port for both nations. Dignified letters passed back and forth, and finally they agreed to disagree and report all negotiations to their respective governments, ask for further instructions, and to meet again at Monterey. Quadra left a Spanish garrison at Nootka, in charge of Lieutenant Fidalgo, who quitted the Neah Bay post, bringing to Nootka all the live stock and other properties. Quadra sailed away in the *Active*, and with him went the other Spanish vessels. It is altogether likely, however, that the troops mentioned by Alberni as being at "Nuca" remained for that winter under Fidalgo.

During the negotiations between the two commissioners, Quadra asked that some geographic feature be named for them jointly to commemorate their historic meeting at Nootka. Vancouver at once christened the large island he had discovered and, courteously putting the Spaniard's name first, he called it "Quadra and Vancouver's Island." This partnership name endured for half a century, but now the name of Quadra has almost disappeared. Victoria, the chief city on the island, has an avenue named in his honor. The principal government steamer also bears his name. In addition, Mr. R. E. Gosnell, Secretary of the Natural History Society of Victoria, writes that an island north of Vancouver being found to be two islands instead of one, the name of Quadra has been bestowed upon one of them. All this will help to preserve the memory of a brave and patriotic man.

On Tuesday, November 26, 1792, Vancouver and his little fleet, now consisting of the *Discovery*, the *Chatham*, and the *Dædalus*, arrived at the Spanish port of Monterey and exchanged courtesies with the Spaniards. Señor Quadra again renewed his pleasant attentions. He told Vancouver that on his return from Nootka he found orders from Spain directing him to arrest all vessels on the North American coast, except those under the flag of Great Britain. The Spaniard readily agreed to aid Lieutenant Broughton to pass through New Spain to the Atlantic coast so as to enable him the sooner to reach London with Vancouver's despatches. The winter months were spent by Vancouver in exploring about the Sandwich Islands.

On May 20, 1793, Vancouver again appeared at Nootka, where he saluted the Spanish fort, which salute was answered by Lieutenant Fidalgo. The visit on this occasion was pleasant, but had no effect upon the settlement of the Nootka controversy. From this time Vancouver busied himself with the work of exploring the Alaskan coast.

The year 1794 was also devoted to explorations on the Alaskan coast. As the summer drew toward a close Vancouver determined to return to Nootka, thinking that by this time despatches would certainly be there in answer to those sent home by Lieutenant Broughton. He cast anchor in Friendly Cove on the evening of September 2, 1794. Here he found the Spanish armed vessels *Princesa*, *Aranzazu*, and *San Carlos*.

Fidalgo had been to San Blas and had returned the evening before in the *Princesa*, and he brought with him Brigadier-General Don Jose Manuel Alava. Under date of Tuesday, September 2, 1794, Vancouver tells why Alava was at Nootka and at the same time pays a fine tribute to Quadra as follows: —

"The appointment of this gentleman as governor of Nootka had taken place in consequence of the death of our highly valuable and much esteemed friend Señor Quadra, who in the month of March had died at St. Blas, universally lamented. Having endeavoured, on a former occasion, to point out the degree of admiration and respect with which the conduct of Señor Quadra towards our little community had impressed us during his life; I cannot refrain, now that he is no more, from rendering that justice to his memory to which it is so amply intitled, by stating, that the unexpected melancholy event of his decease operated on the minds of us all, in a way more easily to be imagined than described; and whilst it excited our most grateful acknowledgments, it produced the deepest regret for the loss of a character so amiable, and so truly ornamental to civil society."

The other occasion referred to by Vancouver was during the visit of his little fleet of three vessels in the harbor of Monterey, California. At that time he paid such deference to the generosity of Quadra that a full quotation from his journal is here made in the hope that it will aid toward a better appreciation of this character. Vancouver wrote at the end of December, 1792, as follows: —

"The well known generosity of my other Spanish friends, will, I trust, pardon the warmth of expression with which I must ever advert to the conduct of Señor Quadra; who, regardless of the difference in opinion that had arisen between us in our diplomatic capacities at Nootka, had uniformly maintained towards us a character infinitely beyond the reach of my powers of encomium to describe. His benevolence was not confined to the common rights of hospitality, but was extended to all occasions, and was exercised in every instance, where His Majesty's service, combined with my commission, was in the least concerned.

"To Señor Quadra we were greatly indebted, for waiting our arrival at Monterey, for the friendly and hospitable reception we experienced, and afterwards for remaining there for the sole purpose of affording me an opportunity of transwriting through the medium of his kind offices, my dispatches to England; when his time, no doubt, would have passed infinitely more to his satisfaction at the town of Tepic, the place of his residence in the vicinity of St. Blas. Such sacrifices did not however fill the measure of Señor Quadra's liberality; for, on my requesting an account of the expenses incurred for the refreshments, with which the three vessels under my command had been so amply supplied, here and at St. Francisco, together with the charges attendant on the cattle, sheep, corn, etc., etc., put on board the *Dædalus* for His Majesty's infant colony in New South Wales, he not only revolted at the idea of receiving any payment, but gave strict orders that no account whatever should be rendered; nor would he accept of the most common voucher, or other acknowledgment, for the very liberal supply we had received, of such essential importance not only to our health and comfort at the time, but to our subsequent welfare.

"On my first arrival at Monterey I had questioned Señor Quadra, as to the supply of refreshments, and the price of the different species we should require. To the first he assured me that everything the country afforded was at our service; and as to the last, he said that could be easily settled on our departure. On this ground I now strongly urged his compliance with his former promise, especially as the account between us was of a public nature; but all my remonstrances were to no effect; he insisted that he had fulfilled his promise, since the only *settlement* in which he could possibly engage was that of seeing we were accommodated to the extent of our wishes, with every supply the country could bestow; adding, that repayment would most amply be made, by the promised success attending every creature and production, that we had either received for our own use, or that were destined for other purposes. And as it was probable our respective courts would become acquainted with our several transactions, he should submit all further acknowledgment to their determination.

"The venerable, and respectable father president of the Franciscan missionaries, with all the excellent and worthy members of that religious order, together with Señors Caamano, Arguello, Sal, and the whole of the Spanish officers with whom we had the honor of being acquainted, demand from us the highest sentiments of esteem and gratitude. Even the common people were entitled to our good opinion and respect, as they uniformly subscribed to the exemplary conduct of their superiors, by a behaviour that was very orderly and obliging.

"To the reverence, esteem, and regard, that was shown Señor Quadra by all persons and on all occasions, I must attribute some portion of the respect and friendship we received; and consider the general disposition in our favor

THE NOOTKA MONUMENT.
Erected at Friendly Cove by the Washington University State Historical Society, in August, 1903.

to have acquired no little energy, by the noble example of that distinguished character."

Knowing these pleasant testimonies as to the excellence of Quadra's character, it was a delight to honor his memory by the erection of the monument at Nootka as already described. After visiting the place and studying the scenes of these notable transactions, the anxiety to know more about Quadra was greater than ever. Vancouver's life work is largely told in his published journal. He also gives us a glimpse of Quadra, but there are few published records that show the real life and work of Quadra. His voyage in 1775 was recorded by Maurelle, the pilot, and in 1781 an English version was published by Daines Barrington in his "Miscellanies." This abbreviated account tells of the bravery, industry, and kindness of Quadra on that famous voyage in the little *Sonora*. It is a scant record, however, to reflect the life of a big man.

In the quest for more information, pictures of the Nootka monument were sent, with appeals for facts about Quadra, to Mexico, Peru, and to the Royal Academy of History at Madrid, Spain. The last-named institution responded generously. With the extreme dignity and politeness for which the Spanish people are justly famous, Cesareo Fernandez Duro, Secretary of the Royal Academy, wrote as follows: —

"This Royal Academy, to which I have given an account of your communication of the 12 of December, 1903, has conferred upon me the charge of answering it, beginning by expressing its gratitude to your Society for the honor done to the Spanish Navy in the person of Don Juan Francisco de la Bodega y Quadra, by engraving his name on the monument erected in Nootka (British Columbia), and continuing by gathering together the biographical data concerning the distinguished hydrographer, which may serve to satisfy your desires.

"The facts are not many: I do not know of any special biographer of Quadra, nor do I believe there exists any portrait of him; from data scattered in various works, I have formed the adjoining account, and it will please me greatly if it be of any use to you."

The adjoining account to which he refers consists of four printed pages, evidently from the proceedings of the Royal Academy of History, dated at Madrid, January 15, 1904, and signed like the letter by Señor Duro. The account is, of course, in the Spanish language, a translation of which is given here because of the light thrown upon the little-known career of Quadra, who richly deserves to be rescued from threatening oblivion. It will be noticed that the coasts of California and British Columbia are confused. Under the caption of "Monument Erected in California to Vancouver and Bodega y Quadra," the document is as follows:—

"In the month of August of the past year, 1903, there was erected at the port of Nutka (Coast of California), under the direction of Mr. Edmond S. Meany, Secretary of the Washington University State Historical Society, in honourable recognition, a prismatic and quadrangular monolith of granite, sustained by a simple parallelopiped of the same material. The inscription in the English language, engraved on the anterior face of the prism, explains its object, reading: 'Vancouver and Quadra met here in August, 1792, under the treaty between Spain and Great Britain of October, 1790. — Erected by the Washington University State Historical Society, August, 1903.' Which translated into Spanish reads: (Then follows the same inscription in Spanish.)

"The monument, then, relates to the services of the captain in the Spanish Navy, Don Juan Francisco de la Bodega y Quadra, Knight of the Order of Santiago, and especially to those which are here mentioned as follows:—

"In a meeting of authorities of the viceroyalty of New Spain, at the initiative of the visitador Don Jose Galvez, in the year 1768, they agreed upon the occupation of the ports of San Diego and Monterey, on the coast of California, by founding military garrisons and missions for religious purposes, to which end they despatched by sea the packet boats *San Antonio* and *San Carlos*, constructed for this purpose at the naval station of San Blas, sending at the same time auxiliary expeditions by land.

"In the first part of the year 1775 there was organized another maritime expedition in charge of the lieutenant of a man-of-war, Don Bruno de Heceta, who commanded the frigate *Santiago*, having under his orders the schooner *Sonora*, captained by Don Juan Francisco de la Bodega y Quadra, above mentioned. They conducted a notable and profitable campaign: they went as far north as 56° 47' of latitude and no farther, because the cold and the epidemic of scurvy harassed the crews terribly. Nevertheless they examined ports, coves, rivers, capes, seldom seen or entirely unknown; they gave names to the harbors of la Trinidad, los Martires, Guadalupe, Remedios, Bucarelli; they drew maps, corrected the general chart of the coast; they gathered ethnographic notes and gained honorable recognition among discoverers.

"Two corvettes constructed in Guayaquil, the *Princesa* and the *Favorita*, continued the exploration in February of 1779, in command of the lieutenants of the Navy, Don Ignacio de Arteaga and the above mentioned Bodega y Quadra. They were to go north, according to their instructions, as far as 70° of latitude, and amplify what had been formerly observed. They did so with regard to orography and the variety of minerals, plants, birds, and fish; they drew a sketch of the port of Bucarelli, the Bay of Regla with the contiguous island and its channels, prolonging the work so that in the autumn it came to be very laborious, and they could go north as far as 61° only.

"While these examinations were suspended, on account of the war with Great Britain, Russian expeditions crossed Bering Strait and secretly established trading houses on the islands of Trinidad, Onalaska and Nutka, until this fact having been found out diplomatic claims were set on foot with complete success, and they dislodged the intruders. The port of San Lorenzo de Nutka was settled and fortified in consequence, by sending an expedition to that effect in 1788. [This is evidently a mistake of one year. It should be 1789.]

"Ships from the United States of America and from Portugal tried to enter into transactions, without result, and shortly after, in July, 1789, there appeared there the English packet boat *Argonaut*, whose captain declared he had received orders from the British Company of the South, to which he belonged to take up station and instal a commercial trading post for sea-otter skins; the Spanish commandant denied such claims and as the conduct of the said captain was not suited to his station as foreign guest, the ship was detained and sent to San Blas, an event which was the origin of remonstrances on the part of the English Government and a question of gravity which came to the point of rupture.

"It was concluded amicably, the treaty or agreement being signed at San Lorenzo del Escorial the 28th of October, 1790, in which were settled the differences relative to fishing, shipping and trading points on the Pacific Ocean. There remained pendent only the details of execution, in order to determine the which there were designated on the part of England the celebrated navigator and discoverer Vancouver, who went directly to Nutka with the ships *Discovery* and *Chatham;* on the part of Spain Don Juan de la Bodega y Quadra, at the time commandant of the naval station San Blas in California. The definite treaties of Whitehall on the 12th of February, 1793, and that of Madrid of the 11th of January, 1794, were the result of these conferences.

"Bodega died this same year.

"I have no information that there has been written any especial biography of this famous sailor nor do I know of any portrait of him, but eulogies are paid him in the hydrographical Annals, above all in the works cited below:

"D. Luis de Salazar, 'Discurso sobre la Hidrografia.'

"D. Martin Fernandez de Navarrete, 'Biblioteca Maritima,' II, 190.

"Idem, 'Noticia de las expediciones en busca del paso de oro.'

"'Anuario de la Direccion de Hidrografia,' ano III. Madrid, 1865.

"D. Manuel de Mendiburu, 'Diccionario biografico historico del Peru.' Lima, 1876, V, 50.

"'Catalogo de manuscritos espanoles del Museo Britanico,' II, 366.

"Fernandez Duro, 'Armada espanola,' t. VII y VIII.

"The especial achievement alluded to by the above works is the following:

"General map concerning what, up to to-day, has been discovered and explored by the Spaniards on the northern coast of California formed on very positive knowledge, according to the meridian of San Blas, which is 88° 15' to the West of Tenerife, by D. Juan Francisco de la Bodega y Quadra, of the order Santiago, Captain of a battleship of the Royal Navy and Commandant of the Department. Year of 1791.

"The following series as its complement:

"'The Voyage of the frigates *Santa Gertrudis*, *Aranzazu*, *Princesa* and the schooner *Active* to the northwest coast of northern America in 1792,' by the same Bodega.

"Villavicencio engraved in Mexico, in 1788, another geographical chart of the west coast of California, by the same author.

"In the document of proofs in order to obtain the insignia of the Order of Santiago commenced in December, 1775, and concluded in the following year, the original of which is preserved in the Archivo Historico Nacional (Madrid), it is stated that D. Juan Francisco de la Bodega was then about thirty or thirty two years old, that is to say, that he was born about 1744, in Lima, the capital of Peru, his parents being D. Tomas de la Bodega, a native of San Julian de Musques in the valley of Somorrostro, under the laws of Viscaya, and Dona Francisca Mollinedo, a native of Lima.

"His paternal grand-parents were D. Juan de la Bodega and Dona Agustina de las Llanas, both natives of the same San Julian de Musques.

"His maternal grand-parents, D. Manuel De Mollinedo, a native of Bilbao, and Dona Josefa Losada, who was from the town of Chamcay in Peru, but of Galician descent.

"His paternal great grandmother was Dona Isabel de la

Quadra and this surname the candidate for the insignia used in the second place, doubtless because his father also had adopted it, and because the latter moved to Peru, at the instigation of his relative, D. Antonio de la Quadra, a gentleman who was there established in a good position.

"Twenty four witnesses convoked in Madrid, in San Julian de Musques, in Bilbao and in San Salvador del Castro de Oro (Galicia), for proving the nobility of the family; declared in the writs that they had an ancestral house and coat of arms in San Julian, and that the ancestors had been mayors, magistrates and captains, on account of all of which, and in view of the documents proving it, the insignia was conceded to Don Juan Francisco in 1776, at that time lieutenant in the Royal Navy, stationed in California."

Fragmentary as the record seems, it is enough to show that Bodega y Quadra was a man of great bravery, warm-hearted, kind, and dignified. He had wrought out his own career and had achieved success, climbing to high station by the force of his own character. He deserves to be remembered by all who care for the early history of this western land.

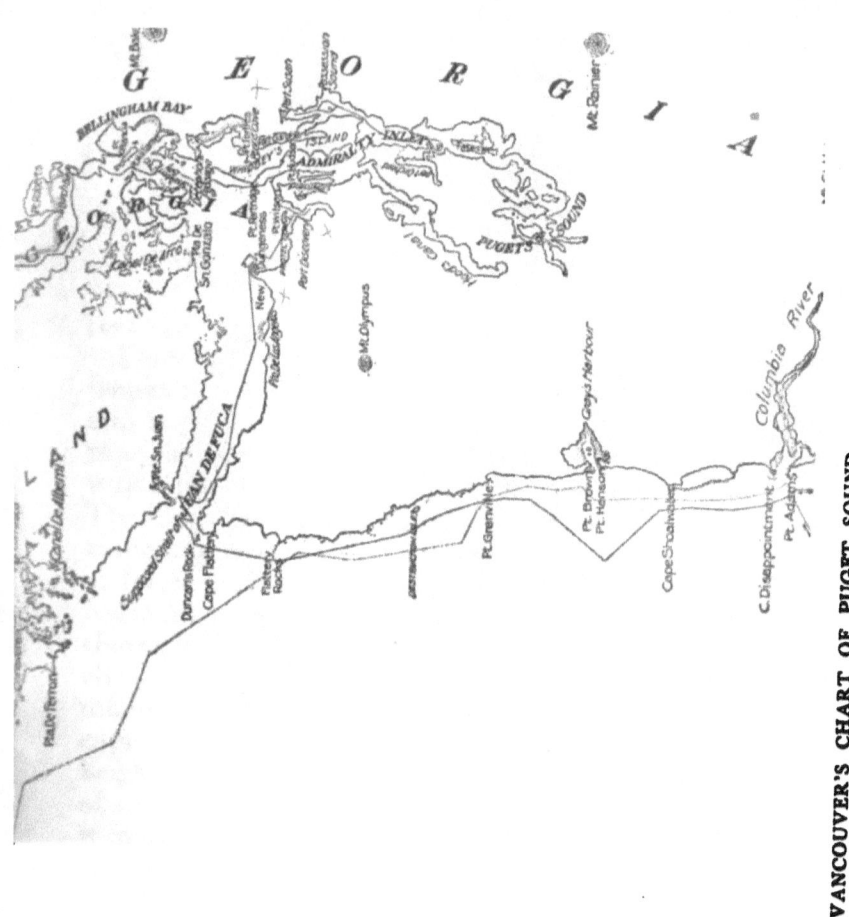

VANCOUVER'S CHART OF PUGET SOUND.
Reproduced from the map in the original Atlas, London, 1798.

CHAPTER V

ENTER THE SUPPOSED STRAITS OF JUAN DE FUCA

[April, 1792.] [Original Journal, Pages 33-34, Book II, Chapter III.]

From cape Look-out, which is situated in latitude 45° 32′, longitude 236° 11′, the coast takes a direction about N. 8 W. and is pleasingly diversified with eminences and small hills near the sea shore, in which are some shallow sandy bays, with a few detached rocks lying about a mile from the land. The more inland country is considerably elevated; the mountains stretch towards the sea, and at a distance appeared to form many inlets and projecting points; but the sandy beach that continued along the coast renders it a compact shore, now and then interrupted by perpendicular rocky cliffs, on which the surf breaks violently. This mountainous inland country extends about 10 leagues to the north from cape Look-out, where it descends suddenly to a moderate height; and had it been destitute of its timber, which seemed of considerable magnitude and to compose an intire forest, it might be deemed low land. Noon brought us up with a very conspicuous point of land composed of a cluster of hummocks, moderately high, and projecting into the sea from the low land before mentioned. These hummocks are barren, and steep near the sea, but their tops are thinly covered with wood.

On the south side of this promontory was the appearance of an inlet, or small river, the land behind not indicating it to be of any great extent; nor did it seem accessible for vessels of our burthen, as the breakers extended from the above point two or three miles into the ocean, until they joined those on the beach nearly four leagues further south. On reference to Mr. Meares's description of the coast south of this promontory, I was at first induced to believe it to be cape Shoalwater, but on ascertaining its latitude, I presumed it to be that which he calls cape Disappointment; and the opening to the south of it, Deception bay. This cape was found to be in latitude 46° 19', longitude 236° 6'.

The sea had now changed from its natural, to river coloured water; the probable consequence of some streams falling into the bay, or into the ocean to the north of it, through the low land. Not considering this opening worthy of more attention, I continued our pursuit to the N. W. being desirous to embrace the advantages of the prevailing breeze and pleasant weather, so favorable to our examination of the coast, which now took a direction N. 12 W.; the latitude at this time was 46° 14'; longitude 236° 1½'; and the variation of the compass 18° eastwardly. In this situation we had soundings at the depth of 33 fathoms, black sandy bottom; the northernmost land seen from the deck bore by compass north; the promontory of cape Disappointment, from N. 14 E. to N. 32 E.; this, the nearest shore, was about two leagues distant; and the southernmost land in sight bore S. E. by S.

The country before us presented a most luxuriant landscape, and was probably not a little heightened in beauty by the weather that prevailed. The more interior parts were somewhat elevated, and agreeably diversified with hills, from which it gradually descended to the shore, and terminated in a sandy beach. The whole had the appearance of a continued forest extending as far north as the eye could reach, which made me very solicitous to find a port in the vicinity of a country presenting so delightful a prospect of fertility; our attention was therefore earnestly directed to this object, but the sandy beach bounded by breakers extending three or four miles into the sea, seemed to be completely inaccessible until about four in the afternoon, when the appearance of a tolerably good bay presented itself. For this we steered, in the hope of finding a division in the reef, through which, should admittance be gained, there was great reason to expect a well sheltered anchorage; but on approaching within two or three miles of the breakers, we found them produced by a compact reef, extending from a low projecting point of land along the shores to the southward, until they joined the beach to the north of cape Disappointment. This projecting point is somewhat more elevated than the rest of the coast, and is situated in latitude 46° 40'; longitude 236°. Not a little disappointed, we resumed our route along the shores of this pleasant country. The projecting point, at six, bore compass N. 10 E.; the center of the bay, and the nearest part of the reef in a line N. 69 E.; distant from the former about seven, and from the latter, about three miles. Immediately within the point, the interior country is more elevated than to the north or south of it; rising in gradual ascent to land of a moderate height. In respect of latitude, this point answered nearly to Mr. Meares's cape Shoalwater; but, from his description of the adjacent country, it should rather appear to be his Low Point; and the bay we endeavoured to enter to the south of it, Shoalwater bay; as in it there appeared two openings, the one taking a northerly, and the other an eastwardly direction. Mr. Meares likewise states, "that, with their glasses, they traced the line of the coast to the south of cape Shoalwater, which presented no opening that promised like an harbour"; those to the south of both these points flattered our expectations, until the breakers, extending across each of them, gave us reason to consider them inaccessible, and unworthy any loss of time whilst accompanied by so favorable a breeze. At sun-set we again shortened sail, and as usual hauled our wind to preserve our station until morning. Our soundings were from 24 to 43 fathoms, dark brown sandy bottom. It was calm for a few hours during the evening and night, attended with a heavy fall of rain.

The next morning, Saturday 28th, at 4 o'clock, with a light breeze at E. S. E. we again steered in for the land, and found that we had been materially affected by a northern current. The land we had been abreast of the preceding evening, now bore by compass S. E. six or seven leagues distant; and the coast to the north of it still continuing to appear a straight and compact shore, I did not attempt gaining a nearer view, but passed on to the northward, keeping at about a league from the land which now took an almost north direction, to a point that, after the Right Honorable Lord Grenville, I named POINT GRENVILLE, situated in latitude 47° 22', longitude 235° 53½'; whence the coast tends N. N. W. Lying off point Grenville are three small rocky islets, one of which, like that at cape Look-out, is perforated.

From hence, as we proceeded to the north, the coast began to increase regularly in height, and the inland country, behind the low land bordering on the sea shore, acquired a considerable degree of elevation. The shores we passed

---

Lord Grenville. There is but one Lord Grenville. He won the title in the course of his political career, and as he died without issue that title passed with him to the grave. William Wyndham Grenville was born on October 25, 1759. He was educated at Eton and Oxford, studied at the Inns of Court, but did not practise at the bar. When less than twenty-three years of age he was elected to Parliament for the county of Buckingham. In September of the same year, 1782, he became secretary to his brother, the Marquis of Buckingham, who had been made Lord Lieutenant of Ireland. Returning to England on the overthrow of Lord Shelburne's cabinet in 1783, he was appointed Paymaster of the Forces by his cousin, Pitt. In 1789 he was chosen Speaker of the House of Commons, but during the same year he became Secretary of State and was thereupon transferred to the Upper House with the title of Lord Grenville. In 1791 he exchanged his office for that of Secretary of Foreign Affairs. He sympathized strongly with Pitt's desire to remove political disabilities from the Catholics, and on the king's declining to make any concessions on this point he resigned with Pitt in 1801. Pitt resumed office in 1804, but did not stipulate for Catholic emancipation, on which account Grenville not only refused to join his ministry, but went into close alliance with Fox. On the death of Pitt in 1806 the Government known as "All the Talents" was organized with Grenville as the nominal head. This Government abolished the slave trade, but was otherwise unsuccessful and was greatly weakened by the death of Fox, the real leader. In March, 1807, the king demanded of Grenville an assurance that he would not initiate any measures for the relief of the Catholics, whereupon he resigned. Some of his colleagues disapproved this conscientiousness, and Sheridan voiced their sentiment as follows, "I have known many men to knock their heads against a wall, but I never before heard of a man collecting bricks and building a wall for the express purpose of knocking

LORD GRENVILLE.

From the painting by J. Hoppner, in the National Portrait Gallery, London. Photograph copyrighted by Walker & Cockrell. Rights secured for this work in England and America. Engraving made in England for this work.

[April, 1792.]

this morning, differed in some respects from those we had hitherto seen. They were composed of low cliffs rising perpendicularly from a beach of sand or small stones; had many detached rocks of various romantic forms, lying at the distance of about a mile, with regular soundings, between 16 and 19 fathoms, soft sandy bottom. Noon brought us in sight of land, which was considered to be that named by Mr. Barclay, Destruction island; bearing by compass from N. 14 W. to N. 17 W.; the southernmost land in sight, S. 53 E.; the northernmost N. 36 W.; and the nearest shore N. 65 E. at the distance of about four miles; in this situation our observed latitude was 47° 30′, longitude 235° 49′, and the variation of the compass 18° eastwardly.

---

out his own brains against it." He never held office again. He continued one of the principal advocates for Catholic emancipation and generally voted with the Whigs. He died at his home, Dropmore, Buckinghamshire, January 12, 1834.

Lord Grenville was not a great statesman, but he wielded considerable influence by his industry, straightforwardness, and political knowledge. He also attained some rank in literature. Among other things he edited the letters from the Earl of Chatham to his nephew, Thomas Pitt, afterwards Lord Camelford, who has been referred to in the biography of Vancouver. In 1809 Grenville was chosen Chancellor of the University of Oxford. In 1792 he married Anne Pitt, daughter of the first Lord Camelford.

Destruction Island. This island has an interesting history. On July 14, 1775, Quadra took shelter on its lee while Heceta in the *Santiago* a few miles south took formal possession of the land in the usual Spanish manner. He landed with Padre Sierra, Surgeon Davales, and Second Pilot Cristobal Reveilla. These were the first civilized men to touch foot to soil in Oregon or Washington. On landing they took possession and, erecting a cross on the shore, they planted at its foot a bottle sealed with wax in which was placed a record of the event. While this ceremony was in progress, Quadra was witnessing a terrible tragedy. The Indians had given every evidence of friendliness. As with Perez at Nootka in 1774, so now with Quadra, these Indians, though startled at the first appearance of white men, seemed sure that the visitors would bring wealth. They held up bits of iron and copper and in unmistakable sign language asked for more. Native copper has been found in the western river gravel, but the iron was a mystery. Indian tradition and even written records as, for example, Nathaniel J. Wyeth's letter, published as an appendix to Washington Irving's "Adventures of Captain Bonneville," tell of Japanese junks being wrecked on the western coasts.

[Original Journal, Pages 38-39.] [April, 1792.]

In the afternoon the wind we had been so happily favored with died away, and was succeeded by calms and light variable breezes. These, with a current or tide setting rapidly in shore, obliged us to anchor in 21 fathoms, on a bottom of soft sand and mud: the coast, which now formed a straight and compact shore, bore by compass from N. 30 W. to S. 49 E.; the nearest part of the main land, cast, about five miles; Destruction island being the nearest land N. 5 E. to N. 5 W. about a league distant, some breakers extending from its north point N. 8 W.

This island is situated in latitude 47° 37'; longitude 235° 49'; and is by far the largest detached land yet observed on the coast. It is about a league in circuit, low, and nearly flat on the top, presenting a very barren aspect, and producing only one or two dwarf trees at each end. A canoe

---

This may account for these Indians having iron. The *Sonora* needing water, Quadra sent ashore six men under Boatswain Pedro Santa Ana. An ambush of savages rushed out, killed the men, threw their bodies into the sea, tore the boat to pieces for the iron and copper fastenings, and then fled into the woods. Quadra was furious and wanted to march at the head of thirty men to seek revenge. He was overruled by a council of officers and was forced to sail away after calling the place "Isla de Dolores," or the "Island of Sorrows."

Twelve years later, in July, 1787, Captain Barclay saw the little river near this island. He sent a boat ashore for fresh water. The crew of five men, under Mr. Millar, were all killed by the Indians. He called the place "Destruction River." The next year, 1788, John Meares found among the Indians at Nootka a seal that had belonged to Mr. Millar and the hand of a white man, probably cut from the body of Millar or one of his unfortunate companions.

Since that time the names have been shifted and we have "Destruction Island," while the river is known by the Indian name Hoh, sometimes given on maps as Ohalat.

In the summer of 1905 the present writer made the journey on foot from Gray's Harbor to Neah Bay. It may be imagined what thoughts filled his mind as he visited the scenes of these tragedies of the long ago. The native village at the mouth of Hoh River gives evidence of having existed there for ages. The winding foot-path leading back into the forest from the village was explored for about a mile. Quadra would certainly have been defeated if he had sought revenge from Indians in that kind of a place, with its tangled undergrowth, and logs, rocks, and huge trees to serve as fortifications for the lurking savage warriors.

[April, 1792.]

or two were seen paddling near the island. It was a fact not less singular than worthy observation, that, on the whole extensive coast of New Albion, and more particularly in the vicinity of those fertile and delightful shores we had lately passed, we had not, excepting to the southward of cape Orford and at this place, seen any inhabitants, or met with any circumstances, that in the most distant manner indicated a probability of the country being inhabited.

Notwithstanding the serenity and pleasantness of the weather, our voyage was rendered excessively irksome by the want of wind; our progress was slow, and our curiosity was much excited to explore the promised expansive mediterranean ocean, which, by various accounts, is said to have existence in these regions. The several large rivers and capacious inlets that have been described as discharging their contents into the pacific, between the 40th and 48th degree of north latitude, were reduced to brooks insufficient for our vessels to navigate, or to bays, inapplicable as harbours, for refitting; excepting that one of which Mr. Dalrymple informs us, that "it is alledged that the Spaniards have recently found an entrance in the latitude of 47° 45' north, which in twenty-seven days course brought them to the vicinity of Hudson's bay; this latitude exactly corresponds to the ancient relation of John De Fuca, the Greek pilot, in 1592."*

---

* *Vide* Mr. Dalrymple's plan for promoting the fur trade, etc., page 21, 1789.

Straits of Juan de Fuca. This is one of the great geographical puzzles of the world.

Samuel Purchas (1577–1626), an English clergyman and author, published in 1613 "Purchas his Pilgrimage, or Relations of the World and the Religions observed in all ages and places, etc." After a second edition in 1614 there were added four succeeding volumes, comprising articles from Hakluyt's publications and manuscripts, which appeared in 1625 under the title, "Hakluytus Posthumus, or Purchas his Pilgrimes: containing a history of the World, in Sea Voyages and Land Travels by Englishmen and Others." In this work Purchas included a note from Michael Lok, a man well known for his interest in geographical matters. Lok had met in Venice in 1596 Juan de Fuca, a native of Cephalonia, whose real Greek name was Apostolos Valerianos. He claimed to have been for forty

[Original Journal,
Page 40.]
[April, 1792.]

This inlet could be now only ten miles from us; and another that had been visited by Mr. Meares and other traders on the coast, was not more than twenty leagues distant. We had been extremely fortunate in the favorable winds that had attended us along this coast, and their absence at this juncture made us impatient for their return. Our anxiety was, however, of no long duration; as by three o'clock on Sunday morning the 29th, we were indulged with a pleasant breeze, with which at day-light we weighed and stood along the shore to the N. W. Whilst at anchor we found a constant current, without intermission, setting in the line of the coast to the northward, at an uniform rate of near half a

---

years in the Spanish service as pilot in the West Indies. While on the coast of California in 1587 he had been captured and robbed by the English Captain Cavendish and thereafter he had escaped and had been sent by the viceroy of New Spain to find the supposed Straits of Anian. Lok's note in "Purchas his Pilgrimes" then continues as follows:—

"Also he said, that shortly after the said Voyage was so ill ended, the said Viceroy of Mexico sent him out againe Anno 1592, with a small Caravela, and a Pinnace, armed with Mariners onely, to follow the said Voyage, for a discovery of the same Straits of Anian, and the passage thereof, into the Sea which they call the North Sea, which is our North-west Sea. And that he followed his course in that Voyage West and North-west in the South Sea, all alongst the coast of Nova Spania, and California, and the Indies, now called North America (all which Voyage hee signified to me in a great Map, and a Seacard of mine owne, which I laied before him) untill hee came to the Latitude of fortie seven degrees, and that there finding that the Land trended North and North-east, with a broad Inlet of Sea, between 47 and 48 degrees of Latitude: hee entred thereinto, sayling therein more than twentie dayes, and found that Land trending still sometime North-west and North-east, and North, and also East and South-eastward, and very much broader Sea then was at the said entrance, and that he passed by diuers Ilands in that sayling. And that at the entrance of this said Strait, there is on the North-west coast thereof, a great Hedland or Iland, with an exceeding high Pinacle, or spired Rocke, like a piller thereupon.

"Also he said, that he went on Land in divers places, and that he saw some people on Land, clad in Beasts skins: and that the Land is very fruitfull, and rich of gold, Silver, Pearle, and other things, like Nova Spania.

"And also he said, that he being entred thus farre into the said Strait, and being come into the North Sea already, and finding the Sea wide enough every where, and to be about thirtie or fortie leagues wide in the mouth of the

[April, 1792.]

league per hour. Since we had passed cape Orford, we had been regularly thus affected, and carried further to the north by ten or twelve miles per day than we expected.

At four o'clock, a sail was discovered to the westward standing in shore. This was a very great novelty, not having seen any vessel but our consort, during the last eight months. She soon hoisted American colours, and fired a gun to leeward. At six we spoke her. She proved to be the ship *Columbia*, commanded by Mr. Robert Gray, belonging to Boston, whence she had been absent nineteen months. Having little doubt of his being the same person who had formerly commanded the sloop *Washington*, I desired he

---

Straits, where hee entred; hee thought he had now well discharged his office, and done the thing he was sent to doe."

This is the famous first announcement of the discovery of the long-supposed Straits of Anian. Many writers who followed Purchas copied and credited the story, which is now generally believed to have been a fable and myth foisted upon Lok by the Greek mariner who was seeking a good employment at the hands of the English. Years upon years of search have failed to reveal one shred of contemporaneous evidence of Fuca's ever having made the voyage he claimed. It is not necessary here to enter into the long debate on the subject by three centuries of writers. In drawing the record of his "Voyage" to a close Vancouver says: "By my having continued the name of De Fuca in my journal and charts a tacit acknowledgment of his discoveries may possibly, on my part, be inferred; this however I must positively deny, because there has not been seen one leading feature to substantiate his tradition: on the contrary, the sea coast under the parallels between which this opening is said to have existed, is compact and impenetrable; the shores of the continent have not any opening whatever, that bears the least similitude to the description of De Fuca's entrance; and the opening which I have called the 'supposed straits of Juan de Fuca,' instead of being between the 47th and 48th degrees, is between the 48th and 49th degrees of north latitude, and leads not into a far broader sea or Mediterranean ocean. The error, however, of a degree in latitude may, by the advocates of De Fuca's merits, be easily reconciled, by the ignorance in those days, or in the incorrectness in making such common astronomical observations; yet we do not find that Sir Francis Drake, who sailed before De Fuca, was liable to such mistakes."

George Davidson, the justly famous modern geographer of the Pacific Coast says in the "Pacific Coast Pilot," edition of 1889, page 520, "There is not a single statement in the so-called narrative of Juan de Fuca as given by

would bring to, and sent Mr. Puget and Mr. Menzies on board to acquire such information as might be serviceable in our future operations.

The most remarkable mountain we had seen on the coast of New Albion, now presented itself. Its summit, covered with eternal snow, was divided into a very elegant double fork, and rose conspicuously from a base of lofty mountains clothed in the same manner, which descended gradually to hills of a moderate height, and terminated like that we had seen the preceding day, in low cliffs falling perpendicularly on a sandy beach; off which were scattered many rocks and rocky islets of various forms and sizes. This was generally considered, though it was not confirmed by its latitude, to be the mount Olympus of Mr. Meares; it being the only conspicuous mountain we had observed on the part of the coast we had visited. Mount Olympus is placed in latitude 47° 10'; whereas our latitude now was 47° 38'; and as this mountain bore N. 55 E. it must consequently be to the north of us; although we were unable to determine its precise situation, by the thick hazy weather which shortly succeeded.

On the return of the boat, we found our conjectures had not been ill grounded, that this was the same gentleman

---

Matthew [Michael] Locke, the elder, that applies to this strait. The whole story is a fabrication."

The Spaniards had no record of De Fuca's discovery. In Daines Barrington's "Miscellanies," published in London in 1781, is the first English version of Bodega y Quadra's voyage of 1775. The journal was kept by Don Francisco Antonio Maurrelle, second pilot of the fleet. On page 493 is this entry, "On the 9th of July I conceived myself to be in the latitude of the mouth of a river [footnote says 'perhaps gulf (boca)'], discovered by John de Fuca (according to the French map) which we therefore endeavored to make for."

So these Spaniards of New Spain depended on the French map for their knowledge of De Fuca's supposed voyage. The Englishmen depended upon Purchas of 1625 and his successors. Meares had these statements and restatements in mind when on Sunday, June 29, 1788, he saw the actual inlet and named it after its "original discoverer Juan de Fuca." This has fixed the name for all subsequent geographers. Captain Barclay had noted the inlet in 1787, but did not attempt to explore or name it.

who had commanded the sloop *Washington* at the time, we are informed, she had made a very singular voyage behind Nootka. It was not a little remarkable that, on our approach to the entrance of this inland sea, we should fall in with the identical person who, it had been stated, had sailed through it. His relation, however, differed very materially from that published in England. It is not possible to conceive any one to be more astonished than was Mr. Gray, on his being made acquainted, that his authority had been quoted, and the track pointed out that he had been said to have made in the sloop *Washington*. In contradiction to which, he assured the officers, that he had penetrated only 50 miles into the straits in question, in an E. S. E. direction; that he found the passage five leagues wide; and that he understood from the natives, that the opening extended a considerable distance to the northward; that this was all the information he had acquired respecting this inland sea, and that he returned into the ocean by the same way he had entered. The inlet he supposed to be the same that De Fuca had discovered, which opinion seemed to be universally received by all the modern visitors. He likewise informed them of his having been off the mouth of a river in the latitude of 46° 10′, where the outset, or reflux, was so strong as to prevent his entering for nine days. This was, probably, the opening passed by us on the forenoon of the 27th; and was, apparently, inaccessible, not from the current, but from the breakers that extended across it. He had also entered another inlet to the northward, in latitude 54½°; in which he had sailed to the latitude of 56°, without discovering its termination. The south point of entrance into De Fuca's straits he stated to be in 48° 24′, and conceived our distance from it to be about eight leagues. The last winter he had spent in port Cox, or, as the natives call it, Clayoquot, from whence he had sailed but a few days. During the winter he had built a small vessel, in which he had dispatched a mate and ten men to barter for furs on Queen Charlotte's islands, and was himself now commencing his summer's trade along the coast to the southward. Whilst he remained at Clayoquot,

Wicananish, the chief of the district, had concerted a plan to capture his ship, by bribing a native of Owyhee, whom Mr. Gray had with him, to wet the priming of all the firearms on board, which were constantly kept loaded; upon which the chief would easily have overpowered the ship's crew, by a number of daring Indians who were assembled for that purpose. This project was happily discovered, and the Americans being on their guard the fatal effects of the enterprize were prevented.

Having obtained this information, our course was again directed along the coast to the northward. It continued to increase in height as we advanced, with numberless detached rocky islets, amongst which were many sunken rocks, extending in some places a league from the shore. As we passed the outermost of these rocks at the distance of a mile, we plainly distinguished the south point of entrance into De Fuca's straits, bearing by compass N. 8 W.: the opposite side of the straits, though indistinctly seen in consequence of the haze, plainly indicated an opening of considerable extent. The thick rainy weather permitted us to see little of the country, yet we were enabled to ascertain that this coast, like that which we had hitherto explored from cape Mendocino, was firm and compact, without any opening into the Mediterranean sea, as stated in latitude 47° 45'; or the least appearance of a safe or secure harbour, either in that latitude, or, from it southward to cape Mendocino; notwithstanding that, in that space, geographers have thought it expedient to furnish many. Those, however, who from such ideal reports may be induced to navigate, in the confidence of meeting such resorts for shelter or refreshment, will, it is greatly to be apprehended, be led into considerable error, and experience like myself no small degree of mortification.

We now saw several villages scattered along the shore, whose inhabitants came off for the purpose, as we supposed, of trading; as the *Columbia* brought to for a short time, and again made all the sail she could after us; which led us to conjecture, that Mr. Gray had not been perfectly satisfied with the account given by our officers, and suspected that our object was of a commercial nature like his own, as he had informed our gentlemen that he was immediately going a considerable way southward. We were at this time within two or three miles of the shore; the wind blew a fresh gale, attended with thick rainy weather from the E. S. E. But as it was favourable for entering this inlet, we were eager to embrace the opportunity it afforded, and shortened sail that the *Chatham* might take the lead.

About noon, we reached its south entrance, which I understand the natives distinguish by the name of Classet*; it is a projecting and conspicuous promontory; and bore, by compass, from N. 56 E. to N. 39 E. distant from its nearest part about two miles. Tatooche's island, united to the promontory by a ledge of rocks over which the sea violently breaks, bore from N. 17 E. to N. 30 E.; and the rock lying off the island, as described by Mr. Duncan in his excellent sketch of the entrance into the inlet, N. 14 E. In the latitude, however, there appears to be an error of ten miles; which, from Mr. Duncan's accuracy in other respects, I was induced to attribute to the press. The south entrance is by him stated to be in 48° 37'; whereas, by our run, and making every allowance, we could not place it so far north as Mr. Gray.

* Cape Flattery.

Cape Flattery. It is noticed that Vancouver mentions the Indian name of Classet in the text, and in the footnote gives the name of Cape Flattery, which had been applied by Captain Cook on Sunday, March 22, 1778. Vancouver was with Cook when that name was given. He writes it full and clear on his chart, but the journal seems to indicate that he really preferred the other name. Cook's journal of the last voyage, Volume II, page 263, gives the reason for the name as follows:—

"Between this island or rock, and the Northern extreme of the land, there appeared to be a small opening, which flattered us with the hopes of finding an harbour. These hopes lessened as we drew nearer; and at last, we had some reason to think, that the opening was closed by low land. On this account I called the point of land to the North of it Cape Flattery."

After this he stood off from the shore, was overtaken by a gale, and, when he next approached the shore on Sunday, March 29, 1778, he was on the west coast of what was later known as Vancouver Island and this caused him to deny the existence of the Strait of Juan de Fuca.

VANCOUVER'S DISCOVERY

[Original Journal, Pages 46-47.]

[April, 1792.]

No great violence of tide was experienced; nor did we observe the Pinnacle rock, as represented by Mr. Meares and Mr. Dalrymple, in order to identify these as De Fuca's straits, or any other rock more conspicuous than thousands along the coast, varying in form and size; some conical, others with flat sides, flat tops and almost every other shape that can be figured by the imagination.

We followed the *Chatham* between Tatooche's island and the rock, hauling to the eastward along the southern shore of the supposed straits of De Fuca. This rock, which rises just above the surface of the water, and over which the surf breaks with great violence, I called ROCK DUNCAN, in commemoration of that gentleman's discovery. It is situated, as he represents, about N. 20 E. nearly half a league from Tatooche's island; forming a passage, to all appearance, perfectly clear. The island of Tatooche is of an oblong shape, lying nearly in a N. W. and S. E. direction, about half a league in circuit, bearing a verdant and fertile appearance, without any trees. On the east side is a cove which nearly divides the island into two parts; the upper part of the cliff in the center of the cove, had the appearance of having been separated by art for the protection or conveniency of the village there situated; and has a communication from cliff to cliff above the houses of the village by a bridge or causeway, over which the inhabitants were seen passing and repassing. On the beach were seen several canoes, and some of them would most probably have visited us, had we thought proper to shorten sail. This promontory, though not greatly elevated, rises very abruptly from the sea in steep barren cliffs;

Duncan Rock. The naming of this rock at Cape Flattery, so well known to all mariners who enter the Strait of Juan de Fuca, is thus recorded by R. E. Gosnell in the 1897 edition of the Year Book of British Columbia, page 78: "After Captain Charles Duncan, of the merchant ship *Princess Royal*, named by Vancouver in 1792, to whom Duncan had given valuable information relating to the North-West Coast. Duncan had served in the Royal Navy as Master."

Duncan Rock is a serious menace to navigation. Keepers of the lighthouse at Cape Flattery say the United States government has had estimates made on the feasibility and probable cost of removing the rock.

above these it seems well wooded; but the badness of the weather that obscured the adjacent country, prevented also our ascertaining its situation. From the north-west part of Tatooche's island, which bears from the north point of the promontory of Classet N. 79 W. distant about two miles, the exterior coast takes a direction nearly south about ten leagues; where, as we passed, I anxiously looked out for the point which Captain Cook had distinguished by the name of Cape Flattery, of which I could not be completely satisfied, on account of the difference in latitude. A shallow bay, however, does extend about three leagues to the southward of Classet, which falls some distance back from the general line of the coast; and the base of the inland mountains which preject there, and form deep ravines, present at a distance the appearance of a safe and secure port; but, on a nearer approach, the whole was found firmly connected by a sandy beach. This, most probably, is the bay which the *Resolution* and the *Discovery* stood into; and Classet is the point, with an island lying off it, which Captain Cook called Cape Flattery. The difference in latitude, (if Mr. Gray is correct, who has passed it several times, and always made it nearly the same,) may have been occasioned by a current similar to that which we had lately experienced along the coast; affecting the *Resolution* in the same manner, between noon, when their latitude was observed, and late in the evening, when Captain Cook hauled off the coast.

As we proceeded along the shore, we passed the village of Classet, which is situated about two miles within the Cape, and has the appearance of being extensive and populous. As the fresh southwardly wind became much moderated by the intervention of the high land we were now under, some of the inhabitants found no difficulty in visiting us; this they did in a very civil, orderly, and friendly manner, requesting permission before they attempted to enter the ship; and on receiving some presents, with assurances of our friendship, they very politely and earnestly solicited us to stop at their village. The situation of the anchorage however being much exposed, and wishing for some snug port where, with ease and convenience, the various necessary services we now required might be performed, I declined their very cordial invitation, and directed our course up the inlet, entertaining no doubt that we should soon be enabled to accommodate ourselves with a more advantageous station.

The few natives who came off resembled, in most respects, the people of Nootka. Their persons, garments, and behaviour, are very similar; some difference was observed in their ornaments, particularly in those worn at the nose; for instead of the crescent, generally adopted by the inhabitants of Nootka, these wore straight pieces of bone. Their canoes, arms, and implements, were exactly the same. They spoke the same language, but did not approach us with the formality observed by those people on visiting the *Resolution* and *Discovery;* which may probably be owing to their having become more familiar with strangers. The wind veering to the S. E. obliged us to turn up along shore on the southern side of the straits, which, from cape Classet, takes a direction S. 70 E. About two miles within the village we passed a small open bay, with a little island lying off its eastern side, apparently too insignificant to answer our purpose of refitting. The weather becoming more unpleasant as the day advanced, at seven in the evening we came to anchor in 23 fathoms water, on a bottom of black sand and mud, about a mile from the shore.

I now became acquainted that after we had passed within Tatooche's island a rock was noticed, and supposed to be that represented as De Fuca's pinnacle rock; this however was visible only for a few minutes, from its being close to the shore of the main land, instead of lying in the entrance of the straits; nor did it correspond with that which has been so described.

It was somewhat remarkable, that although we rode all night by the wind, the *Chatham*, though anchored not a quarter of a mile in shore of us, rode to a regular six hours tide, running near half a league per hour; and, by the appearance of the shores, the ebb and flow seemed to have been very considerable.

CHAPTER VI

THE WORK IN AND AROUND PORT DISCOVERY

[April, 1792.] [Original Journal, Pages 52-53, Book II, Chapter IV.]

THE evening of the 29th brought us to an anchor in very thick rainy weather, about eight miles within the entrance on the southern shore of the supposed straits of De Fuca. The following morning, Monday the 30th, a gentle breeze sprang up from the N. W. attended with clear and pleasant weather, which presented to our view this renowned inlet. Its southern shores were seen to extend, by compass, from N. 83 W. to E.; the former being the small island we had passed the preceding afternoon, which, lying about half a mile from the main land, was about four miles distant from us: its northern shore extends from N. 68 W. to N. 73 E.; the nearest point of it, distant about three leagues, bore N. 15 W. We weighed anchor with a favorable wind, and steered to the east along the southern shore, at the distance of about two miles, having an uninterrupted horizon between east and N. 73 E. The shores on each side the straits are of a moderate height; and the delightful serenity of the weather permitted our seeing this inlet to great advantage. The shores on the south side are composed of low sandy cliffs, falling perpendicularly on beaches of sand or stones. From the top of these eminences, the land appeared to take a further gentle moderate ascent, and was entirely covered with trees chiefly of the pine tribe, until the forest reached a range of high craggy mountains, which seemed to rise from the woodland country in a very abrupt manner, with a few scattered trees on their steril sides, and their summits covered with snow. The northern shore did not appear quite so high: it rose more gradually from the sea-side to the tops of the mountains, which had the appearance of a compact range, infinitely more uniform, and much less covered with snow than those on the southern side.

Our latitude at noon was 48° 19'; longitude 236° 19'; and the variation of the compass 18° eastwardly. In this situation, the northern shore extended by compass from N. 82 W. to N. 51 E.; between the latter, and the eastern extremity of the southern shore, bearing N. 88 E., we had still an unbounded horizon; whilst the island before mentioned, continuing to form the west extremity of the southern shore, bore S. 84 W. By these observations, which I have great reason to believe were correctly taken, the north promontory of Classet is situated in latitude 48° 23¼'; longitude 235° 38'. The smoothness of the sea, and clearness of the sky, enabled us to take several sets of lunar distances, which gave the longitude to the eastward of the chronometer, and served to confirm our former observations, that it was gaining very materially on the rate as settled at Otaheite. As the day advanced, the wind, which as well as the weather was delightfully pleasant, accelerated our progress along the shore. This seemed to indicate a speedy termination to the inlet; as high land now began to appear just rising from that horizon, which, a few hours before, we had considered to be unlimited. Every new appearance, as we proceeded, furnished new conjectures; the whole was not visibly connected; it might form a cluster of islands separated by large arms of the sea, or be united by land not sufficiently high to be yet discernable. About five in the afternoon, a long, low, sandy point of land was observed projecting from the craggy shores into the sea, behind which was seen the appearance of a well-sheltered bay, and, a little to the S. E. of it, an opening in the land, promising a safe and extensive port. About this time a very high conspicuous craggy mountain, bearing by compass N. 50 E. presented itself, towering above the clouds: as low down as they allowed it to be visible, it was covered with snow; and south of it, was a long ridge of very rugged snowy mountains, much less elevated, which seemed to stretch to a considerable distance.

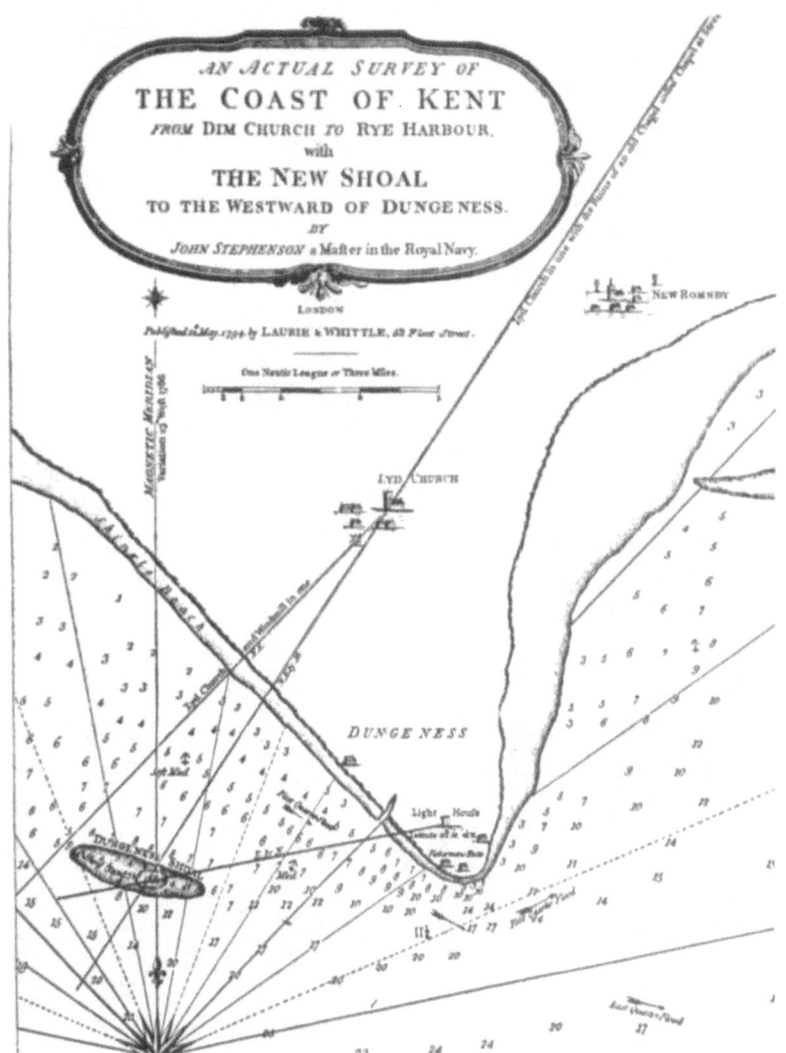

DUNGENESS ON THE ENGLISH CHANNEL.
Photograph of this old chart secured by special permission of the Lords Commissioners of the Admiralty.

[April, 1792.]

As my intention was to anchor for the night under the low point, the necessary signals were made to the *Chatham;* and at seven we hauled round it, at the distance of about a mile. This was, however, too near, as we soon found ourselves in three fathoms water; but, on steering about half a mile to the north, the depth increased to ten fathoms, and we rounded the shallow spit, which, though not very conspicuous, is shewn by the tide causing a considerable rippling over it. Having turned up a little way into the bay, we anchored on a bottom of soft sand and mud in 14 fathoms water. The low sandy point of land, which from its great resemblance to Dungeness in the British channel, I called NEW DUNGENESS, bore by compass N. 41 W. about three

---

New Dungeness. The word is sometimes spelled Dengeness, as by Montague Burrows, "Cinque Ports," page 236, "that tract of land with the separate borough of Dengemarsh of which the mooring Dengeness or Dungeness is the extreme point." Halliwell's Dictionary, 1847, gives a meaning of "den" as "a sandy tract near the sea as at Exmouth and at other places." Murray's great dictionary traces "den" and "dene" to "dune." "Ness" is easily traced to the Anglo-Saxon "naess," meaning cape. It is interesting to observe that the Indians of the Pacific Coast through their Chinook jargon call a cape, "nose." Dungeness, then, means a sandy or dunelike cape.

The journal of the Royal Geographical Society, volume IX, 1897, page 536, has a paper called "Dungeness the Foreland," by F. P. Gulliver. The author produces a chart, comparing Dungeness Foreland with West Point, north of Seattle, and also with "False Dungeness Harbor, Port Angeles," probably in this last case confusing Port Angeles with New Dungeness. On page 546 of the same journal appears the following: "English sailors have recognized in other parts of the world forms similar to Dungeness Foreland and have applied the same name to two widely separated deposits, both having a similar geological structure. One is in Puget Sound and the other is South of Patagonia in the Strait of Magellan."

The *Illustrated London News* for February 1, 1873, in describing a wreck, used the following: "Dungeness is fourteen miles from Folkestone by road from Romney, the last four being a track over a shingly beach. The Ness runs out from the highland more than a couple of miles and creates a kind of breakwater."

During the search for Vancouver's reason for giving this name to the first harbor he found in Northwestern America, special permission was obtained from the Lords Commissioners of the Admiralty to photograph an old chart.

miles distant, from whence the low prejecting land extends until it reaches a bluff cliff of a moderate height, bearing from us S. 60 W. about a league distant. From this station the shores bore the same appearance as those we had passed

---

The chart was published on May 12, 1794, while Vancouver was exploring Cook's Inlet in Alaska. It is therefore practically contemporaneous with the naming of New Dungeness.

Search was also being made for a picture of the old lighthouse at Dungeness when the Lords Commissioners sent word through their Secretary, Evan MacGregor, that they had no picture of the lighthouse. "My Lords would suggest reference to the Trinity House for accurate information, as the light was originally established by the Elder Brethren." At Trinity House was found a water-color drawing of the old lighthouse as damaged by lightning. The Elder Brethren kindly gave their permission for a photograph to be made for this work, and in regard to the damages indicated in the picture, T. Matthews of Trinity House writes: "I have had search made, but regret that we are unable to fix the exact date when the lighthouse at Dungeness was struck with lightning. There is, however, a reference in one of the documents, dated 5th May 1846, to the effect that the brickwork of the Tower walls was shaken 'by lightning many years back.'"

The Corporation of Trinity House is an exceedingly interesting institution of itself. It is an association of English mariners and got its first charter from Henry VIII in 1514, when it was described as the "guild or fraternity of the most glorious and undividable Trinity of St. Clement." Henry VIII intrusted it with the direction of the new naval dockyard at Deptford. Elizabeth, in 1573, conferred a grant of arms and gave it authority to erect beacons and other marks for the guidance of navigators along the coasts of England. In 1604 the Elder Brethren received control while the other members were called Younger Brethren. The corporation was dissolved by act of Parliament in 1647, but was restored in 1660. In 1836 Trinity House was empowered to buy all lighthouses and maintain them by tolls, the surplus to go toward the maintenance of indigent mariners. In 1853 the control of the funds passed to the Board of Trade. They still erect lighthouses, buoys, and beacons, and serve, in an advisory capacity, the High Court of Admiralty.

According to the records of Trinity House, the first lighthouse at Dungeness was built in 1615. It was rebuilt in 1792. In 1904 a finer and higher lighthouse was built, bearing this inscription, "This lighthouse and that on the Point together with the Fog Signal were erected in the year 1904 to supersede the lighthouse built in 1792."

A clipping from an English newspaper of 1904 gives some interesting information about the new lighthouse as follows: "The new lighthouse at

OLD LIGHTHOUSE AT DUNGENESS, ENGLAND.
Photograph of a water-color drawing, secured by special permission of the Elder Brethren of Trinity House.

[April, 1792.]

in the morning, composing one entire forest. The snowy mountains of the inland country were, however, neither so high nor so rugged, and were further removed from the sea shore. The nearest parts bore by compass from us, south about half a league off; the apparent port S. 50 E. about two leagues; and the south point of an inlet, seemingly very capacious, S. 85 E.; with land appearing like an island, moderately elevated, lying before its entrance, from S. 85 E.; to N. 87 E.; and the S. E. extremity of that which now appeared to be southern shore, N. 71 E. From this direction round by the N. and N. W. the high distant land formed, as already observed, like detached islands, amongst which the lofty mountain, discovered in the afternoon by the third

---

Dungeness, which next to Cape Gris Nez, on the French Coast, has the most powerful light in the English Channel, was used for the first time last night. It has taken two years to construct, and supersedes the old building, which has been in existence for 114 years, but which now, owing to the accumulation of shingle, stands nearly half a mile inland. The illuminant is oil-gas, burnt on the incandescent principle, the intensity of the flash is 144,000 candle power, and the light is visible for seventeen and a half miles. There is also a subsidiary light in the same tower which can be seen for thirteen miles."

This reference to the changing of the beach at old Dungeness in England recalls a recorded change at New Dungeness near Puget Sound. Professor George Davidson, in his "Pacific Coast Pilot," page 530, discusses the curious harbor as follows: "This point is so low that vessels bound in or out of the harbor, before the erection of the Light-house, were upon it before they were aware of their danger. Several had run ashore on the outside beach; and in 1855, while we were anchored close under the point, with the weather thick and hazy, a vessel from Admiralty Inlet had been set out of her course by the currents, and came driving in with studding sails set, and only saw her mistake and danger when the black hull of our vessel attracted her attention." Then in a footnote on the same page: "On the 2nd of December, 1871, there was a violent gale of wind from the northwest, during which the sea made a breach across the spit nearly fifty yards in width, cutting off communication along the spit from the main land to the Light-house, except at low water and with a smooth sea. This cut was temporary. The sea also cut over one hundred feet into the spit northeast of the Light-house and reduced the distance of the Light-house from the water by that amount. At times during this gale clouds of sand arose and completely enveloped the top of the tower."

VANCOUVER'S DISCOVERY

[Original Journal, Pages 56-57.]

[April, 1792.]

lieutenant, and in compliment to him called by me MOUNT BAKER, rose a very conspicuous object, bearing by compass N. 43 E. apparently at a very remote distance. A small Indian village was near us on the south side of the bay, but we had not yet been visited by any of the inhabitants. We had now advanced further up this inlet than Mr. Gray, or (to our knowledge) any other person from the civilized world; although it should hereafter be proved to be the same which is said to have been entered by De Fuca, in support of which oral testimony is the only authority produced; a tradition rendered still more doubtful by its entrance differing at least 40′ in latitude.

Considering ourselves now on the point of commencing an examination of an entirely new region, I cannot take leave

---

Third Lieutenant Joseph Baker. Diligent and extensive search has thus far failed to bring a portrait or biographical sketch of this young officer in whose honor was named one of the finest mountains on the Pacific Coast. The Muster Book of his Majesty's sloop *Discovery*, now on file in the Public Record Office, London, carries the name of Joseph Baker as Third Lieutenant, whose commission was issued on December 18, 1790. Unfortunately, however, the place of birth and age are omitted for most of the officers, though given for the others. So we do not have even those items. By the muster table of the *Discovery* at the time of paying off from October 1 to November 3, 1795, it is shown that Vancouver had promoted Baker to be Second Lieutenant on September 26, 1792, and to be First Lieutenant on November 25, 1794. It probably took some time to have these promotions confirmed. At any rate, we have the record that he died in 1817 after attaining the rank of Captain. Besides the honor conferred upon him by Vancouver, this same young officer was honored by Lieutenant Broughton in the *Chatham*, who named a group of islands found in the Columbia River, Baker Islands, "after the second lieutenant of the *Discovery*," which recognizes his promotion after the discovery of the mountain.

Finally, Vancouver, as he bids farewell to his ship, speaks of Baker as follows: "and the following day, after having seen the *Discovery* safely moored, and giving such instructions, as circumstances demanded, to my first lieutenant, Mr. Baker, in whose zeal for the service, and abilities as an officer, a long experience justified me in implicitly confiding; I resigned my command of the *Discovery* into his hands, and with such books, papers and charts as had been previously selected, as being essential to the illustration of the services we had performed, I took leave of my officers and crew; not, however, without emotions which, though natural, on parting with a society

of the coast already known, without obtruding a short remark on that part of the continent, comprehending a space of nearly 215 leagues, on which our inquiries had been lately employed under the most fortunate and favorable circumstances of wind and weather. So minutely had this extensive coast been inspected, that the surf had been constantly seen to break on its shores from the masthead; and it was but in a few small intervals only, where our distance precluded its being visible from the deck. Whenever the weather prevented our making free with the shore, or on our hauling off for the night, the return of fine weather and of day-light uniformly brought us, if not to the identical spot we had departed from, at least within a few miles of it, and never beyond the northern limits of the coast which we had previously seen. An examination so directed, and circumstances happily concurring to permit its being so executed, afforded the most complete opportunity of determining its various turnings and windings; as also the position of all its conspicuous points, ascertained by meridional altitudes for the latitude, and observations for the chronometer, which we had the good fortune to make constantly once, and in general twice every day, the preceding one only excepted.

It must be considered as a very singular circumstance that, in so great an extent of sea-coast, we should not until now have seen the appearance of any opening in its shores, which presented any certain prospect of affording shelter; the whole coast forming one compact, solid, and nearly straight barrier against the sea.

The river Mr. Gray mentioned should, from the latitude he assigned to it, have existence in the bay, south of cape Disappointment. This we passed on the forenoon of the

---

with whom I had lived so long, shared so many dangers, and from whom I had received such essential services, are yet more easily to be imagined than I have the power to describe; and in the course of a few days I arrived at the Admiralty, where I deposited my several documents."

The chart in the published journal showing part of the coast of Northwest America bears a legend to the effect that it was prepared by Lieutenant Joseph Baker, under the "immediate inspection" of Captain Vancouver.

27th; and, as I then observed, if any inlet or river should be found, it must be a very intricate one, and inaccessible to vessels of our burthen, owing to the reefs and broken water which then appeared in its neighborhood. Mr. Gray stated that he had been several days attempting to enter it, which at length he was unable to effect, in consequence of a very strong outset. This is a phenomenon difficult to account for, as, in most cases where there are outsets of such strength on a sea coast, there are corresponding tides setting in. Be that however as it may, I was thoroughly convinced, as were also most persons of observation on board, that we could not possibly have passed any safe navigable opening, harbour, or place of security for shipping on this coast, from cape Mendocino to the promontory of Classet; nor had we any reason to alter our opinions, notwithstanding that theoretical geographers have thought proper to assert, in that space, the existance of arms of the ocean, communicating with a mediterranean sea, and extensive rivers, with safe and convenient ports. These ideas, not derived from any source of substancial information, have, it is much to be feared, been adopted for the sole purpose of giving unlimited credit to the traditionary exploits of ancient foreigners, and to undervalue the laborious and enterprizing exertions of our own countrymen, in the noble science of discovery.

Since the vision of the southern continent, (from which the Incas of Peru are said to have originated,) has vanished; the pretended discoveries of De Fuca and De Fonte have been revived, in order to prove the existence of a northwest passage. These have been supported by the recent concurring opinions of modern traders, one of whom is said to conceive, that an opening still further to the north is that which De Fuca entered. Under this assertion, should any opening further to the northward be discovered leading to a N. W. passage, the merit of such discovery will necessarily be ascribed to De Fuca, De Fonte, or some other favorite voyager of these closet philosophers.

The preceding evening brought us to an anchor under New Dungeness. Our May-day, Tuesday, was ushered in by a

morning of the most delightfully pleasant weather, affording us, from the broken appearance of the coast before us, the prospect of soon reaching a safe and commodious harbour. Indeed, our present situation was far from ineligible, as it promised to admit us as near the shore as we might think proper to take our station. Mr. Whidbey was therefore dispatched in the cutter, to sound, and search for fresh water.

The appearance of the huts we now saw, indicated the residence of the natives in them to be of a temporary nature only; as we could perceive with our glasses, that they differed very materially from the habitations of any of the American Indians we had before seen, being composed of nothing more than a few mats thrown over cross sticks; whereas those we had passed the preceding day, in two or three small villages to the eastward of Classet, were built exactly after the fashion of the houses erected at Nootka.* The inhabitants seemed to view us with the utmost indifference and unconcern; they continued to fish before their huts as regardless of our being present, as if such vessels had been familiar to them, and unworthy of their attention. On the low land of New Dungeness were erected perpendicularly, and seemingly with much regularity, a number of very tall straight poles, like flag-

* *Vide* Cook's last Voyage.

Tall Poles at New Dungeness. Vancouver here meets with work of the Indians which puzzled him throughout his explorations. He refers to such tall poles several times in his journal and always with the same mystery. While at Port Townshend, Artist Sykes drew a sketch of the place showing four of these remarkable poles. That sketch makes one of the fine steel engravings in the original publication. The present writer counts it a piece of good fortune that he has been able to learn from the Indians themselves just what use were made of these great poles. During the summer of 1905 he visited the eighteen Indian Reservations in the State of Washington, gathering materials for another work in course of preparation. On the Lummi Reservation, Bellingham Bay, were found the ruins of an old potlatch house from the site of which a long sand spit formed a connection with the lower islandlike portion of the Reservation. It is called by the Indians "Swolhasen." At the present time the place is a favorite stand for the duck hunters from Bellingham and neighboring cities. Ducks fly low there in passing from Bellingham Bay to the outer waters. The old Indians gave this in-

staves or beacons, supported from the ground by spurs. Their first appearance induced an opinion of their being intended as the uprights for stages on which they might dry their fish; but this, on a nearer view, seemed improbable, as their height and distance from each other would have required spars of a greater size to reach from one to the other, than the substance of the poles was capable of sustaining. They were, undoubtedly, intended to answer some particular purpose; but whether of a religious, civil, or military nature, must be left to some future investigation.

Mr. Whidbey found from ten to three fathoms water close to the shore. He landed at the upper part of the bay, but could not find any water; nor did he see the appearance of any along the shore near the inhabitations of the Indians, who remained as before described, or fishing on the water, without paying any more attention to the cutter, than if she had been one of their own canoes.

On receiving this report, the *Chatham's* cutter with the *Discovery's* yawl and cutter, were ordered to be armed and supplied with a day's provision; with which we set off to examine the two apparent openings nearest to us. We found the surface of the sea almost covered with aquatic birds of various kinds, but all so extremely shy that our sportsmen were unable to reach them with their guns, although they made many attempts. The first opening to the S. E. appeared to be formed by two high bluffs; the elevated land within them seemingly at a considerable distance. It proved, however, to be a close and compact shore, the apparent vacant space being occupied by a very low sandy beach, off

---

formation: Long ago their people had no muskets, but they got many canoeloads of ducks by large nets. They set great high poles in the ground. From one of these to another they stretched nets woven of willow twigs. At night or in hazy weather the ducks would strike these nets when the watchers would pull a rope of twisted roots or twigs fastened to a loop of the net and down would come a flap, holding in the strong meshes of willow the entire flock of ducks. It was practically a fish net made to work on land. The Indian tradition clears away the mystery found by the first white man to visit this inland sea.

which extended a flat of very shallow soundings. From hence we made the best of our way for land, appearing like an island, off the other supposed opening; from whose summit, which seemed easy of access, there was little doubt of our ascertaining whether the coast afforded any port within reach of the day's excursion. On landing on the west end of the supposed island, and ascending the eminence which was nearly a perpendicular cliff, our attention was immediately called to a land-scape, almost as enchantingly beautiful as the most elegantly finished pleasure grounds in Europe. From the height we were now upon, our conjectures of this land being an island situated before the entrance of an opening in the main land were confirmed. The summit of this island presented nearly a horizontal surface, interspersed with some inequalities of ground, which produced a beautiful variety on an extensive lawn covered with luxuriant grass, and diversified with an abundance of flowers. To the northwestward was a coppice of pine trees and shrubs of various sorts, that seemed as if it had been planted for the sole purpose of protecting from the N. W. winds this delightful meadow, over which were promiscuously scattered a few clumps of trees, that would have puzzled the most ingenious designer of pleasure grounds to have arranged more agreeably. Whilst we stopped to contemplate these several beauties of nature, in a prospect no less pleasing than unexpected, we gathered some gooseberries and roses in a state of considerable forwardness. Casting our eyes along the shore, we had the satisfaction of seeing it much broken, and forming to all appearance many navigable inlets. The inlet now before us did not seem so extensive as we had reason to believe it to be from the ships; yet there was little doubt of its proving sufficiently secure and convenient for all our purposes. We therefore proceeded to its examination, and found its entrance to be about a league wide, having regular good soundings from 10 fathoms close to the shores, to 30, 35, and 38 fathoms in the middle, without any apparent danger from rocks or shoals. Fresh water, however, seemed hitherto a scarce commodity, and yet, from the general face of the country, a deficiency in this respect was not to be apprehended. The shores of the harbour were of a moderate height; its western side, bounded at no very great distance by a ridge of high craggy mountains covered with snow, were, as I conceived, connected with the mountain we took for mount Olympus. In quest of the only great object necessary for constituting this one of the finest harbours in the world, we prosecuted our researches; until almost despairing of success, I suddenly fell in with an excellent stream of very fine water. The design of our excursion was thus happily accomplished; and, after taking some little refreshment, we returned towards the ships, and arrived on board about midnight, perfectly satisfied with the success of our expedition, and amply rewarded for our labour.

During my absence, some of the natives had been trading with the vessels in a very civil and friendly manner. They did not appear to understand the Nootka language; as those of our people who had some knowledge of it were by no means able to make themselves understood.

A light pleasant breeze springing up, we weighed on Wednesday morning the 2d and steered for the port we had discovered the preceding day, whose entrance about four leagues distant bore S. E. by E. The delightful serenity of the weather greatly aided the beautiful scenery that was now presented; the surface of the sea was perfectly smooth, and the country before us exhibited everything that bounteous nature could be expected to draw into one point of view. As we had no reason to imagine that this country had ever been indebted for any of its decorations to the hand of man, I could not possibly believe that any uncultivated country had ever been discovered exhibiting so rich a picture. The land which interrupted the horizon between the N. W. and the northern quarters, seemed, as already mentioned, to be much broken; from whence its eastern extent round to the S. E. was bounded by a ridge of snowy mountains, appearing to lie nearly in a north and south direction, on which mount Baker rose conspicuously; remarkable for its height, and the snowy mountains that stretch from its base to the north and south. Between us and this snowy range, the land, which on the sea shore terminated like that we had lately passed, in low perpendicular cliffs, or on beaches of sand or stone, rose here in a very gentle ascent, and was well covered with a variety of stately forest trees. These, however, did not conceal the whole face of the country in one uninterrupted wilderness, but pleasingly clothed its eminences, and chequered the valleys; presenting, in many directions, extensive spaces that wore the appearance of having been cleared by art, like the beautiful island we had visited the day before. As we passed along the shore near one of these charming spots, the tracks of deer, or of some such animal, were very numerous, and flattered us with the hope of not wanting refreshments of that nature, whilst we remained in this quarter.

A picture so pleasing could not fail to call to our remembrance certain delightful and beloved situations in Old England. Thus we proceeded without meeting any obstruction to our progress; which, though not rapid, brought us before noon abreast of the stream that discharges its water from the western shore near five miles within the entrance of the harbour; which I distinguished by the name of PORT DISCOVERY, after the ship. There we moored, in 34 fathoms, muddy bottom, about a quarter of a mile from the shore.

The entrance of this harbor is formed by low projecting points, extending, on each side, from the high woodland cliffs which in general bound the coast; bearing by compass from N. 48 W. to N. 54 W. in a line with two corresponding points from the island already described, lying off this harbour. Had this insular production of nature been designed by the most able engineer, it could not have been placed more happily for the protection of the port, not only from the N. W. winds to the violence of which it would otherwise be greatly exposed, but against all attempts of an enemy, when properly fortified; and hence I called it PROTECTION ISLAND.

The stream of water, near which we had taken a very convenient station, appeared to have its source at some distance from its outfal, through one of those low spits of sand already mentioned, which constitute most of the projecting points we had seen ever since our having entered this inlet. These usually acquire a form somewhat circular, though irregular; and, in general, are nearly steep to, extending from the cliffy woodland country, from one to six hundred yards towards the water's edge, and are composed of a loose sandy soil. The surface of some was almost entirely occupied by a lagoon of salt water, or brackish swamp; others were perfectly dry; no one of them produced any trees; but were mostly covered with a coarse spiry grass, interspersed with strawberries, two or three species of clover, samphire, and a great variety of other small plants; some of which bore very beautiful flowers. On a few of the points were some shrubs that seemed to thrive excessively; such as roses, a species of sweet briar, gooseberries, raspberries, currants, and several other small bushes, which, in their respective seasons, produce most probably the several fruits common to this and the opposite side of America. These all appeared to grow very luxuriantly; and, from the quantity of blossoms with which they were loaded, there was great reason to believe them very productive.

We had little trouble in clearing a sufficient space for our encampment, which was very commodiously situated close to the north side of the stream or brook. The tents, observatory, chronometers and instruments, guarded by a party of marines, were sent on shore after dinner; and, whilst they were properly arranging, I made a short excursion up the harbour. It extended nearly in a south direction, about four miles from the ship, and then terminated in a muddy flat across its head, about a quarter of a mile from the shore. The water, which was seven fathoms deep close to the flat, gradually deepened to 10, 20, and 30 fathoms, good holding ground. On this bank were found some small indifferent oysters. The shores beyond it are low and thickly wooded, and through them there appeared to run a very considerable stream of water, with several smaller ones, emptying themselves into the harbour. The back country had the appearance of a swampy fen for a considerable distance. We landed not far from the largest rivulet, where we found a deserted village capable of containing an hundred inhabitants. The houses were built after the Nootka fashion, but did not seem to have been lately the residence of the Indians.

The habitations had now fallen into decay; their inside, as well as a small surrounding space that appeared to have been formerly occupied, were over-run with weeds; amongst which were found several human sculls, and other bones, promiscuously scattered about.

On Thursday morning the 3d we sat seriously to work on board, and on shore where the sailmakers were repairing and altering the sails; coopers inspecting the casks; gunners airing the powder; and parties cutting wood, brewing spruce beer, and filling water: whilst those on board were as busily employed in necessary repairs about the rigging; getting the provisions to hand; clearing the main and after holds for the reception of shingle ballast, of which we had for some time stood in much need; some of our carpenters were stopping leaks about the bows, and the rest assisted in caulking the *Chatham's* sides. The serenity of the climate and season was extremely favorable to the execution of their several duties, as also to our astronomical inquiries. The part of the coast that we had now reached being nearly destitute of inhabitants, few circumstances occurred to divert our attention, or interfere with the pursuits in which we were all engaged.

So little leisure or rest had been afforded in the several ports we had hitherto visited since we left Cape of Good Hope, that it was not until this morning, Sunday the 6th, that our people could be indulged with a holiday, for the purpose of taking some recreation and exercise on shore.

A few of the natives in two or three canoes favored us with their company, and brought with them some fish and venison for sale. The latter was extremely good, and very acceptable, as we had not hitherto obtained any; though on our first arrival we had entertained hopes of procuring a supply, from the numerous tracks of deer which appeared fresh, and in all directions.

These people, in their persons, canoes, arms, implements,

etc. seemed to resemble chiefly the inhabitants of Nootka; though less bedaubed with paint, and less filthy in their external appearance. They wore ornaments in their ears, but none were observed in their noses; some of them understood a few words of the Nootka language; they were clothed in the skins of deer, bear, and some other animals, but principally in a woolen garment of their own manufacture, extremely well wrought. They did not appear to possess any furs. Their bows and implements they freely bartered for knives, trinkets, copper, etc.; and, what was very extraordinary, they offered for sale two children, each about six or seven years of age, and, being shewn some copper, were very anxious that the bargain should be closed. This, however, I peremptorily prohibited, expressing, as well as I was able, our great abhorrence of such traffic.

As our several employments, on board and on shore, would still require some time before they could be fully completed; and as I was desirous of obtaining some further knowledge of this inlet, in order that, when the vessels should be ready, we might extend our researches without fear of interruption; I directed the *Discovery's* yawl and launch, with the *Chatham's* cutter, properly armed, and supplied with stores for five days, to be in readiness early the next morning. I committed to Mr. Broughton the charge of the ships, and to Mr. Whidbey that of the observatory and encampment, with directions to make a survey of the port, and such further necessary observations as circumstances would admit during my absence.

Mr. Menzies, with two of the young gentlemen, accompanied me in a yawl, Mr. Puget commanded the launch, and Mr. Johnstone the *Chatham's* cutter. With these arrangements, about five o'clock on Monday morning the 7th, we took our departure for the purpose of becoming more intimately acquainted with the region in which we had so very unexpectedly arrived. The day did not promise to be very auspicious to the commencement of our examination. That uninterrupted serenity of weather that we had experienced the last seven days, seemed now to be materially changed;

the wind which, in the day-time, had constantly blown from the N. W. with light southwardly airs, or calms, from sunset until eight or ten o'clock in the forenoon, had now blown, since the preceding evening, a moderate gale from the S. E.; and, before we had proceeded a mile from the ship, brought with it a very thick fog, through which we steered, keeping the starboard, or continental shore, on board, trusting that towards noon the fog would disperse itself and clear away.

On our arrival in port Discovery, we passed to the S. W. of Protection island; another channel, equally as safe and convenient, we now found to the S. E. of it. Having rowed against a strong tide along the shore about two or three leagues to the N. E. from the entrance of port Discovery, we rounded a low projecting point, and though the fog prevented our seeing about us, yet there was no doubt of our having entered some other harbour or arm in the inlet that took a southwardly direction. Here I proposed to wait until the weather should be more favorable, and in the mean time to haul the seine; which was done, along the beach to the southward, with little success.

Prosecuting our labours as fishermen along the beach, we were led near a point similar to that we had passed, and distant from it about two miles; here the fog entirely dispersing, afforded an opportunity of ascertaining its latitude to be 48° 7′ 30″, its longitude 237° 31½′. A very spacious inlet now presented itself, whose N. E. point, in a line with its S. W. being the point from which we had last departed, bore by compass N. 25 W. and seemed about a league asunder: mount Baker bore N. 26 E.; a steep bluff point opposite to us, appearing to form the west point of another arm of this inlet, S. 87 E. about four miles distant; the nearest eastern shore S. 50 E. about two miles; and a very remarkable high round mountain, covered with snow, apparently at the southern extremity of the distant range of snowy mountains before noticed, bore S. 45 E.: the shores of this inlet, like those in port Discovery, shoot out into several low, sandy, projecting points, the southernmost of which bore S. 9 E. distant about two leagues, where this branch of the inlet seemed to terminate, or take some other direction. Here we dined, and having taken the necessary angles, I directed Mr. Puget to sound the mid-channel, and Mr. Johnstone to examine the larboard or eastern shore, whilst I continued my researches on the continental shore, appointing the southernmost low point for our next rendezvous. As we advanced, the country seemed gradually to improve in beauty. The cleared spots were more numerous, and of larger extent; and the remote lofty mountains covered with snow, reflected greater luster on the fertile productions of the less elevated country. On arriving near our place of rendezvous, an opening was seen, which gave to the whole of the eastern shore under the examination of Mr. Johnstone, the appearance of being an island. For this we steered, but found it closed by a low sandy neck of land, about two hundred yards in width, whose opposite shore was washed by an extensive salt lake, or more probably by an arm of the sea stretching to the S. E. and directing its main branch towards the high round snowy mountain we had discovered at noon: but where its entrance was situated we could not determine, though conjecture led to suppose it would be found round the bluff point of land we had observed from our dinner station.

In the western corner of this isthmus was situated a deserted Indian village, much in the same state of decay as that which we had examined at the head of port Discovery. No signs of any inhabitants were discernible; nor did we visit it, it being expedient we should hasten to our appointed station, as night was fast approaching, during which Mr. Johnstone did not join us; this led us to suppose he had found some entrance into the above lake or inlet that had escaped my notice; and which afterwards proved to have been the cause of his absence. Having determined the extent of this inlet, whose south extremity is situated in latitude 47° 59′, longitude 237° 31′; at day-break the next morning, Tuesday the 8th, we embarked in pursuit of the entrance into the lake or inlet that we had discovered the preceding evening. About this time we heard and answered the report of a swivel gun. A very strong run of water was now observed, but

THE MARQUIS OF TOWNSHEND.

From a mezzotint by C. Turner after Sir Joshua Reynolds. Photograph copyrighted by Augustin Rischgitz. Rights secured for this work in England and America.

being brackish, we were under the necessity of carrying kegs near a mile into the country to replenish them, not having found any fresh water since we left the ships. Whilst we were engaged, Mr. Johnstone came up. He had found a narrow channel into the inlet, which had flattered him with returning by the isthmus that had opposed our progress; but to his great mortification he found it closed, and was obliged to keep rowing the greater part of the night, in order that he might join us by the same passage he had entered, which he had now just effected. Its southern entrance was found to be navigable for small boats only, from half flood to half ebb, and was dry at low water; but as its northern part formed a snug little port, and, with its tide, seemed likely to be made useful in careening; Mr. Johnstone was induced to prosecute its examination. The survey of this inlet, which had occupied our time since the preceding day at noon, having been finally accomplished by the joining of the boats, it proved to be a very safe and more capacious harbour than port Discovery; and rendered more pleasant by the high land being at a greater distance from the water-side. Its soundings also give it a further advantage, being very regular from side to side, from 10 to 20 fathoms depth of water, good holding ground: but, with respect to fresh water, so far as we could determine by our transitory visit, it was very deficient, as has been already observed. To this port I gave the name of PORT TOWNSHEND, in honor of the noble Marquis of that name.

Marquis Townshend. For many years Port Townsend (this is a case where the Americans, and not the English, drop an "h") has been the principal port of entry for the entire Customs District of Puget Sound. As such it has become well known to mariners and commercial men throughout the world. It is clear from the text what Townshend was honored by Vancouver in this case, and yet there are probably but few men among those familiar with the geographical term who remember the remarkable history of the man who bore that name. How few students who have been thrilled by the dramatic scene on the Plains of Abraham back of Quebec, which culminated in the death of the immortal Wolfe, recall the fact that the command of that British army then fell to Brigadier-General George Townshend! His life was full

VANCOUVER'S DISCOVERY

[Original Journal, Pages 76-77.]

[May, 1792.]

Mr. Johnstone, who had a much better opportunity than I had of seeing the above lake or inlet, represented it as appearing very extensive and divided into two or three branches; but he had not been able to determine its communication either with the ocean or the main inlet, although he had great

---

of interest, in which all was not glamour or greatness. There were foibles and selfishness which have not been overlooked by his own countrymen, as is evidenced from the thoroughgoing sketch written by Robert Dunlop in the "National Dictionary of Biography."

George Townshend was born on February 28, 1724, and at his baptism had King George I as one of his sponsors. He graduated as Master of Arts from St. John's College, Cambridge, on July 3, 1749, and completed his education by travelling on the continent. Before his graduation, while visiting at The Hague in January, 1745, he was offered high military command and actually accepted the post of captain of dragoons, serving under the Duke of Cumberland. He was advanced in military rank, becoming lieutenant-colonel in 1748. Then the young man met with a backset. For family reasons he had been placed in the family of the Duke of Cumberland, who now took great offence because of Townshend's indiscreet use of his talent as a caricaturist. He retired from the service in 1750 and the next year the breach with his royal patron was widened by the appearance of a harsh pamphlet attributed to him, criticising the military capacity of the Duke of Cumberland. He hated Fox and tried to draw his brother Charles into opposition to the Duke of Newcastle. His hostility to the Duke of Cumberland and his dread of a standing army caused him to advocate the bill which became a law in 1757, establishing the militia on a national basis. He was proud of this and later acts along that line. In his portrait, while he was Lord-Lieutenant of Ireland and had not yet attained the title of Marquis, painted by Thomas Hudson, he holds in his hand a document inscribed, "A Bill Intitled An Act for the Better Order of the Militia Forces &c."

His penchant for caricaturing bred him hosts of enemies, calling out among other evidences a bitter pamphlet called "Art of Political Lying."

On the retirement of the Duke of Cumberland, Townshend returned to the army and was promoted Colonel on May 6, 1758, being assigned to the staff of George II. He asked Pitt to be remembered if any services were intended against France, and in February, 1759, he was appointed Brigadier-General in America under Major-General James Wolfe, in the expedition against Quebec. He took part in all those operations, but as the summer wore on he grew dissatisfied and wrote to his wife: "General Wolfe's health is but very bad. His generalship, in my poor opinion, is not a bit better: this only between us. He never consulted any of us until the latter end of August, so that we have nothing to answer for, I hope, as to the success of this campaign."

reason to believe it did communicate by the way of the bluff point already mentioned; which about noon was confirmed. In our way thither, we found on one of the low points projecting from the eastern shore, two upright poles set in the ground, about fifteen feet high, and rudely carved.

The consultation referred to was the letter written by Wolfe from his sick bed on August 29, asking his three Brigadiers — Monckton, Townshend, and Murray — to meet and consider the best method of attack. The plan then adopted was the one that led to victory, and friends of Townshend claimed it was his suggestion. Monckton was disabled when Wolfe was killed at the very moment of victory. The command of the army therefore devolved upon Townshend. The battle was on September 13, and four days later the city capitulated to Townshend, and on September 20 he sent to the Secretary of State an account of the battle and his own success. This was in language much more stilted than the famous message from Wolfe. George Augustus Selwyn, meeting Charles Townshend, exclaimed, "Charles, if your brother wrote Wolfe's despatch, who the devil wrote your brother George's?"

Monckton recovered, Murray was made Governor of Quebec, and Townshend sailed away home in the fleet, "there to parade his laurels and to claim more than his share of the honors of victory." The last are the words of Francis Parkman, the American historian in his "Montcalm and Wolfe." Hot pamphlets appeared and Townshend was accused of enmity toward the nation's hero, Wolfe. He challenged the Earl of Albemarle, but the meeting was averted.

He was sworn a privy councillor on December 2, 1760, and with the rank of Major-General he was appointed Lieutenant-General of Ordnance on May 14, 1763, which position he held until 1767. On March 12, 1764, he had succeeded to his father's title and became fourth Viscount Townshend. On August 12, 1767, he was appointed Lord-Lieutenant of Ireland. Here he found stormy experiences for five years. Mr. Lecky, in his "History of England," says: "Lord Townshend is one of the very small number of Irish viceroys who have been personally disliked . . . his abilities were superior to those of many of his predecessors and successors; but he was utterly destitute of tact and judgment. . . . He sought for popularity by sacrificing the dignity and decorum of his position, and he brought both his person and his office into contempt."

In his effort to be popular he wore Irish cloth. There is no doubt that he sympathized with the toiling peasants. In his "Meditations upon a Late Excursion in Ireland" are some verses beginning: —

"Ill-fated kingdom with a fertile soil,
Whose factors mock the naked peasants' toil."

VANCOUVER'S DISCOVERY

[Original Journal, Pages 77–78.]

[May, 1792.]

On the top of each was stuck a human head, recently placed there. The hair and flesh were nearly perfect; and the heads appeared to carry the evidence of fury or revenge, as, in driving the stakes through the throat to the cranium, the sagittal, with part of the scalp, was borne on their points some inches above the rest of the skull. Between the stakes a fire had been made, and near some calcined bones were observed, but none of these appearances enabled us to satisfy ourselves, concerning the manner in which the bodies had been disposed of.

The situation of this point is a little to the southward of the narrow passage Mr. Johnstone had gone through; the north extremity of which is formed by a very long sandy spit, where seventeen of the long supported poles were seen like those before described on New Dungeness. These poles had frequently presented themselves, though in less numbers than on the present occasion; but though these afforded us an opportunity of examining them, they did not contribute the least instruction concerning the purpose for which they were intended. They were uniformly placed in the center of the low sandy spit, at the distance of about eighty yards from

---

In the midst of his troubles with the Irish Parliament, Townshend allowed his pencil to betray his feelings. He drew caricatures of himself, showing his hands tied and his mouth open.

He was recalled from Ireland in September, 1772. The eventful portion of his life was ended. He was promoted to General on November 20, 1782, and to Field Marshal, July 30, 1796. He received a host of appointments to offices, such as Governor of Hull, Governor of Chelsea Hospital, Governor of Jersey, Lord-Lieutenant and Vice-Admiral of the County of Norfolk. On October 31, 1786, he was created Marquis Townshend of Rainham. It was this newly conferred honor that Vancouver remembered as he sailed from England in 1791.

The Marquis died at Rainham on September 14, 1807, and was buried in the family vault there on September 28.

Besides the portrait by Hudson already referred to there is another full-length painting by Sir Joshua Reynolds. This was painted in his later days after he had become Marquis. This painting recently sold at Christie's for £2205. As this portrait shows the man as he was when Vancouver placed his name upon his chart, it has been chosen for an illustration of the present work.

PETER RAINIER, Admiral of the Blue.
Photograph from the collection of Augustin Rischgitz, London.

each other; and it should seem that they were required to be of certain definite heights, although not all equally high. They were, in general, about six inches in diameter at the bottom, and perfectly straight; and, when too short, a piece was added, which was very neatly scarfed on; the top of each terminating in two points like a crescent, or rather like the straight spreading horns of an ox. The tallest of these poles I should suppose to be about one hundred feet, the shortest not so high by ten or fifteen feet. Between several of them large holes were dug in the ground, in which were many stones that had been burnt, which gave these holes the resemblance of the cooking places in the South-Sea islands. There was, however, no appearance of any recent operations of that kind.

In most of my excursions I met with an indurated clay, much resembling fuller's-earth. The high steep cliff, forming the point of land we were now upon, seemed to be principally composed of this matter; which, on a more close examination, appeared to be a rich species of the marrow stone, from whence it obtained the name of MARROW-STONE POINT. East of this cliff, the shore is extended about a quarter of a mile by one of those sandy projecting points we had so frequently met with. Here we dined, and had an excellent view of this inlet, which appeared to be of no inconsiderable extent. The eastern shore stretched by compass from N. 41 W. to S. 51 E.; the south extremity of the western shore bore S. 26 E.; and, between these latter bearings, the horizon was occupied by islands, or land appearing much broken. The weather was serene and pleasant, and the country continued to exhibit, between us and the eastern snowy range, the same luxuriant appearance. At its northern extremity, mount Baker bore by compass N. 22 E.; the round snowy mountain, now forming its southern extremity, and which, after my friend Rear Admiral Rainier, I distinguished by the name of MOUNT RAINIER, bore N. [S.] 42 E.

Rear-Admiral Rainier. The United States government has created the Mount Rainier National Park. And now, in order to make more available

VANCOUVER'S DISCOVERY

[Original Journal, Pages 79-80.]

[May, 1792.]

Having finished all our business at this station, the boats received the same directions as before; and having appointed the western part of some land appearing like a long island, and bearing S. E. by S. four leagues distant, for our evening's rendezvous, we left Marrow-Stone point with a pleasant gale, and every prospect of accomplishing our several tasks. The favourable breeze availed us but little; for we had not advanced a league before we found the influence of so strong an ebb tide that, with all the exertions of our oars in addition to our sails, we could scarcely make any progress along the

---

to the citizens the wonders and beauties of that park, the government is building through it a road of easy grades. The mountain itself is one of the highest and most beautiful on the whole American hemisphere. For a score or more of years there has been a rather heated contest over changing the name to "Tacoma," supposed to have been the name used by the Indians living within sight of it along the shores of Puget Sound. For these reasons there ought to be a desire to know something of the life of the man whom Vancouver so greatly honored on that Monday, May 7, 1792.

Upon the revocation of the Edict of Nantes, among the Huguenots who went to England, was a Poitevan family who spelled their name Regnier. Daniel Regnier had a son, who, being an Englishman born and bred was called Peter Rainier of Sandwich. He took to himself an English wife named Sarah Spratt, and to this pair was born about the year 1741 a son who received the full name of his father and became a famous sailor. He is the subject of this brief sketch.

When about fifteen years old, in 1756, he entered the British navy on board the *Oxford*. He served on her two years and then in the *Yarmouth* to the East Indies for service on the *Tiger*. He was in the actions of April 29 and August 3, 1758, and September 10, 1759. In June, 1760, he was moved to the *Norfolk* under Rear-Admiral Stevens at the siege of Pondicherry and later at the reduction of Manila under Vice-Admiral Cornish. The *Norfolk* was paid off in England in 1764, and for the next ten years Rainier saw no service in the navy, though he was carried on the lists. He passed his examination, February 2, 1768, his certificate stating that he was then over twenty-six years old. He was promoted to the rank of lieutenant on May 26, 1768. During these years he seems to have been employed under the East India Company.

In 1774 his active work in the navy was resumed. He went to the West Indies in the *Maidstone* under Captain Alan Gardner, whose name figures often in this book. On May 3, 1777, Vice-Admiral Clark Gayton promoted young Rainier to the command of the *Ostrich* sloop. This was the time of the American War for Independence, and of course Lieutenant Rainier was

[May, 1792.]

coast. Towards sunset, both the wind and the weather materially changed; the former became light and variable, from the southern quarter, and brought with it incessant torrents of rain. We persevered, however, in our endeavors to gain our destined point, but without success, until about eleven at night; when, having collected the boats by signal, we bore up for the western, which was nearest the shore, and landed about one in the morning, completely drenched. With some difficulty we got a fire, and found a tolerable place for our tents. This, though uncomfortable, protected us in some degree from the inclemency of the weather, which de-

---

on the British side. In his newly acquired command, on July 8, 1778, he captured a large American privateer after a severe struggle. In this fight Rainier was severely wounded. His victory met with warm approval. The Admiralty advanced him to post rank, October 29, 1778, and in the following January he was given command of the *Burford*, of sixty-four guns. In her, under Sir Edward Hughes, he took part in all the engagements in the East Indies, including the reduction of Negapatam and Trincomalee. After the war the *Burford* returned to England and Rainier was put on half-pay.

His active service seems to have been revived in 1790 when he commanded the *Monarch* in the Channel. Early in 1794 he sailed again for the East Indies, this time in the *Suffolk*, of seventy-four guns. He was Commodore and Commander-in-Chief, and with the *Suffolk*, went a large convoy. This fleet arrived at Madras in November without having made a stop, which was in that day considered a great achievement.

He was promoted to the active rank of Rear-Admiral on June 1, 1795, and to that of Vice-Admiral on February 14, 1799. He continued as Commander-in-Chief on the East India station until 1804. During that time he assisted in the capture of several ports yielding immense booty, his share of which made him a rich man. His principal duty in the East Indies was to protect British subjects and British interests. His long experience in that section fitted him to render this service well, and even after he returned to England and retired from active service the ministry continued to consult him on East Indian affairs.

In the Trafalgar promotions of November 9, 1805, Rainier was advanced to the rank of Admiral of the Blue. He was elected to Parliament for Sandwich in May, 1807. On April 7, 1808, he died at his house on Great George Street, Westminster. In his will he left one-tenth of his property, proved at £250,000, toward the extinguishment of the national debt. He was a bachelor; but there have been nephews, grand nephews, and great-grand nephews by the name of Rainier in the British navy from the days of Admiral Peter to the present time.

tained us all the next day. On Wednesday morning the 9th, we found ourselves near the south extremity of the narrow shoal passage through which Mr. Johnstone had passed from port Townshend, in a very fine cove, affording good anchorage from 10 to 25 fathoms, excellent holding ground, and sufficiently capacious to accommodate many vessels. We traversed its northern shores, but could not find any water, except such as dripped in small quantities from the rocks. Whilst detained by this unfavorable weather, some of the young gentlemen in their excursions found several oak-trees, of which they produced specimens; but stated that they had not seen any exceeding three or four feet in circumference. In consequence of this valuable discovery, the place obtained the name of OAK COVE.

The weather in some measure clearing up soon after daybreak on Thursday the 10th, we again embarked, and continued on the same western or continental shore, making a very slow progress, owing to a strong ebb tide, and a fresh S. E. wind, against us.

We had not been long out of Oak cove, when we descried some Indians paddling slowly under the lee of a rocky point, with an apparent intention of waiting our approach. In this they were soon gratified, and on our arrival, they did not seem to express the least doubt of our friendly disposition towards them. They courteously offered such things as they possessed, and cordially accepted some medals, beads, knives, and other trinkets, which I presented to them, and with which they appeared to be highly pleased. We were now employed in taking such necessary angles as the weather permitted us to obtain, and in acquiring some further information of this inlet. It appeared to be divided into two branches; the most extensive one took its direction to the south-eastward of land appearing like a long, low island; the other, apparently much less, stretched to the south-westward of the same land; the shores of which terminating in a high perpendicular bluff point, was, in consequence of the change we experienced in its neighborhood, called FOULWEATHER BLUFF.

OF PUGET SOUND

[May, 1792.]

As my intentions were not to depart from the continental boundary, the western arm was the first object of our examination; and we directed our course towards a high lump of land that had the appearance of an island, entertaining little doubt of finding a way into the south eastern, or main arm, south of the supposed long low island. Off this point lie some rocks above water, with others visible only at low tide, extending at the distance of three fourths of a mile, and nearly a mile along the shore. The country thereabouts presented a very different aspect from that which we had been accustomed to see. Instead of the sandy cliffs that form the shores within the straits, these were composed of solid rocks. On them the herbage and shrubs seemed to flourish with less luxuriance, though the trees appeared to form a much greater variety. Having landed about nine o'clock to breakfast, and to take the advantage of the sun and wind to dry some of our clothes, our friends the Indians, seventeen in number, landed also from six canoes about half a mile ahead of us, and then walked towards our party, attended by a single canoe along the shore; they having hauled up all the others. They now approached us with the utmost confidence, without being armed, and behaved in the most respectful and orderly manner. On a line being drawn with a stick on the sand between the two parties, they immediately sat down, and no one attempting to pass it, without previously making signs, requesting permission for so doing.

In their persons, dress, canoes, etc. they much resembled the Indians of port Discovery; they had not the most distant knowledge of the Nootka language, and it was with some difficulty that any of their numerals were acquired. They had not any thing to dispose of excepting their bows, arrows and some few of their woollen and skin garments; amongst the latter appeared to be the skin of a young lioness. These they exchanged for trinkets, and other things of little value, and in the traffic conducting themselves in a very fair and honest manner.

After we had embarked they examined the place where we had been sitting, and then paddling towards their village, which was situated in a very pleasant cove a little to the S. W. and built with wood, after the fashion of the deserted ones we had before seen. The wind blowing strong from the southward so much retarded our progress, that at noon we had only reached the N. W. point of the arm we had been steering for, and which was not more than five miles from our station in Oak cove, in a direction S. 14 E.; its observed latitude was 47° 53', longitude 237° 36', Foulweather bluff forming the opposite point of entrance into the arm, bore east about half a league distant. The strength of the ebb tide obliged us to stop near two hours, and from its rapidity we were induced to believe, as we had before suspected, that either the eastern shore was an island, or that the tide had extensive inland communication.

On the flood returning, we resumed our route, and found our supposed high round island connected with the main by a low sandy neck of land, nearly occupied by a salt-water swamp. Into the bay, formed between this point and that we had departed from, descended a few small streams of fresh water; with which, so far as we were enabled to judge, the country did not abound. This opinion was sanctioned by the Indians who visited us this morning, bringing with them small square boxes filled with fresh water, which we could not tempt them to dispose of. Hence this branch of the inlet takes a direction about S. W. ½ S. near 13 miles, and is in general about half a league wide. Its shores exhibited by no means the luxuriant appearance we had left behind, being nearly destitute of the open verdant spots, and alternately composed of sandy or rocky cliffs falling abruptly into the sea, or terminating on a beach; whilst in some places the even land extended from the water side, with little or no elevation. The low projecting points cause the coast to be somewhat indented with small bays, where, near the shore, we had soundings from five to twelve fathoms; but in the middle of the channel, though not more than two miles in width, no bottom could be reached with 110 fathoms of line.

We had not advanced more than two or three miles before we lost the advantage of the flood tide, and met a stream that ran constantly down. This, with a very fresh S. W. wind, so retarded our progress, that it was not until Friday the 11th at noon that we reached the extent above mentioned, which we found to be situated due south of our observatory in port Discovery, in the latitude of 47° 39'. From this station, which I called HAZEL POINT in consequence of its producing many of those trees, the channel divides into two branches, one taking a direction nearly due north, the other S. W. We still continued on the right hand, or continental shore, and found the northern arm terminate at the distance of about seven miles in a spacious bason, where bottom could not be found with 70 fathoms of line. As we returned to take up our abode for the night at the S. W. point of this arm, we observed some smoke on shore, and saw a canoe hauled up into a small creek; but none of the inhabitants could be discovered, nor did we hear or see any thing of them during the night.

The next morning, Saturday the 12th, at four o'clock, we again embarked. Having been supplied for five days only, our provisions were greatly exhausted, and the commencement of this, which was the sixth, threatened us with short allowance. Our sportsmen had been unable to assist our stock; and the prospect of obtaining any supplies from the natives was equally uncertain. The region we had lately passed seemed nearly destitute of human beings. The brute creation also had deserted the shores; the tracks of deer were no longer to be seen; nor was there an aquatic bird on the whole extent of the canal; animated nature seemed nearly exhausted; and her awful silence was only now and then interrupted by the croaking of a raven, the breathing of a seal, or the scream of an eagle. Even these solitary sounds were so seldom heard, that the rustling of the breeze along the shore, assisted by the solemn stillness that prevailed, gave rise to ridiculous suspicions in our seamen of hearing rattlesnakes, and other hideous monsters, in the wilderness, which was composed of the productions already mentioned, but which appeared to grow with infinitely less vigour than we had been accustomed to witness.

[May, 1792.]

To the westward and N. W. lay that range of snowy mountains, noticed the morning we spoke with the *Columbia*. These gradually descended in a southern direction, whilst the summit of the eastern range now and then appearing, seemed to give bounds to this low country on that side. Between the S. E. and S. W. a country of a very moderate height seemed to extend as far as the eye could reach; and, from its eminences and vallies, there was reason to believe that this inlet continued to meander a very considerable distance, which made me much regret that we were not provided for a longer excursion. Yet, having proceeded thus far, I resolved to continue our researches, though at the expense of a little hunger, until the inlet should either terminate, or so extensively open, as to render it expedient that the vessels should be brought up; which would be a very tedious and disagreeable operation, in consequence of the narrowness of the channel, and the great depth of the water. Soundings in some places only could be gained close to the shore; and in the middle no bottom had anywhere been found with 100 fathoms of line, although the shores were in general low, and not half a league asunder.

Having very pleasant weather, and a gentle favorable breeze, we proceeded, and passed several runs of fresh water. Near one of the largest we observed our latitude at noon to be 47° 27'; and once again had the pleasure of approaching an inhabited country. A canoe, in which there were three men, went alongside the launch, and bartered a few trifles for beads, iron, and copper, but declined every invitation from us to come on shore. From Mr. Puget I learned, that they appeared to be very honest in their dealings, and had used their utmost endeavors to prevail on the party in the launch to attend them home, which he understood to be at the distance of about a league, and for which they seemed to make the best of their way, probably to acquaint their friends with the approach of strangers. Soon after we had dined, a smoke was observed near the supposed place of their residence; made, as we concluded, for the purpose of directing us to their habitations, for which we immediately set off, agreeably to their very civil invitation.

OF PUGET SOUND

[May, 1792.]

An idea during this excursion had occurred to us, that part of the brute creation have an aversion to the absence of the human race; this opinion seemed now in some measure confirmed, by the appearance for the first time during the last three days, of several species of ducks, and other aquatic birds. I do not, however, mean absolutely to infer, that it is the affection of the lower orders of the creation to man, that draws them to the same spots which human beings prefer, since it is highly probable that such places as afford the most eligible residence in point of sustenance to the human race, in an uncivilized state, may be, by the brute creation, resorted to for the same purpose.

The habitations of our new friends appeared to be situated nearly at the extremity of this inlet, or where it appeared to take a very sharp turn to the S. E. still favoring our hopes of returning by the great eastern arm. These, however, vanished on landing, as we found its S. W. direction terminate in land, apparently low and swampy, with a shoal extending some distance from its shores, forming a narrow passage to the south-eastward into a cove or bason, which seemed its termination also in that direction.

Here we found the finest stream of fresh water we had yet seen; from the size, clearness, and rapidity of which, little doubt could be entertained of its having its source in perpetual springs. Near it were two miserable huts with mats thrown carelessly over them, protecting their tenants neither from the heat nor severity of the weather; these huts seemed calculated to contain only the five or six men then present, though previously to our quitting the boats we supposed a greater number of persons had been seen; those were probably their women, who on our approach had retired to the woods.

These good people conducted themselves in the most friendly manner. They had little to dispose of, yet they bartered away their bows and arrows without the least hesitation, together with some small fish, cockles, and clams; of the latter we purchased a large quantity, a supply of which was very acceptable in the low condition of our stock. They made us clearly to understand, that in the cove to the S. E. we should find a number of their countrymen, who had the like commodities to dispose of; and being anxious to leave no doubt concerning a further inland navigation by this arm of the sea, and wishing to establish, as far as possible, a friendly intercourse with the inhabitants of the country, which, from the docile and inoffensive manners of those we had seen, appeared a task of no great difficulty, we proceeded to a low point of land that forms the north entrance into the cove. There we beheld a number of natives, who did not betray the smallest apprehension at our approach; the whole assembly remained quietly seated on the grass, excepting two or three whose particular office seemed to be that of making us welcome to their country. These presented us with some fish, and received in return trinkets of various kinds, which delighted them excessively. They attended us to their companions, who amounted in number to about sixty, including the women and children. We were received by them with equal cordiality, and treated with marks of great friendship and hospitality. A short time was here employed in exchanges of mutual civilities. The females on this occasion took a very active part. They presented us with fish, arrows, and other trifles, in a way that convinced us they had much pleasure in so doing. They did not appear to differ in any respect from the inhabitants we had before seen; and some of our gentlemen were of opinion that they recognized the persons of one or two who had visited us on the preceding Thursday morning; particularly one man, who had suffered very much from the small pox. This deplorable disease is not only common, but it is greatly to be apprehended is very fatal amongst them, as its indelible marks were seen on many; and several had lost the sight of one eye, which was remarked to be generally the left, owing most likely to the virulent effects of this baneful disorder. The residence of these people here was doubtless of a temporary nature; few had taken the trouble of erecting their usual miserable huts, being content to lodge on the ground, with loose mats only for their covering.

LORD HOOD.

From the painting by Lemuel F. Abbott, in the National Portrait Gallery, London. Photograph copyrighted by Walker & Cockrell. Rights secured for this work in England and America. Engraving made in England for this work.

[May, 1792.]

From this point, which is situated nearly at the south extremity of the channel in latitude 47° 21′, longitude 237° 6½′, little doubt existed of the cove terminating its navigation. To ascertain this, whilst I remained with these civil people, Mr. Johnstone was directed to row round the projection that had obstructed our view of the whole circumference of the cove, which is about two miles; and, if it were not closed, to pursue its examination. Our former conjectures being confirmed, on his return we prepared to depart; and, as we were putting off from the shore, a cloak of inferior sea otter skins was brought down, which I purchased for a small piece of copper. Upon this they made signs that if we would remain, more, and of a superior quality, should be produced; but as this was not our object, and as we had finished our proposed talk sooner than was expected this morning, to the no small satisfaction of our whole party, we directed our course back towards port Discovery, from which we were now about 70 miles distant.

A fresh northwardly wind, and the approach of night, obliged us to take up our abode about two miles from the Indians, some of whom had followed us along the beach until we landed, when they posted themselves at the distance of about half a mile, to observe our different employments; at dark they all retired, and we neither heard nor saw any thing more of them. The rise and fall of the tide, although the current constantly ran down without any great degree of rapidity, appeared to have been nearly ten feet, and it was high water 3h 50′ after the moon passed the meridian.

Early on Sunday morning the 13th, we again embarked; directing our route down the inlet, which, after the Right Honorable Lord Hood, I called Hood's Channel; but our

---

Lord Hood. Any one visiting the shores of Hood's Canal, that beautiful inlet of the sea, running parallel with and counted a part of what is now generally known as Puget Sound, will be confused with the theories advanced as to the origin of the name. These theories cluster around the local tradition that years ago one of the first settlers bore the name of Hood, and, being killed by the Indians, his name was given to the waterway. The falsity of this tradition and its accompanying theories is seen by a perusal of

VANCOUVER'S DISCOVERY

[Original Journal, Page 93.]

[May, 1792.]

progress homeward was so very slow, that it was Monday afternoon, the 14th, before we reached Foulweather bluff. This promontory is not ill named, for we had scarcely landed, when a heavy rain commenced, which continuing the rest of the day, obliged us to remain stationary. This detention I endeavoured to reconcile with the hope that the next morning

---

Vancouver's journal, wherein on Sunday, May 13, 1792, the discoverer names the waterway Hood's Channel, "after the Right Honorable Lord Hood." It is a curious fact that Vancouver named many places "channels" in his journal, but wrote them down as "canals" on his excellent charts. This was the case with Hood's Canal.

Lord Hood was again honored by this expedition. In October, 1792, while Lieutenant Broughton was exploring the Columbia River he saw a fine mountain and on receiving his report, Vancouver wrote in his journal as follows: "The same remarkable mountain that had been seen from Belle Vue point, again presented itself, bearing at this station S. 67 E.; and though the party were now nearer to it by 7 leagues, yet its lofty summit was scarcely more distinct across the intervening land which was more than moderately elevated. Mr. Broughton honored it with Lord Hood's name; its appearance was magnificent; and it was clothed in snow from its summit, as low down as the high land, by which it was intercepted, rendered it visible. Mr. Broughton lamented that he could not acquire sufficient authority to ascertain its positive situation, but imagined it could not be less than 20 leagues from their then station." The station referred to is now occupied by the city of Vancouver.

Rumors and traditions about the Canal's name are not the only confusing matter, for it is unexpectedly discovered that there is also confusion in the biographies of the Hoods. There have been many of them prominent in English history. Two of them, cousins, bore the same name, were contemporaneous, and each attained high rank in the Royal Navy. However, the Samuel Hood who could be referred to in 1792 as the "Right Honorable Lord" is the one in whom we are interested at this moment, and there is but one such among all the Hoods of that day.

He was born on December 12, 1724. His father was vicar of Butleigh in Somerset. His education was that of a sailor, for on May 6, 1741, he entered the navy as captain's servant under Captain Thomas Smith, popularly known as "Tom of Ten Thousand." Hood's junior service was in ships along the coast of Scotland, in the North Sea, and in the British Channel, always, however, under splendid officers. He became a lieutenant in 1746 and experienced considerable service in American and other stations until he was posted to the *Lively* on July 22, 1756. This promotion was deserved, but just as his chance seemed best he was transferred to the *Grafton*, which soon returned to England and was paid off.

would permit some examination, or at least afford us a view of the great eastern arm, before we returned to the ships; but in this I was disappointed. After waiting until ten o'clock in the forenoon of Tuesday the 15th, without the least prospect of an alteration for the better, we again set out with a fresh breeze at S. S. E. attended with heavy squalls and torrents

---

In January, 1757, Hood wrote to Lord Temple that he was "no ways inclined to be idle ashore while anything can be got to employ me." He offered his services to take temporary command of any ship whose captain was absent on the court-martial of Admiral Byng. He then received several such temporary appointments, and while in one of them he drove a French ship of fifty guns ashore and captured two privateers. In approving this the Admiralty gave him permanent command. Sailing in the *Vestal* for America under Commodore Holmes he overtook the French frigate *Bellona*, which was captured by Hood after a severe single-handed fight. Returning to England, he was employed along the coast of France.

In 1760 he requested and received service in the Mediterranean for the benefit of failing health. In 1765 he carried a regiment of foot soldiers to North America in the *Thunderer*, and in April, 1767, he was appointed Commander-in-Chief in North America. He returned to England in 1771.

Hood's career up to this time was successful but not remarkable. It was thought to have come to a close in January, 1778, when he was appointed Commissioner at Portsmouth and Governor of the Naval Academy. This idea was emphasized in May when the king, on visiting Portsmouth, created Hood a Baronet. It was a matter of surprise, therefore, when in September, 1780, Hood was promoted to the rank of Rear-Admiral of the Blue and was sent with a strong squadron to reënforce Sir George Rodney in the West Indies. Under Rodney and later under Admiral Hugh Pigot, Hood remained as second in command in the American waters until the peace of 1783. He took part in nearly all of the stirring naval engagements that marked the close of the American War for Independence. He received his share of the severe criticism for the failure to relieve Cornwallis at Yorktown. The entire campaign was counted a success, and Hood's participation was especially approved. Before his return to England, on September 12, 1782, he was raised to the Irish peerage as Baron Hood of Catherington, Hampshire. On his return he was presented with the freedom of London in a gold box, and was elected to Parliament for Westminster in 1784. In September, 1787, he became Vice-Admiral of the Blue, and in July, 1788, was made a member of the Board of Admiralty under the Earl of Chatham. In this capacity he signed the original instructions for Vancouver's voyage, which is probably another reason for his being honored by the discoverer.

Admiral Hood remained in this position until the outbreak of the war of the French Revolution, when he again saw active service. He captured

of rain; and about four in the afternoon arrived on board, much to the satisfaction I believe of all parties, as great anxiety had been entertained for our safety, in consequence of the unexpected length of our absence. The swivels fired from our boat and that of the *Chatham's* the morning after our departure, were heard on board, and were the cause of much alarm after the expiration of the time appointed for our return. Such attention had been paid to the several common occupations going forward when I left the ships, that I had the satisfaction to find everything accomplished. But from Mr. Whidbey I understood, that the weather had been so unfavorable to our astronomical pursuits, that he had not been able to obtain any lunar distances, though he had suc-

---

Corsica, but the major portion of his work in this campaign was in the famous case of Toulon. The situation was one of terrible confusion, viewed from Hood's position. There was the disaffection of the French themselves, the presence of the Spaniards and the English. When the crisis was reached and Hood decided to leave Toulon, the populace clamored to be carried away to safety. Fifteen thousand of these were embarked, including all who seemed liable to punishment, and yet of those who were left a number estimated at from one thousand to six thousand were guillotined or shot by officers of the Convention. On leaving Toulon, Hood gave orders to destroy the French ships, which orders were imperfectly carried out. Toulon was a failure, but Corsica was a brilliant success. Lord Nelson, then a captain under Hood, wrote to his brother, "All has been done by seamen and troops embarked to serve as marines, except a few artillery under the orders of Lord Hood, who has given in this instance a most astonishing proof of the vigour of his mind and of his zeal and judgment."

But Hood was recalled and on that occasion Nelson wrote, "The fleet must regret the loss of Lord Hood, the best officer, take him altogether, that England has to boast of; great in all situations which an admiral can be placed in." When recalled Hood was succeeded by his friend Sir William Hotham, who wrote of him: "I never saw an officer of more intrepid courage or warmer zeal; no difficulties stood in his way, and he was a stranger to any feeling of nervous diffidence of himself. Without the least disposition to severity, there was something about him which made his inferior officers stand in awe of him. He was so watchful upon his post himself that those who acted with him were afraid to slumber; and his advanced age at the time he was last employed appears neither to have impaired the vigour of his understanding nor in any way cooled the ardour of his zeal. . . . He was exceedingly liberal, and never was nor would have been a rich man."

MONUMENT TO LORD HOOD AND OTHERS.

In the old cemetery at Greenwich Hospital. Photograph secured by special permission of the Lords Commissioners of the Admiralty.

[May, 1792.]

ceeded in ascertaining the rate of the chronometers. Having, however, acquired sufficient authority of this nature for correcting our survey, and carrying it further into execution, I determined to depart as soon as the weather should break up. This did not happen until Thursday afternoon the 17th; when the tents and observatory were re-embarked, and every thing got in readiness for sailing the next morning, Friday the 18th. A light air from the S. E. and pleasant weather, favored our departure; and about breakfast time, the ship arriving at the entrance of the port, I landed on the east end of Protection island, in order, from its eminence, to take a more accurate view of the surrounding shores. In most directions, they seemed much broken, particularly in the northern quarter, being there occupied by an archipelago of islands of various sizes. On my return on board, I directed Mr. Broughton

---

Before his recall he had been elected an Elder Brother of Trinity House on March 25, 1795, and on April 12 of the same year he was promoted to the rank of Admiral. In March, 1796, he was appointed Governor of Greenwich Hospital, a post he held until his death. On June 1, 1796, he was created Viscount Hood in the peerage of Great Britain. In 1815, on the restoration of the Order of the Bath, Hood received the Grand Cross of the Bath. His friend Hotham is authority for this, "He was very attentive to his religious duties, and talked of and viewed his approaching dissolution with the courage of a strong mind and the hope of a religious one." Though attaining to the age of ninety-two years, he retained his faculties to the last. He died on January 27, 1816, and was buried in the old cemetery of Greenwich Hospital.

There are several portraits of this famous man in existence. The one selected for reproduction in this work is Number 628 in the National Portrait Gallery. It was painted by Lemuel F. Abbott. In seeking information about his last resting place, special permission was obtained from the Director of Greenwich Hospital to secure a photograph of the magnificent monument to Hood and others buried in the old cemetery. This monument was erected by order of the Lords Commissioners of the Admiralty in 1892. Part of the inscription reads, "In memory of the gallant officers and men of the Royal Navy and marines, the number of about 20,000, formerly inmates of Greenwich Hospital, whose remains were interred in the cemetery between the years 1749 and 1869." In a letter on this subject the Director says, "I may add that the original grave of Viscount Hood was not interfered with for the erection of this monument, and I am not aware that reference has been made to the monument in any book or published document."

to use his endeavors, in the *Chatham,* to acquire some information in that line, whilst I continued my examination with the *Discovery* up the inlet which we had discovered in the boats, to the eastward of Foulweather bluff; appointing the first inlet to the south-eastward of that point on the starboard, or continental shore, as our place of rendezvous. We parted about noon in pleasant weather, and with a fine breeze directed our vessels agreeably to our respective pursuits.

As a more particular description of port Discovery and the surrounding country would have interfered with our primary object of ascertaining the boundary of this coast, I shall reserve it for the subject of the following short chapter; and shall conclude this with such astronomical and nautical observations as circumstances permitted us to make whilst in port, as well as those made previous to our arrival and after our departure; which have assisted in fixing its longitude, as well as that of the exterior coast of New Albion southward to cape Mendocino.

A part of this coast, prior to our visit, had been seen by different navigators, and the position of certain head lands, capes, etc. given to the world. Several of these I have found myself under the necessity of placing in different latitudes and longitudes, as well those seen by Captain Cook, as others laid down by the different visitors who have followed him. This, however, I have not presumed to do, from a consciousness of superior abilities as an astronomer, or integrity as an historian; but from the conviction, that no one of my predecessors had the good fortune to meet so favorable an opportunity for the examination: under the happy circumstances of which I have been induced to assign, to the several conspicuous head lands, points, etc. the positions ascertained by the result of our several observations; from which, as it evidently appeared that our chronometer had materially accelerated on its Otaheitean rate, it may not be unacceptable to state the mode I adopted for the correction of that error.

In our passage towards, and during our stay amongst, the Sandwich islands, the chronometer, agreeably to its

OF PUGET SOUND

[May, 1792.] [Original Journal, Pages 96–98.]

Otaheitean rate, seemed to have been accurate to a scrupulous degree of nicety; but, by some observations made prior to the 26th of March, it appeared to have deviated manifestly from the truth. The observations made on that day were the most remote ones I made use of on this occasion; and, by the mean result of all made since in port Discovery, instead of the chronometer gaining at the rate of 4″ 3‴ per day only, it was found to be gaining 11″ 55‴ per day; and therefore, instead of the allowance of the former rate, from the 26th of March to our arrival on the coast, it was increased to 8″ per day; and from the 17th of April, 11″ 30‴ were allowed as the rate of the chronometer, for the purpose of reducing all our observations from that period to our arrival in port Discovery; which medium, I trust, will hereafter be found fully to answer my expectations. The following will serve to exhibit the different observations made to establish this point, comprehending two hundred and twenty sets of lunar distances, each set containing six observations, taken by the several officers and gentlemen on board, as follows:

Mr. Puget, nine sets taken between the 28th March and 9th of April...237° 19′ 5″
Mr. Whidbey, fifty-eight ditto, the 26th March and 12th of June...237° 23′ 38″
Mr. Orchard, fifty-three ditto, ditto.......................237° 22′
Mr. J. Stewart, twenty-four ditto, 27th March and 29th April..237° 25′ 50″
Mr. Ballard, thirty-eight ditto, do......................237° 22′ 50″
Myself thirty-eight ditto, the 28th of March and 5th of May...237° 21′ 9″

Hence the longitude of the observatory deduced from the mean result of the above observed distances of the sun, moon and stars was...237° 22′ 19″
On our arrival in port Discovery, the chronometer, by the Portsmouth rate, on the 4th of May, showed............237° 51′
By the Otaheitean rate....................................235° 59′
Mr. Arnold's chronometer on board the *Chatham*, by the Otaheitean rate..235° 27′

From the above observations, and nine days corresponding altitudes, Kendal's chronometer was found, on the 13th of

May at noon, to be fast of mean time at Greenwich 45′ 46″, and to be gaining on mean time at the rate of 11″ 55‴ per day. By the same observations, Mr. Arnold's, on the 13th of May at noon, was fast of mean time at Greenwich 2h 56′ 49″, and was gaining on mean time at the rate of 27′ per day.

The latitude of the observatory, by the mean result of nine meridian altitudes was.................................. 48° 2′ 30″

The variation, by all our compasses in eleven sets of azimuths, differing from 20° to 26°, gave their mean result.......... 21° 30′

The vertical inclination of the magnetic needle.
Marked end North face East .... 73° 50′
Ditto   West............................ 75° 57′
Ditto   South face East............................ 72° 17′
Ditto   West............................ 75° 55′

Mean vertical inclination of the North point of the marine dipping needle.. 74° 30′

In port Discovery, the tide was observed to flow on the full of the moon, about ten feet; and was high water 3h 50′ after the moon passed the meridian.

CHAPTER VII

DESCRIPTION OF THE COUNTRY AND THE NATIVE PEOPLES

[May, 1792.] [Original Journal, Pages 100-101, Book II, Chapter V.]

I SHALL now proceed to relate such matters respecting the country of New Albion as appeared entitled to notice, and which are not inserted in the preceding narrative.

Port Discovery, already mentioned as a perfectly safe and convenient harbor, has its outer points $1\frac{3}{4}$ miles asunder, bearing from each other S. 63 W. and N. 63 E.; its entrance is situated in latitude 48° 7′, longitude 237° $20\frac{1}{2}$′, whence the port first takes a direction S. 30 E. about eight miles, and then terminates S. W. by W. about a league further. If it lies under any disadvantage, it is in its great depth of water; in which respect, however, we found no inconvenience, as the bottom was exceedingly good holding ground, and free from rocks. Towards the upper part of the harbor it is of less depth; but I saw no situation more eligible than that in which the vessels rode, off the first low sandy point on the western shore, about $4\frac{1}{2}$ miles within the entrance. Here our wooding, watering, brewing, and all other operations were carried on with the utmost facility and convenience. The shores of Protection island form on its south side, which is about two miles long, a most excellent roadstead, and a channel into port Discovery, near two miles wide on either side, without any interruption, which, with other nautical particulars, are exhibited in the chart.

The country in the neighborhood of this port may generally be considered of a moderate height, although bounded on the west side by mountains covered with snow, to which the land from the water's edge rises in a pleasing diversity by hills of gradual ascent. The snow on these hills probably dissolves as the summer advances, for pine trees were produced on their very summits. On the sea shore the land generally terminated in low sandy cliffs; though in some spaces of considerable extent it ran nearly level from high water mark. The soil for the most part is a light sandy loam, in several places of very considerable depth, and abundantly mixed with decayed vegetables. The vigor and luxuriance of its productions proved it to be a rich fertile mould, which possibly might be considerably improved by the addition of the calcareous matter contained in the marrow stone that presented itself in many places. In respect to its mineral productions no great variety was observed. Iron ore, in its various forms, was generally found; and from the weight and magnetic qualities of some specimens, appeared tolerably rich, particularly a kind much resembled the blood stone. These, with quartz, agate, the common flint, and a great intermixture of other silicious matter, (most of the stones we met with being of that class) with some variety of calcareous magnesian, and argilaceous earths, were the mineral productions generally found.

The parts of the vegetable kingdom applicable to useful purposes appeared to grow very luxuriantly, and consisted of the Canadian and Norwegian hemlock, silver pines, the Tacamahac and Canadian poplar, arbor-vitæ, common yew, black and common dwarf oak, American ash, common hazel, sycamore, sugar, mountain, and Pennsylvanian maple, oriental arbutus, American alder, and common willow; these, with the Canadian alder, small fruited crab, and Pennsylvania cherry trees, constituted the forests, which may be considered rather as encumbered, than adorned, with underwood; although there were several places where, in its present state, the traveller might pass without being in the least incommoded, excepting by the undecayed trunks of trees which had fallen. Of esculent vegetables we found but few; the white or dead nettle, and samphire, were most common; the wild orache, vulgarly called fat-hen, with the vetch. Two or three sorts of wild peas, and the common hedge mustard, were frequently though not always met with, and were considered by us as excellent of their kinds, and served to relish our salt provisions, on which, with a very scanty supply of fish, all hands subsisted. Amongst the more minute productions, Mr. Menzies found constant amusement; and, I believe, was enabled to make some addition to the catalogue of plants.

The knowledge we acquired of the animal kingdom was very imperfect. The skins of the animals already noticed were such as are commonly found amongst the inhabitants on the sea coasts under the same parallel, and towards Nootka; these were mostly of the coarser and more common sorts. Garments of sea otter skins were not worn, nor did many such skins appear amongst the inhabitants. The only living quadrupeds we saw, were a black bear, two or three wild dogs, about as many rabbits, several small brown squirrels, rats, mice, and the skunk, whose effluvia were the most intolerable and offensive I ever experienced.

Few of the feathered tribe were procured, although, on our first arrival, the aquatic birds were so numerous, that we expected a profuse supply of wild fowl; but these were all so extremely shy and watchful, that our guns seldom reached them; and, on being fired at, they disappeared. About the shores and on the rocks, we found some species of the tern, the common gull, sea pigeon of Newfoundland, curlews, sandlarks, shags, and the black sea pye, like those in New Holland and New Zealand; these were however not so abundant as the others. Nor did the woods appear to be much resorted to by the feathered race; two or three spruce partridges had been seen; with few in point of number, and little variety, of small birds: amongst which the humming birds bore a great proportion. At the outskirts of the woods, and about the water side, the white headed and brown eagle; ravens, carrion crows, American king's fisher, and a very handsome woodpecker, were seen in numbers; and in addition to these on the low projecting points, and open places in the woods, we frequently saw a bird with which we were wholly unacquainted, though we considered it to be a species of the crane or heron; some of their eggs were found of a bluish cast, considerably larger than that of a turkey, and well tasted. These birds have remarkably long legs and necks, and their bodies seemed to equal in size the largest turkey. Their plumage is uniformly of a light brown, and when erect, their height, on a moderate computation, could not be less than four feet. They seemed to prefer open situations, and used no endeavors to hide or screen themselves from our sight, but were too vigilant to allow our sportsmen taking them by surprise. Some blue, and some nearly white herons of the common size were also seen.

The sea was not much more bountiful to us of its animal productions than was its shores. The scanty supply of fish we were enabled to procure, consisted in general of the common sorts of small flat-fish, elephant fish, sea bream, sea perch, a large sort of sculpin, some weighing six or eight pounds, with a greenish color about their throat, belly, and gills; these were very coarse, but no ill effects were consequent on eating them. The above, with a few trout, a small sort of eel extremely well tasted, of a yellowish green color, were the fishes we most generally caught. A small common black snake, a few lizards and frogs, together with a variety of common insects, none of which could be considered as very troublesome, were the only creatures of the reptile tribe we observed.

This country, regarded in an agricultural point of view, I should conceive is capable of high improvement, notwithstanding the soil in general may be considered to be light and sandy. Its spontaneous productions in the vicinity of the woods are nearly the same, and grow in equal luxuriance with those under a similar parallel in Europe; favoring the hope, that if nutritious exotics were introduced and carefully attended to, they would succeed in the highest degree. The mildness of the climate, and the forwardness of every species of plants, afforded strong grounds in support of this opinion.

The interruptions we experienced in the general serenity of the weather, were probably no more than were absolutely requisite in the spring of the year to bring forward the annual productions. These were attended with no violence of wind, and the rain which fell, although disagreeable to travellers, was not so heavy as to beat down and destroy the first efforts of vegetation. Under all these favorable circumstances, the country yet labors under one material disadvantage in the scarcity of fresh water. The streams however that we met with appeared sufficient to answer all purposes, in the domestic economy of life, to a very numerous body of inhabitants: and, were the country cleared and searched, there can be little doubt that a variety of eligible situations might be found for establishments, where, with proper exertions, wholesome water might be procured.

What the low country before us toward the range of snowy mountains may produce, remains for future investigation; but judging from what we had seen, it seemed more than probable, that those natural channels of the sea wind in various directions; and that they are capable of affording great advantages to commercial pursuits, by opening communications with parts of the interior country commodiously and delightfully situated. The great depth of water may be offered as an insuperable objection; yet, on a more minute examination, it is likely that many eligible and convenient stopping places might be found for the security of such vessels as would necessarily be employed in those occupations.

Having considered with impartiality the excellencies and defects of this country, as far as came under our observation, it now remains to add a few words on the character of its inhabitants.

None being resident in port Discovery, and our intercourse with them having been very confined, the knowledge we may have acquired of them, their manners, and customs, must necessarily be very limited, and our conclusions drawn chiefly from comparison. From New Dungeness we traversed nearly one hundred and fifty miles of their shores without seeing that number of inhabitants. Those who came within our notice so nearly resembled the people of Nootka, that the best delineation I can offer is a reference to the description of those people, which has before been so ably and with so much justice given to the public.* The only difference I observed

---

* *Vide* Captain Cook's last Voyage.

was, that in their stature they did not generally appear quite so stout; and in their habits were less filthy; for though these people adorn their persons with the same sort of paint, yet it is not laid on in that abundance, nor do they load their hair with that immense quantity of oil and coloring matter, which is so customary amongst the people of Nootka; their hair, as before mentioned, being in general neatly combed and tied behind.

In their weapons, implements, canoes, and dress, they vary little. Their native woollen garment was most in fashion, next to it the skins of deer, bear, etc.; a few wore dresses manufactured from bark, which, like their woollen ones, were very neatly wrought.

Their spears, arrows, fishgigs, and other weapons, were shaped exactly like those of Nootka; but none were pointed with copper, or with muscle shell. The three former were generally barbed, and those pointed with common flint, agate, and bone, seemed of their original workmanship. Yet more of their arrows were observed to be pointed with thin flat iron, than with bone or flint, and it was very singular that they should prefer exchanging those pointed with iron to any of the others. Their bows were of a superior construction: these in general were from two and a half to three feet in length; the broadest part in the middle was about an inch and a half, and about three quarters of an inch thick, neatly made, gradually tapering to each end, which terminated in a shoulder and a hook, for the security of the bow string. They were all made of yew, and chosen with a naturally inverted curve suited to the method of using them. From end to end of the concave side, which when strung became the convex part, a very strong strip of an elastic hide is attached to some, and the skins of serpents to others, exactly the shape and length of the bow, neatly and firmly affixed to the wood by means of a cement, the adhesive property of which I never saw, or heard of being, equalled. It is not to be affected by either dry or damp weather, and forms so strong a connection with the wood, as to prevent a separation without destroying the component parts of both. The bow string is made of the

[May, 1792.]

sinew of some marine animal laid loose, in order to be twisted at pleasure, as the temperature of the atmosphere may require to preserve it at a proper length. Thus is this very neat little weapon rendered portable, elastic, and effective in the highest degree, if we may be allowed to judge by the dexterity with which it was used by one of the natives at port Discovery.

We had little opportunity of acquiring any satisfactory information with regard to the public regulations, or private economy, of these people. The situation and appearance of the places we found them generally inhabiting, indicated their being much accustomed to a change of residence; the deserted villages tended to strengthen the conjecture of their being wanderers. Territorial property appeared to be of little importance; there was plenty of room for their fixed habitations, and those of a temporary nature, which we now found them mostly to occupy, being principally composed of cross sticks, covered with a few mats, as easily found a spot for their erection, as they were removed from one station to another, either as inclination might lead, or necessity compel: and having a very extensive range of domain, they were not liable to interruption or opposition from their few surrounding neighbors.

From these circumstances alone, it may be somewhat premature to conclude that this delightful country has always been thus thinly inhabited; on the contrary, there are reasons to believe it has been infinitely more populous. Each of the deserted villages was nearly, if not quite, equal to contain all the scattered inhabitants we saw, according to the custom of the Nootka people; to whom these have great affinity in their persons, fashions, wants, comforts, construction of these their fixed habitations, and in their general character. It is also possible, that most of the clear spaces may have been indebted, for the removal of their timber and underwood, to manual labor. Their general appearance furnished this opinion, and their situation on the most pleasant and commanding eminences, protected by the forest on every side, except that which would have precluded a view of the sea, seemed to encourage the idea. Not many years since, each of these vacant places might have been allotted to the habitations of different societies, and the variation observed in their extent might have been conformable to the size of each village; on the scite of which, since their abdication, or extermination, nothing but the smaller shrubs and plants had yet been able to rear their heads.

In our different excursions, particularly those in the neighborhood of port Discovery, the scull, limbs, ribs, and back bones, or some other vestiges of the human body, were found in many places promiscuously scattered about the beach, in great numbers. Similar relics were also frequently met with during our survey in the boats; and I was informed by the officers, that in their several perambulations, the like appearances had presented themselves so repeatedly, and in such abundance, as to produce an idea that the environs of port Discovery were a general cemetery for the whole of the surrounding country. Notwithstanding these circumstances do not amount to a direct proof of the extensive population they indicate, yet, when combined with other appearances, they warranted an opinion, that at no very remote period this country had been far more populous than at present. Some of the human bodies were found disposed of in a very singular manner. Canoes were suspended between two or more trees about twelve feet from the ground, in which were the skeletons of two or three persons; others of a larger size were hauled up into the outskirts of the woods, which contained from four to seven skeletons covered over with a broad plank. In some of these broken bows and arrows were found, which at first gave rise to a conjecture, that these might have been warriors, who after being mortally wounded, had, whilst their strength remained, hauled up their canoes for the purpose of expiring quietly in them. But on a further examination this became improbable, as it would hardly have been possible to have preserved the regularity of position in the agonies of death, or to have defended their sepulchres with the broad plank with which each was covered.

The few skeletons we saw so carefully deposited in the

canoes, were probably the chiefs, priests, or leaders of particular tribes, whose followers most likely continue to possess the highest respect for their memory and remains: and the general knowledge I had obtained from experience of the regard which all savage nations pay to their funeral solemnities, made me particularly solicitous to prevent any indignity from being wantonly offered to their departed friends. Baskets were also found suspended on high trees, each containing the skeleton of a young child; in some of which were also small square boxes filled with a kind of white paste, resembling such as I had seen the natives eat, supposed to be made of saranne root; some of these boxes were quite full, others were nearly empty, eaten probably by the mice, squirrels, or birds. On the next low point, south of our encampment, where the gunners were airing the powder, they met with several holes in which human bodies were interred slightly covered over, and in different states of decay, some appearing to have been very recently deposited. About half a mile to the northward of our tents, where the land is nearly level with high water mark, a few paces within the skirting of the wood, a canoe was found suspended between two trees, in which were three human skeletons; and a few paces to the right was a cleared place of nearly forty yards round; where, from the fresh appearance of the burnt stumps, most of its vegetable productions had very lately been consumed by fire. Amongst the ashes we found the sculls, and other bones, of near twenty persons in different stages of calcination; the fire, however, had not reached the suspended canoe, nor did it appear to have been intended that it should. The skeletons found thus disposed, in canoes, or in baskets, bore a very small proportion to the number of sculls and other human bones indiscriminately scattered about the shores. Such are the effects; but of the cause or causes that have operated to produce them, we remained totally unacquainted; whether occasioned by epidemic disease, or recent wars. The character and general deportment of the few inhabitants we occasionally saw, by no means countenanced the latter opinion; they were uniformly civil and friendly, without manifesting the least sign of fear or suspicion at our approach; nor did their appearance indicate their having been much inured to hostilities. Several of their stoutest men had been seen perfectly naked, and contrary to what might have been expected of rude nations habituated to warfare, their skins were mostly unblemished by scars, excepting such as the small pox seemed to have occasioned; a disease which there is great reason to believe is very fatal amongst them. It is not, however, very easy to draw any just conclusions on the true cause from which this havoc of the human race proceeded: this must remain for the investigation of others who may have more leisure, and a better opportunity, to direct such an inquiry: yet it may not be unreasonable to conjecture, that the present apparent depopulation may have arisen in some measure from the inhabitants of this interior part having been induced to quit their former abode, and to have moved nearer the exterior coast for the convenience of obtaining in the immediate mart, with more ease and at a cheaper rate, those valuable articles of commerce, that within these late years have been brought to the sea coasts of this continent by Europeans and the citizens of America, and which are in great estimation amongst these people, being possessed by all in a greater or less degree.

CHAPTER VIII

DISCOVERY OF PUGET SOUND — THE COUNTRY CALLED NEW GEORGIA

[May, 1792.] [Original Journal, Pages 116-117, Book II, Chapter VI.]

AGREEABLY to the proposed destination of each vessel, the *Discovery* and *Chatham*, at noon, on Friday the 18th of May, directed their course towards the objects of their respective pursuits; and as I had already traced the western shore in the boats, we now kept the eastern side on board, which, like the other, abounds with those verdant open places that have been so repeatedly noticed. On one of these beautiful lawns, nearly a league within the entrance of the inlet, about thirty of the natives came from the surrounding woods, and attentively noticed us as we sailed along. We did not discover any habitations near them, nor did we see any canoes on the beach. On the south side of the lawn, were many uprights in the ground, which had the appearance of having formerly been the supporters of their large wooden houses. We used our endeavors to invite these good people on board, but without effect. After advancing about four leagues up the inlet, the pleasant gale, which had attended us from the N. W. died away, and a strong ebb making against us, we were compelled to anchor for the night, in 18 fathoms water, about half a mile from the eastern shore: Marrow-Stone point bearing by compass N. 56 W.; the N. E. point of Oak-cove S. 48 W.; and the Foulweather bluff S. 51 E.

During the night, we had a gentle southerly breeze, attended by a fog which continued until nine o'clock on Saturday morning the 19th, when it was dispersed by a return of the N. W. wind, with which we pursued our route up the inlet; our progress was, however, soon retarded by the fore-topsail yard giving way in the slings; on examination it appeared to have been in a defective state some time. The spare fore-topsail yard was also very imperfect; which obliged us to get the spare main-topsail yard up in its room; and it was a very fortunate circumstance, that these defects were discovered in a country abounding with materials to which we could resort; having only to make our choice from amongst thousands of the finest spars the world produces.

To describe the beauties of this region, will, on some future occasion, be a very grateful task to the pen of a skilful panegyrist. The serenity of the climate, the innumerable pleasing landscapes, and the abundant fertility that unassisted nature puts forth, require only to be enriched by the industry of man with villages, mansions, cottages, and other buildings, to render it the most lovely country that can be imagined; whilst the labour of the inhabitants would be amply rewarded, in the bounties which nature seems ready to bestow on cultivation.

About noon, we passed an inlet on the larboard or eastern shore, which seemed to stretch far to the northward; but, as it was out of the line of our intended pursuit of keeping the continental shore on board, I continued our course up the main inlet, which now extended as far as, from the deck, the eye could reach, though, from the masthead, intervening land appeared, beyond which another high round mountain covered with snow was discovered, apparently situated several leagues to the south of mount Rainier, and bearing by compass S. 22 E. This I considered as a further extension of the eastern snowy range; but the intermediate mountains, connecting it with mount Rainier, were not sufficiently high to be seen at that distance. Having advanced about eight leagues from our last night's station, we arrived off a projecting point of land, not formed by a low sandy spit, but rising abruptly in a low cliff about ten or twelve feet from the water side. Its surface was a beautiful meadow covered with luxuriant herbage; on its western extreme, bordering on the woods, was an Indian village, consisting of temporary habitations, from whence several of the natives assembled to view the ship as we passed by; but none of them ventured off, though several of their canoes were seen on the beach. Here the inlet divided into two extensive branches, one taking a south-eastwardly, the other a south-western direction. Near this place was our appointed rendezvous with the *Chatham;* and under a small island to the S. W. of us, appeared an eligible spot, in which, with security, we might wait her arrival; but, on approaching it, we found the depth of water no where less that 60 fathoms, within a cable's length of the shore. This obliged us to turn up towards the village point, where we found a commodious roadstead; and about seven o'clock in the evening, anchored about a mile from the shore in 38 fathoms water, black sand and muddy bottom. The village point bore by compass N. 4 E.; the nearest opposite shore of the main inlet N. 52 E. about a league distant; and the direction of its southern extent S. E.; the above island lying before the branch leading to the south-westward, bore from S. 36 E. to south, about half a league distant; and the appearance of a small inlet or cove, west, about the same distance. We had no sooner anchored than a canoe in which were two men, paddled round the ship. We attempted to induce them, but they were not to be prevailed upon, to enter the vessel; and having satisfied their curiosity, they hastily returned to the shore. Before the evening closed in, I proceeded to acquire some information respecting the small opening to the westward. It was nearly dark before I reached the shore, which seemed to form a small cove about half a mile in width, encircled by compact shores, with a cluster of rocks above water, nearly in its center, and little worthy of further notice. On my return on board, I directed that a party, under the command of Lieutenant Puget and Mr. Whidbey, should, in the launch and cutter, proceed, with a supply of provisions for a week, to the examination of that branch of the inlet leading to the south-westward; keeping always the starboard or continental shore on board; which was accordingly carried into execution, at four o'clock the next morning.

VANCOUVER'S DISCOVERY

[Original Journal, Pages 120-122.] [May, 1792.]

Our situation being somewhat incommoded by the meeting of different tides, we moved nearer in, and anchored in the same depth, and on the same bottom as before, very conveniently to the shore. Our eastern view was now bounded by the range of snowy mountains from mount Baker, bearing by compass north to mount Rainier, bearing N. [S.] 54 E. The new mountain was hid by the more elevated parts of the low land; and the intermediate snowy mountains in various rugged and grotesque shapes, were seen just to rear their heads above the lofty pine trees, which appearing to compose one uninterrupted forest, between us and the snowy range, presented a most pleasing landscape; nor was our western view destitute of similar diversification. The ridge of mountains on which mount Olympus is situated, whose rugged summits were seen no less fancifully towering over the forest than those on the eastern side, bounded to a considerable extent our western horizon; on these however, not one conspicuous eminence arose, nor could we now distinguish that which on the sea coast appeared to be centrally situated, and forming an elegant bi-forked-mountain. From the southern extremity of these ridges of mountains, there seemed to be an extensive tract of land moderately elevated and beautifully diversified by pleasing inequalities of surface, enriched with every appearance of fertility.

On Sunday the 20th, in the meadow and about the village many of the natives were seen moving about, whose curiosity seemed little excited on our account. One canoe only had been near us, from which was thrown on board the skin of some small animal, and then it returned instantly to the shore.

Our carpenters were busily engaged in replacing the topsail yards with proper spars, which were conveniently found for that purpose. Some beer was brewed from the spruce, which was here very excellent, and the rest of the crew were employed in a variety of other essential services. The gentle N. W. wind generally prevailed in the day, and calms, or light southerly breezes during the night.

Towards noon I went on shore to the village point, for the purpose of observing the latitude; on which occasion I visited the village, if it may be so dignified, as it appeared the most lowly and meanest of its kind. The best of the huts were poor and miserable, constructed something after the fashion of a soldier's tent, by two cross sticks about five feet high, connected at each end by a ridge-pole from one to the other, over some of which was thrown a coarse kind of mat, over others a few loose branches of trees, shrubs, or grass, none however appeared to be constructed for protecting them, either against the heat of summer, or the inclemency of winter. In them were hung up to be cured by the smoke of the fire they kept constantly burning, clams, muscles, and a few other kinds of fish, seemingly intended for their winter's subsistence. The clams perhaps were not all reserved for that purpose, as we frequently saw them strung and worn about the neck, which, as inclination directed, were eaten, two, three, or half a dozen at a time. This station did not appear to have been preferred for the purpose of fishing, as we saw few of the people so employed; nearly the whole of the inhabitants belonging to the village, which consisted of about eighty or an hundred men, women, and children, were busily engaged like swine, rooting up this beautiful verdant meadow in quest of a species of wild onion, and two other roots, which in appearance and taste greatly resembled the saranne, particularly the largest; the size of the smallest did not much exceed a large pea: this Mr. Menzies considered to be a new genus. The collecting of these roots was most likely the object which attached them to this spot; they all seemed to gather them with much avidity, and to preserve them with great care, most probably for the purpose of making the paste I have already mentioned.

These people varied in no essential point from the natives we had seen since our entering the straits. Their persons were equally ill made, and as much besmeared with oil and different colored paints, particularly with red ochre, and a sort of shining chaffy mica, very ponderous, and in color much resembling black lead; they likewise possessed more ornaments, especially such as were made of copper, the article most valued and esteemed amongst them. They seemed not wanting in offers of friendship and hospitality; as on our joining their party, we were presented with such things as they had to dispose of: and they immediately prepared a few of the roots, and some shell fish for our refreshment, which were very palatable. In these civil offices, two men who appeared the most active, and to be regarded by their countrymen as the most important persons of the party, were particularly assiduous to please. To each of them I made presents, which were received very thankfully; and on my returning towards the boat, they gave me to understand by signs, the only means we had of conversing with each other, that it would not be long ere they returned our visit on board the ship. This they accordingly did in the afternoon, with no small degree of ceremony. Beside the canoes which brought these two superior people, five others attended, seemingly as an appendage to the consequence of these chiefs, who would not repair immediately on board, but agreeably to the custom of Nootka, advanced within about two hundred yards of the ship, and there resting on their paddles a conference was held, followed by a song principally sung by one man, who at stated times was joined in chorus by several others, whilst some in each canoe kept time with the handles of their paddles, by striking them against the gunwhale or side of the canoe, forming a sort of accompanyment, which though expressed by simple notes only, was by no means destitute of an agreeable effect. This performance took place whilst they were paddling slowly round the ship, and on its being concluded, they came along side with the greatest confidence, and without fear or suspicion immediately entered into a commercial intercourse with our people. The two chiefs however required some little intreaty before they could be induced to venture on board. I again presented them with some valuables, amongst which was a garment for each of blue cloth, some copper, iron in various shapes, and such trinkets as I thought would prove most acceptable. In this respect either my judgment failed, or their passion for traffic and exchange is irresistable; for no sooner had they quitted the cabin, than, excepting the copper, they bartered away on deck nearly every article I had given them, for others of infinitely less utility or real value, consisting of such things as they could best appropriate to the decoration of their persons, and other ornamental purposes, giving uniformly a decided preference to copper.

In the morning of Monday the 21st, fell a few showers of rain, which were neither so heavy as to retard our business on shore, nor to prevent the friendly Indians paying us a visit on board.

Convinced of our amicable disposition towards them, near the whole of the inhabitants, men, women and children, gratified their curiosity in the course of the day by paddling round the ship; for neither the ladies nor the children ventured on board. This was the case also with the generality of the men, who contentedly remained in their canoes, rowing from side to side, bartering their bows and arrows; which, with their woollen and skin garments, and a very few indifferent sea-otter skins, composed the whole of their assortment for trading; these they exchanged, in a very fair and honest manner, for copper, hawk's bells, and buttons, articles that greatly attracted their attention. Their merchandise would have been infinitely more valuable to us, had it been comprised of eatables, such as venison, wild fowl or fish, as our sportsmen and fishermen had little success in either of these pursuits. All the natives we had as yet seen, uniformly preferred offering such articles as composed their dress, arms, and implements for sale, rather than any kind of food, which might probably arise either from the country not affording them a superabundance of provisions, or from their having early discovered that we were more curious than hungry.

In the evening, some of the canoes were observed passing from the village to the opposite shore, for the purpose, as we supposed, of inviting their neighbors to partake of the advantages of our commerce. This was confirmed the next morning, Tuesday the 22d, by the return of our friends, accompanied by several large canoes, containing near eighty persons, who after ceremoniously paddling round the ship, came alongside without the least hesitation, and conducted themselves with the utmost propriety. The principal number of these evidently belonged to the other side of the inlet; they were infinitely more cleanly than our neighbors; and their canoes were of a very different form. Those of our friends at the village, exactly corresponded with the canoes at Nootka, whilst those of our new visitors were cut off square at each end; and were in shape precisely like the canoes seen to the southward of cape Orford, though of greater length, and considerably larger. The commodities they brought for sale were trifles of a similar description to those offered by the other society: in all other respects, they corresponded with the generality of the few inhabitants of the country with whom we had become acquainted.

On Wednesday the 23d, we had some lightning, thunder, and rain, from the S. E.; this continued a few hours, after which the day was very serene and pleasant. Some of our gentlemen having extended their walk to the cove I had visited the first evening of our arrival, found it to communicate by a very narrow passage with an opening apparently of some extent. In consequence of this information, accompanied by Mr. Baker in the yawl, I set out the next morning, Thursday the 24th, to examine it, and found the entrance of the opening situated in the western corner of the cove, formed by two interlocking points, about a quarter of a mile from each other; these formed a channel about half a mile long, free from rocks or shoals, in which there was not less than five fathoms water. From the west end of this narrow channel the inlet is divided into two branches, one extending to the S. W. about five or six miles, the other to the north about the same distance, constituting a most complete and excellent port, to all appearance perfectly free from danger, with regular soundings from four fathoms near the shores, to nine and ten fathoms in the middle, good holding ground. It occupied us the whole day to row round it, in doing which we met a few straggling Indians, whose condition seemed excessively wretched and miserable. The country that surrounds this harbor varies in its elevation; in some places the shores are low level land, in others of a moderate height, falling in steep low cliffs on the sandy beach, which in most places binds the shores. It produces some small rivulets of water, is thickly wooded with trees, mostly of the pine tribe, and with some variety of shrubs. This harbor, after the gentleman who discovered it, obtained the name of PORT ORCHARD. The best passage into it is found by steering from the village point for the south point of the cove, which is easily distinguished, lying from the former S. 62 W. at the distance of about 2½ miles, then, hauling to the N. W. into the cove, keeping on the larboard or S. W. shore, passing between it and the rocks in the cove; in this channel the depth of water is from nine to fifteen fathoms, gradually decreasing to five fathoms in the entrance into the port. There is also another passage round to the north of these rocks, in which there is seven fathoms water; this is narrow, and by no means so commodious to navigate as the southern channel.

On my return to the ship I understood that few of our friendly neighbors had visited the vessel. The party was evidently reduced, and those who still remained having satisfied their curiosity, or being compelled by their mode of life,

---

H. M. Orchard. Rumors and traditions as to the origin of the name of Port Orchard are quite as numerous and equally as groundless as in the case of Hood's Canal. In this instance the traditions have to do with the early planting of fruit trees. It is quite clear from the journal that the place was named for a member of the expedition. An examination of the muster tables of both the *Discovery* and *Chatham* discloses but one man by that name. H. M. Orchard was mustered in as clerk on the *Discovery*. His birthplace was given as Cornwall. He was older than many others of the crew, his age being given as thirty-one years. When paid off at the end of the voyage, he is shown by the muster table to have been appointed midshipman on December 1, 1792, but was again listed as clerk on December 1, 1794. It is regretted that no further facts in the history of this man have come to light. Since the United States government has located in this harbor the Puget Sound Navy Yard, the name of Port Orchard has attained added importance. Future researches may yield more information about the discoverer of this important harbor.

It may be well to add that in October, 1792, Lieutenant Broughton, while exploring the Columbia River, named a small tributary east of Gray's Bay, Orchard's River.

were preparing to depart with all their stock and effects. These it required little labor to remove, consisting chiefly of the mats for covering their habitations, wherever it may be convenient to pitch them; their skin and woollen garments, their arms, implements, and such articles of food as they had acquired during their residence; which, with their family and dogs, all find accommodation in a single canoe; and thus the party is easily conveyed to any station, which fancy, convenience, or necessity, may direct. The dogs belonging to this tribe of Indians were numerous, and much resembled those of Pomerania, though in general somewhat larger. They were all shorn as close to the skin as sheep are in England; and so compact were their fleeces, that large portions could be lifted up by a corner without causing any separation. They were composed of a mixture of a coarse kind of wool, with very fine long hair, capable of being spun into yarn. This gave me reason to believe that their woollen clothing might in part be composed of this material mixed with a finer kind of wool from some other animal, as their garments were all too fine to be manufactured from the coarse coating of the dog alone. The abundance of these garments amongst the few people we met with, indicates the animal from whence the raw material is procured, to be very common in this neighborhood; but as they have no one domesticated excepting the dog, their supply of wool for their clothing can only be obtained by hunting the wild creature that produces it; of which we could not obtain the least information.

The weather continued delightfully serene and pleasant; the carpenters had executed their task, and the topsail yards were replaced.

In the course of the forenoon of Friday the 25th, some of our Indian friends brought us a whole deer, which was the first intire animal that had been offered to us. This they had killed on the island, and from the number of persons that came from thence, the major part of the remaining inhabitants of the village, with a great number of dogs, seemed to have been engaged in the chase. This and another deer, parts of which remained in one of their canoes, had cost all these good people nearly a day's labor, as they went over to the island for this purpose the preceding evening; yet they were amply rewarded for their exertions by a small piece of copper not a foot square. This they gladly accepted as a full compensation for their venison, on which the whole party could have made two or three good meals; such is the esteem and value with which this metal is regarded!

About four in the afternoon, agreeably to our expectations, the *Chatham* was seen from the mast head over the land, and about sun-set she arrived and anchored near us. Mr. Broughton informed me, that the part of the coast he had been directed to explore, consisted of an archipelago of islands lying before an extensive arm of the sea stretching in a variety of branches between the N. W. north, and N. N. E. Its extent in the first direction was the most capacious, and presented an unbounded horizon.

On due consideration of all the circumstances that had fallen under my own observation, and the intelligence now imparted by Mr. Broughton, I became thoroughly convinced, that our boats alone could enable us to acquire any correct or satisfactory information respecting this broken country; and although the execution of such a service in open boats would necessarily be extremely laborious, and expose those so employed to numerous dangers and unpleasant situations, that might occasionally produce great fatigue, and protract their return to the ships; yet that mode was undoubtedly the most accurate, the most ready, and indeed the only one in our power to pursue for ascertaining the continental boundary.

The main arm of the inlet leading towards mount Rainier still remained unexplored. It became evident from the length of time Mr. Puget and Mr. Whidbey had been absent, that the inlet they had been sent to examine, had led them to a considerable distance. We had no time to spare, and as it was equally evident none ought to be lost, I directed that Mr. Johnstone, in the *Chatham's* cutter, should accompany me in the morning, in the *Discovery's* yawl, for the purpose of examining the main arm; and that Mr. Broughton, on the return of our boats, which were now hourly expected, should take Mr. Whidbey in one of them, and proceed immediately to the investigation of that arm of this inlet, which we had passed on the eastern shore, stretching to the N. N. E.; and I desired that the *Chatham* might be anchored within its entrance in some conspicuous place on the starboard side, where the *Discovery* or the boats would easily find her, in case the result of my inquiries should render it expedient for the vessels to proceed further in that direction.

On Saturday morning the 26th, accompanied by Mr. Baker in the yawl, and favored by pleasant weather and a fine northwardly gale, we departed, and made considerable progress. Leaving to the right the opening which had been the object of Mr. Puget and Mr. Whidbey's expedition, we directed our route along the western shore of the main inlet, which is about a league in width; and as we proceeded the smoke of several fires were seen on its eastern shore. When about four leagues on a southwardly direction from the ships, we found the course of the inlet take a south-westerly inclination, which we pursued about six miles with some little increase of width. Towards noon we landed on a point on the eastern shore, whose latitude I observed to be 47° 21', round which we flattered ourselves we should find the inlet take an extensive eastwardly course. This conjecture was supported by the appearance of a very abrupt division in the snowy range of mountains immediately to the south of mount Rainier, which was very conspicuous from the ship, and the main arm of the inlet appearing to stretch in that direction from the point we were then upon. We here dined, and although our repast was soon concluded, the delay was irksome, as we were excessively anxious to ascertain the truth, of which we were not long held in suspense. For having passed round the point, we found the inlet to terminate here in an extensive circular compact bay, whose waters washed the base of mount Rainier, though its elevated summit was yet at a very considerable distance from the shore, with which it was connected by several ridges of hills rising towards it

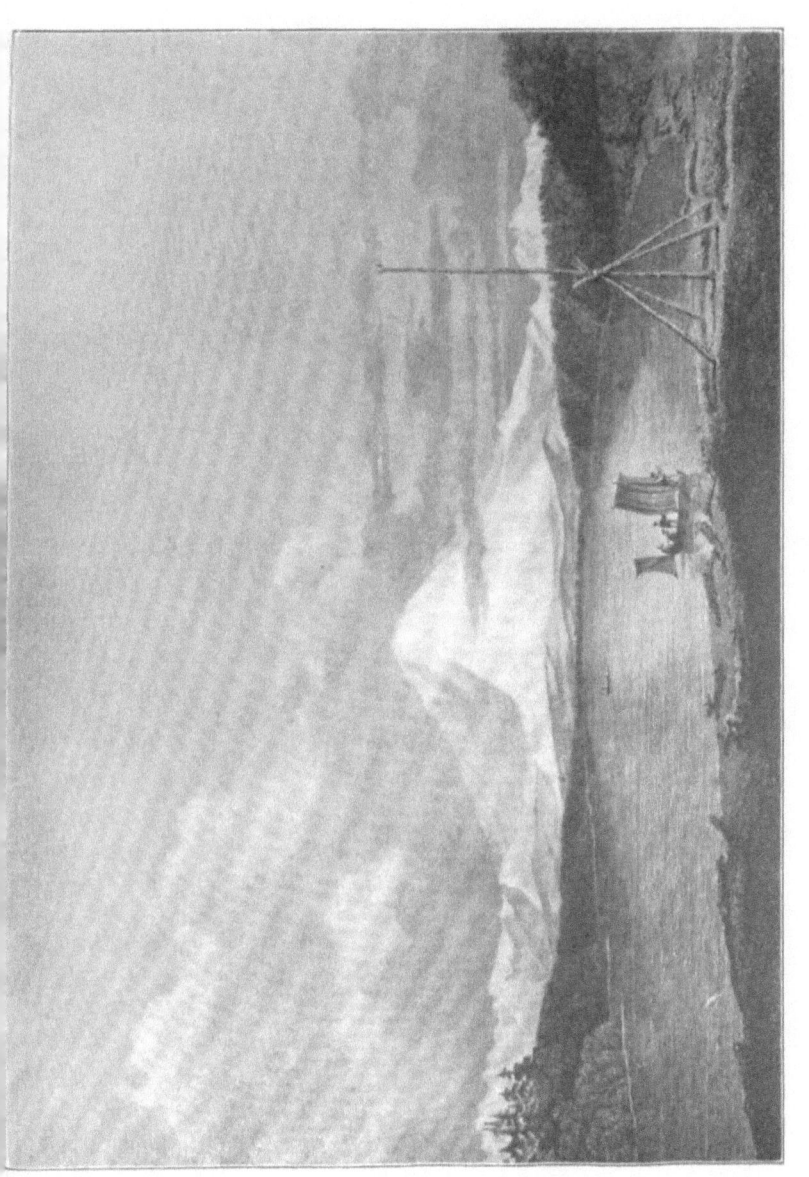

FIRST PICTURE OF MOUNT RAINIER.

From the steel engraving by J. Landseer in Vancouver's Journal. Drawn by W. Alexander from a sketch made by J. Sykes from the southern part of Admiralty Inlet, probably at Point Defiance.

with gradual ascent and much regularity. The forest trees, and the several shades of verdure that covered the hills, gradually decreasing in point of beauty, until they became invisible; when the perpetual clothing of snow commenced, which seemed to form a horizontal line from north to south along this range of rugged mountains, from whose summit mount Rainier rose conspicuously, and seemed as much elevated above them as they were above the level of the sea; the whole producing a most grand, picturesque effect. The lower mountains as they descended to the right and left, became gradually relieved of their frigid garment; and as they approached the fertile woodland region that binds the shores of this inlet in every direction, produced a pleasing variety. We now proceeded to the N. W. in which direction the inlet from hence extended, and afforded us some reason to believe that it communicated with that under the survey of our other party. This opinion was further corroborated by a few Indians, who had in a very civil manner accompanied us some time, and who gave us to understand that in the north western direction this inlet was very wide and extensive; this they expressed before we quitted our dinner station, by opening their arms, and making other signs that we should be led a long way by pursuing that route; whereas, by bending their arm, or spreading out their hand, and pointing to the space contained in the curve or the arm, or between the fore-finger and thumb, that we should find our progress soon stopped in the direction which led towards mount Rainier.

The little respect which most Indians bear to truth, and their readiness to assert what they think is most agreeable for the moment, or to answer their own particular wishes and inclinations, induced me to place little dependance on this information, although they could have no motive for deceiving us.

About a dozen of these friendly people had attended at our dinner, one part of which was a venison pasty. Two of them, expressing a desire to pass the line of separation drawn between us, were permitted to do so. They sat down by us, and ate of the bread and fish that we gave them without the least hesitation; but on being offered some of the venison, though they saw us eat it with great relish, they could not be induced to taste it. They received it from us with great disgust, and presented it round to the rest of the party, by whom it underwent a very strict examination. Their conduct on this occasion left no doubt in our minds that they believed it to be human flesh, an impression which it was highly expedient should be done away. To satisfy them that it was the flesh of the deer, we pointed to the skins of the animal they had about them. In reply to this they pointed to each other, and made signs that could not be misunderstood, that it was the flesh of human beings, and threw it down in the dirt, with gestures of great aversion and displeasure. At length we happily convinced them of their mistake by showing them a haunch we had in the boat, by which means they were undeceived, and some of them ate of a remainder of the pye with a good appetite.

This behavior, whilst in some measure tending to substantiate their knowledge or suspicions that such barbarities have existance, led us to conclude, that the character given of the natives of North-West America does not attach to every tribe. These people have been represented not only as accustomed inhumanly to devour the flesh of their conquered enemies; but also to keep certain servants, or rather slaves, of their own nation, for the sole purpose of making the principal part of the banquet, to satisfy the unnatural savage gluttony of the chiefs of this country, on their visits to each other. Were such barbarities practiced once a month, as is stated, it would be natural to suppose these people, so inured, would not have shown the least aversion to eating flesh of any description; on the contrary, it is not possible to conceive a greater degree of abhorrence than was manifested by these good people, until their minds were made perfectly easy that it was not human flesh we offered them to eat. This instance must necessarily exonerate at least this particular tribe from so barbarous a practice; and, as their affinity to the inhabitants of Nootka, and of the sea-coast, to the south of that place, in their manners and customs, admits of little difference, it is but charitable to hope those also, on a more minute inquiry, may be found not altogether deserving such a character. They are not, however, free from the general failing attendant on a savage life. One of them having taken a knife and fork to imitate our manner of eating, found means to secrete them under his garment; but, on his being detected, gave up his plunder with the utmost good humor and unconcern.

They accompanied us from three or four miserable huts, near the place where we had dined, for about four miles; during which time they exchanged the only things they had to dispose of, their bows, arrows, and spears, in the most fair and honest manner, for hawk's bells, buttons, beads, and such useless commodities.

The first information of the natives we found perfectly correct; and it was not long before we had every reason to give credit to the second, by finding the inlet divided into two branches, one taking a northwardly direction towards the ships, giving that which, in the morning, we had considered to be the western shore of the main inlet, the appearance of an island, eight or nine leagues in circuit; the other stretched to the southwestward; and into which ran a very strong tide. Although there was little doubt of our having been preceded in the examination of this branch, yet, as the strength of the influx indicated its extremity to be at some distance, I determined, as we were well supplied for the excursion, to embrace the advantage of so favorable an opportunity of keeping the larboard shore on board, and of examining such inlets as might be found leading to the left; that, in the event of Mr. Puget having been unable to accomplish the task assigned him, our survey might be completed without another expedition into this region. With the assistance of the strong tide, we rapidly passed through a fair navigable channel, near half a league wide, with soundings from 24 to 30 fathoms, free from any appearance of shoals, rocks, or other interruptions. The eastern shore was found nearly straight and compact; but on the western, three wide openings were seen, whose terminations were not distinguishable; and the strength with which the tide flowed into the two northernmost, induced us to consider them as very extensive.

Having advanced in a direction S. 32 W. about three leagues from the south, or inner point of entrance, into an opening, situated in latitude 47° 19½', longitude 237° 42', we halted about eight in the evening for the night, on a small island, lying about a mile from the eastern shore. The general character of the situation in which we had now arrived, indicated it to be a continuation of the main branch of the inlet, we had been thus long navigating. The insular appearance of its western side, the rapidity of the flood tide, and its increasing width, gave us reason to suppose we should find it still more extensive. Whilst employed in arranging our matters for the night, we discovered, coming out of the southernmost opening, two small vessels, which, at first, were taken for Indian canoes, but, on using our glasses, they were considered to be our two boats. The evening was cloudy; and, closing in very soon, prevented a positive decision. The original idea was, however, somewhat confirmed on firing two muskets, which were not answered.

During the night, we had some rain, with a fresh gale from the S. E. which abated by the morning; the rain still continued, but not so violently as to prevent our proceeding. At four o'clock on Sunday morning, the 27th, we again embarked, and steered about S. W. by S.; in which direction the inlet seemed to stretch to some distance; and the appearance of the southern land gave rise to an opinion of its terminating in a river. The space we had so considered was, by seven o'clock, proved to be a low swampy compact shore, forming the southern extremity of the inlet in this direction, about two leagues from our last resting place. The inlet here terminated in an expansive though shallow bay, across which a flat of sand extended upwards of a mile from its shores; on which was lying an immense quantity of drift wood, consisting chiefly of very large trees. The country behind for some distance, was low, then rose gradually to a moderate height; and, like the eastern shores of the inlet, was covered with wood, and diversified with pleasant inequalities of hill and dale, though not enriched with those imaginary parks and pleasure grounds we had been accustomed to behold nearer to the sea coast; the whole presenting one uninterrupted wilderness.

From hence the direction of the inlet was about N. W. by N. still preserving a considerable width; the western shore appearing to be formed by a group of islands. Our progress was a little retarded by the rain in the forenoon; but, about mid-day the clouds dispersed, though not sufficiently early to procure an observation for the latitude. We had now reached a point on the larboard shore, where the inlet was again divided into two other large branches, one leading to the south-westward, the other towards the north. As my plan was to pursue the examination of the larboard shore, the south-west branch became our first object. This we found divided into two narrow channels, leading to the southward, with the appearance of two small coves to the northward. Up the westernmost of the former, about six miles we took up our abode for the night, which was serene and pleasant.

Early in the morning, Monday 28th, we again started, and soon found the channel to terminate about a league from the place where we had slept the night before, as the rest had done, in low swampy ground, with a shallow sandy bank extending to some distance into the channel. Here we met, as had been frequently the case, a few miserable Indians in their temporary habitations; these either had nothing to dispose of, or were not inclined to have intercourse with us; the latter seemed most probable, as our visit was not attended with that cordial reception we had generally experienced. This however might have been occasioned by our having disturbed them unusually early from their rest; we made them some presents which they accepted very coolly, and having satisfied ourselves with the extent of the inlet in this direction we returned, and about nine o'clock landed to breakfast about two miles within the main entrance of the south-west branch. We left behind us to the westward the appearance of two or three small islands or points, that might form similar inlets to those we had already examined, leading to the south. These could be of little extent, as scarcely any visible tide was found in the narrowest parts.

From the length of time also that the other boats had been absent previous to our departure from the ships, together with the appearance and direction of the inlet, I entertained little doubt that the greater part of what we had seen, as also that which we were now leaving unexplored, had undergone the examination of Mr. Puget and Mr. Whidbey. This induced me to return on board, considering we were now passing our time to little purpose; and as the branch of the main inlet before us stretching to the northward, presented every prospect of communicating with some of those we had passed on Saturday evening, we pursued that route. The situation we quitted this morning, according to my survey, was in latitude 47° 3', longitude 237° 18', about 17 leagues from the sea coast of New Albion, towards which, from the moderate height of the country, there could be little doubt of an easy intercourse by land. About noon we landed on a point of the eastern shore, whose latitude is 47° 15½', longitude 237° 17½'. From hence we proceeded with a pleasant southerly gale, to ascertain if any communication existed, as we had before conjectured. The further we advanced the more doubtful it became, until at length, about three leagues north of the above point, it terminated like all the other channels in a shallow flat before a low swampy bog. Here we dined, and about four in the afternoon set out on our return by the way we had come, purposing to stop for the night at a cove a little to the south of the point we were upon at noon, where we arrived about nine in the evening. Mr. Johnstone, who had kept along the western shore in order to look into a small opening we had passed in sailing down, had the advantage by being on the weather shore, and had arrived a short time before us. He informed me the opening was very narrow, and could extend but a little way before it joined that which we had quitted this morning. Whilst he was on shore for the purpose of taking the necessary angles,

ADMIRAL JAMES VASHON.

From a mezzotint by John Young after George Watson. Photograph copyrighted by Walker & Cockrell. Rights secured for this work in England and America.

OF PUGET SOUND

[May, 1792.]

[Original Journal, Pages 144-145.]

a deer came down to the beach, which Mr. Le Mesurier, the gentleman who had attended him in the boat, fired at, and fortunately killed. It proved to be a very fine buck, and afforded our people a good fresh meal, which was some compensation for the disappointment we experienced in not finding a passage home by the route we had lately pursued.

About day-break, as usual, on Tuesday morning the 29th, we again resumed our voyage towards the ships, which were now distant about 45 miles. Towards noon we landed on the north point of entrance into the second opening we had passed on Saturday evening; the latitude of which is 47° 15½'. The strength of the ebb tide facilitated our progress, and our conjectures were soon proved to have been well founded in this being the same inlet, which I had directed the other party to examine. We were carried with great rapidity for some time up the branch leading to the northward, and through this channel we arrived in the evening on board, without seeing any other opening leading to the westward. The land composing the eastern shore of this channel, and the western shore of that we had pursued on Saturday morning, was now ascertained to be the most extensive island we had yet met with in our several examinations of this coast; which after my friend Captain Vashon of the navy, I have distinguished by the name of VASHON'S ISLAND.

Captain Vashon. The large island that bears this name extends for more than half the distance between Seattle and Tacoma, the two principal cities of Puget Sound. It is natural, therefore, that the question should often be asked as to the origin and meaning of the name Vashon.

Vancouver is clear as to whom he wished to honor. Vashon was a contemporary of his in the British Navy, and saw service under the same excellent officers, some of which officers were also honored by the explorer, notably Sir Alan Gardner.

James Vashon was the son of James Volant Vashon, the vicar of Eye in Herefordshire. He was born at Ludlow on August 9, 1742. Like many other successful and famous seamen, he grew up in the navy. When thirteen years old, in August, 1755, he began service in the *Revenge* under Captain Frederick Cornewall. In this ship the boy was present at the battle of Minorca on May 20, 1756. On his captain being called to England to attend the trial of Admiral Byng, young Vashon was transferred into the *Lancaster*

VANCOUVER'S DISCOVERY

[Original Journal, Page 145.]

[May, 1792.]

Late on the preceding Saturday night, or rather on Sunday morning, our other party had returned. It was them we had seen the first evening of our excursion from the island, and they very distinctly saw our fire; but as they did not hear the report of the muskets, concluded it a fire of the natives, not having the least idea of any of our boats being in that

---

with Captain Edgecumbe and took part in the reduction of Louisbourg in July, 1758. The *Lancaster* went to the West Indies and under Commodore John Moore participated in the reduction of Guadaloupe.

Vashon was then moved into the *Cambridge*, the Commodore's flagship, and under Captain Goostrey and Rear-Admiral Charles Holmes continued at Jamaica. He saw sharp service in the *Boreas*, being frequently lent to that ship employed in cutting out privateers. In the summer of 1761, Captain Goostrey asked Rear-Admiral Holmes to make Vashon a lieutenant. Holmes said he would some day, but then he looked too much like a boy. Holmes died in November, 1761, and Goostrey was killed in the attack on Morro Castle, Havana, July 1, 1762. These two deaths were serious to Vashon. He passed his examination on September 7, 1763, and continued active service in the West Indies and the Newfoundland station, and yet he was not promoted until June 1, 1774, when Sir George Rodney made him a lieutenant of the *Maidstone*. In 1777 the *Maidstone* was refitted in England and sent to the coast of North America under Captain Alan Gardner, where she was engaged in active cruising early in 1778. In March Lieutenant Vashon commanded the boats in setting fire to a ship which had been driven on shore. In this work he was defended by several field pieces. After carrying news of the French fleet to Lord Howe in New York in July, he rejoined the *Maidstone* and helped to capture the *Lion*, a large armed ship. With twenty-four men, Vashon was put in charge of the prize and some two hundred prisoners. The boat was unseaworthy and the condition was dangerous. Vashon made his prisoners work the pumps and took his prize in safety to Antigua.

For this service Vashon was promoted to the rank of Commander on August 5, 1779, was ordered home, appointed to the *Alert*, and again sent to the West Indies. Early in 1781 he was sent home with despatches from Jamaica, and after some service in the North Sea under Sir Hyde Parker he returned to the West Indies under Rodney, and the *Alert* was stationed off Martinique as a lookout ship. On April 12, 1782, Vashon was with the fleet in the action off Dominica and took possession of the *Glorieuse*. He was active in saving people blown up in the *Cesar*. It was quite appropriate that he should have been promoted to the rank of Captain in a commission bearing this same date. Rodney transferred him to the *Formidable* as flag captain and, when Rodney was superseded, Vashon was transferred to the *Sibyl* in which he served until the peace.

From 1786 to 1789 Vashon was captain of the *Europa* with Commodore

neighborhood. They had explored all those parts of the inlet we had passed by, and found the three openings we had left unexamined, the first afternoon, leading to the westward, to be channels dividing that shore into three islands; and those we had not attended to on Monday morning formed two small branches leading to the S. W.; the westernmost of which extends to the latitude 47° 6', about two leagues to the westward of our researches in that direction; that in which the deer was shot communicated with the S. W. branch of the inlet by a very narrow channel. They had also passed the opening we had pursued leading towards mount Rainier; but agreeably to my directions had not prosecuted its examination; the termination of every other opening in the land they had ascertained. Thus by our joint efforts, we had completely explored every turning of this extensive inlet; and to commemorate Mr. Puget's exertions, the south extremity of it I named PUGET'S SOUND.

The *Chatham* had sailed on Monday, and Mr. Whidbey had departed in the *Discovery's* launch for the purpose of carrying into effect the orders I had left with Mr. Broughton.

Gardner's broad pennant on board. In the great Spanish armament of 1790, which broke up the first-planned expedition to the Northwest Coast of America, Vashon had command of the *Ardent*. During the war of the French Revolution, in 1793, he commanded the *St. Albans* in the convoy service to the Mediterranean and to Jamaica. Later he commanded the *Pompee* off Brest and during the Spithead mutiny. After that outbreak was quelled, there was another on the *Pompee*. It was promptly suppressed and the ringleaders sentenced to death, but Vashon asked to be relieved of that command. He later served in the *Neptune*, the *Dreadnaught*, and *Princess Royal*.

On April 23, 1804, Vashon was made a Rear-Admiral and for four years commanded the ships at Leith and on the coast of Scotland. On April 28, 1808, he was made Vice-Admiral of the Blue, and on June 4, 1814, was advanced to the rank of Admiral.

He died June 4, 1827, at Ludlow, the place of his birth. He left one son in holy orders.

The portrait used in this work is from an engraving by John Young, "Engraver in Mezzotints to His Royal Highness, the Prince of Wales," from a painting by George Watson. The painting was made while Vashon was Vice-Admiral of the Blue.

VANCOUVER'S DISCOVERY

[Original Journal, Page 146.]

[May, 1792.]

Mr. Puget had little more to communicate respecting his late expedition than what had fallen under my own observation, excepting the disorderly behavior of an Indian tribe

---

Lieutenant Peter Puget. The first whites to settle in this region were the Hudson Bay Company men who organized the Puget Sound Agricultural Company and established Fort Nisqually near the mouth of Nisqually River. The first entry in the "Journal of Occurrences at Nisqually House" is dated May 30, 1833. This settlement was made as a necessary station on the route from Fort Vancouver on the Columbia River to Fort Langley, established near the mouth of Fraser River in 1827. The first American settlements were made at Jackson Prairie and Tumwater near Olympia, in 1845 and 1846. These settlements (except Fort Langley) were near the southern extremity of this inland sea — the very portion which Vancouver named Puget's Sound. That name became the familiar one, and as the white settlements moved northward along the shores that name was carried along regardless of other names, like Admiralty Inlet, Port Gardner, the Gulf of Georgia, and Strait of Juan de Fuca. Puget Sound became the generic name for the whole region and is largely so used at the present time. It may interest some to know that the Indians call this waterway by the name of "Whulge."

Because of this enormous and rapidly increasing importance of Puget Sound as a geographic term, the present writer has been extremely anxious to secure a portrait and biography of Peter Puget. A few years ago Judge James Wickersham, then of Tacoma, now of Alaska, declared that he and others interested had for years been searching for a portrait and biography of Puget — all in vain. This was discouraging, but not wholly disheartening. A systematic search was undertaken in England and, though the results are lamentably meagre, they are certainly better than nothing and far more complete than have ever been assembled before.

Mr. Frederick V. James, who conducted this search in England, writes about this particular case as follows: "This important name has caused most research as very little is recorded of his services. The 'Dictionary of National Biography,' the *Gentleman's Magazine*, the Annual Register, have all been drawn blank." The extensive and valuable "Dictionary of National Biography" draws largely upon the talents of Professor J. K. Laughton for biographies of distinguished mariners and naval men. He omitted the life of Puget, but an appeal was made to him personally. From 9 Pepys Road, Wimbledon, he writes: "I have no notes about Captain (died Rear-Admiral) Puget. In the Record Office there is a Service Book made up of returns from the several admirals and captains living in 1817. Puget is (or ought to be — some few did not send in the returns) in this, and will give you all his service. In the 'Blockade of Brest' (issued by the Navy Record Society: you can see it at the British Museum), II, 3, is a biographical note; and there are several interesting papers relating to him in the volume.

he had met with at some distance up the first arm leading to the westward within the narrows, whose conduct had materially differed from that of the natives in general; and in particular from that of a party consisting of about twenty natives whom they had before seen in that route, and who had behaved with their usual friendship and civility. In this

---

Probably in the *Gentleman's Magazine* there will be a biographical notice as an obituary. I don't know the exact date of his death, but I believe 1821 or 1822. Leyland speaks of him as alive in 1821. Marshall does not count him so in 1823." Such was the statement of probably the best-informed man on such subjects in all England. An appeal was then made to the Board of Admiralty, bringing from Evan MacGregor, the Secretary, this reply: "With reference to your letter of the 17th (October, 1903) instant, requesting permission to inspect documents relative to Rear-Admiral Peter Puget who died about 1820, I am commanded by my Lords Commissioners of the Admiralty to inform you that the Admiralty records for the period in question are lodged at the Public Record Office, Chancery Lane, and are open to the public for purposes of research up to the end of year 1830." Thus it became a case of the Public Record Office and the wide open field outside.

Puget's return for the Service Book mentioned by Professor Laughton was found. It gives in skeleton form his entire active career in the navy. It is headed "Memorandum of the Services of Captain Peter Puget, C.B.," and is signed "Peter Puget, Capt. R.N." It is a large double foolscap sheet, on which the information is arranged in tabulated form. Being by far the most important document in existence relating to the life of Puget, each scrap of information is here reproduced.

He evidently entered the navy on August 1, 1778, as midshipman under Captain Milligen in the *Dunkirk*. He may have had the usual boy's time as captain's servant before that, but, if so, he makes no account of it. On December 12, 1779, he was transferred to the *Syren* under Captain E. Dodd, seeing service in the North Sea. On June 13, 1780, he followed Captain Dodd into the *Lowestoft* on the West Indies station. On November 16, 1782, he was sent to the *Thetis*, and under Captain J. Blanket saw service at Gibraltar. On May 16, 1783, he went, still as midshipman, to the *Europa*, in which he saw four years of service in the West Indies under Admiral Gambier, Captain Smith; Admiral Innes, Captain Fisher; Admiral Sir Alan Gardner, Captain Vashon. From this service he was discharged on July 22, 1787, and then had his first vacation until May 3, 1788, when he was returned to the *Lowestoft*, Captain Dodd, with whom he served in the Channel. From November 25, 1788, to June 10, 1790, he was midshipman on the *Prince* (West Indianman) under Captain R. Dundas, going to the East Indies. On June 11, 1790, he was shipped as mate on the *Discovery* under Captain R. (probably meant for H.) Roberts. He continued on this rating until

[Original Journal, Page 147.] [May, 1792.]

arm they found the shores in general low and well wooded. About eight in the evening, attended by some of the natives in two canoes, they landed for the night. These people could not be invited nearer our party than about an hundred yards, where they remained attentive to all the operations until the

---

November 22, 1790, and the station is given as Deptford. This is evidence that, when the excitement over the Nootka troubles caused the scattering of officers in the great Spanish Armament, Puget remained with the sloop *Discovery* at Deptford. On November 23, 1790, he is booked as lieutenant on the *Discovery* under Captain Vancouver for a voyage "Round the World." On January 14, 1793, he was transferred as commander to the armed tender *Chatham* and continued the "Voyage Round the World." From the *Chatham* he was discharged on October 17, 1795. His next service was as commander in the *Adelphi*, taking advance stores to Gibraltar from February to September, 1796. He was then transferred to the *Esther* with despatches from Gibraltar, September 21, 1796, to January 9, 1797. His last service as commander was in the *Theseus* under Captain Aylmer to Lisbon from February 14 to April 28, 1797. He was then posted to the rank of Captain on the *St. Nicholas* on April 29, 1797, and in September was sent in a packet with despatches to England. During the year 1798 he was captain of the *Van Tromp*, no station being given. From December, 1798, to December, 1800, he served on the Channel station as captain of the *Temeraire*, the *Barfleur*, and the *Temeraire* again, always under Rear-Admiral Whitshed. From March, 1801, to May 22, 1802, he was under Rear-Admiral Sir T. Graves on the Yarmouth station as captain of the *Monarch*. In the *Fondroyant* under the same admiral he served on the Brest station from February, 1804, to June, 1805. From April to September, 1806, he served as agent of prisoners in France. From January, 1807, to January, 1809, he served as captain of the *Goliath* in the North Sea and off Copenhagen. He served under the Commissioners of the Navy at Flushing from May to December, 1809, and at Madras from May 24, 1810, to February 21, 1818, still having the rank of Captain in the Royal navy.

This brief outline shows an active, varied, and successful career in the navy for the period of forty years. Such faithfulness deserved the fullest recognition. Had he lived to the ripe old age attained by some of his companions, he would undoubtedly have received greater honors. As it was, after the Order of the Bath was reorganized in 1815, he became Companion of that ancient institution. In addition to this, in 1821, just a year before his death, he was advanced to the rank of Rear-Admiral of the Blue.

Vancouver fully appreciated the abilities of his lieutenant, as is shown by the frequent occasions on which he used him for important duties, and especially the promotion to command the *Chatham* after Lieutenant Broughton had been sent home with despatches. In this new capacity Puget had a

tents were pitched, when it became necessary to discharge some loaded muskets, the noise of which they heard without any apparent surprize, and exclaimed *poo!* after every report. They soon afterwards paddled away to the westward. The next morning Mr. Puget proceeded up the arm, which took

---

large share in the explorations of Cook's Inlet, Prince William Sound, and especially in Yakutat Bay or Port Mulgrave, which Puget surveyed while Vancouver was busy in Prince William's Sound. Vancouver again honored Puget by naming for him Cape Puget, near Montagu Island, at the entrance to Prince William Sound. This high regard for Puget was apparently shared by other members of the expedition, for when Lieutenant Broughton was examining the Columbia River, while the *Discovery* had gone on to the Spanish settlements in California, he discovered a large island in the river which he named Puget's Island.

That others, who are in a position to learn more than one living on the shores of Puget Sound, are beginning to appreciate the importance of Puget's life and to grope around for facts, is shown by the "Despatches and Letters relating to the Blockade of Brest, 1803-1805," edited by John Leyland and issued by the Navy Records Society, London, 1902. Facing the title-page of Volume II is "Captain Peter Puget's Plan for the Destruction of the French Fleet in Brest Harbour, June 23, 1804. Original in Possession of Colonel Cornwallis West." A note on page 3 of the same work is as follows: "Captain Peter Puget was an officer of whose career too little is known. As a lieutenant he was a companion of Vancouver, and the deep inlet of Puget Sound was named after him. Greatly esteemed as a surveyor, when Broughton came home in 1793, Puget succeeded him in command of the *Chatham*. Promoted captain April 29, 1797. In 1807, in command of the *Goliath*, he took part in the expedition to Copenhagen, which brought about the surrender of the Danish fleet and was hotly engaged inside the Treknor. He also accompanied the expedition to the Baltic in 1808. Captain Puget became a Rear-Admiral in 1821 and died in that rank."

The *London Times* of November 6, 1822, announces Puget's death as follows: "Admiral Puget who died on Thursday last at Bath was one of the Companions of the Order of the Bath, sailed round the world with Captain Vancouver and many years was Commissioner at Madras."

The same event was announced by the *Bath Chronicle* in its issue of November 7, 1822, as follows: "Died on Thursday 31 October 1822 at his home in Grosvenor Place, after a long and painful illness Rear-Admiral Puget, C.B. This lamented officer had sailed round the world with the late Captain Vancouver, had commanded various men-of-war, and was many years Commissioner at Madras, the climate of which place greatly contributed to the destruction of his health."

Most prominent or successful men of that day sat to artists for their por-

VANCOUVER'S DISCOVERY

a N. E. direction about a mile wide, narrowing as they advanced to one-fourth of that width; the soundings were found regular from eight to thirteen fathoms. In this situation they saw a canoe making towards them, on which they rested on their oars to wait its approach. The canoe suddenly stopped, and no offers of presents, nor signs of friendly inclinations, could induce the Indians to venture near the boat. In order to remove their apprehensions, Mr. Puget fastened some medals, copper, and trinkets, to a piece of wood which he left floating on the water;. and when the boat was at a sufficient distance, the Indians picked it up. After repeating this twice or thrice they ventured, though not without some trepidation, alongside the boats. In their persons they seemed more robust than the generality of the inhabit-

---

traits. Puget seems to have been an exception. Failing to find trace of a picture of the man, it was thought that a picture of his grave would not be without interest in the present work. Helping in the search, Mr. I. F. Meehan wrote: "Rear-Admiral Peter Puget, C.B., died at 21 Grosvenor Place (now known as Grosvenor), Walcot Parish, where his widow was living as late as 1829. A search in Walcot Parish Records may find other information. I have several hundred Bath portraits but none of Puget." The parish clerk of Walcot stated that, although Grosvenor was in that parish, there was no such name as Peter Puget in the Walcot Register of Burials. He suggested a trial at Bath Abbey, but Prebendary Boyd gave the information that the Registers there do not show the name.

The Admiralty Registers of Salaries and Pensions, Volume 47, in the Public Record Office, London, show that Rear-Admiral Peter Puget's half pay of £1.5.0 per diem ended on 31 October, 1822, as he was dead and certified. The number of days due were 31, and the amount was paid to Thomas Stillwell for the widow Hannah, executrix. A query was then sent to Stillwell & Sons of 42 Pall Mall, London, who wrote: "We beg to inform you that we have no record of Admiral Peter Puget beyond his ledger account. This was balanced by a payment to his widow in 1823. Subsequently a sum of 1.17.0 entered as *Chatham* Prize Money was credited in 1825, and that amount was sent to Mrs. Hannah Puget on 22 August, 1834, but to what place we are now unable to say."

The City Librarian of Bath was unable to trace the date of Mrs. Puget's death, though he also found she was living at 21 Grosvenor Place as late as 1826.

Here the search has ended for the present. Some day we may learn more about Peter Puget, or at least find his last resting place.

ants; most of them had lost their right eye, and were much pitted with the small pox. They now attended the boats for a short time, and having received some additional presents, returned to the shore. The whole of their conduct exhibited much suspicion and distrust. When any question was endeavored to be put to them, they replied by *poo! poo!* pointing at the same time to a small island on which the party had breakfasted, and where some birds had been shot. They seemed well acquainted with the value of iron and copper, but would not dispose of their weapons, or any other article in exchange for either. About noon the party landed to dine; and whilst they were preparing to haul the seine before a fresh water brook, six canoes were seen paddling hastily round the point of the cove they were in, and directing their course towards the boats. The suspicious behaviour of those whom they had parted with in the morning, rendered it highly expedient that they should be upon their guard against any hostile design of these people; on whose approach, a line on the beach was drawn, to separate the two parties from each other; which was readily understood, and obeyed. They now divided their numbers into two sets, one remaining on shore with their bows and quivers, the other retiring to their canoes, where they quietly seated themselves.

Thus, with every appearance of good order being established, the officers went to dinner, on an elevated spot a few yards from the water-side, where the crews were dining in their respective boats, and in readiness to act in case of any alarm. On a seventh canoe joining the Indian party, those on the beach immediately embarked; and the whole number, amounting to twenty four persons, evidently entered into a consultation, during which they frequently pointed to those in the boats, as well as to the officers on the hill. This conduct tended to increase the suspicions that their inclinations were otherwise than friendly, however imprudent they might deem it, on the present moment, to carry their intentions into execution. But as our party could not be surprized, and as they were ready to act immediately on the defensive, Mr. Puget and the other gentlemen did not consider their situation alarming, and preferred quietly finishing their repast, to that of indicating any signs of distrust or apprehension, by a precipitate retreat. Towards the conclusion of their conference, three of their canoes were stealing near to the boats; but, on finding they were discovered by the officers, instantly returned. At this time, an eighth canoe joined the party; on which all of them paddled to the beach, jumped on shore and strung their bows. This was manifestly preparing for an attack, as they had not ever been seen, on any former occasion, with their bows strung. The very man who appeared the principal in the canoe, they had met in the morning, and with whom so much trouble was taken to obtain his good opinion, now seemed the leader of this party; and, with an arrow across his bow in readiness for immediate use, advanced towards the station of the officers, whilst others of the party were moving that way. Such measures however were prudently resorted to, without proceeding to extremities, as obliged them all to retreat to the line of separation, where they again held a close and long consultation; and our gentlemen having now no object to detain them on shore, they re-embarked, leaving the Indians at the line of separation, sharpening their arrows and spears on stones, apparently much inclined, though irresolute, to attempt hostilities. In this undecided state of their minds, Mr. Puget thought it might answer a good purpose to fire a swivel, shotted; the effect of which, might teach them to respect, hereafter, our powers of defence, and induce them, on the present occasion, to prefer a pacific deportment, and preserve the lives of many, that must have been lost, had they been so injudicious as to have commenced an attack. Although, on the report of the gun, or the distant effect of the shot, which was fired over the water, not the least visible astonishment or apprehension was expressed, yet, the measure was almost instantly attended with every expected good consequence. Their bows were soon unstrung; and instead of their menacing a combat, their weapons became articles of traffic, in common with other trifles they had to dispose of, for copper, buttons, knives, beads, and other ornaments; in which friendly intercourse, they accompanied the boats until towards the evening, when they peaceably took their leave, and returned to their home.

From Mr. Puget I likewise understood, that, in the course of his excursion, himself and party had visited, and had received the visits of several tribes of Indians, whose behavior had been uniformly civil, courteous, and friendly. Why this party, whose unfriendly intentions were too evident to be mistaken, should have been induced to assume, without the least provocation, a character so diametrically opposite to that which, in every other instance, seemed to govern their general conduct, is certainly very mysterious, and renders the foregoing an extraordinary circumstance, for which it is difficult to account.

The country we had mutually explored, did not appear, to either party, from our transient view of it, materially to differ from that which had already been described, either in its several productions from the soil, or in its general appearance of fertility. It did not, however, possess that beautiful variety of landscape; being an almost impenetrable wilderness of lofty trees, rendered nearly impassable by the underwood, which uniformly incumbers the surface.

By the termination of the western range of snowy mountains in their southern direction, taking place considerably to the northwestward, and the more elevated land intercepting the view of such mountains as may extend from the eastern range, southward of mount Rainier, we were presented with more than the whole southern horizon of land moderately high, extending as far as the eye could reach, diversified by eminences and vallies, affording a probability of an easy intercourse by land with the sea coast; where some places of shelter for small vessels may possibly still be found, which, in the event of an establishment being formed, would prove highly advantageous.

The scarcity of water has before been mentioned as the only disadvantage that the interior country seemed to labor under; but in Mr. Puget's survey, a greater supply of water was found than in the inlets and bays that underwent my

VANCOUVER'S DISCOVERY

[Original Journal, Page 153.]

[May, 1792.]

own particular examination. The country had also been considered by us as nearly destitute of inhabitants; but this opinion we found to be erroneous, from the other party having, by accident, fallen in with near 150 Indians, and having seen several deserted villages.

The point near our present station, forming the north point of the bay, hitherto called the Village point, I have distinguished by the name of RESTORATION POINT, having cele-

---

Restoration Point. Lying opposite the city of Seattle, this point is passed by every ship going to or from the city of Tacoma, and every vessel going to the Puget Sound Navy Yard must pass around it. For these reasons it is a prominent and well-known geographical feature. For years it was locally known as Bean's Point, because an early settler of that name had been killed by Indians there. A few years ago a meeting of pilots and masters in Seattle was addressed by a will-informed captain of the United States Coast and Geodetic Survey. In the course of his address he referred to this point, saying that Vancouver so named it because he had there restored his vessels. That is just where the captain made a slip. Vancouver says he gave the name because he had "celebrated that memorable event, whilst at anchor under it."

The word "Restoration" stands for different things in history. In Jewish history it means the return of the Jews to Palestine about 537 B.C.; and also their future return and possession of the Holy Land as expected by many. In French history there are two Restorations: first, the return of the Bourbons to power after the Napoleonic upheaval in 1814; second, after the "Hundred Days" in 1815. In English history there is but one "Restoration," and that is the return of the "Merrie Monarch," Charles II, after the fall of the Cromwellian Commonwealth. Charles was convoyed from Holland to the coast of Kent landing, on May 25, 1660. Lord Macaulay speaks of that event as follows: "When he landed, the cliffs of Dover were covered by thousands of gazers, among whom scarcely one could be found who was not weeping with delight. The journey to London was a continued triumph."

The anniversary of this restoration of the English monarchy was celebrated for more than a century. It is clear what Vancouver meant by giving the name to that point. If, however, another proof is needed, it is only necessary to turn over the pages of his journal for just one year. They were near Queen Charlotte's Islands, where they had found a safe harbor and had remained for some time, having created an observatory on shore. On June 10, 1793, Vancouver makes this entry, "and in the afternoon we weighed and towed out of the cove, which I distinguished by the name of Restoration Cove, having there passed and celebrated the anniversary of that happy event."

brated that memorable event, whilst at anchor under it; and from the result of my observations made on the spot, it is situated in latitude 47° 30', longitude 237° 46'. During our stay the tides were observed to be materially affected, by the direction or force of the winds, not only in respect to their rise and fall, but as to the time of high water. The former seldom exceeded seven or eight feet: and the latter generally took place about 4h 10' after the moon passed the meridian. The variation of the compass, by six sets of azimuths taken on board, differing from 18° to 22°, gave the mean result of 19° 36' east variation.

Nothing occurring to detain us, on Wednesday morning, the 30th, with a pleasant southerly breeze, we directed our course to the opening under the examination of Mr. Broughton; the entrance of which lies from Restoration point, N. 20 E. five leagues distant. The breeze, as was usual, dying away, we advanced very slowly; towards noon, it was succeeded by a N. W. wind, accompanied with the flood-tide, so that, by the time we had worked up the opening, the ebb tide was returning not only with great strength, but attended by a sort of counter-tide, or under tow, that so affected the ship, as to render her almost unmanageable, notwithstanding we had a fresh breeze, and were assisted in working in by our boats. Having advanced about three miles within the entrance, which we found about half a league across, and, in the evening, seeing no appearance of the *Chatham*, a gun was fired, which was immediately answered from behind a point of land, on the starboard, or eastern shore, where, soon afterwards, we saw the *Chatham* bearing a light at her mast-head for our guidance; and, though within the distance of two miles, it was near midnight before we anchored in 32 fathoms water, about a cable's length from her; not having been able to gain soundings with 110 fathoms of line, until we reached this station.

The next morning, Thursday 31st, we found ourselves about a cable's length from the shore, in a capacious sound; whose entrance bore by compass from S. 2 W. to S. 30 W., about six miles from us, from whence it extended in a true

N. N. E. direction. To the north was a high round island, bearing from N. 18 W. to N. 33 W.; on each side of which an opening was seen stretching to the northward. These openings were separated by a high narrow slip of land, which also appeared to be insular. The eastern side of the sound formed a deep bay, apparently bounded by solid compact land of a moderate height.

Mr. Broughton informed me; he had navigated the east side of the round island in the brig, and had examined the eastern shore of the sound, which was, as it appeared to be, a compact shore. Mr. Whidbey, in our launch, accompanied by Lieutenant Hanson in the *Chatham's*, had, on the 29th, been dispatched to the two openings to the northward, with directions to examine the right hand, or easternmost, first; and, on finding its termination, to return with such information to the *Chatham*, before they proceeded to visit the other; that, in the event of the *Discovery's* arrival previous to their return, the vessels might follow them in such pursuit, observing to keep on the eastern shore until they should find it divided into two branches. This being the third day of their absence, it was concluded they had found the easternmost opening to be of considerable extent; in consequence of which I determined to follow them, but the weather being calm and gloomy, with some rain, we were prevented moving. On a low point of land near the ship, I observed the latitude to be 47° 57½′, longitude 237° 58′. A light favorable breeze sprang up shortly after noon; but before the anchor was at the ship's bows it again fell calm, with much rain, which obliged us to remain quiet. The *Chatham* however weighed, and being soon off the bank, which does not reach a quarter of a mile from the shore, was instantly out of soundings, and was driven by the ebb-tide until nine in the evening to the entrance of the sound. At this time a fresh southerly breeze springing up we weighed, and directed our course northward, to pass on the western side of the round island.

We had now been stationary upwards of 20 hours, and during that time the tide or current had constantly sat out; the like was observed by Mr. Broughton during his continuance in the same place. The southerly wind, attended by a heavy fall of rain, soon became so faint, that by eleven at night we had proceeded only five miles. Here we were obliged to anchor in twenty fathoms water, hard sandy bottom, near half way between the island and the point that divides the two openings, which are about a league asunder.

About six in the morning of Friday, June the First, assisted by the flood tide, and a light south-easterly wind, we proceeded up the eastern arm; the entrance of which is about a mile wide, with soundings from 75 to 80 fathoms, dark sandy bottom. The weather being rainy, calm, or attended with light variable winds, most of the forenoon we made little progress. During this interval the *Chatham* gained some advantage of us, and about noon proceeded with a favorable breeze from the southward up the opening. The haze which had obscured the land all the fore part of the day, gave the inlet an extensive appearance, without any visible termination: but on the fog's dispersing, it seemed to be closed in every direction, excepting that by which we had entered; but as soundings could not be gained with fifty fathoms of line, we continued our course up the inlet until about two o'clock, at which time we had advanced six miles from the entrance; and being perfectly satisfied that the inlet finished in the manner common to all we had hitherto examined, the signal was made for the *Chatham* to bring up, and we shortened sail accordingly. In a few minutes she was discovered to be a-ground, and had made the signal for assistance. On this we stood towards her, and anchored about a mile from her in 20 fathoms water, sandy bottom, and about half that distance from the eastern shore, which was the nearest land. Our boats were immediately sent to her relief; but as the tide subsided very fast, they could only lay out anchors for heaving her off on the returning flood. Although the upper part of the inlet had appeared to be perfectly closed, yet it was not impossible a channel might exist on the western or opposite shore, which by interlocking points might have been invisible to us on board, and through which our absent party might have found a passage. To ascertain this fact, I went in a yawl, and found the depth of water suddenly to decrease on leaving the ship to ten, seven, and two fathoms. We continued our researches in one and two fathoms water to the opposite side, where we landed nearly abreast of the ship, and found the shores of the inlet to be straight, compact, and about two miles apart. In several places we attempted to land near the upper end, but found ourselves as often repulsed by a flat sandy shoal, which extended directly across. The land there seemed of a swampy nature, was thinly wooded, and through it was the appearance of a shallow rivulet falling into the sea; further back it was more elevated, and the surrounding country being covered with a similar growth of timber to that before noticed, made us conclude the land to be equally fertile.

This examination perplexed me extremely to account for an error that had certainly taken place. For under the conviction that this inlet had been found navigable by the boats, I should not have hesitated to have prosecuted my way hither in the ship at midnight, in consequence of the party not having made any report to the contrary. This could only be attributed to a misunderstanding of the orders given, or to some unfortunate accident having befallen them. The latter we had no reason to apprehend, unless from an attack of the Indians, which was not very likely to have happened, as we saw not the least indication of either permanent or temporary habitations. I called on board the *Chatham* on my return, and was happy to understand that there was little probability of her receiving any injury, having grounded on a muddy bank; and that there was every prospect of her floating off the next tide. In sounding to lay out their anchors, it became evident that in the very direction in which they had sailed to their then station, they had run upwards of half a mile on this bank in two fathoms water, in consequence of the unpardonable negligence of the man at the lead, who had announced false soundings, and for which he was deservedly punished. She was hove off about midnight, and anchored near us without having received the least damage.

The *Chatham* being in readiness by ten the next morning,

OF PUGET SOUND

[June, 1792.]

Saturday the 2d, with a light northerly breeze, attended with gloomy weather and some rain, we directed our route back by the way we had come, and it was not until three o'clock that we reached the sound, where we again anchored in fifty fathoms, a quarter of a mile from the eastern shore, and about six times that distance to the eastward of the arm we had quitted, which forms an excellent harbour, well sheltered from all winds; but during our short stay there we saw no appearance of any fresh water. Here our position was before a small bay, into which flowed two excellent streams, but these were so nearly on a level with the sea, that it became necessary either to procure the water at low tide, or at some distance up the brook; which latter was easily effected, as our boats were admitted to where the fresh water fell from the elevated land. In this situation the observed latitude was 48° 2$\frac{1}{2}$', longitude 237° 57$\frac{1}{2}$', being six miles S. S. E. from our last anchorage.

As there was little doubt now remaining that the party had proceeded to the examination of the other inlet, and as the weather was thick and hazy with some rain, a gun was now and then fired to direct them to the ships in case they should be on their return.

In the course of the afternoon we were tolerably successful with the seine, as we had also been in the above harbor, in taking a quantity of fish similar to those we procured in port Discovery. About eight in the evening we had the satisfaction of hearing our gun answered; and at nine the boats safely returned to the vessels.

Mr. Whidbey informed me, that on his return from the survey of the port we had quitted in the morning, he saw the *Chatham* working off the east end of the round island at so little distance, that he concluded the boats could not have escaped the observation of those on board; and under that impression, and his anxiety to forward this tedious service, he had availed himself of a favorable southerly wind, and flood tide, to prosecute his examination of the other branch, whose entrance he had found something wider than the harbor we had left, having sixty fathoms depth of water, with a soft muddy bottom. Its general direction led N. N. W. Having advanced about four miles, they found, on a low projecting point of the western shore, a village containing a numerous tribe of the natives. But as my orders, as well as the general inclination of the officers, were to prevent by all possible means the chance of any misunderstanding, it was the uniform practice to avoid landing in the presence of considerable numbers; and as it was now the dinner time of our party, Mr. Whidbey very prudently made choice of the opposite shore, in the hope of making a quiet meal without the company of the Indians. Having reached the place where they intended to land, they were met by upwards of two hundred, some in canoes with their families, and others walking along the shore, attended by about forty dogs in a drove, shorn close to the skin like sheep. Notwithstanding their numbers, it was important to land for the purpose of taking angles; and they had the satisfaction of being received on shore with every mark of cordial friendship. Mr. Whidbey however, thought it prudent to remain no longer in their society than was absolutely necessary; and having finished the business for which he had landed, he instantly embarked, and continued his route up the inlet until the evening, when he landed for the night about nine miles within its entrance. In the morning they again pursued their inquiry, and soon after they had landed to breakfast, they were visited by a large canoe full of Indians, who were immediately followed by an hundred more of the natives, bringing with them the mats for covering their temporary houses, and, seemingly, every other article of value belonging to them.

On landing, which they did without the least hesitation, their behavior was courteous and friendly in the highest degree. A middle-aged man, to all appearance the chief or principal person of the party, was foremost in showing marks of the greatest hospitality; and perceiving our party were at breakfast, presented them with water, roasted roots, dried fish, and other articles of food. This person, in return, received some presents, and others were distributed amongst the ladies and some of the party. The chief, for so we must distinguish him, had two hangers, one of Spanish, the other of English manufacture, on which he seemed to set a very high value. The situation of the spot where they had landed was delightful; the shores on each side the inlet being composed of a low country, pleasingly diversified by hills, dales, extensive verdant lawns, and clear spaces in the midst of the forest, which, together with the cordial reception they had met from the natives, induced Mr. Whidbey to continue his examination on shore; on this occasion he was accompanied by the chief and several of the party, who conducted themselves with the greatest propriety; though with no small degree of civil curiosity in examining his clothes, and expressing a great desire to be satisfied as to the color of the skin they covered; making signs, that his hands and face were painted white, instead of being black or red like their own; but when convinced of their mistake by opening his waistcoat, their astonishment was inexpressible. From these circumstances, and the general tenor of their behavior, Mr. Whidbey concluded they had not before seen any Europeans, though, from the different articles they possessed, it was evident a communication had taken place; probably by the means of distant trading tribes. The people, who had been met in that inlet removing with their families, and all their moveable property, were not unlikely to be of this commercial description; particularly, as their voyage was towards the sea-coast, where, in some convenient situation near to the general resort of Europeans, they might fix their abode until an opportunity was afforded them to barter their commodities for the more valuable productions of Europe, which are afterwards disposed of to the inhabitants of the interior country at a very exorbitant price. This circumstance tends, in some degree, to corroborate an opinion hazarded on a former occasion to this effect.

On the boats being ordered on shore to receive Mr. Whidbey and the gentlemen who had attended him in his walk, the launch grounded, which was no sooner perceived by the Indian chief, than he was foremost in using every exertion to shove her off. This being effected, and the gentlemen embarked, most of these good people took their leave, and seemed to part with their newly-acquired friends with great reluctance. The chief, and a few others, accompanied our party, until they had advanced about fourteen miles from the entrance, when they, very civily, took their departure; here the arm branched off from its former direction of about N. N. W., to the westward, and N. E. The latter being the object of their pursuit, they soon arrived off another extensive and populous village, whence several canoes came off with not less than seventy of the natives in them; and several others were seen coming from the different parts of the shore. Those who approached the boats conducted themselves with the utmost propriety, shewing, by repeated invitations to their dwellings, the greatest hospitality, and making signs that they had plenty of food to bestow. In these entreaties the ladies were particularly earnest, and expressed much chagrin and mortification that their offers of civility were declined. As the boats sailed past the village those in the canoes returned to the shore.

The direction which the land took to the N. E. conducted them to a considerable branch whose outer points lie from each other N. 20 W., about a league asunder. From its eastern shore a shallow flat of sand, on which are some rocky islets and rocks, runs out, until within half a mile of the western shore, forming a narrow channel, navigated by them in nearly a N. N. W. direction, for about three leagues. The depth, at its entrance, was twenty fathoms; but gradually decreased to four, as they advanced up the channel which is formed by the western shore, and the sand-bank, continuing with great regularity, about half a mile wide, to the latitude of 48° 24', longitude 237° 45', where it then ceased to be navigable for vessels of any burthen, in consequence of the rocks and overfalls from three to twenty fathoms deep, and a very irregular and disagreeable tide. On meeting these impediments, the party returned, with intention of exploring the opening leading to the westward. As they repassed the village, they were again visited by their friendly chief, attended by two or three canoes only, who presented them with a most welcome supply of very fine small fish which, in many respects, resembled, and most probably were, a species of the smelt. He accepted, with apparent pleasure, an invitation into the launch, where he remained with Mr. Whidbey until evening, ate and drank of such things as were offered with the greatest confidence, and on being made acquainted that the party was going to rest, bad them farewell with every mark of respect and friendship.

In the morning, the examination of the western branch was pursued, and found to terminate in a very excellent and commodious cove or harbor, with regular soundings from 10 to 20 fathoms, good holding ground. Its western extent situated in latitude 48° 17', longitude 237° 38', is not more than a league from the eastern shore of the main inlet, within the straits. On each point of the harbor, which in honor of a particular friend I call PENN'S COVE, was a deserted village; in one of which were found several sepulchers formed exactly like a sentry box. Some of them were open, and contained skeletons of many young children tied up in blankets; the smaller bones of adults were likewise noticed, but no one of the limb bones could here be found, which gave rise to an opinion that these, by the living inhabitants of the neighborhood, were appropriated to useful purposes, such as pointing their arrows, spears, or other weapons. The surrounding country, for several miles in most points of view, presented a delightful prospect, consisting chiefly of spacious meadows elegantly adorned with clumps of trees; amongst which the oak bore a very considerable proportion, in size from four to six feet in circumference. In these beautiful pastures, bordering on an expansive sheet of water, the deer were seen

---

Friend Penn. There were undoubtedly many Penns in England at that time. The explorer does not leave a shred of information by which his "particular friend" may be identified. The "Century Cyclopedia of Names" gives two who were living in 1791 when Vancouver left England. These were John Penn (1729–1795) and Richard Penn (1736–1811). Both were grandsons of William Penn. Both were born in England, and each served as lieutenant-governor of Pennsylvania. It probably never will be known whether or not it was one of these whom Vancouver thus honored.

playing about in great numbers. Nature had here provided the well-stocked park, and wanted only the assistance of art to constitute that desirable assemblage of surface, which is so much sought in other countries, and only to be acquired by an immoderate expense in manual labor. The soil principally consisted of a rich, black vegetable mould, lying on a sandy or clayey substratum; the grass, of an excellent quality, grew to the height of three feet, and the ferns, which, in the sandy soils, occupied the clear spots, were nearly twice as high. The country in the vicinity of this branch of the sea is, according to Mr. Whidbey's representation, the finest we had yet met with, notwithstanding the very pleasing appearance of many others; its natural productions were luxuriant in the highest degree, and it was, by no means, ill supplied with streams of fresh water. The number of its inhabitants he estimated at about six hundred, which I should suppose would exceed the total of all the natives we had before seen; the other parts of the sound did not appear, by any means, so populous, as we had been visited by one small canoe only, in which were five of the natives, who civilly furnished us with some small fish. The character and appearance of their several tribes here seen did not seem to differ in any material respect from each other, or from those we have already had occasion to mention.

A fortnight had now been dedicated to the examination of this inlet; which I have distinguished by the name of ADMIRALTY INLET: we had still to return about forty miles through this tedious inland navigation, before we could arrive on a new field of enquiry. The broken appearance of the region before us and the difficulties we had already en-

---

Admiralty Inlet. The body of water which Vancouver intended should bear this name extends from Port Townsend to Tacoma. It is rarely so used now except on official charts. The name of Puget Sound has supplanted it in common use. The Board of Admiralty supervises the work of the Royal Navy of Great Britain. In addressing this body the members are referred to as "My Lords Commissioners of the Admiralty." Vancouver sought to honor this important portion of the British government by writing this name upon his chart.

KING GEORGE III.

From the painting by Allan Ramsay, now in the National Portrait Gallery, London. Engraved in England for this work.

countered in tracing its various shores, incontestibly proved, that the object of our voyage could alone be accomplished by very slow degrees. Perfectly satisfied with the arduousness of the task in which we were engaged, and the progress we were likely to make, I became anxiously solicitous to move the instant an opportunity should serve. The two following days were however unfavorable to that purpose, and after the great fatigue our people had lately undergone, were well appropriated to holidays. Sunday, the 3d, all hands were employed in fishing with tolerably good success, or in taking a little recreation on shore; and on Monday, the 4th, they were served as good a dinner as we were able to provide for them, with double allowance of grog to drink the King's health, it being the anniversary of His Majesty's birth; on which auspicious day, I had long since designed to take formal possession of all the countries we had lately been employed in exploring, in the name of, and for His Britannic Majesty, his heirs and successors.

To execute this purpose, accompanied by Mr. Broughton and some of the officers, I went on shore about one o'clock, pursuing the usual formalities which are generally observed on such occasions, and under the discharge of a royal salute from the vessels, took possession accordingly of the coast, from that part of New Albion, in the latitude of 39° 20′ north, and longitude 236° 26′ east, to the entrance of this inlet of the sea, said to be the supposed straits of Juan de Fuca; as likewise all the coast islands, etc. within the said straits, as well on the northern as on the southern shores; together with those situated in the interior sea we had discovered, extending from the said straits, in various directions, between the north-west, north, east, and southern quarters; which interior sea I have honored with the name of THE GULF OF GEORGIA, and the

---

George III. The name of Gulf of Georgia has been retained, though greatly restricted from its original extent, and changed on all modern charts to Strait of Georgia. The land binding the Gulf of Georgia and extending southward to the 45th degree of north latitude, Vancouver called New Georgia. The mainland just north and northwest of New Georgia he called New Hanover, in honor of the "House" of the reigning family. By a pecul-

[Original Journal, Page 170.]

VANCOUVER'S DISCOVERY

[June, 1792.]

continent binding the said gulf, and extending southward to the 45th degree of north latitude, with that of NEW GEOR-

---

iar irony of fate both of these intensely English names have been supplanted by two intensely American names, — Washington and British Columbia. George II ruled from 1727 to 1760, so it was he who was honored by the name given to the English colony planted by James Edward Ogelthorpe in the southeastern corner of the United States, just as his grandson was honored by the attempt to place his name on the land that was destined to become the northwestern corner.

The other name of Possession Sound was given, as recorded in the journal, to commemorate the act of taking possession. On Vancouver's chart it is written on the bay where now stands the city of Everett. Recent maps show it moved southward from that bay to the channel between the south end of Whidbey Island and the mainland.

It is not necessary that there should be attempted here a sketch of the life of George III. It is easily accessible in any cyclopædia or standard work of history. Queen Victoria reigned sixty-four years from 1837 to 1901. Next to that the reign of George III, from 1760 to 1820, was the longest in English history. That long span of sixty years witnessed many events of prime importance to the history of the world. The French and Indian War in America, and the contest for control in India, were settled by the Treaty of Paris, 1763. The American War for Independence was successfully ended. The entire period of disturbances known as the French Revolution and the Napoleonic Era fell wholly within the time of this reign.

Few monarchs have impressed their personalities upon their governments to the extent that George III did from beginning to end. This was the cause of much turmoil, but it was a time when turmoil was natural. There was much of governmental evolution in the time of George III. Born on June 4, 1738, he was the eldest son of the Prince of Wales, Frederick Louis. The boy loved his father and was greatly shocked by his death in March, 1751. His education was in the hands of lords, bishops, and tutors, but more particularly was it watched over by his mother, an exceedingly ambitious princess, who whispered continually in her son's ears, "George, be king." This motherly advice may have been the inspiration of the king's life. His prevailing trait was called by himself "firmness"; by those opposed to him it was called "obstinacy." The first two Georges had been ruled by the great Whig families. This new king would break that influence. He wanted no party government. So he struggled on with one ministry after another, seeking to restore the prerogatives of the crown, while slowly but surely, in spite of his opposition, the elements of the present constitution were being developed. There is a sense in which George III may be called the last of the "unconstitutional" monarchs of Great Britain.

With all his other faults, he was personally a sincerely pious man and a clean one in domestic life. Queen Charlotte declared that from the day

ADMIRAL SIR ALAN GARDNER.

From an engraving by Fenner after Sir William Beechey. Photograph copyrighted by Walker & Cockrell. Rights secured for this work in England and America.

OF PUGET SOUND

GIA; in honor of His present Majesty. This branch of Admiralty inlet obtained the name of POSSESSION Sound; its western arm, after Vice Admiral Sir Alan Gardner, I distinguished by the name of PORT GARDNER, and its smaller eastern one by that of PORT SUSAN.

---

of her wedding to the day of the king's first illness she had never known a day of real sorrow. This illness was a mental malady, developing periods of insanity. During his last nine years this malady was constant, and added to it was that of blindness. In perfect darkness he was led about the palace or its gardens, waiting for the call to rest which came on January 29, 1820.

Vancouver was a sailor. He was no politician. In selecting the names of great men to be honored during his explorations, he chose friends and enemies of the king with reckless impartiality. In one sense this was inevitable if he honored those great men at all. In his struggle with ministries the king had alternately loved and hated, trusted and suspected, almost every one of the great men of his realm. Take, for example, Lord Grenville, whose name Vancouver gave to that magnificent headland on the western coast of the State of Washington. George III trusted Grenville's father, but, as minister, he scolded and lectured the king about his stubborn blundering until George III hated him. But Grenville was powerful and was eventually called back to office. The king struggled against that necessity and petulantly declared, "I would rather see the devil in my closet than George Grenville." The son of this man was also suspected and then trusted, raised to the peerage, and made prime minister. Contrasted with this is the case of the Earl of Bute, whom the ministers hated and opposed as the king's favorite. Vancouver honored him also by naming in his honor Bute Canal, now Bute Inlet.

The portrait used in this work is Number 223 in the National Portrait Gallery. It is the work of Allan Ramsay, a Scottish portrait painter, son of the poet of the same name. Fortunately, the portrait of Queen Charlotte is by the same artist, as is also the one of the Earl of Bute. Evidently all three were painted in the same palace, for the same Corinthian pillar appears in each, suggesting the similarity of background found in a series of photographs made in a gallery of the present day. The setting, the artist, and all suggest also the time when Bute was a prime favorite of the king.

Sir Alan Gardner. This is one of the names that is loved and respected by British seamen everywhere. It is a matter of regret that the name Port Gardner is gradually disappearing from the geographies of Puget Sound. Originally Vancouver applied it to the waterway extending from Deception Pass to Possession Sound, or the present site of Everett. Now that waterway is charted as Saratoga Passage and occasionally we see the name Port Gardner applied to the bay of Everett. At this rate it will be the matter of but a few years when Port Gardner will be extinct as a geographic term.

Not so is the name of Port Susan as applied to the waterway between Camano Island and the mainland. Alan has been dismissed, but the geographers have remained constant to Susan. For more than a century Vancouver's curt and brief honor to Susan has proved a baffling enigma. It has often been suggested that Susan was the sweetheart in England whom Vancouver did not live long enough to wed. The mystery is cleared away, however, when it is learned that Captain Alan Gardner, while serving in the West Indies, met, wooed, and wed a widow and heiress at Jamaica in 1769. Her name was Susanna Hyde Turner. Vancouver had served under Gardner and the latter recommended Vancouver, who had just returned with him from the West Indies, to be second in command of the proposed expedition under Captain Henry Roberts. This was the very expedition of which Vancouver was later given the chief command. Then it was that Gardner as one of the Lords of the Admiralty signed his "Additional Instructions" for his great voyage. Therefore, when he named one port after Admiral Gardner, he named the other after the admiral's esteemed lady.

Alan Gardner, the son of Lieutenant-Colonel Gardner of the Eleventh Dragoon Guards, was born at Uttoxeter, Staffordshire, on April 12, 1742. Like most of the British naval heroes, he entered service at a tender age, joining the *Medway*, under Captain Peter Denis, in May, 1755. In January, 1758, he followed Captain Denis into the *Dorsetshire* and was present at the battle of Quiberon Bay. He was promoted to be lieutenant of the *Bellona*, still under Denis, but he remained with that ship after she passed to the command of Captain Faulknor. He took part in the capture of the *Courageux* on August 14, 1761.

On April 12, 1762, he was promoted to be commander of the *Raven* fire-ship. On May 17, 1766, he was advanced to post rank and given command of the *Preston*. In her he went to Jamaica as flagship of Rear-Admiral Parry. In 1768 he was removed to the *Levant* frigate, which he commanded on the same station until 1771. It was while in command of this frigate that he married Susan.

In 1775 he received command of the *Maidstone* of twenty-eight guns, and was again sent to the West Indies. In 1778 he was sent to join Lord Howe on the North American coast, and carried the first news of the approach of the French fleet. On November 3, 1778, he captured a French merchantship, which he carried with him to Antigua. He was then appointed to the *Sultan* of seventy-four guns, and had a share in the battle of Grenada on July 6, 1779. In 1781, in the *Duke* of ninety-eight guns, he accompanied Sir George Rodney to the West Indies and took part in the victory of April, 1782.

After the peace of 1783 he returned to England, but in 1786 he went again to the West Indies as commander-in-chief. His flag as commodore was in the *Europa*. During part of this time the captain of his flagship was James Vashon, and during the whole of the cruise one of his midshipmen was Peter Puget.

He returned to England in 1787 and was appointed to a seat at the Board of Admiralty in January, 1790, which he held until March, 1795. During the famous Spanish Armament in 1790 he commanded the *Courageux* for a short time. In February, 1793, having been appointed Rear-Admiral, he went once more to the West Indies with a large squadron, his own flag being in the *Queen*. This expedition against the French colonies was a failure, through lack of troops to coöperate with the navy. On returning to England he was attached to the grand fleet under Lord Howe and took part in the battle of June 1, 1794, when the loss of the battleship *Queen* proved a severe matter. However, for his share in this action, Gardner was created a Baronet, and on July 4, 1794, was advanced to the grade of Vice-Admiral. Vancouver evidently took it for granted that the advance was due to arrive, for he uses that as Gardner's rank in 1792. Gardner was again with the fleet under Lord Bridfort, but had little share in the action of June 23, 1795, off Lorient.

During this time Gardner was also a member of Parliament, being elected in 1790 for Plymouth, which seat he held until 1796, when he was elected for Westminster.

At the time of the mutiny at Spithead, in April, 1797, Gardner had his flag in the *Royal Sovereign*. He had a conference with the delegates on board the *Queen Charlotte*, in which Gardner lost his temper. He seized one of the delegates by the collar and threatened to have him and his companions hanged. The admiral with difficulty escaped from the human tempest stirred up by his hasty threat.

He was promoted to be Admiral of the Blue on February 14, 1799, and in August, 1800, was appointed Commander-in-Chief on the coast of Ireland. In December, 1800, he was created a peer of Ireland, with the title of Baron Gardner. He was still being returned to Parliament by Westminster until he was transferred to the upper House by being raised in 1806 to the peerage of the United Kingdom, with the title of Baron Gardner of Uttoxeter.

In 1807 he was appointed to command the Channel Fleet, but his health was failing. He resigned his command in 1808, and on January 1, 1809, he died.

CHAPTER IX

WORK AROUND BELLINGHAM BAY AND THE GULF OF GEORGIA, NOW CALLED WASHINGTON SOUND

[Original Journal, Pages 171-172, Book II, Chapter VII.] [June, 1792.]

A LIGHT breeze springing up from the N. W. about seven in the morning of Tuesday the 5th of June, we sailed down Possession sound. This wind brought with it, as usual, serene and pleasant weather. Whilst we were passing gently on, the chief, who had shown so much friendly attention to Mr. Whidbey and his party, with several of his friends came on board, and presentd us with some fruit and dried fish. He entered the ship with some reluctance, but was no sooner on deck than he seemed perfectly reconciled; and with much inquisitive earnestness regarded the surrounding objects, the novelty of which seemed to fill his mind with surprise and admiration. The unaffected hospitable attention he had shewn our people, was not likely upon this occasion to be forgotten. After he had visited the different parts of the ship, at which he expressed the greatest astonishment, I presented him and his friends with an assortment of such things as they esteemed to be most valuable; and then they took their leave, seemingly highly pleased with their reception.

The N. W. wind was unfavorable after we were clear of Possession sound, and obliged us to work to windward, which discovered to us a shoal lying in a bay, just to the westward of the north point of entrance into the sound, a little distance from the shore. It shews itself above the water, and is discoverable by the soundings gradually decreasing to ten, seven, and five fathoms, and cannot be considered as any material impediment to the navigation of the bay. As the ebb-tide was greatly in our favor, I did not wait to examine

OF PUGET SOUND

it further, but continued plying to windward until midnight, when being unable to gain any ground against the strength of the flood, we anchored in 22 fathoms water about half a mile from the western shore of Admiralty inlet, and about half way between Oak cove and Marrowstone point; the *Chatham* having anchored before us some distance astern.

The ebb again returned at the rate of about three miles per hour; but as it was calm we did not move until the N. W. wind set in about seven in the morning of Wednesday the 6th, when we worked out of the inlet.

Having reached its entrance, we were met by several canoes from the westward. Some of the headmost, when they had advanced near to the ship made signs of peace, and came alongside, giving us to understand that their friends behind wished to do the same, and requested we would shorten sail for that purpose. They seemed very solicitous to dissuade us from proceeding to the northward by very vociferous and vehement arguments; but as their language was completely unintelligible, and their wishes not appertaining to the object of our pursuit, so far as we were enabled to comprehend their meaning, we treated their advice with perfect indifference, on which they departed, joined the rest of their countrymen, and proceeded up Admiralty inlet, whose north point, called by me POINT PARTRIDGE, is situated in latitude 48° 16', longitude 237° 31', and is formed by a high white sandy cliff, having one of the verdant lawns on either side of it. Passing at the distance of about a mile from this point we very suddenly came on a small space of ten fathoms water, but immediately again increased our depth to 20 and 30 fathoms. After advancing a few miles along the eastern shore of the gulf, we found no effect either from the ebb or flood tide, and the wind being light and variable from the northward, at

---

Point Partridge. It is probable that this name came from seeing there a pheasant or a grouse, or something that reminded them of a partridge. No individual bearing that name was listed with either the *Discovery* or the *Chatham.* If the name were that of some friend at home, the fact would likely be mentioned.

three in the afternoon we were obliged to anchor in 20 fathoms water, sandy bottom.

In this situation New Dungeness bore by compass S. 54 W.; the east point of Protection island S. 15 W.; the west point of Admiralty inlet, which after my much esteemed friend Captain George Wilson of the navy, I distinguished by the name of POINT WILSON, S. 35 E. situated in latitude 48° 10′, longitude 237° 31′; the nearest shore east, two leagues distant; a low sandy island, forming at its west end a low cliff, above which some dwarf trees are produced from N. 26 W. to N. 40 W.; and the proposed station for the vessels during the examination of the continental shore by the boats, which, from Mr. Broughton who had visited it, obtained the name of STRAWBERRY BAY, N. 11 W. at the distance of about six leagues, situated in a region apparently much broken and divided by water. Here we remained until seven in the evening; we then weighed, but with so little wind, that after having drifted to the southward of our former station, we were obliged again to anchor until six the next morning, Thursday the 7th, when we made an attempt to proceed, but were soon again compelled to become stationary near our last situation.

On reflecting that the summer was now fast advancing, and that the slow progress of the vessels occasioned too much delay, I determined, rather than lose the advantages which the prevailing favorable weather now afforded for boat expeditions, to dispatch Mr. Puget in the launch, and Mr. Whidbey in the cutter, with a week's provisions, in order that the shores should be immediately explored to the next intended station of the vessels, whither they would proceed as soon as circumstances would allow. In this arrangement

---

George Wilson. Here Vancouver mentions one of his friends in the navy. He evidently did not attain high rank or much prominence. Usual sources of information about such are blank about this George Wilson. He was post captain on the active list in 1793, and was still a captain in 1797 at the capture of Trinidad. He was at one time with the *Bellona* of seventy-four guns. These meagre facts are mentioned casually in the records of others.

I was well aware, it could not be considered judicious to part with our launch, whilst the ship remained in a transitory unfixed state in this unknown and dangerous navigation; yet she was so essentially necessary to the protection of our detached parties, that I resolved to encounter some few difficulties on board, rather than suffer the delay, or lose so valuable an opportunity for the prosecution of the survey. In directing this, orders were given not to examine any openings to the northward, beyond Strawberry bay, but to determine the boundaries of the continental shore leading to the north and eastward, as far as might be practicable to its parallel, whither they were to resort after performing the task assigned. On this service they departed, and directed their course for the first opening on the eastern shore about 3 or 4 leagues distant, bearing by compass from the ship N. by E.

Having repaired to the low sandy island already noticed, for the purpose of taking some angles, I found some rocks lying on its western side nearly three quarters of a mile from its shores; and that the eastern part of it was formed by a very narrow low spit of land, over which the tide nearly flowed. Its situation is in latitude 48° 24′, longitude 237° $26\frac{1}{2}$′. Amongst the various bearings that it became necessary to take here, were those of the two remarkably high snowy mountains so frequently mentioned. Mount Baker bore N. 63 E.; mount Rainier S. 27 E.; and from a variety of observations purposely made for fixing their respective situations, it appeared that mount Baker was in latitude 48° 39′, longitude 238° 20′, and mount Rainier in latitude 47° 3′, longitude 238° 21′. To the southward of these were now seen two other very lofty, round, snowy mountains, lying apparently in the same north and south direction, or nearly so; but we were unable to ascertain their positive situation. The summits of these were visible only at two or three stations in the southern parts of Admiralty inlet; they appeared to be covered with perpetual snow as low down as we were enabled to see, and seemed as if they rose from an extensive plain of low country.

VANCOUVER'S DISCOVERY

When due attention is paid to the range of snowy mountains that stretch to the southward from the base of mount Rainier, a probability arises of the same chain being continued, so as to connect the whole in one barrier along the coast, at uncertain distances from its shores; although intervals may exist in the ridge where the mountains may not be sufficiently elevated to have been discernable from our several stations. The like effect is produced by the two former mountains, whose immense height permitted their appearing very conspicuously, long before we approached sufficiently near to distinguish the intermediate range of rugged mountains that connect them, and from whose summits their bases originate.

About six in the evening, with a light breeze from the S. W. we weighed and stood to the northward; but after having advanced about 11 miles, the wind became light and obliged us to anchor about nine that evening, in 37 fathoms water, hard bottom, in some places rocky; in this situation we were detained by calms until the afternoon of the following day, Friday the 8th. Our observed latitude here, was 48° 29′, longitude 237° 29′: the country, occupying the northern horizon in all directions, appeared to be excessively broken and insulated. Strawberry bay bore, by compass, N. 10 W. about three leagues distant; the opening on the continental shore, the first object for the examination of the detached party, with some small rocky inlets before its entrance that appeared very narrow, bore, at the distance of about five miles, S. 87 E.; point Partridge S. 21 E.; the low sandy island south; the south part of the westernmost shore, which is composed of islands and rocks, S. 37 W. about two miles distant; the nearest shore was within about a mile; a very dangerous sunken rock, visible only at low tide, lies off from a low rocky point on this shore, bearing N. 79 W.; and a very unsafe cluster of small rocks, some constantly, and others visible only near low water, bore N. 15 W. about two miles and a half distant.

This country presented a very different aspect from that which we had been accustomed to behold further south.

The shores now before us were composed of steep rugged rocks, whose surface varied exceedingly in respect to height, and exhibited little more than the barren rock, which in some places produced a little herbage of a dull color, with a few dwarf trees.

With a tolerably good breeze from the north, we weighed about three in the afternoon, and with a flood tide, turned up into Strawberry bay, where, in about three hours, we anchored in 16 fathoms, fine sandy bottom. This bay is situated on the west side of an island, which, producing an abundance of upright cypress, obtained the name of CYPRESS ISLAND. The bay is of small extent, and not very deep; its south point bore by compass S. 40 E.; a small islet, forming nearly the north point of the bay, round which is a clear good passage west; and the bottom of the bay east, at the distance of about three quarters of a mile. This situation, though very commodious, in respect to the shore, is greatly exposed to the winds, and sea in a S. S. E. direction.

In consequence of the wind ceasing, the *Chatham*, whilst endeavoring to gain this anchorage, was, by a strong flood tide, driven to the eastward of the island, where she was compelled to anchor. The next morning, Saturday 9th, received from Mr. Broughton a letter acquainting me, that, having been obliged to anchor on a rocky bottom, on account of the strength and irregularity of the tide, their stream cable had been cut through by the rocks; and that, after several attempts to recover the anchor, the rapidity of the tide had rendered all their efforts ineffectual; and he was very apprehensive that, remaining longer in that situation, for the purpose of repeating his endeavors, might endanger the loss also of the bower anchor by which they were then riding. In reply, I desired, if the anchor could not be regained by the next slack tide, that they would desist, rather than run a risk of still greater importance.

A fine sandy beach, forming the shores of the bay, gave us the hope of procuring a good supply of fish, as the *Chatham*, on her former visit, had been very successful, we were however, unfortunately mistaken; the seine was repeatedly hauled, but to no effect.

The *Chatham* arrived in the bay on Sunday morning, the 10th, with the loss of her stream anchor; and in the afternoon the boats returned from their survey.

From the officers, I became acquainted, that the first inlet communicated with port Gardner, by a very narrow and intricate channel, which, for a considerable distance, was not forty yards in width, and abounded with rocks above and beneath the surface of the water. These impediments, in addition to the great rapidity and irregularity of the tide, rendered the passage navigable only for boats or vessels of very small burthen. This determined all the eastern shore of the gulf, from S. W. point of this passage, in latitude 48° 27′, longitude 237° 37′, to the north point of entrance into Possession sound, in latitude 47° 53′, longitude 237° 47′, to be an island, which, in its broadest part, is about ten miles across; and in consequence of Mr. Whidbey's circumnavigation, I distinguished by the name of WHIDBEY'S ISLAND: and this northern pass, leading into port Gardner, DECEPTION PASSAGE.

Hence they proceeded to the examination of the continental coast leading to the northward, and entered what appeared to be a spacious sound, or opening, extending widely in three directions to the eastward of our present station. One,

---

Joseph Whidbey. This is another aggravating case of a name attaining increasing importance in geography while the life of its original owner is lost in oblivion. All that is now known of Joseph Whidbey is gleaned from Vancouver's journal of the voyage. Whidbey was mustered in as master on the *Discovery* and he remained in that position throughout the cruise. Being one of the officers, his name and rank only are recorded in the muster tables, while his age and birthplace are omitted. His name is frequently mentioned in the journals, for he was one of the most useful men on the expedition. He often had charge of crews in the small boats sent on side trips of exploration. It was in this way that he found the large island that bears his name. When the party started south from Nootka, Whidbey was directed to take one of the *Discovery's* boats into the storeship *Dædalus* and proceed with a survey of Gray's Harbor. This work he did in his usual thorough manner, and Vancouver records the result with a chart of the harbor in his journals.

leading to the southward, and another, to the eastward, they examined, and found them to terminate alike in deep bays, affording good anchorage, though inconvenient communication with the shores; particularly towards the head of each bay, on account of a shallow flat of sand or mud, which met them at a considerable distance from the land. Having fixed the boundaries of the continent as far to the north as the latitude of this island, agreeably to their directions, they returned, leaving unexplored a large opening which took a northern direction, as also the space that appeared to be the main arm of the gulf, to the north-westward, where the horizon was unbounded, and its width seemed very considerable. The country they had seen to the north-east of Deception passage, is much divided by water, and bore nearly the same sterile appearance with that of our present situation; excepting near the heads of the two large bays, which they had examined on the continental shore. There the land was of a moderate height, unoccupied by rocky precipices, and was well wooded with timber. In the course of this expedition, several deserted villages had been seen, and some of the natives met with, who differed not, in any material particular, as to their persons, nor in their civil and hospitable deportment, from those we had been so happy, on former occasions, to call our friends.

As our present anchorage was much exposed, and supplied us with no sort of refreshment, excepting a few small wild onions or leeks, I determined, on this information, to proceed with the vessels up the gulf, to the N. W. in quest of a more commodious situation, from whence Mr. Whidbey might be dispatched, to complete the examination of the arm which had been left unfinished, and another party, prosecute their inquiries to the N. W. or in such other direction as the gulf might take.

With a light breeze from the S. E. about four o'clock in the morning of Monday the 11th, we quitted this station, and passed between the small island and the north point of the bay to the north-westward, through a cluster of numerous islands, rocks, and rocky islets. On Mr. Broughton's first visit hither, he found a great quantity of very excellent strawberries, which gave it the name of Strawberry bay; but, on our arrival, the fruit season was passed. The bay affords good and secure anchorage, though somewhat exposed; yet, in fair weather, wood and water may be easily procured. The island of Cypress is principally composed of high rocky mountains, and steep perpendicular cliffs, which, in the center of Strawberry bay, fall a little back, and the space between the foot of the mountains and the sea-side is occupied by low marshy land, through which are several small runs of most excellent water, that find their way into the bay by oozing through the beach. It is situated in latitude 48° 36½′, longitude 237° 34′. The variation of the compass, by eighteen sets of azimuths differing from 18° to 21° taken on board, and on shore, since our departure from Admiralty inlet, gave the mean result of 18° 5′ eastwardly. The rise and fall of the tide was inconsiderable, though the stream was rapid: the ebb came from the east, and it was high water 2h 37′ after the moon had passed the meridian.

We proceeded first to the north-eastward, passing the branch of the gulf that had been partly examined, and then directed our course to the N. W. along that which appeared a continuation of the continental shore, formed by low sandy cliffs, rising from a beach of sand and stones. The country moderately elevated, stretched a considerable distance from the N. W. round to the south-eastward, before it ascended to join the range of rugged snowy mountains. This connected barrier, from the base of mount Baker, still continued very lofty, and appeared to extend in a direction leading to the westward of north. The soundings along the shore were regular, from 12 to 25 and 30 fathoms, as we approached, or increased our distance from, the land, which seldom exceeded two miles: the opposite side of the gulf to the south-westward, composed of numerous islands, was at the distance of about two leagues. As the day advanced, the S. E. wind gradually died away, and, for some hours, we remained nearly stationary.

In the evening, a light breeze favoring the plan I had in

contemplation, we steered for a bay that presented itself, where, about six o'clock, we anchored in six fathoms water, sandy bottom, half a mile from the shore. The points of the bay bore by compass S. 32 W. and N. 72 W.; the westernmost part of that which we considered to be the main land west, about three leagues distant; to the south of this point appeared the principal direction of the gulf, though a very considerable arm seemed to branch from it to the northeastward. As soon as the ship was secured, I went in a boat to inspect the shores of the bay, and found, with little trouble, a very convenient situation for our several necessary duties on shore; of which the business of the observatory was my chief object, as I much wished for a further trial of the rate of the chronometers, now that it was probable we should remain at rest a sufficient time to make the requisite observations for that purpose. Mr. Broughton received my directions to this effect, as also, that the vessels should be removed, the next morning, about a mile further up the bay to the N. E. where they would be more conveniently stationed for our several operations on shore; and as soon as the business of the observatory should acquire a degree of forwardness, Mr. Whidbey, in the *Discovery's* cutter, attended by the *Chatham's* launch, was to proceed to the examination of that part of the coast unexplored to the S. E.; whilst myself, in the yawl, accompanied by Mr. Puget in the launch, directed our researches up the main inlet of the gulf.

Matters thus arranged, with a week's provision in each boat, I departed at five o'clock in the morning of Tuesday the 12th. The most northerly branch, though attracting our first attention, caused little delay; it soon terminated in two open bays; the southernmost, which is the smallest, has two small rocks lying off its south point; it extends in a circular form to the eastward, with a shoal of sand projecting some distance from its shores: This bay affords good anchorage from seven to ten fathoms water: the other is much larger, and extends to the northward; these, by noon, we had passed round, but the shoals attached to the shores of each, and particularly to those of the latter, prevented our reaching within four or five miles of their head. The point constituting the west extremity of these bays, is that which was seen from the ship, and considered as the western part of the main land, of which it is a small portion, much elevated at the south extremity of a very low narrow peninsula; its highest part is to the S. E. formed by high white sand cliffs falling perpendicularly into the sea; from whence a shoal extends to the distance of half a mile round it, joining those of the larger bay; whilst its southwest extremity, not more than a mile in an east and west direction from the former, is one of those low projecting sandy points, with ten to seven fathoms water, within a few yards of it. From this point, situated in latitude 48° 57', longitude 237° 20', (which I distinguished by the name of POINT ROBERTS, after my

---

Captain Henry Roberts. Vancouver is the principal biographer of this man. His life is not included in the "Dictionary of National Biography" or any of the other standard sources of such information. However, in the introduction to his narrative, Vancouver gives a fine record of part of his life as follows: —

"Captain Henry Roberts, of known and tried abilities, who had served under Captain Cook during his two last voyages, and whose attention to the scientific part of his profession had afforded that great navigator frequent opportunities of naming him with much respect, was called upon to take charge of, and to command, the proposed expedition.

"At that period, I had just returned from a station at Jamaica under the command of Commodore (now Vice-Admiral) Sir Alan Gardner, who mentioned me to Lord Chatham and the Board of Admiralty; and I was solicited to accompany Captain Roberts as his second. In this proposal I acquiesced, and found myself very pleasantly situated, in being thus connected with a fellow traveler for whose abilities I bore the greatest respect, and in whose friendship and good opinion I was proud to possess a place. And as we had sailed together with Captain Cook on his voyage towards the south pole, and as both had afterwards accompanied him with Captain Clerke in the *Discovery* during his last voyage, I had no doubt that we were engaged in an expedition, which would prove no less interesting to my friend than agreeable to my wishes."

There followed the excitement over the Nootka episode and the Spanish Armament, in which Captain Roberts was sent away to be ready to fight the Spaniards in the West Indies should war actually ensue. The treaty was signed, and because Captain Roberts was away the command of the expedition "Round the World" was given to Commander George Vancouver.

[June, 1792.]

esteemed friend and predecessor in the *Discovery*) the coast takes a direction N. 28 W. and presented a task of examination to which we conceived our equipment very unequal. That which, from hence, appeared the northern extreme of

---

On the title-page of the published account of Captain Cook's last voyage is this phrase, "Illustrated with maps and charts, from the original drawings made by Lieut. Henry Roberts, under the direction of Captain Cook." It is well known that Captain Cook lost his life on the Sandwich Islands before the completion of his last voyage. The editor who prepared the journals for publication pays this tribute to Roberts: "Lieutenant Roberts was also frequently consulted, and was always found to be a ready and effectual assistant, when any nautical difficulties were to be cleared up."

In the same introduction to the 1784 edition of Cook's last voyage may be found a long letter signed by Henry Roberts and dated at Shoreham, Sussex, May 18, 1784. The scarcity of materials about the life and work of Roberts will justify the insertion here of the first paragraph of that letter as follows: —

"Soon after our departure from England, I was intrusted by Captain Cook to complete a map of the world as a general chart, from the best materials he was in possession of for that purpose; and before his death this business was in a great measure accomplished; That is, the grand outline of the whole was arranged, leaving only those parts vacant or unfinished, which he expected to fall in with and explore. But on our return home, when the fruits of our voyage were ordered by the Lords Commissioners of the Admiralty to be published, the care of the general chart being consigned to me, I was directed to prepare it from the latest and best authorities; and also to introduce Captain Cook's three successive tracks, that all his discoveries, and the different routes he had taken might appear together, by this means to give a general idea of the whole. This task having been performed by me, it is necessary, for the information of the Reader, to state the heads of the several authorities which I have followed in such parts of the chart as differ from what was drawn up immediately under the inspection of Captain Cook: and when the Public are made acquainted, that many materials, necessary to complete and elucidate the work, were not, at the time, on board the *Resolution*, or in his possession, the reason will appear very obvious, why these alterations and additions were introduced contrary to the original drawing."

Then follows a thorough discussion of the authorities used in preparing the general chart.

The peculiar situation of Point Roberts will always draw attention to this name. The international boundary, along the forty-ninth parallel, cuts across the peninsula south of the mouth of the Fraser River and thus gives this important point to the United States, while the balance of the peninsula belongs to the Dominion of Canada.

the continental shore, was a low bluff point, that seemed to form the southern entrance into an extensive sound, bearing N. 25 W. with broken land stretching about 5° farther to the westward. Between this direction and N. 79 W. the horizon seemed uninterrupted, excepting by the appearance of a small though very high round island, lying N. 52 W. apparently at the distance of many leagues. Having thus early examined and fixed the continental shore to the furthest point seen from the ship, I determined to prosecute our inquiries to the utmost limits that care and frugality could extend our supplies; and, having taken the necessary angles, we proceeded, but soon found our progress along the eastern or continental shore materially impeded by a shoal that extends from point Roberts N. 80 W. seven or eight miles, then stretches N. 35 W. about five or six miles further, where it takes a northerly direction towards the above low bluff point. Along the edge of this bank we had soundings from ten to one fathom, as we increased or decreased our distance from the eastern shore; to approach which all our endeavors were exerted to no purpose, until nine in the evening, when the shoal having forced us nearly into the middle of the gulf, we stood over to its western side, in order to land for the night, and to cook our provisions for the ensuing day, which being always performed by those on watch during the night, prevented any delay on that account, in the day time. As we stood to the westward, our depth soon increased to 15 fathoms, after which we gained no bottom until we reached the western shore of the gulf, where, on our arrival about one o'clock in the morning, it was with much difficulty we were enabled to land on the steep rugged rocks that compose the coast, for the purpose of cooking only, and were compelled, by this unfavorable circumstance, to remain and sleep in the boats.

At five in the morning of Wednesday the 13th, we again directed our course to the eastern shore, and landed about noon, on the above mentioned low bluff point. This, as was suspected, formed the south point of a very extensive sound, with a small arm leading to the eastward: the space, which seemed to be its main direction, and appeared very extensive, took a northerly course. The observed latitude here was 49° 19', longitude 237° 6', making this point (which, in compliment to my friend Captain George Grey of the navy, was called POINT GREY) seven leagues from point Roberts. The intermediate space is occupied by very low land, apparently a swampy flat, that retires several miles, before the country rises to meet the rugged snowy mountains, which we found still continuing in a direction nearly along the coast. This low flat being very much inundated, and extending behind point Roberts, to join the low land in the bay to the eastward of that point; gives its high land, when seen at a distance, the appearance of an island: this, however, is not the case, notwithstanding there are two openings between this point and point Grey. These can only be navigable for canoes, as the shoal continues along the coast to the distance of seven or eight miles from the shore, on which were lodged, and especially before these openings, logs of wood, and stumps of trees innumerable.

From point Grey we proceeded first up the eastern branch of the sound, where, about a league within its entrance, we passed to the northward of an island which nearly terminated its extent, forming a passage from ten to seven fathoms deep,

---

Captain George Grey. The name of this point is still retained on all the charts. It is a finely defined geographic feature at the entrance to Burrard Inlet. From Point Roberts to Point Grey, Vancouver passed the three mouths of the great Fraser River. Two of them he indicates as slight bays in the coast line. Later, as will be seen in the journal, he met Galliano and Valdes, the Spanish explorers. They reported to him that they had seen drift and other indications of a large river which, Vancouver says, was "Named by one of their officers Rio Blancho, in compliment to the then prime minister of Spain." Elsewhere the minister's name is spelled "Blanca." As in the case of the first report of the Columbia River, Vancouver denied the existence of this new river, which was finally discovered in 1806 by Simon Fraser by the overland route.

Captain Grey so signally honored in this case is little known. He does not figure in the usual collections of biographies. He was probably one of the earlier companions of Vancouver who dropped from public view before attaining distinction.

not more than a cable's length in width. This island lying exactly across the channel, appeared to form a similar passage to the south of it, with a smaller island lying before it. From these islands, the channel, in width about half a mile, continued its direction about east. Here we were met by about fifty Indians, in their canoes, who conducted themselves with the greatest decorum and civility, presenting us with several fish cooked, and undressed, of the sort already mentioned as resembling the smelt. These good people, finding we were inclined to make some return for their hospitality, shewed much understanding in preferring iron to copper.

For the sake of the company of our new friends, we stood on under an easy sail, which encouraged them to attend us some little distance up the arm. The major part of the canoes twice paddled forward, assembled before us, and each time a conference was held. Our visit and appearance were most likely the objects of their consultation, as our motions on these occasions seemed to engage the whole of their attention. The subject matter, which remained a profound secret to us, did not appear of an unfriendly nature to us, as they soon returned, and, if possible, expressed additional cordiality and respect. This sort of conduct always creates a degree of suspicion, and should ever be regarded with a watchful eye. In our short intercourse with the people of this country, we have generally found these consultations take place, whether their numbers were great or small; and though I have ever considered it prudent to be cautiously attentive on such occasions, they ought by no means to be considered as indicating at all times a positive intention of concerting hostile measures; having witnessed many of these conferences, without our experiencing afterwards any alteration in their friendly disposition. This was now the case with our numerous attendants, who gradually dispersed as we advanced from the station where we had first met them, and three or four canoes only accompanied us up a navigation which, in some places, does not exceed an hundred and fifty yards in width.

We landed for the night about half a league from the head of the inlet, and about three leagues from its entrance. Our Indian visitors remained with us until by signs we gave them to understand we were going to rest, and after receiving some acceptable articles, they retired, and by means of the same language, promised an abundant supply of fish the next day; our seine having been tried in their presence with very little success. A great desire was manifested by these people to imitate our actions, especially in the firing of a musket, which one of them performed, though with much fear and trembling. They minutely attended to all our transactions, and examined the color of our skins with infinite curiosity. In other respects they differed little from the generality of the natives we had seen: they possessed no European commodities, or trinkets, excepting some rude ornaments apparently made from sheet copper; this circumstance, and the general tenor of their behavior, gave us reason to conclude that we were the first people from a civilized country they had yet seen. Nor did it appear that they were nearly connected, or had much intercourse with other Indians, who traded with the European or American adventurers.

The shores in this situation were formed by steep rocky cliffs, that afforded no convenient space for pitching our tent, which compelled us to sleep in the boats. Some of the young gentlemen, however, preferring the stony beach for their couch, without duly considering the line of high water mark, found themselves incommoded by the flood tide, of which they were not apprized until they were nearly afloat; and one of them slept so sound, that I believe he might have been conveyed to some distance, had he not been awakened by his companions.

Perfectly satisfied with our researches in this branch of the sound, at four in the morning of Thursday the 14th, we retraced our passage in; leaving on the northern shore, a small opening extending to the northward, with two little islets before it of little importance, whilst we had a grander object in contemplation; and more particularly so, as this arm or channel could not be deemed navigable for shipping. The tide caused no stream; the color of its water, after we had passed the island the day before, was green and perfectly clear, whereas that in the main branch of the sound, extending nearly half over the gulf, and accompanied by a rapid tide, was nearly colorless, which gave us some reason to suppose that the northern branch of the sound might possibly be discovered to terminate in a river of considerable extent.

As we passed the situation from whence the Indians had first visited us the preceding day, which is a small border of low marshy land on the northern shore, intersected by several creeks of fresh water, we were in expectation of their company, but were disappointed, owing to our travelling so soon in the morning. Most of their canoes were hauled up into the creeks, and two or three only of the natives were seen straggling about on the beach. None of their habitations could be discovered, whence we concluded that their village was within the forest. Two canoes came off as we passed the island, but our boats being under sail, with a fresh favorable breeze, I was not inclined to halt, and they almost immediately returned.

The shores of this channel, which, after Sir Harry Burrard of the navy, I have distinguished by the name of BURRARD'S CHANNEL, may be considered, on the southern side, of a

---

Sir Harry Burrard. The name of this channel or canal has been changed on modern charts to Burrard Inlet. It has come into great prominence through the building there of the Canadian Pacific Railway's "Terminal City," called by the honored name of Vancouver.

In honoring the name of Burrard, Vancouver saved subsequent students much trouble by adding the phrase "of the navy." There were two other Sir Harry Burrards, both prominent in the British army and in politics. They were the uncle and the cousin of Sir Harry Burrard of the navy. Still the student is not without his troubles, for this Sir Harry Burrard was really Sir Harry Burrard Neale and is so recorded in the "National Dictionary of Biography." This new name was assumed by royal license, dated April 8, 1795, granting him the privilege of using the name and arms of Neale upon his marriage on April 15 with Grace Elizabeth, daughter and coheiress of Robert Neale of Shaw House, Wiltshire.

SIR HARRY BURRARD NEALE.
From a mezzotint by C. Turner after the painting by Matthew Brown. Photograph from the collection of Augustin Rischgitz, London.

OF PUGET SOUND

[June, 1792.]

moderate height, and though rocky, well covered with trees of a large growth, principally of the pine tribe. On the northern side, the rugged snowy barrier, whose base we had now nearly approached, rose very abruptly, and was only

---

Burrard was born on September 16, 1765, and in 1778 he entered the navy on the *Roebuck* under Sir Andrew Snape Hamond. In this ship he was present at the reduction of Charlestown in April, 1780. Moved to the *Chatham* under Captain Douglas, he took part in the capture of the French frigate *Magicienne*, off Boston, on September 2, 1781. He returned to England in 1783 as acting-lieutenant of the *Perseverance*. After service in the *Hector* under Sir John Hamilton, he went to the West Indies in the *Europa* and was officially thanked for saving five men from a wreck during a hurricane.

On September 29, 1787, he was promoted to be lieutenant of the *Expedition*. In 1790 he was in the *Southampton* with Keats and later in the *Victory*, Lord Hood's flagship. On November 3, 1790, he was promoted to be commander of the *Orestes*.

On April 12, 1791, his uncle, Sir Harry Burrard, died and he then succeeded to the baronetcy. On February 1, 1793, he was advanced to post rank and accompanied Lord Hood to the Mediterranean, where he saw active service, returning to England at the end of 1794.

Shortly after his marriage Neale was appointed to the command of the *San Fiorenzo* of forty-two guns, stationed at Weymouth, in attendance on the king. In company with the *Nymphe*, the *San Fiorenzo*, on March 9, 1797, captured the French frigates *Resistance* and *Constance* off Brest. Neale and his crew won honors a little later during the mutiny at the Nore. This crew refused to join the mutiny, and the ship was ordered to anchor under the stern of the *Sandwich*. In a few days she made her escape, running past a fierce fire from the mutinied ships. This escape was fatal to the mutiny. On June 7 a meeting at the Royal Exchange of London merchants and shipowners thanked Neale, his officers and seamen, for their faithfulness and spirit.

Neale continued in the same ship and, on April 9, 1779, in company with the *Amelia* of thirty-eight guns, was off Lorient where three large French frigates were lying in the outer road, ready for sea. The *Amelia* was partly dismasted by a sudden squall off the land, seeing which the French frigates slipped their cables and dashed for the lone *San Fiorenzo*. The *Amelia* soon patched up her troubles and rejoined her mate. The two ships then compelled the three frigates to retire to Lorient after severe losses.

Appointed to the *Centaur* of seventy-four guns in 1801, Neale was soon after moved into the royal yacht. In May and June, 1804, he was one of the Lords of the Admiralty, but in July returned to the royal yacht. In 1805, in the *London* of ninety-eight guns, he was with a small squadron under Sir

protected from the wash of the sea by a very narrow border of low land. By seven o'clock we had reached the N. W. point of the channel, which forms also the south point of the main branch of the sound: this also, after another particular friend, I called POINT ATKINSON, situated north from point Grey, about a league distant. Here the opposite point of the entrance into the sound bore by compass west, at the

---

John Borlase Warren, and had a remarkable fight on March 13, 1806, with the French ships *Marengo* and *Belle Poule*, both of which were captured. The *Marengo* of seventy-four guns, in command of Admiral Linois, struck to the *London* after a running fight of four hours. In 1808 Neale was captain of the fleet under Lord Gambier during the abortive attack on the French ships on Basque Roads. On July 31, 1810, he was advanced to the rank of Rear-Admiral and commanded a squadron on the coast of France from 1811 to 1814. On June 4, 1814, he became a vice-admiral.

On January 2, 1815, he was nominated a Knight Commander of the Bath, and on September 14, 1822, he received the Grand Cross of the same order. From 1823 to 1826 he was commander-in-chief in the Mediterranean, which position, according to a rule then in force, carried with it a nomination for the Grand Cross of St. Michael and St. George.

In 1824 he compelled the Dey of Algiers to obey the terms of the treaty of 1816. Neale became an admiral on July 22, 1830, and on the death of Sir Thomas Foley in January, 1833, he was offered command at Portsmouth on condition of his resigning his seat in Parliament. Neale, pointing out that such a condition was unprecedented and insulting, declined the command. The affair was probed in the Commons, but the Admiralty made their point stick.

Neale died at Brighton on February 15, 1840. Leaving no issue, his baronetcy fell to his brother, Rev. George Burrard, rector of Yarmouth. Neale was Lord of the Manor in the town of Lymington, which he had represented in Parliament for forty years. On Mount Pleasant, opposite this town, a handsome obelisk has been erected to the memory of Neale. The fine portrait used in this work was engraved in mezzotint by C. Turner from a painting by Matthew Brown.

Point Atkinson. There was one member of the expedition who bore this name. He was Edmund Atkinson, master's mate of the *Chatham*. When mustered in he gave his age at twenty-two years and his birthplace as Carlisle. There is no likelihood that Vancouver had reference to him when he named this point "after another particular friend." Point Atkinson, on the northern entrance to Burrard Inlet, has a lighthouse and is altogether a prominent feature. It is a pity that the man thus honored cannot be identified. There were many Atkinsons contemporaries of Vancouver in Great Britain, but thus far no clew to the right one has been discovered.

distance of about three miles; and nearly in the center between these two points, is a low rocky island producing some trees, to which the name of PASSAGE ISLAND was given. We passed in an uninterrupted channel to the east of it, with the appearance of an equally good one on the other side.

Quitting point Atkinson, and proceeding up the sound, we passed on the western shore some detached rocks, with some sunken ones amongst them, that extend about two miles, but are not so far from the shore as to impede the navigation of the sound; up which we made a rapid progress, by the assistance of a fresh southerly gale, attended with dark gloomy weather, that greatly added to the dreary prospect of the surrounding country. The low fertile shores we had been accustomed to see, though lately with some interruption, here no longer existed; their place was now occupied by the base of the stupendous snowy barrier, thinly wooded, and rising from the sea abruptly to the clouds; from whose frigid summit, the dissolving snow in foaming torrents rushed down the sides and chasms of its rugged surface, exhibiting altogether a sublime, though gloomy spectacle, which animated nature seemed to have deserted. Not a bird, nor living creature was to be seen, and the roaring of the falling cataracts in every direction precluded their being heard, had any been in our neighborhood.

Towards noon I considered that we had advanced some miles within the western boundary of the snowy barrier, as some of its rugged lofty mountains were now behind, and to the southward of us. This filled my mind with the pleasing hopes of finding our way to its eastern side. The sun shining at this time for a few minutes afforded an opportunity of ascertaining the latitude of the east point of an island which, from the shape of the mountain that composes it, obtained the name of ANVIL ISLAND, to be 49° 30', its longitude 237° 3'. We passed an island the forenoon of Friday the 15th, lying on the eastern shore, opposite to an opening on the western, which evidently led into the gulf nearly in a S. W. direction, through a numerous assemblage of rocky islands and rocks, as also another opening to the westward of this island, that seemed to take a similar direction. Between Anvil island and the north point of the first opening, which lies from hence S. by W. five miles distance, are three white rocky islets, lying about a mile from the western shore. The width of this branch of the sound is about a league; but northward from Anvil island it soon narrows to half that breadth, taking a direction to the N. N. E. as far as latitude 49° 39', longitude 237° 9', where all our expectations vanished, in finding it to terminate in a round bason, encompassed on every side by the dreary country already described. At its head, and on the upper part of the eastern shore, a narrow margin of low land runs from the foot of the barrier mountains to the water-side, which produced a few dwarf pine trees, with some little variety of underwood. The water of the sound was here nearly fresh, and in color a few shades darker than milk; this I attributed to the melting of the snow, and its water passing rapidly over a chalky surface, which appeared probable by the white aspect of some of the chasms that seemed formerly to have been the course of water-falls, but were now become dry.

The gap we had entered in the snowy barrier seemed of little importance, as through the vallies, caused by the irregularity of the mountain's tops, other mountains more distant, and apparently more elevated, were seen rearing their lofty heads in various directions. In this dreary and comfortless region, it was no inconsiderable piece of good fortune to find a little cove in which we could take shelter, and a small spot of level land on which we could erect our tent; as we had scarcely finished our examination when the wind became excessively boisterous from the southward, attended with heavy squalls and torrents of rain, which continuing until noon the following day, Friday the 15th, occasioned a very unpleasant detention. But for this circumstance we might too hastily have concluded that this part of the gulf was uninhabited. In the morning we were visited by near forty of the natives, on whose approach, from the very material alteration that had now taken place in the

ADMIRAL EARL HOWE.

From the painting by Henry Singleton, in the National Portrait Gallery, London. Photograph copyrighted by Walker & Cockrell. Rights secured for this work in England and America.

face of the country, we expected to find some difference in their general character. This conjecture was however premature, as they varied in no respect whatever, but in possessing a more ardent desire for commercial transactions; into the spirit of which they entered with infinitely more avidity than any of our former acquaintances, not only in bartering amongst themselves the different valuables they had obtained from us, but when that trade became slack, in exchanging those articles again with our people; in which traffic they always took care to gain some advantage, and would frequently exult on the occasion. Some fish, their garments, spears, bows and arrows, to which these people wisely added their copper ornaments, comprized their general stock in trade. Iron, in all its forms, they judiciously preferred to any other article we had to offer.

The weather permitting us to proceed, we directed our route along the continental or western shore of the sound, passing within two small islands and the main island, into the opening before mentioned, stretching to the westward from Anvil island. At the distance of an hundred yards from the shore, the bottom could not be reached with 60 fathoms of line, nor had we been able to gain soundings in many places since we had quitted point Atkinson with 80 and 100 fathoms, though it was frequently attempted; excepting in the bason at the head of the sound, where the depth suddenly decreased from sixty fathoms to two. We had advanced a shore distance only in this branch, before the color of the water changed from being nearly milk white, and almost fresh, to that of oceanic and perfectly salt. By sun-set we had passed the channel which had been observed to lead into the gulf, to the southward of Anvil island; and about nine o'clock landed for the night, near the west point of entrance into the sound, which I distinguished by the name of HOWE'S SOUND, in honor of Admiral Earl Howe;

Admiral Earl Howe. Of all the geographical names bestowed by Vancouver in his "Voyage Round the World" there is not one that suggests to an American reader more of his country's early history than does this name of Howe's Sound. Emanuel Scrope Howe, second Viscount Howe, had four sons, three of whom impressed American history. The eldest was George Augustus Howe, a great favorite with the Colonials, who fell at Ticonderoga in 1758 during the French and Indian War. The second was the great Admiral Richard Howe, and the third was the great General William Howe.

The general arrived at Boston in March, 1775, with reënforcements for General Gage. He had desired to avoid Boston on account of the friendly feeling there for his brother who had fallen at Ticonderoga. Gage directed him to attack the American position on Charlestown Heights, which resulted in the famous battle of Bunker Hill on June 17, 1775. Howe led the attack, and it is said that for a time he stood alone on the fiery slope, every officer and man around him being shot down. On October 10, 1775, he succeeded Gage with the rank of General in America. There followed Washington's siege of Boston, and Howe on March 6, 1776, withdrew to Halifax. Reënforcements arrived in the summer of 1776 in ships commanded by his brother, Admiral Richard Howe. Then came the Long Island Campaign, the winter in New York, the following winter in Philadelphia. He resigned and embarked for England on May 24, 1778.

Admiral Howe, who held the rank of Commander-in-Chief in America, assisted his brother's movements of troops. There was no American fleet to fight and, on the whole, he was exceedingly clever but unsuccessful in coping with the superior French fleet that arrived in July, 1776, under d'Estaing. He had asked to be relieved as early as November 23, 1777, but would not leave while a superior opposing force was present. When reënforcements arrived, he resigned the command to Rear-Admiral Gambier (whose name has since been given to the principal island in Howe's Sound) and arrived in Portsmouth on October 25, 1778.

Both these brothers seem to have had great respect for the Americans. Admiral Howe was a friend of Franklin. For this reason the brothers had been commissioned to treat for settlement with the colonies. The admiral did not arrive, however, until after the Declaration of Independence of July 4, 1776, which he could not accept, and so the peaceful commission ended. Both were subjected to harsh criticism. Both complained of poor support from the home government. An investigation by Parliament proved nothing. After the American peace and the change of ministers, both resumed commands and attained further distinctions.

It was Richard Howe whom Vancouver honored by the name given to the sound lying west and north of Burrard Inlet. He was born in London on March 8, 1726, and died on August 5, 1799. At the age of fourteen, on July 3, 1740, he entered the navy in the *Severn* and accompanied Anson in his voyage round the world. During those fifty-nine years, until his death, he saw a tremendous amount of service. A few times he was not popular, but for most of his career he was continually hailed as a hero. Personally he was a quiet sort of man. Horace Walpole describes him in one of those famous epigrams, "Undaunted as a rock and as silent." Frequently in a position where he could not grant all claims, he was called by the unsatisfied ones, "Haughty, morose, hard-hearted, and inflexible." He was loved by his officers and men, one proverb running: "I think we shall have the fight to-day. Black Dick has been smiling."

His junior service, though passed in widely separated seas, was not particularly eventful. He was posted to captain's rank on April 10, 1746. In January, 1755, he was appointed to the *Dunkirk* of sixty-four guns, and in April sailed with Boscawen for North America. On June 7 he fell in with a French fleet off the mouth of the St. Lawrence. The next morning he came up with the *Alcide* and Howe requested her to await the arrival of his admiral. On being refused, Howe opened fire and captured the *Alcide*. This was the first gun of the so-called Seven Years' War. During this war, Howe commanded a small squadron in the British Channel. In 1758 his squadron with land forces under Lieutenant-General Bligh destroyed Cherbourg as a naval post. It was during this time that Prince Edward, second son of Frederick, Prince of Wales, entered the navy and was put in charge of Commodore Howe on the *Essex*. Many years afterward Howe wrote in a private letter, "He came, not only without bed and linen almost of every kind, but I paid also for his uniform clothes, which I provided for him, with all other necessaries at Portsmouth." In 1762 Prince Edward became a rear-admiral, and Howe, at his own request, became his flag captain.

At the peace in 1763 Howe entered the Board of Admiralty and in 1765 was made treasurer of the navy. At that time this was a lucrative position, but Howe refused to profit by the interest on the large funds, and "the balance was regularly brought up." He resigned this position on October 18, 1770, when he was promoted to the rank of Rear-Admiral. On December 7, 1775, he was advanced to the grade of Vice-Admiral, and was then sent to North America as already recorded.

In 1782 Howe with rather weak fighting force convoyed relief ships to Gibraltar and eluded the combined French and Spanish fleets. This achievement was greatly praised. There was one exception. Lord Henry published a letter reflecting on Howe, who called him out. They met, but the duel was stopped by Henry making a complete retraction.

In January, 1783, Howe became first Lord of the Admiralty, which important post he filled, with one brief interim, until July, 1788, when he was succeeded by the Earl of Chatham, who held the place during Vancouver's voyage.

During the Spanish Armament in 1790 Howe, then Senior Admiral of the White, was given command of the fleet in the Channel and was ordered to fly the union flag at the main in compliment to himself and other distinguished officers in his fleet. Not long after this came the war of the French Revolution, and Howe added more glory to his record in the latter part of May, 1794, by whipping the French fleet. It was a day of enthusiasm when Howe took his fleet to Spithead on June 13, 1794, with six French prizes. The king, queen, and three princesses visited Howe on his flagship. The king

and this point, situated in latitude 49° 23′, longitude 236° 51′, POINT GOWER; between which and point Atkinson, up

---

presented Howe with a diamond-hilted sword and promised to make him a Knight of the Garter. Gold chains were given to all the other admirals.

Later there was some friction with Viscount Bridport, but Howe was promoted to be Admiral of the fleet in March, 1796. He reluctantly resigned the post of Vice-Admiral of England, which he considered next to that of Lord High Admiral. He consented to hold nominal command at the behest of the king but his final resignation was accepted in May, 1797, and even after that he consented to go to Spithead and settle the famous mutiny.

He repaired to Bath for relief from the severe attacks of gout. In the summer of 1799, while his regular physician was absent, he was persuaded to try electricity, then thought to be a cure-all. It was afterward claimed that this drove the trouble to his head, for he died on August 5, 1799. He was buried in the family vault at Langar, where a monument was erected. A larger one was erected at public expense in St. Paul's Cathedral.

Howe had become fourth Viscount Howe on the death of his elder brother in 1758. This Irish title now went to his brother, General William Howe, at whose death it became extinct. Richard Howe was elected to Parliament by Dartmouth in 1757 and held that seat until 1782, when he was raised to the British peerage by being created Earl Howe.

The portrait used in this work is from the painting by Henry Singleton, now in the National Portrait Gallery.

Sir Erasmus Gower. This name of Point Gower presents one of the most peculiar incidents encountered in this entire research. The journal both in its first and second editions spells the word "Gower," while the chart published with the first edition indicates the cape at the northwest entrance of Howe's Sound as Point Gore. Vancouver does not mention whether the honor is intended for a personal friend or prominent citizen. He simply issues the name without comment. Most of his names were for friends in the navy. The research developed that Sir John Gore (1772–1836) attained the rank of Vice-Admiral and was a lieutenant when Vancouver sailed from home. This was likely the right man if the chart name was to stand. But the journal says "Gower" and so do the British charts of the present. Therefore it must be taken that Sir Erasmus Gower was the man honored.

At thirteen he entered the navy, in 1755, under his maternal uncle, Captain Donkley. He was passed for lieutenant in 1762. He saw service under several noted captains. In 1779 he was selected by Sir George Rodney as first lieutenant of his flagship, the *Sandwich*, and took part in the capture of the Spanish convoy on January 9, 1780, and later saw active service in the East Indies. From 1786 to 1789 he was on the Newfoundland station, and from 1792 to 1794 he commanded the *Lion*, taking to China Lord Macartney and his embassy. For this service he was knighted. He was commodore on the *Neptune* during the mutiny at the Nore. He was

to Anvil island, is an extensive group of islands of various sizes. The shores of these, like the adjacent coast, are composed principally of rocks rising perpendicularly from an unfathomable sea; they are tolerably well covered with trees, chiefly of the pine tribe, though few are of a luxuriant growth.

At four o'clock on Saturday morning the 16th, we resumed our course to the northwestward, along the starboard or continental shore of the gulf of Georgia, which from point Gower takes a direction about W. N. W. and affords a more pleasing appearance than the shores of Howe's sound. This part of the coast is of a moderate height for some distance inland, and it frequently jets out into low sandy projecting points. The country in general produces forest trees in great abundance, of some variety and magnitude; the pine is the most common, and the woods are little encumbered with bushes or trees of inferior growth. We continued in this line about five leagues along the coast, passing some rocks and rocky islets, until we arrived at the north point of an island about two leagues in circuit, with another about half that size to the westward of it, and a smaller island between them. From the north point of this island, which forms a channel with the main about half a mile wide, and is situated in latitude 49° 28½′, longitude 236° 31′, the coast of the continent takes a direction for about eight miles N. 30 W. and is composed of a rugged rocky shore, with many detached rocks lying at a little distance. The track we thus pursued had not the appearance of the main branch of the gulf, but of a channel between the continent and that land, which, from point Roberts, seemed like a small though very high round island. This now appeared of considerable extent, its N. E. side formed a channel to the N. W. as far as the eye could reach, about five miles in width. The main branch of the gulf, apparently of infinitely greater extent, took a direction to the south-westward of this land, which

---

promoted to the rank of Rear-Admiral on February 14, 1799; to Vice-Admiral on April 23, 1804; and to Admiral on April 23, 1809. He died at Hambledon in Hampshire on June 21, 1814.

now looked more like a peninsula than an island. Along this rocky shore of the main land we passed in quest of a resting place for the night, to no effect, until after dark; when we found shelter in a very dreary uncomfortable cove near the south point of an island, about a mile long, and about two miles to the S. S. E. of a narrow opening leading to the northward. This on the return of day-light on Sunday the 17th, we proceeded to examine; and passed through a very narrow, though navigable channel, amongst a cluster of rocks and rocky islets, lying just in the front of its entrance, which is situated in latitude 49° 35½′, longitude 236° 26′. It is about half a mile wide, winding towards the N. N. E. for about three leagues, where it divides into two branches, one stretching to the eastward, the other to the westward of north, with an island before the entrance of the latter. Agreeably to our general mode of proceeding, the north-easterly branch became the first object of our attention, and was found from hence to continue in an irregular course to the latitude of 49° 49′, longitude 236° 35½′; where, finding a tolerably comfortable situation, we rested for the night.

We had seen about seventeen Indians in our travels this day, who were much more painted than any we had hitherto met with. Some of their arrows were pointed with slate, the first I had seen so armed on my present visit to this coast; these they appeared to esteem very highly, and like the inhabitants of Nootka, took much pains to guard them from injury. They however spoke not the Nootka language, nor the dialect of any Indians we had conversed with; at least, the few words we had acquired were repeated to them without effect; in their persons they differed in no other respect, and were equally civil and inoffensive in their behavior. The shores we passed this day are of a moderate height within a few miles of this station, and are principally composed of craggy rocks, in the chasms of which a soil of decayed vegetables has been formed by the hand of time; from which pine trees of an inferior dwarf growth are produced, with a considerable quantity of bushes and underwood. We passed a few rocky islets near the division of the inlet. These seemed steep, as soundings with the hand line could not be gained; nor had we any where in mid-channel been able to reach the bottom with 100 fathoms of line, although the shores are not a mile asunder.

The next morning, Monday the 18th, as usual, at four o'clock, we proceeded up the inlet about three miles in a N. N. W. direction, whence its width increases about half a league in a direction nearly N. E. to a point which towards noon we reached, and ascertained its latitude to be 50° 1', longitude 236° 46'. The width of this channel still continuing, again flattered us with discovering a breach in the eastern range of snowy mountains, notwithstanding the disappointment we had met with in Howe's sound; and although since our arrival in the gulf of Georgia, it had proved an impenetrable barrier to that inland navigation, of which we had heard so much, and had sought with sanguine hopes and ardent exertions hitherto in vain, to discover.

By the progress we had this morning made, which comprehended about six leagues, we seemed to have penetrated considerably into this formidable obstacle; and as the more lofty mountains were now behind us, and no very distant ones were seen beyond the vallies caused by the depressed parts of the snowy barrier in the northern quarters, we had great reason to believe we had passed the center of this impediment to our wishes, and I was induced to hope we should yet find this inlet winding beyond the mountains, by the channel through which we had thus advanced upwards of 11 leagues, though for the most part it was not more than half a mile wide. Under these circumstances, our reduced stock of provisions was a matter of serious concern, fearing we might be obliged to abandon this pursuit without determining the source of this branch of the sea, having now been absent six days with subsistence for a week only, which would consequently very materially retard our survey, by rendering a second visit to this inlet indispensibly necessary. The surrounding country presented an equally dreary aspect with that in the vicinage of Howe's sound; and the serenity of the weather not adding at present to the natural gloominess of the prospect, was counterbalanced by the rugged surface of the mountains being infinitely less productive. A few detached dwarf pine trees, with some berry, and other small bushes, were the only signs of vegetation. The cataracts here rushed from the rugged snowy mountains in greater number, and with more impetuosity than in Howe's sound; yet the color of the water was not changed, though in some of the gullies there was the same chalky aspect. Hence it is probable, that the white appearance of the water in Howe's sound, may arise from a cause more remote, and which we had no opportunity of discovering.

Having dined, we pursued our examination. The inlet now took a N. W. by W. direction, without any contraction in its width, until about five o'clock in the evening, when all our hopes vanished, by finding it terminate, as others had done, in a swampy low land producing a few maples and pines, in latitude 50° 6', longitude 236° 33'. Through a small space of low land, which extended from the head of the inlet to the base of the mountains, that surrounded us, flowed three small streams of fresh water, apparently originating from one source in the N. W. or left hand corner of the bay, formed by the head of this inlet; in which point of view was seen an extensive valley, that took nearly a northerly uninterrupted direction as far as we could perceive, and was by far the deepest chasm we had beheld in the descending ridge of the snowy barrier, without the appearance of any elevated land rising behind. This valley much excited my curiosity to ascertain what was beyond it. But as the streams of fresh water were not navigable, though the tide had risen up to the habitations of six or seven Indians, any further examination of it in our boats was impracticable, and we had no leisure for excursions on shore. From the civil natives who differed not in any respect from those we had before occasionally seen, we procured a few most excellent fish, for which they were compensated principally in iron, being the commodity they most esteemed and sought after. In all these arms of the sea we had constantly observed, even to their utmost extremity, a visible, and sometimes a material rise and fall of the tide, without experiencing any other current than a constant drain down to the seaward, excepting just in the neighborhood of the gulf.

On our approach to the low land, we gained soundings at 70 fathoms, which soon decreased as we advanced, to 30, 14, and 3 fathoms, on a bank that stretches across the head of the inlet, similar to all the others we had before examined. So far as these soundings extended, which did not exceed half a league, the color of the water was a little affected, probably by the discharge of the fresh water rivulets, that generally assumed a very light color. Beyond these soundings the water again acquired its oceanic color, and its depth was unfathomable.

Not a little mortified that our progress should be so soon stopped, it became highly expedient to direct our way towards the ships, to whose station, by the nearest route we could take, it was at least 114 miles. This was now to be performed, after the time was nearly expired for which our supply of provisions had been calculated. Necessity directed that no time should be lost; especially as I was determined to seek a passage into the gulf by the branch of the inlet that we had passed the preceding day, leading to the N. W. conceiving there was a great probability that this branch might lead into the gulf at some distance beyond where we had entered this inlet; in which course we should have an opportunity of fixing the boundaries of the continent to the utmost extent that our present equipment would afford. For as our people had become wise by experience, I entertained little doubt of their having so husbanded their provisions as to enable our effecting this service; by which means any other excursion this way would be rendered unnecessary.

About two leagues from the head of the inlet we had observed, as we passed upwards on the northern shore, a small creek with some rocky islets before it, where I intended to take up our abode for the night. On our return, it was found to be full of salt water, just deep enough to admit our boats

[June, 1792.]

against a very rapid stream, where at low tide they would have grounded some feet above the level of the water in the inlet. From the rapidity of the stream, and the quantity of water it discharged, it was reasonable to suppose, by its taking a winding direction up a valley to the N. E. that its source was at some distance. This not answering our purpose as a resting place, obliged us to continue our search along the shore for one less incommodious, which the perpendicular precipices precluded our finding until near eleven at night, when we disembarked on the only low projecting point the inlet afforded.

At four, on the morning of Tuesday the 19th, we again started, but having a strong southerly gale against us, it was past nine at night before we reached a small bay, about a mile to the north of the north point of the arm leading to the north-westward, where we rested for the night; and, at day-light, proceeded as usual, along the continental shore.

This first stretched a little way to the north-westward, and then to the S. W. into the gulf, as I had imagined it would; forming, irregularly, a much more spacious channel than that by which we had entered, having an island lying between the two channels about three leagues in length, with several small islets about it. This island, and its adjacent shores, like those in the other channel, are of a moderate height, and wear a similar appearance. It was nearly noon before we reached the north point of the inlet; which, producing the first Scotch firs we had yet seen, obtained the name of SCOTCH-FIR POINT, and is situated in latitude 49° 42′, longitude 236° 17′. To this arm of the sea, I gave the name of JERVIS'S CHANNEL, in honor of Admiral Sir John Jervis.

Admiral Sir John Jervis. The name "Channel" is changed to "Canal" on Vancouver's chart, and on the present maps it appears as Jervis Inlet. The man for whom the waterway was named is one of the most picturesque and interesting characters in the history of the British Navy, and that is acknowledged to be a strong statement.

John Jervis was born at Meaford on January 9, 1715. His father was a barrister-at-law, of an old but impoverished family. They intended the son should also follow the law and started him at school. In 1747 the

ADMIRAL SIR JOHN JERVIS, EARL OF ST. VINCENT.
From a mezzotint after the painting by Sir William Beechey. Photograph copyrighted by Walker & Cockrell. Rights secured for this work in England and America.

[June, 1792.]

The boundary of the continental shore I now considered as determined to this point, from a full conviction that the

---

family moved to Greenwich on the father's becoming solicitor to the Admiralty and treasurer of Greenwich Hospital. Here the atmosphere of the navy was too strong for the boy and on January 4, 1749, he entered the navy as an able seaman. For six years he put in his time on the Jamaica and other stations until he passed his examination on January 22, 1755. Then his real climbing and his forceful career began. In this same year he was with Boscawen at the mouth of the St. Lawrence, where the Seven Years' War was begun. In 1756 he went to the Mediterranean with Rear-Admiral Saunders and in May, 1758, returned to England in command of the *Foudroyant*.

In 1795 he went again with Saunders to North America. In command of the *Porcupine* he had the difficult task of leading the squadron past Quebec. General James Wolfe was favorably impressed with Jervis, and it is said that he intrusted to him his last message to the lady to whom he was engaged, and that Jervis delivered that message in person. He was sent to England with despatches and immediately sent back with important messages to General Amherst.

He was posted to captain's rank on October 13, 1760, and in 1762 was with Lord Colvill at the recapture of Newfoundland. He was sent to Genoa in 1769 in the *Alarm* with a freight of $200,000 for the merchants. On September 9 two Turkish slaves escaped from a galley to one of the *Alarm's* boats from which they were seized by pursuers. For this violation of the British flag, Jervis demanded instant apologies and the restitution of the slaves, both of which were granted on a show of spunk by the captain. On March 30, 1770, while at Marseilles, his ship was driven in a violent gale on the rocks. He saved her and wrote to his father, "A glorious action in the midst of a war could not be more applauded than the gallantry of the officers and crew."

In the years 1773 and 1774 he spent his time in an unusual way. He was supposed to be resting. He travelled in France, Germany, Denmark, Russia, and Holland, and returned to England with a vast collection of notes and figures that would be wonderfully useful to the future admiral.

In command of the *Foudroyant* he served in the Channel and in relief cruises to Gibraltar. On April 19, 1782, Barrington's squadron encountered a French convoy, which scattered, and the *Foudroyant* took after the largest, the *Pegase*, and at midnight captured her. For this action Jervis was made a Knight of the Bath. In 1783 he was married, promoted to the rank of Commodore, and elected to Parliament. In 1785 and 1786 he served on the commission to consider the desirability of fortifying Portsmouth and Plymouth. They reported against the plan, and though it was supported by the government, the Commons sided with the commission.

He was promoted to the rank of Rear-Admiral on September 24, 1787, and

VANCOUVER'S DISCOVERY

[Original Journal, Page 208.] [June, 1792.]

inlet under the examination of Mr. Whidbey, would terminate like those we had visited. Presuming our time to

---

to that of Vice-Admiral on February 1, 1793. In 1794 he assisted General Sir Charles Grey in the campaign against Guadeloupe and Martinique. Returning to England, he was made Admiral on July 1, 1795.

He was then sent to the Mediterranean, and during the four years that followed he accomplished two significant things. The combination of the French and Spanish fleets would make them supreme in the Mediterranean. England was greatly alarmed. If those fleets defeated Jervis and sailed for the Channel, there was no telling what damage they would do. Jervis was determined that they would not pass him. He posted himself off Cape Saint Vincent and waited. The Spanish fleet approached and at noon, February 14, 1797, the battle took place. Four Spanish ships were captured and the rest fled. The danger to England was over. Parliament voted its thanks, and granted a pension of £3000 a year to Jervis. The city of London voted the freedom of the city in a gold box and this was imitated by other cities. The king had previously nominated him for a peerage, and now the monarch selected the title and on July 16 he was created the Earl of Saint Vincent.

The other significant event was the new and severe discipline which he introduced. Mutiny was rife. The danger was great and Jervis was austere, hanging the culprits whenever caught and proven guilty. This system stamped out mutiny, but it raised a clamor against Jervis. His health began to fail and his temper grew swift and hot. One writer said, "On stirring occasions of unofficer or unseamanlike conduct, or when retarded by laziness or factiousness, a torrent of impetuous reproof in unmeasured language would violently rush from his lips."

Worn out, he relinquished his command on June 15, 1799, and returned home for rest. As soon as he recovered a little he consented to take command of the Channel fleet, saying it mattered little to him whether he died afloat or ashore. He then began his severe discipline and aroused an enormous clamor, but kept at it until he succeeded.

In 1801 Saint Vincent became first Lord of the Admiralty and in that capacity undertook his greatest struggle. The administration of the navy had become extremely corrupt. He hunted out the culprits, brought about reforms, caused Parliament to investigate, and all the former clamors were mild riffles compared to the one that now threatened to ingulf him. Again he gained his point and those ancient grafters were exposed and driven from their places.

In 1806 he again took command of a fleet, but on April 24, 1807, he was permitted to retire. He then attended the sittings of the House of Lords. He made his last appearance there in 1810, and Sheridan put it beautifully when he said he retired "with his triple laurel, over the enemy, the mutineer, and the corrupt."

have been not ill spent, we directed our course to the station where we had left the ships now at the distance of 84 miles, steering for the opposite shore, being the land before adverted to, as appearing to form an extensive island, or peninsula; the nearest part of which was about five miles across from Scotch-fir point; and with the continental shore still formed a passage, to all appearance, of the same width, in a direction N. 62 W., with an uninterrupted horizon in that point of view; so that, whether it was an island or peninsula, remains still to be determined.

The shores of this land, nearly straight and compact, are principally formed of rocky substances of different sorts; amongst which, slate was in abundance; and the trees it produced were of infinitely more luxuriant growth than those on the opposite shore. In the forenoon of Thursday the 21st, we passed the south point of this land, and in remembrance of an early friendship, I called it POINT UPWOOD, situated in latitude 49° 28½', longitude 236° 24'. This land, though chiefly composed of one lofty mountain, visible at the distance of 20 leagues and upwards, is very narrow, appearing to form, with the western shore of the gulf, a channel nearly parallel to that which we had last quitted; though considerably more extensive, and containing some small islands. Its horizon was bounded by the summits of high distant detached mountains.

As we were rowing, on the morning of Friday the 22d, for point Grey, purposing there to land and breakfast, we discovered two vessels at anchor under the land. The idea

---

On the coronation of George IV this old admiral was promoted one more grade, as Admiral of the fleet. It was an unusual honor and grateful to the worn-out earl. He died on March 14, 1823.

Sir William Beechey made two paintings of Earl Saint Vincent. One of them belongs to the Fishmongers' Company and the other belonged to Admiral Sir William Parker. The photograph for this work is of the last-named portrait.

Point Upwood. It has not been possible thus far to trace this "early friendship" of Vancouver's. The name is still used on modern maps for the southern end or point of Texada Island.

which first occurred was, that, in consequence of our protracted absence, though I had left no orders to this effect, the vessels had so far advanced in order to meet us; but on a nearer approach, it was discovered, that they were a brig and a schooner, wearing the colors of Spanish vessels of war, which I conceived were most probably employed in pursuits similar to our own; and this on my arrival on board, was confirmed. These vessels proved to be a detachment from the commission of Señor Malaspina, who was himself employed in the Phillippine islands; Señor Malaspina had, the preceding year, visited the coast; and these vessels, his Catholic Majesty's brig the *Sutil*, under the command of Señor Don D. Galiano, with the schooner *Mexicana*, commanded by Señor Don C. Valdes, both captains of frigates in the Spanish navy, had sailed from Acapulco on the 8th of March, in order to prosecute discoveries on this coast. Señor Galiano, who spoke a little English, informed me, that they had arrived at Nootka on the 11th of April, from whence they had sailed on the 5th of this month, in order to complete the examination of this inlet, which had, in the preceding year, been partly surveyed by some Spanish officers whose chart they produced.

I cannot avoid acknowledging that, on this occasion, I experienced no small degree of mortification in finding the external shores of the gulf had been visited, and already examined a few miles beyond where my researches during the excursion, had extended; making land, I had been in doubt about, an island; continuing nearly in the same direction, about four leagues further than had been seen by us; and, by the Spaniards, named Favida. The channel, between it and the main, they had called Canal del Neustra Signora del Rosario, whose western point had terminated their examination; which seemed to have been entirely confined to

---

Texada Island. Vancouver here misunderstood the word in writing down that the Spaniards had called this island "Favida." Elisa's chart of 1791, as reproduced in H. H. Bancroft's works, XXVII, 245, shows the island with the name Isla de Texada. It is still known as Texada Island, and is coming into prominence because of its deposits of iron ore.

the exterior shores, as the extensive arms, and inlets, which had occupied so much of our time, had not claimed the least of their attention.

The Spanish vessels, that had been thus employed last year, had refitted in the identical part of port Discovery, which afforded us similar accommodation. From these gentlemen, I likewise understood, that Señor Quadra, the commander in chief of the Spanish marine at St. Blas and at California, was, with three frigates and a brig, waiting my arrival at Nootka, in order to negotiate the restoration of those territories to the crown of Great Britain. Their conduct was replete with that politeness and friendship which characterizes the Spanish nation; every kind of useful information they cheerfully communicated, and obligingly expressed much desire, that circumstances might so concur as to admit our respective labors being carried on together; for which purpose, or, if from our long absence and fatigue in an open boat, I would wish to remain with my party as their guest, they would immediately dispatch a boat with such directions as I might deem necessary for the conduct of the ships, or, in the event of a favorable breeze springing up, they would weigh and sail directly to their station: but being intent on losing no time, I declined their obliging offers, and having partaken with them a very hearty breakfast, bad them farewell, not less pleased with their hospitality and attention, than astonished at the vessels in which they were employed to execute a service of such a nature. They were each about forty-five tons burthen, mounted two brass guns, and were navigated by twenty-four men, bearing one lieutenant, without a single inferior officer. Their apartments just allowed room for sleeping places on each side, with a table in the intermediate space, at which four persons, with some difficulty, could sit, and were, in all other respects, the most ill calculated and unfit vessels that could possibly be imagined for such an expedition; notwithstanding this, it was pleasant to observe, in point of living, they possessed many more comforts than could reasonably have been expected. I shewed them the sketch I had made of our excursion, and pointed out the only spot which I conceived we had left unexamined, nearly at the head of Burrard's channel: they seemed much surprized that we had not found a river said to exist in the region we had been exploring, and named by one of their officers Rio Blancho, in compliment to the then prime minister of Spain; which river these gentlemen had sought for thus far to no purpose. They took such notes as they chose from my sketch, and promised to examine the small opening in Burrard's channel, which, with every other information they could procure, would be at my service on our next meeting.

From these new and unexpected friends we directed our course along the shoal already noticed, which I now called STURGEON BANK, in consequence of our having purchased of the natives some excellent fish of that kind, weighing from fourteen to two hundred pounds each. To avoid this bank, which stretches from point Roberts to point Grey, a most excellent leading mark was observed along its western extremity, being Passage and Anvil islands in one, which lead by its edge in six fathoms water, deepening suddenly to the westward, and in many places to the eastward, shoaling as suddenly to three, two, and one fathom. The circle which this bank occasioned us to make, made the distance to point Roberts upwards of 30 miles. We were likewise unfortunate in having two flood tides against us. These, together with a light southerly breeze that prevailed the whole time, obliged us to be constantly rowing from nine in the forenoon until after midnight, before we could reach the point, which was at length effected; though not before we were nearly exhausted by fatigue. Here we slept, and in the morning of Saturday the 23d, against a strong easterly breeze, about ten

---

Sturgeon Bank. In looking at the chart and the journal at this interesting point the reader feels like shouting out to Vancouver in his small boats to turn in shore and discover that great river. He is rowing past the mouth. The habit of the sturgeon in seeking rivers should have prompted him to look more carefully. The Spaniards hinted at the river, as already related, but Vancouver calls the place Sturgeon Bank and moves on. The name is still found on the United States Coast and Geodetic Survey chart of Georgia Strait, Number 6300.

in the forenoon we reached the ships, after having traversed in our boats upwards of 330 miles.

The broken part of the coast that Mr. Whidbey had been employed in examining, was found to extend but a few miles to the northward of the spot where his former researches had ended; forming altogether an extensive bay, which I have distinguished as BELLINGHAM'S BAY. It is situated behind a cluster of islands, from which a number of channels lead into it: its greatest extent in a north and south direction, is

---

Sir William Bellingham. It is rather provoking to have Vancouver give this name in such an offhand way without indicating the man whom he sought thus to honor. Master Joseph Whidbey is the one who discovered and explored the bay while the Captain was away on his expedition to Texada Island. The Spanish chart by Elisa in 1791, as reproduced by Bancroft, shows the bay clearly enough, but it is given no name, although Spanish names are sprinkled liberally on other places. Some have been retained, like the San Juan Archipelago, Guemes Island, Port Angeles, but most of them have been changed. Davidson's "Pacific Coast Pilot," page 572, says that Elisa named this place Bahia de Gaston, and for a time the admiralty charts showed the upper part of the large bay as Gaston Bay, but even that has now disappeared. Vancouver's name for Bellingham's Bay has remained and, what makes the name still more important, the fine city on the bay has recently assumed the name of Bellingham. There were formerly three cities, Whatcom, Sehome, and Fairhaven. They have united under the one name. There was no one by the name of Bellingham on the muster books of the Vancouver expedition; but when they took on their stores and supplies on leaving England, their accounts were checked over and approved by Sir William Bellingham, Knight. He was thus one of the last administrative officers to come in contact with Vancouver and his officers. His office was controller of the storekeeper's accounts of his Majesty's Navy. It is claimed in Clowe's "Navy" that the office was discontinued on August 2, 1796. It is quite clear that this Bellingham is the one honored. Thus far no picture or biography of him has been discovered.

There is another bit of evidence to prove that this is the man honored by Vancouver. As was the case in other places, the explorer named the southern point at the entrance of the big bay after the knight's first or Christian name, and to this day it is known as Point William. He wrote the name on the chart, but did not mention the fact in the journal. Within the bay he also wrote the name of Point Francis, now Point Frances, on the charts. This name he also overlooked in the journal. There is no intimation as to the person for whom this last honor was intended. The name still stands at the original place at the southern extremity of the Lummi peninsula.

VANCOUVER'S DISCOVERY

from the latitude 48° 36′, to 48° 48′; the longitude of its eastern extremity 237° 50′. It everywhere affords good and secure anchorage; opposite to its north point of entrance the shores are high and rocky, with some detached rocks lying off it. Here was found a brook of most excellent water. To the north and south of these rocky cliffs the shores are less elevated, especially to the northward, where some of those beautiful verdant lawns were again presented to our view. Near the north entrance into this bay, the two Spanish vessels had been described by Mr. Whidbey, who returned, and communicated the intelligence to the ships; in consequence of which the *Chatham* weighed and spoke them off point Roberts; they having passed our ships during the night undiscovered.

Having now fixed the continental shore so far as from this station was within our reach, and having obtained sufficient observations for correcting the rate of our chronometers, every thing was immediately re-embarked, and we were in readiness to proceed in the morning.

During my absence, the boats of the *Discovery* and *Chatham* had been employed in attempting to gain some further knowledge of the numerous islands we passed on our arrival in this bay; but they were found so abundantly dispersed as to preclude any correct examination, without having sufficient leisure for the purpose.

Nothing further occurred at this station worthy of notice, if we except an observation which had been repeatedly made, that in proportion as we advanced to the northward, the forests were composed of an infinitely less variety of trees, and their growth was less luxuriant. Those most commonly seen were pines of different sorts, the arbor vitæ, the oriental arbutus, and I believe, some species of cypress. On the islands some few small oaks were seen, with the Virginian juniper; and at this place the Weymouth pine, Canadian elder, and black birch; which latter grew in such abundance, that it obtained the name of BIRCH BAY. The S. E. part

---

Black Birch. Betula occidentalis was described and named by the English botanist Hooker. In Sargent's "Silva," IX, 64–66, its discovery is

OF PUGET SOUND

[June, 1792.] [Original Journal, Pages 215–217.]

of this bay is formed by nearly perpendicular rocky cliffs, from whence the higher woodland country retires a considerable distance to the north eastward, leaving an extensive space of low land between it and the sea, separated from the high ground by a rivulet of fresh water that discharges itself at the bottom, or northern extremity of the bay. On the low land very luxuriant grass was produced, with wild rose, gooseberry, and other bushes in abundance.

I shall conclude this chapter by stating that, by the mean result of eleven meridional altitudes of the sun, we found Birch Bay situated in latitude 48° 53½′; the longitude 237° 33′, was deduced from the observations made use of for settling port Discovery, including twenty-eight sets of lunar distances taken at this station, whence on the 22d, at noon, Kendall's chronometer was found to be 54′ 11″ 29‴ fast of mean time Greenwich, and by six days corresponding altitudes, to be gaining on mean time at the rate of 12″ 45‴ per day. Mr. Arnold's on board the *Chatham*, from the same authority was, on the same day at noon, fast of mean time at Greenwich, 3h 14′ 46″, and gaining at the rate of 25″ 15‴ per day. The variation of the compass, by nineteen sets of azimuths, differing from 17½ to 21 degrees, gave a mean result of 19° 30′ eastwardly variation.

The vertical inclination of the marine dipping needle,

Marked end, North face	East	....	72°	81′
Ditto,	Ditto	West	73	—
Ditto,	South face	East............................	73	28′
Ditto,	Ditto	West	74	20
The mean vertical inclination of the magnetic needle		....	73	13

The tides were found to be very inconsiderable, but were not particularly noticed.

---

credited to the Lewis and Clark expedition of 1803–1806, who found it on the banks of the Jefferson River at the eastern base of the Rocky Mountains. "It was afterwards found by Dr. John Scouler near the coast of British Columbia." It is quite likely that this is the same species, and if so its real discovery should be accredited to Archibald Menzies at Birch Bay in 1792.

CHAPTER X

THROUGH THE STRAIT OF GEORGIA AND JOHNSTONE'S STRAITS

[Original Journal, Pages 218-219, Book II, Chapter VIII.] [June, 1792.]

WITH a fine breeze, and very pleasant weather, we sailed out of Birch bay, on Midsummer morning; and, with the wind from the eastward, we directed our course up the gulf, to the north-westward. About two in the afternoon of Sunday the 24th, we were joined by the Spanish vessels, who saluted by cheering. This was returned; after which their respective commanders favored me with their company on board the *Discovery;* and we pursued our way up the gulf together.

Señor Galiano informed me, that they had examined the small branch I had passed by in Burrard's channel, which was found very narrow, leading in a north direction nearly three leagues, where it terminated in a small rivulet. They favored me with a copy of their sketch of it, as also with their good company until sun-set, when they returned to their vessels; point Roberts then bearing by compass S. 68 E. point Grey, N. 64 E.; which, being the nearest part of the continental or eastern shore, was at the distance of about three leagues; and the nearest part of the opposite shore of the gulf, bearing S. W. was distant about two leagues.

During the night, and until noon the next day, Monday the 25th, the winds were light and baffling. In the course of the forenoon a great number of whales were playing about in every direction; and though we had been frequently visited by these animals in this inland navigation, there seemed more about us now, than the whole of those we had before seen, if collected together.

This circumstance, in some measure, favored the assertion in Mr. Meares's publication, that a passage to the ocean would be found by persevering in our present course; though this was again rendered very doubtful, as we had understood, from our Spanish friends, that, notwithstanding the Spaniards had lived upon terms of great intimacy with Mr. Gray and other American traders at Nootka, they had no knowledge of any person having ever performed such a voyage, but from the history of it published in England; and so far were these gentlemen from being better acquainted with the discoveries of De Fuca or De Fonte than ourselves, that from us, they expected much information as to the truth of such reports. Señor Valdes, who had been on the coast the preceding year, and spoke the Indian language fluently, understood, from the natives, that this inlet *did* communicate with the ocean to the northward, where they had seen ships. He was, however, too well acquainted with their characters as reporters, to place much dependence on their information, which was incompetent to the forming of any idea how far remote such ocean might be.

A gentle gale springing up from the eastward, soon after mid-day, we brought to for the Spanish vessels, who were at some distance astern. When they came up, we were honored with the company of the commanders to dinner; and then made sail, directing our course through the channel del Neustra Signora del Rosario, whose whole extent nearly in a direction N. 53 W. is about 10 leagues from point Upwood, the S. E. point, to POINT MARSHALL, the N. W. point of the

---

William Marshall. This northern point of Texada Island was named, of course, for some one that Vancouver held in esteem. The search for such a man in history is hampered by the absence of any suggestion by the explorer. It is quite likely, however, that the right one has been found in William Marshall, the agriculturist and philologist. The reason for believing that he is the right man is found in the title of one of his books "Arbustum Americanum, the American Grove, or an Alphabetical Catalogue of Forest Trees and Shrubs, natives of the American United States." This book appeared in 1785 and most certainly would not be overlooked in fitting the expedition for American exploration in 1790 and 1791. Such a book would be frequently consulted, and nothing is more natural than that the author should be honored in this way. There is no name of Marshall on the muster books of the expedition. There are many Marshalls in English

VANCOUVER'S DISCOVERY

island of Feveda; which point is situated in latitude 49° 48′, longitude 235° 47½′. From Scotch-fir point, the shores of the channel approximated, until they became within two miles of each other, at its western end; and are, as well on the island as on the continental side, nearly straight, perfectly compact, and rise gradually, particularly on the continental shore, from a beach of sand and small stones, to a height that might be considered rather elevated land, well clothed with wood, but without any signs of being inhabited. From hence the continental shore took a N. W. direction. From point Marshall, N. 35 W. about a league distant, lies an island of a moderate height, four miles in circuit, with a smaller one about a mile to the S. W. of it: between this, which I named HARWOOD'S ISLAND, and point Marshall, are some rocky islands and sunken rocks.

On the coast of the main land opposite this island is a small brook, probably of fresh water; from whence, as we advanced, the shores put on a very dreary aspect, chiefly composed of rugged rocks, thinly wooded with small dwarf pine trees. The islands, however, which appeared

---

history, but of all those in the "Dictionary of National Biography" not one fits the case as does this William Marshall.

He was baptized on July 28, 1745, and says himself that he was "born a farmer, and that he could trace his blood through the veins of agriculturists for upwards of four hundred years." He lived for fourteen years in the West Indies, where he probably met many officers of the British Navy visiting those islands, and there he also gleaned and collected for his book on American trees. In 1779 he published a work called "Experiments and Observations concerning Agriculture and Weather."

From 1786 to 1808 he resided in London during the winters and travelled during the summers. His greatest work was in twelve volumes, entitled, "A General Survey, from personal experience, observation, and enquiry, of the Rural Economy of England." He proposed an agricultural college for England, and was erecting a building in which to start it when he died on September 18, 1818.

Edward Harwood. This is probably the man whom Vancouver honored by naming this island. His date and place of birth are not known, but he died in London on January 6, 1814. For many years he was a surgeon in the navy. He is described as "a benevolent friend and an elegant scholar." He made a famous collection of coins and published a book on Numismatics.

before us, were of a moderate height, and presented a scene more pleasing and fertile. About five in the evening we passed between the main and an island lying in an east and west direction, which I named SAVARY'S ISLAND, about two leagues long, and about half a league broad: its N. E. point, situated in latitude 49° 57½', longitude 235° 54½', forms a passage with the continental shore, along which, in a N. W. direction, we continued at a distance from half a mile to half a league. On the south side of Savary's island were numberless sunken rocks, nearly half a league from its shores, visible I believe only at low water.

We seemed now to have forsaken the main direction of the gulf, being on every side encompassed by islands and small rocky islets; some lying along the continental shore, others confusedly scattered, of different forms and dimensions. South-westward of these islands, the main arm of the gulf extended in a north west direction, apparently three or four leagues wide, bounded by high though distant land. Through this very unpleasant navigation we sailed, still keeping close to the continental shore, which was compact. About dark we entered a spacious sound stretching to the eastward. Here I was very desirous of remaining until day-light; but soundings could not be gained though close to the shore.

The night was dark and rainy, and the winds so light and variable, that by the influence of the tides we were driven about as it were blindfolded in this labyrinth, until towards midnight, when we were happily conducted to the north side of an island in this supposed sound, where we anchored in company with the *Chatham* and the Spanish vessels, in 32 fathoms water, rocky bottom. At break of day on Tuesday the 26th, we found ourselves about half a mile from the shores of a high rocky island, surrounded by a detached and broken country, whose general appearance was very inhospitable. Stupendous rocky mountains rising almost perpendicularly from the sea, principally composed the north west, north and

---

Savary's Island. This island lies just north of Harwood's Island. Thus far not even a probable source of the name has been discovered.

eastern quarters; on these, pine trees, though not of luxuriant growth, nor of much variety, were produced in great numbers. The pleasing prospects which the shores on the eastern side of the gulf afforded by their contrast with the mountains of the snowy barrier, giving a grand and interesting character to the landscape, here no longer existed; nor had we been enabled to trace that range of mountains far to the north-westward of Scotch-Fir point, where the line of coast forms a very considerable angle with that of the barrier mountains. It is however probable, that at some distance from our present anchorage, where the perpendicular precipices we were now under would no longer have obstructed our view of the inland country, their lofty summits would have been still visible. The tops of the rugged mountains that compose these shores were not sufficiently elevated to retain the snow in summer, which, in all probability, clothes them during the winter season.

The infinitely divided appearance of the region into which we had now arrived, promised to furnish ample employment for our boats.

To Lieutenant Puget and Mr. Whidbey, in the *Discovery's* launch and cutter, I consigned the examination of the continental shore, from the place where we had lost sight of it the preceding evening. Mr. Johnstone, in the *Chatham's* cutter, accompanied by Mr. Swaine in her launch, were directed to investigate a branch of this sound leading to the North-westward; and Señor Valdes undertook the survey of the intermediate coast; by which arrangement the whole, or if not a very considerable extent, would soon be determined. Whilst the boats were equipping, Mr. Broughton went in quest of a more commodious situation for the ships up the sound to the north west.

The weather, which was serene and extremely pleasant, afforded me an opportunity, in company with Señor Galiano and some of our officers, to visit the shore of the island, near which we were at anchor, and to determine the situation of its west point to be in latitude 50° 6′, longitude 235° 26′. With the former Señor Galiano's observations agreed, but by his chronometer the longitude was made more westerly. My observations being deduced from the watch, according to its rate as settled in Birch bay, which was not very likely to have yet acquired any material error, inclined me to believe we were probably the most correct.

Early in the afternoon Mr. Broughton returned, having found a more eligible anchorage, though in a situation equally dreary and unpleasant. The several gentlemen in the boats being made acquainted with the station to which the ships were about to resort, departed agreeably to their respective instructions.

The wind, that since noon had blown fresh from the S. E. attended with heavy squalls and much rain, drove us, by its increased violence, from our anchorage, and almost instantly into 70 and 80 fathoms water. The anchor was immediately hove up, and we steered for the rendezvous Mr. Broughton had pointed out, where, about six in the evening, we arrived in company with our little squadron. Our situation here was on the northern side of an arm of the sound leading to the north-westward, a little more than half a mile wide, presenting as gloomy and dismal an aspect as nature could well be supposed to exhibit, had she not been a little aided by vegetation; which though dull and uninteresting, screened from our sight the dreary rocks and precipices that compose these desolate shores, especially on the northern side; as the opposite shore, though extremely rude and mountainous, possessed a small space of nearly level land, stretching from the water side, on which some different sorts of the pine tribe, arbor vitæ, maple, and the oriental arbutus, seemed to grow with some vigor, and in a better soil.

The very circumscribed view that we had of the country here rendered it impossible to form the most distant idea of any circumstances relative to the situation in which we had become stationary; whether composed of islands, or of such arms of the sea as we had lately been employed in examining, or how long there was a probability of our remaining in anxious expectation for the return of our friends. Our residence here was truly forlorn; an awful silence pervaded the gloomy forests, whilst animated nature seemed to have deserted the neighboring country, whose soil afforded only a few small onions, some samphire, and here and there bushes bearing a scanty crop of indifferent berries. Nor was the sea more favorable to our wants, the steep rocky shores prevented the use of the seine, and not a fish at the bottom could be tempted to take the hook.

I had absented myself from the present surveying excursions, in order to procure some observations for the longitude here, and to arrange the charts of the different surveys in the order they had been made. These, when so methodized, my third lieutenant Mr. Baker had undertaken to copy and embellish, and who, in point of accuracy, neatness, and such dispatch as circumstances admitted, certainly excelled in a very high degree. To conclude our operations up to the present period some further angles were required. Beside these I was desirous of acquiring some knowledge of the main channel of the gulf we had quitted on Monday afternoon, and to which no one of our boats had been directed.

Early in the morning of Saturday the 30th, I set out in the yawl on that pursuit, with a favorable breeze from the N. W. which shortly shifted to the opposite quarter, and blew a fresh gale, attended with a very heavy rain. Having reached by ten in the forenoon no further than the island under which we had anchored at midnight on the 25th, a prospect of a certain continuance of the unsettled weather obliged me to abandon my design, and return to the ship; where I had the pleasure of hearing the launch and cutter had arrived soon after my departure, after having completed the examination of the continental coast from the place where we had left it, the night we had entered the sound, to about three leagues north-westward of our present station, making the land near which we were then at anchor on our northern side, an island, or cluster of islands of considerable extent. These gentlemen were likewise of opinion, that all the land before us to the westward and N. W. from its insular appearance, formed an immense archipelago; but knowing Mr. Johnstone was directed to examine that quarter, and coming within sight of the ships, they had returned on board for further instructions.

On the commencement of their survey, they found the continental shore continue nearly in its N. W. direction to the eastern point of entrance into this sound, which I called POINT SARAH, and is situated in latitude 50° 4½'; longitude 235° 25½'; its opposite point, which I named POINT MARY, lying N. 72 W. about half a league distant; from point Sarah they proceeded along the continental shore up a very narrow channel, rendered almost inaccessible by the number of sunken rocks and rocky islets which it contained. It was found to lead in a southeasterly direction, almost parallel with, and two or three miles from, the northern shore of the gulf at the distance of about three leagues, with a smaller branch near the middle, extending about a league from its northern shore to the N. N. E. From this channel they continued along the continental shore in an easterly and N. E. direction, which led to that part of the coast under the inspection of Señor Valdes. The eastern shore, for the space of two leagues, was found much indented; and several small islands and rocks were seen lying near it to the latitude of 50° 10', longitude 235° 35'. Here these rocky islets disappeared, and the coast took a winding course N. W. and westward, to a point bearing from the above station N. 35 W. distant about two leagues, and forming the east point of an arm of the sound, whose entrance, about half a league wide, has two islets lying in it. About a mile up this arm they met

---

Point Sarah and Point Mary. It is a great pity that these two names appear without any sidelight as to the reason for putting them on the map. Point Sarah still stands at the southern entrance to Desolation Sound, but Point Mary has been changed. The name is moved to the westward and transferred to a small island. Bute's Canal lies near these points. Both the wife and the eldest daughter of the Earl of Bute bore the names of Mary. This may account for one of the names. There appears no name of Sarah in the Bute household, however, and it seems as though the two common names would have been selected for related reasons. They may have been sisters or sweethearts of the two leaders. It is probable that they were notified by Vancouver and, if so, the letters of notification would be highly prized. They may yet come to light.

Señor Valdes, who informed them he had thoroughly explored that place and that in the channel leading to the north-westward he had spoken with Mr. Johnstone, so that there could be no doubt of a passage to the ships by that route. Señor Valdes intimated that he considered any further investigation of that place totally unnecessary; but the officers not having on this occasion any directions of a discretionary nature, acted according to the directions they had formerly received for the execution of such service, and prosecuted its examination. They found it extend in an irregular north-easterly direction to the latitude of 50° 22', longitude 235° 46', where it terminated in shallow water and a little low land; through which flowed two small rivulets. In these rivulets, and on the shoal parts, several wears were erected. Along the shores of the upper part of this arm, which are mostly composed of high steep barren rocks, were several fences formed by thin laths, stuck either in the ground, or in the chinks of the rocks, with others placed along them; some in horizontal, others in oblique, and different directions. Ranges of these were fixed along the rocky cliffs in the line of the shore, others varied from that direction, and from their appearance were supposed to be intended for the purpose of drying fish; but as similar works, though perhaps not quite so extensive, had been often observed without being appropriated to that use, and always at a considerable distance from any known habitation; the object they were designed for, remained as uncertain to us, as the application of the high beacons we found so frequently erected on the more southern part of New Georgia.

The surrounding country up this arm nearly corresponded with that in the neighborhood of Howe's sound; and, like it, was nearly destitute of inhabitants. Two canoes were seen, which the owners had very recently quitted, as their garments and many of their utensils were remaining in them, to which the officers added some articles of iron, copper, beads, and other trinkets. From hence they directed their course towards the ship, and arrived as before stated. The country they had visited differed little, excepting in one or two small spots, from the region in which we were then stationed: the whole presented one desolate, rude, and inhospitable aspect. It has already been considered as not entirely destitute of the human race; and that it had been more populous than at present, was manifested by the party having discovered an extensive deserted village, computed to have been the residence of nearly three hundred persons. It was built on a rock, whose perpendicular cliffs were nearly inaccessible on every side; and connected with the main, by a low narrow neck of land, about the center of which grew a tree, from whose branches planks were laid to the rock, forming by this means a communication that could easily be removed, to prevent their being molested by their internal unfriendly neighbors; and protected in front, which was presented to the sea, from their external enemies, by a platform, which, with much labor and ingenuity had been constructed on a level with their houses, and overhung and guarded the rock. This, with great stability, was formed by large timbers judiciously placed for supporting each other in every direction; their lower ends were well secured in the chasms of the rocks about half way to the water's edge, admitting the platform to be so projected as to command the foot of the rock against any attempt to storm the village. The whole seemed so skilfully contrived, and so firmly and well executed, as rendered it difficult to be considered the work of the untutored tribes we had been accustomed to meet; had not their broken arms and implements, with parts of their manufactured garments, plainly evinced its inhabitants to be of the same race.

Whilst examining these abandoned dwellings, and admiring the rude citadel projected for their defence, our gentlemen were suddenly assailed by an unexpected numerous enemy, whose legions made so furious an attack upon each of their persons, that unable to vanquish their foes, or to sustain the conflict, they rushed up to their necks in water. This expedient, however, proved ineffectual; nor was it till after all their clothes were boiled, that they were disengaged from an immense hord of fleas, which they had disturbed by examining too minutely the filthy garments and apparel of the late inhabitants.

The weather continued very rainy and unpleasant until the forenoon of Saturday the 1st of July, when, on its clearing up, Mr. Puget and Mr. Whidbey were again dispatched, to execute the task I had the preceding day attempted; as likewise to gain some information of the southern side of the gulf, and the broken country, which existed between it and our present anchorage.

The securities about the head of the *Discovery* being constantly out of repair, our carpenters were now employed on that service; and, here also, we brewed some spruce-beer, which was excellent.

The next day, Monday the 2d, in the afternoon, Mr. Johnstone returned, who, after having met Señor Valdes, as before stated, abandoned his pursuit of that which appeared to him to be the main shore leading to the eastward, and prosecuted his researches in the opposite direction, leading to the west, N. W. and to the north, in a channel of an irregular width, where, after examining a small opening, in a northerly direction, he shortly discovered another, about two miles wide, in latitude 52° 21', longitude 235° 9'; along which, he kept the starboard or eastern shore on board, which was compact; but the western side, for some miles on which some fires were observed, seemed somewhat divided by water. This inlet, in general, from one to two miles wide, led them in an irregular northern direction to the latitude of 50° 52', longitude 235° 19', where, in the usual manner, it terminated by a small tract of low land, from whence a shallow bank stretched into the arm, which soon increased, from 2 to 50, 70, and 100 fathoms in depth, and then became unfathomable. Behind this low small spot of land, the mountains rose very abruptly, divided by two deep vallies, whence issued streams of fresh water, though not sufficiently capacious to admit the boats. In these vallies, and on the low plains, pine-trees grew to a tolerable size; the few seen on the mountains were of very stunted growth. High steep barren rocks, capped with snow, formed the sides

JOHN, EARL OF BUTE.

From an engraving by Richard Purcell after the painting by Allan Ramsay. Photograph copyrighted by Walker & Cockrell. Rights secured for this work in England and America.

of this channel, the water of which at its head, was nearly fresh, and of a pale color, as was that in the arm where Mr. Puget met Señor Valdes. It was noon on the 30th before we reached that part of the western shore, which had appeared broken, and on which the fires of the natives had been observed on entering this channel, which I distinguished by the name of BUTE'S CHANNEL. Here was found an

---

John Stuart, Third Earl of Bute. If there seemed any doubt about the man meant to be honored by the naming of Bute's Canal, the words of Vancouver a little later in the journal would set such doubts at rest. He says, "Lying before the entrance into Bute's channel, nearly a round island three or four leagues in circuit, which obtained the name of Stuart's Island." There was on the muster book of the *Discovery* "Honorable C. Stuart, able seaman, born in London, sixteen years of age." If he were intended, Vancouver would have mentioned the fact as he always did in honoring the young men of his company. This is a clear case of his using the earl's name of Bute for the canal and the family name for the island lying at its entrance.

The Earl of Bute has already been mentioned in the sketch of George III. He was the king's favorite and as such created a furore of opposition, which practically drove him from court, and from London as well. His influence over the king came about, in the first place, through an accident. Frederick, Prince of Wales, was overtaken by a shower of rain at the close of the races at Egham in 1747. Bute was summoned to the royal tent to take a hand at whist while the shower passed. From that hour he was a favorite of the prince. When the latter died, Bute's influence was even increased. He helped the dowager princess instil into the mind of her son George the Bolingbroke theory that a king should not only reign but govern. It is also said that Bute obtained from Blackstone a portion of the manuscript of his "Commentaries" years before they were published, and with them further instructed the prince in his rights and powers.

The dowager princess and Prince George secured Bute's appointment as groom of the stole on November 15, 1756. The old king hated him and would not receive him in his closet to confer the badge of this office, but gave it to the Duke of Grafton, who slipped the golden key into Bute's pocket. He was of a noble family, born on May 25, 1713, and at ten years of age inherited the Scotch earldom. He was elected a Scottish representative peer in April, 1737, and was often though not always reëlected.

On the accession of George III to the throne he was promptly sworn a member of the Privy Council on October 27, 1760, and was also appointed groom of the stole and first gentleman of the bedchamber. Though not of the cabinet, he was practically the prime minister. He undertook three

VANCOUVER'S DISCOVERY

[Original Journal, Page 234.]

[July, 1792.]

Indian village, situated on the face of a steep rock, containing about one hundred and fifty of the natives, some few of whom had visited our party in their way up the channel, and now many came off in the most civil and friendly manner, with a plentiful supply of fresh herrings and other fish, which they bartered in a fair and honest way for nails. These were of greater value amongst them, than any other articles our people had to offer. From the point on which this village is erected, in latitude 50° 24', longitude 235° 8', a very narrow opening was seen stretching to the westward, and through it flowed so strong a current, that the boats,

---

things: to secure peace with France, to break up the Whig oligarchy, and to strengthen the power of the king. In opposition to the old ministers, and by various questionable schemes, he brought about the peace of 1763. He declared that he desired no more glorious epitaph on his tombstone than, "Here lies the Earl of Bute, who in concert with the king's ministers made the peace."

Bute had been made a Knight of the Thistle, but when made first Lord of the Treasury on May 26, 1762, he resigned that knighthood and was made a "Knight of the Most Noble Order of the Garter." He pushed on his plans with the king's full approval. Many Whigs were driven from office, but finally the strain was too great and Bute resigned. His influence at court continued and ministerial troubles thickened. In May, 1765, Grenville obtained the king's promise that Bute should not, directly or indirectly, influence his business. Though still suspected and abused, his interference really ended there. In 1774 Bute was again elected a representative peer of Scotland, which caused Lord North to explain that "a dowager first lord of the treasury has a claim to this distinction, and we do not now want a coup d'état to persuade the most ordinary newspaper politician that Lord Bute is nothing more."

He continued extremely unpopular in England. His house was a favorite point of attack for mobs. He once wrote, "Few men have ever suffered more in the short space I have gone through of political warfare."

He was a cultured man, favoring literature and the arts. He was especially fond of botany and published at the cost of £12,000 twelve engraved copies of Botanical Tables. It is not at all unlikely but that this old earl with his love of botany, hearing of the preparations for the Vancouver expedition, gave the officers help in suggestions and books. He had made great collections of books and paintings, and had also established a collection of living trees and shrubs.

He died in London on March 10, 1792, at the age of seventy-eight years.

VILLAGE OF FRIENDLY INDIANS.

From a steel engraving by J. Landseer in Vancouver's Journal. Drawn by W. Alexander from a sketch on the spot by T. Heddington, at entrance of Bute's Canal.

unable to row against it, were hauled by a rope along the rocky shores forming the passage. In this fatiguing service the Indians voluntarily lent their aid to the utmost of their power, and were rewarded for their cordial disinterested assistance, much to their satisfaction. Having passed these narrows, the channel widened, and the rapidity of the tide decreased. Mr. Johnstone, in the cutter, had alone been able to pass; to whom it was evident that this narrow passage had communication with some very extensive inlet of the sea; but, as the weather was now very boisterous, with heavy rain, and a thick haze, and as the launch had not yet made her appearance, he returned in search of her, and found the party using their utmost endeavors to get through the narrows by the same friendly assistance of the natives he had before experienced; which being now no longer required these good people returned to their habitations, apparently well satisfied with the kind offices they had rendered, and the acknowledgments they had received. The boats now sought shelter from the inclemency of the weather in a small cove on the south side of the arm they had quitted, where the same cause operated to detain them until the morning of the 2d of July, when the time for which they were supplied with provisions being nearly expired, it was deemed most expedient to return to the ships.

By these two expeditions, the boundary of the continental shore was completely ascertained to the above narrow passage; and the strongest presumption induced that the whole of the coast on our western side, southward of that passage was composed of innumerable islands.

The weather being tolerably fair, Mr. Johnstone and Mr. Swaine were the next day, Wednesday the 5th, again dispatched with a week's provisions, to examine the continental shore through the narrow passage from whence they had returned; by the means of which, and the survey then prosecuting under Lieutenant Puget and Mr. Whidbey, who were to commence their inquiries in an opposite point, the whole extent of the gulf would be finally determined; or, in the event of the Indian's information being correct, its

VANCOUVER'S DISCOVERY

further navigable communication to the northward would be discovered.

By what I had seen of the gulf on the evening we entered this sound, though its western extremity was certainly bounded, yet the appearance of the land in that direction favored the opinion of its being composed of islands, though the whole might be united by low land not perceptible at so great a distance.

On Friday the 5th in the afternoon, the officers in the launch and cutter returned, from whom I understood, that they had found the western side of the gulf of Georgia, from that part opposite to point Marshall, to be compact, rising in a gentle ascent from the sea shore to the inland mountains, (some of which were covered with snow) wearing a pleasant and fertile appearance; along this shore they continued their route and entered an inlet, whose eastern side is formed by a long narrow peninsula, the south extreme of which is situated in latitude 50°, longitude 235° 9'. This promontory, after my first lieutenant, who had also discovered the inlet from the top of a mountain he had ascended in this neighborhood, obtained the name of POINT MUDGE.

Zachary Mudge. Vancouver had already given significant honors to second Lieutenant Puget, to third Lieutenant Baker, to Master Joseph Whidbey, and to Clerk H. M. Orchard. Now his first Lieutenant Zachary Mudge is honored. This tardiness is not easily understood unless it be surmised that, in sending out boat parties on side trips, which he often accompanied himself, he left Mudge on board the sloop to command in his temporary absence. This may have prevented Puget Sound from being called Mudge Sound. He had the spirit of an explorer, as is shown in this very case where he climbed a mountain and discovered the channel at whose entrance his name was written on Point Mudge.

Whether or not he felt slighted during the expedition, it is certain that he did feel so when his subsequent promotions came more slowly than should have been the case. Stanford Raffles Fling, B.A., edited a little book called "Mudge Memoirs," which was privately printed in 1883. The edition amounted to only one hundred copies, and the work is therefore rare. W. H. K. Wright, Borough Librarian at Plymouth, England, loaned his copy from which it is gleaned that in 1797 Mudge considered his promotions were being delayed, and he got Richard Rosden, his brother-in-law, to write to Lady Camelford on July 30, 1797, to the following effect: Mudge had

ADMIRAL ZACHARY MUDGE.

Special photograph from the painting by John Opie, now owned by Arthur Mudge, Esq., Sidney of Plympton, Devon.

OF PUGET SOUND

[July, 1792.] [Original Journal, Page 237.]

It forms a channel with the main land of the western side of the gulf of about a mile in width, nearly in a N. N. W.

---

been passed over and Mr. Puget, his junior lieutenant on the first voyage, was made captain before him, and that he had missed the *Chatham* with all this, and she was not to return until 1799. A lieutenant who had been more than two years on a second voyage and altogether had been five years employed as a first lieutenant on voyages of discovery had some claim on the Admiralty. He should not have captains over him who were not even in the navy when he was a first lieutenant of the *Discovery*. Lady Camelford was asked to name his case to Lord Spencer, and get Mudge put on the list of naval commanders. Soon afterward Lady Camelford informed Mr. and Mrs. Rosden that Lord Spencer would immediately send out a commission to Mr. Mudge, which was done, and his promotions were satisfactory from that time on.

Zachary Mudge, the son of Dr. John Mudge, was born at Plymouth on January 22, 1770. His name was borne on the books of the *Foudroyant* under Captain Jervis from November, 1780, and he was with that ship when she captured the *Pegase* on April 21, 1782. For seven years he served as midshipman on the home and North American stations. On May 24, 1789, he was promoted to be a lieutenant. The muster book of the *Discovery* shows that he entered her as second lieutenant on December 15, 1790, and was promoted to first lieutenant on January 3, 1791. After the transactions with Quadra at Nootka had failed, Vancouver sent Lieutenant Mudge with despatches to England by way of China. The journal says he embarked on the *Fenis and St. Joseph*. The "Mudge Memoirs" say it was an open vessel with a crew of fourteen men. In any event, he made the trip safely. Lieutenant Broughton was sent home by the Spanish route from Monterey with further despatches. In February, 1794, before Vancouver's return, Commander Broughton in the *Providence* started on another voyage of discovery and with him went first Lieutenant Mudge.

After this service came the intercession by Lady Camelford and on November 24, 1797, Mudge was promoted to the rank of Commander. In November, 1798, he was appointed to the *Fly* sloop on the coast of North America. He was promoted a captain on November 15, 1800, and on the *Constance* was engaged in convoy service. In September he was moved into the *Blanche* frigate on the West India station. During 1803 and 1804 she made many captures, but on July 15, 1805, she was encountered by a French squadron. Though resisting bravely, she was reduced to a wreck and struck her colors. Soon after she sank. It was questioned whether the best defence had been made, and Mudge was court-martialled. He was acquitted and complimented for his "very able and gallant" conduct. He commanded other ships on coasting cruises until 1815.

He became a rear-admiral on July 22, 1830; a vice-admiral on November

direction; this was pursued about three or four leagues without any apparent termination; the further they advanced the more extensive it was found. The tide, which was regular, was also rapid, and the flood evidently came from the north-westward; all these circumstances indicating the channel to be of considerable extent, they returned to communicate this intelligence.

On point Mudge was a very large village of the natives, many of whom visited the party on their passing and repassing by it, who uniformly conducted themselves with the greatest civility and respect. On the western shore, immediately without the entrance of the inlet, they found a rivulet of excellent fresh water. The passage up the inlet is perfectly free from danger, and affords good anchorage. Round point Mudge, at the distance of about half a mile, is a ledge of sunken rocks; these are, however, easily avoided by the weeds which they produce. From hence their way was directed to the northward, in order to join the ship through the broken land that exists between our present station and point Mudge. This was effected through a very intricate channel full of sunken rocks and rocky islets, leading them to the north point of the island which formed our S. W. shore, and bearing from hence N. 53 W. distant about four miles.

After receiving this information, I waited with no little impatience the return of the other boat party; in the hope that, if no intelligence should be derived to facilitate the progress of the ships, there was yet a great probability of finding a more comfortable resting place than that we then occupied. This afforded not a single prospect that was

---

23, 1841; and admiral on September 15, 1849. He died at Plympton on October 26, 1852, and was buried at Newton Ferrers.

There is a beautiful memorial window in St. Andrew's Church, Plymouth, a photograph of which was secured for this work. Arthur Mudge, Esq., Sydney, Plympton, Devon, possesses a portrait of Admiral Mudge, painted by John Opie in 1800. He gave permission for its reproduction in this work, and the photograph was made by W. Heath & Co. of Plymouth, England.

MUDGE WINDOW.
In Saint Andrew's Church, Plymouth, England.

pleasing to the eye, the smallest recreation on shore, nor animal nor vegetable food, excepting a very scanty proportion of those eatables already described, and of which the adjacent country was soon exhausted, after our arrival. Nor did our exploring parties meet with a more abundant supply, whence the place obtained the name of DESOLATION SOUND; where our time would have passed infinitely more heavily, had it not been relieved by the agreeable society of our Spanish friends.

The week, for which Mr. Johnstone and his party were furnished with supplies, having been expired some time, I began to be anxiously solicitous for their welfare; when, about two in the morning of Thursday the 12th, I had the satisfaction of having their arrival announced, all well, and that a passage leading into the Pacific Ocean to the northwestward had been discovered.

Mr. Johnstone had succeeded in finding his way into the arm leading to the westward through the narrows, where they were assisted by the friendly natives, about a league to the south of the passage by which he had before entered it; making the intermediate land, lying before the entrance into Bute's channel, nearly a round island three or four leagues in circuit, which obtained the name of STUART'S ISLAND. This channel was not less intricate than the other, neither of which he considered a safe navigation for shipping, owing to their being so narrow, to the irregular direction and rapidity of the tides, and to the great depth of water; which even close to the shore, was no where less than sixty fathoms. From this passage the northern shore was pursued, and two small arms leading to the N. W. each about a league in extent, were examined. Here was met a canoe in which were three Indians, who fled to the woods with the utmost precipitation, leaving their canoe on the shore. In it Mr. Johnstone deposited some trifling articles, in the hope of

---

Desolation Sound. This rather objectionable name is still retained on the British Columbia charts, though the area is greatly restricted. Most of the arms and inlets have received other names, and only one bay retains the name near the entrance to the original Desolation Sound.

dissipating by this means, their ill-grounded apprehension of danger. As he proceeded, he passed a spacious opening leading to the S. W. which he supposed communicated with the gulf some distance to the westward of our present station. The principal channel of the western arm still preserving a west direction, was about a mile wide; and as they advanced in it, they arrived at another branch nearly about the same width, in latitude 50° 26' longitude 234° 35', with an islet and some rocks lying off its east point of entrance. Conformably to our mode of tracing the continental shore, they were led up this opening; and in the night found themselves incommoded by the flood tide, although they had conceived from their former observations on the tides, that, at the time of their being disturbed at their resting place on shore, it would be nearly low water, as the moon was then passing the meridian. But, as the tide here varied upwards of four hours earlier than in the gulf of Georgia, and as the night had been still and pleasant, no accidental cause could be referred to, which was likely to have produced so material an alteration: the period of flowing, however, nearly corresponded with that of the tides at Nootka, and on the seacoast to the north of that place; which left little doubt, in the mind of Mr. Johnstone, that this unexpected circumstance had been occasioned by the channel they were in communicating with the ocean to the north-westward. The examination of the arm was continued, the next morning, to the latitude of 50° 46', longitude 234° 41', where it was thought to end. But this appearance proved to be a contraction only of the channel, by two interlocking points, from whence the Spaniards, who afterwards pursued its course, found its final termination in a N. E. by N. direction about three leagues further. They again reached the entrance in the evening, where the party rested for the night. This channel, which I distinguished by the name of LOUGHBOROUGH'S CHANNEL, was about a mile wide, between steep

---

Alexander Wedderburn, First Baron Loughborough. Vancouver here departs from the usual run of naval names and selects for this inlet the

BARON LOUGHBOROUGH.

From the painting by William Owen, now in the National Portrait Gallery, London. Photograph copyrighted by Walker & Cockrell. Rights secured for this work in England and America.

[July, 1792.]

and nearly perpendicular mountains, from whose lofty summits the dissolving snow descended down their rugged sides in many beautiful cascades.

---

name of one Lord Chancellor, the name of the large island fronting it being that of another Lord Chancellor, and a recent British Columbia map shows that others have since called the waterway leading by the island to the inlet, Chancellor Channel.

Wedderburn was a Scotch boy who was possessed of an enormous ambition, and lived to have it gratified. He was born at Edinburgh on February 13, 1733. His father was an advocate, and he was himself educated for the law. His student days were memorable, for he was on familiar terms with Dr. Robertson, the historian; David Hume, the librarian to the faculty of advocates; and Adam Smith, whose friendship was life-long.

He was making good progress in Scotland, but conceived the idea that he could do better in England. After winning a hard case, he was stung by a reproof from the presiding judge and threw off his advocate's gown, left Scotland, and took up his work in England. He took elocution lessons from the elder Sheridan to get rid of his provincial accent. His practice was slow, but he was a close friend of the Earl of Bute, and when the latter became powerful on the accession of George III, Wedderburn's fortunes improved. He was repeatedly elected to Parliament from one electorate or another. He was violently in opposition to Lord North's ministry, but all of a sudden he changed and was given his rival's place as solicitor-general when that rival, Lord Thurlow, was promoted to the attorney-generalship. One English writer refers to this change in Wedderburn as "one of the most flagrant cases of ratting recorded in our party annals."

Wedderburn was at the same time made chancellor to the queen and a privy councillor. In June, 1778, when Thurlow became Lord Chancellor, Wedderburn was made Attorney-General. He was climbing and reaching for the top. The American war problems made his position a difficult one. On June 14, 1780, he was appointed Chief Justice of the Court of Common Pleas, and was raised to the peerage as Baron Loughborough of Loughborough. It was difficult to adjust one's sails to the political winds of that day. Part of the time Loughborough was with North and Fox, but it remained for Pitt to give him the great seal and thus satisfy his life's ambition. On January, 28, 1793, he became Lord Chancellor and allied himself to the "king's friends." The French Revolution threatened to extend its influence into England. In this crisis Loughborough was firm, but he became very unpopular. In March, 1801, Pitt's ministry was dismissed and Loughborough was promptly ousted. He loved the office so much that he continued to attend the cabinet meetings until Premier Addington politely dismissed him.

Still his great services demanded more recognition, and on April 21, 1801,

[Original Journal, Pages 241-243.] [July, 1792.]

In the morning of the 6th, their researches were continued along the western channel, in which they found the tide favoring their former conjectures, by the flood evidently approaching them from the westward. About two leagues to the west of the arm they had quitted, the channel again branched off in two directions, one stretching a little to the northward, the other a little to the southward of west. The former demanded their attention first, and was found to be an intricate channel, containing many sunken rocks and rocky islets, occasioning great irregularity in the tides, which were here extremely violent; this continued about two leagues, where the channel widened, and the water became less agitated. Their course along the continental shore led them into a continuation of the western channel, which they had forsaken for the purpose of pursuing this more northerly one along the shore of the main land, by which means the southern side of the channel they had passed through was proved to be an island, about four leagues in extent. From hence they continued along the northern shore of the great western channel for the most part upwards of half a league wide, in the firm reliance of finding it lead to the ocean. Under this impression, Mr. Johnstone thought it of importance to ascertain that fact as speedily as possible; for which purpose, he steered over to the southern shore, leaving some openings, with some islands and rocks, on the northern side, for future examination. The southern shore was found nearly straight, and entire, rising abruptly from the sea to mountains of great height. Here they passed some small habitations of the natives, but the northern shore presented not the least sign of its being inhabited to the westward of the narrows. A slow progress was now made to the westward, in consequence of a fresh gale from that quarter, most part of the day; and the nights and mornings, often obscured in a thick fog, were generally calm.

---

he was created the first Earl of Rosslyn. He died on January 2, 1805, and having no heir, the titles were allowed to descend to his nephew, Sir James St. Clair Erskine.

On the morning of the 8th, they were much surprized by the report of a gun at no very great distance. This was immediately answered by a swivel; but no return was heard. On the fog clearing away, a small canoe appeared, which attended them until they reached a village of greater consequence, in point of size, than any they had before seen, situated on the front of a hill near the sea-side. The two Indians in the canoe, finding they were seen by those on shore, ventured alongside our boats; and, in the canoe was a musket with its appendages, and an eagle recently shot, which easily accounted for the discharge heard in the fog. As they approached the village several canoes visited the party; each of which was armed with a musket, and provided with ammunition; in one canoe there were three; these were considered as belonging to a chief, who informed them, that the village was under the authority of *Maquinna*,* the chief of Nootka, who, they gave our party reason to believe, was then on shore. The village had the appearance of being constructed with much regularity; its inhabitants numerous, and all seemingly well armed: under these circumstances it was passed by, without further inquiry, agreeable to our established maxim, never to court a danger on shore when necessity did not compel our landing.

A small sandy island, lying to the eastward of the village, affords between it and the land on which the town is situated, a small, but very commodious, anchorage. This is not, however, to be approached by the passage to the south of the island, that being navigable only for very small craft. To the south of the village a valley extended, apparently to a considerable distance, in a south-westerly direction. Through it a very fine stream of fresh water emptied itself into the sea, from the many wears that were seen in it, it was unquestionably well stocked with fish, though not any was offered for sale, notwithstanding the solicitation of our party, in the Nootka language, with which the natives seemed well acquainted.

* So called by the Spaniards, but known by the name of *Maquilla* by the English.

After the chief had received some presents, amongst which copper seemed to him the most valuable, he, with most of his companions, returned to the shore; and, on landing, fired several muskets, to show, in all probability, with what dexterity they could use these weapons, to which they seemed as familiarized as if they had been accustomed to fire-arms from their earliest infancy.

The shores on each side of the channel had materially decreased in height. That to the northward appeared very much broken, and mostly composed of islands; whilst that to the southward, which was pursued, remained compact and entire. The islands to the north were generally formed by low land near the shore, rising to a moderate height, well wooded, and on them the smoke of several fires was observed. This circumstance, together with the number of inhabitants on the southern shore, and the many canoes that were seen passing and repassing, evidently bespoke this country to be infinitely more populous than the shores of the gulf of Georgia.

The evening brought our party to the termination of the compact southern shore in its west direction, by a narrow channel leading to the south; and the main arm, which from that station took a north direction, spread very considerably; but the view to the westward was greatly interrupted by small islands. In the hope of reaching the westernmost island in sight, and by that means of determining the great object of their pursuit, they proceeded with a fresh gale from the east, attended by a great fall of rain, until midnight; when, supposing themselves at the limits they had seen before it was dark, they came to a grapnell under the lee of a small island, which in some degree sheltered them from the inclemency of the night. This extremely unpleasant weather continued without intermission, the whole of the next day, and until the morning of the 10th. They had now been absent six days out of the seven for which they had been provided, and the small remains of their stock were becoming hourly more insufficient for the distant voyage they had yet to perform in returning to the ships, which greatly increased the mortification they experienced by this very unlooked for detention;

but a westerly wind and pleasant weather returning with the morning of the 10th, they rowed to an island conspicuously situated, from whence their expectations were gratified by a clear though distant view of the expansive ocean. The land constituting the different shores of the passage appeared of moderate height, much broken, and seemed to form various other channels to sea. This was however the most capacious; the westernmost land of which, on the northern side, bore by compass N. 62 W. about five leagues; and the westernmost land on the southern side N. 80 W. about four leagues distant. This island obtained the name of ALLEVIATION ISLAND, from whence they directed their course homeward, being upwards of 120 miles from the ships.

Impelled by reasons of the most pressing nature, no time was lost in taking advantage of the prevailing favorable gale, with which they kept on their return until midnight, when as usual, they landed for the night on the southern shore, nearly opposite the west end of the island that forms the south side of the intricate passage they had passed through on the 6th. As the survey from the ship had been carried on by that route, and confined to the examination of the northern or continental shore to that station, through passages rendered by various impediments ineligible as a navigation for the ships, Mr. Johnstone was desirous of pursuing another which led more southerly, and appeared less liable to such objections. Though he much regretted the lost opportunity of returning by the favorable gale that continued all night, he waited the approach of day, and departing with the dawn, had his wishes gratified by sailing through a clear and spacious channel, in width about half a league, without the smallest interruption, or the least irregularity in the tides. The southern shore, which from the large village was nearly straight, afforded some few small bays, the land mostly rising in an abrupt manner from the sea to mountains of considerable height, divided by valleys that appeared to extend a great way back into the country; the shores were tolerably well inhabited by the natives who lived in small villages near the water side. The northern shore was neither so high nor so compact; several detached rocks were seen lying near it, and it was, generally speaking, composed of rugged rocks, in the fissures of which an abundance of pine trees were produced, constituting, as on the southern shore, one intire forest. As they advanced in this channel, leading nearly in an east and west direction, they observed another which led to the south, south eastward, bearing every appearance of being clear, navigable, and communicating with the gulf; and one also stretching to the north-eastward, which they had little doubt was the same they had seen after passing the narrows on the 4th, leading to the S. W. The former of these they much wished to explore, but their provisions being totally exhausted, it became expedient they should join the ships without further delay, and therefore pursued that leading to the north-eastward, by which they arrived as already related.

This information left me scarcely a doubt that the channel Mr. Johnstone had declined pursuing south eastwardly towards the gulf, was the same our boats had entered leading to the northward from point Mudge, and which, on comparing the sketches of the several surveys, was as nearly as possible reduced to a certainty. I derived no small degree of satisfaction in finding my expectations so far advanced, for had our efforts proved ineffectual in discovering a communication with the ocean, it would have occupied the remaining part of the season to have examined the numerous openings on the opposite shores of the gulf, which were now proved to form the northeastern side of an extensive island or archipelago, on whose south-western coast Nootka is situated; hence this task now became unnecessary, and I was flattered with the hope of yet extending our researches during the summer months a considerable distance to the northward.

Señors Galiano and Valdes I made acquainted with our discoveries; and with my intention of departing, in consequence of the information we had gained, the first favorable moment.

When the village was pointed out where *Maquinna* was supposed to have been, Señor Valdes was of opinion, that circumstance was highly probable, knowing he had authority over an extensive country to the north-westward of Nootka.

These gentlemen received such information of all our discoveries up to this period as they required, and now begged leave to decline accompanying us further, as the powers they possessed in their miserable vessels, were unequal to a co-operation with us, and being apprehensive their attendance would retard our progress. Señor Galiano favored me with a copy of his survey, and other particulars relative to this inlet of the sea, which contained also that part of the neighboring coast extending north-westward from the straits of De Fuca, beyond Nootka to the latitude of 50° 3', longitude 232° 48'. He likewise gave me a letter to be forwarded to Señor Quadra at Nootka, by *Maquinna*, or any of his people with whom we might chance to meet, together with an introductory one to Señor Quadra, when I should have the pleasure of meeting him at Nootka. After an exchange of good wishes, we bad each other farewell, having experienced much satisfaction, and mutually received every kindness and attention that our peculiar situation could afford to our little society. From these gentlemen we were assured, that on our arrival at Nootka we should meet a most cordial reception, and be more pleasantly situated than we could imagine, as the houses had lately undergone a thorough repair, and all the gardens had been put and kept in the highest order, for the purpose of being so delivered into our possession.

With a light breeze from the northward, in the morning of Friday the 13th, we weighed and left our Spanish friends at anchor, who intended to pursue their researches to the westward through the channel Mr. Johnstone had discovered; and in commemoration of whose exertions was by me named JOHNSTONE'S STRAITS; and the island described by him on

---

James Johnstone. The journal indicates that Johnstone was a useful member of the expedition. The waterway that bears his name is an important channel, well known to every one who makes the trip to Alaska by the "inside" route. His work in discovering the channel earned for him this great honor. Little is known of his life. He entered the navy as a midshipman on the *Keppel* brig on the American station, under Lieutenant Whit-

the 6th, was in compliment to Mr. Swaine, who commanded the other boat, distinguished by the name of HARDWICKE'S ISLAND, after the noble earl of that title; towards which

---

worth. In 1790 he was mustered on the armed tender *Chatham* under Lieutenant Broughton as master. He held that place until August, 1792, when Vancouver found it necessary to make some promotions upon the arrival of the storeship *Dædalus*, whose lieutenant-commanding had died. Johnstone then became lieutenant of the *Chatham*. He became a commander on June 22, 1802, and was advanced to the rank of captain on June 22, 1806. Afterward he was a commissioner at Bombay.

Philip Yorke, Third Earl of Hardwicke. As seen in the journal, Vancouver bestowed this name of Hardwicke upon the large island lying partly in Johnstone's Strait, "in compliment to Mr. Swaine who commanded the other boat." This has been something of an enigma. No relationship could be traced between the earl and the sailor. There was every reason for complimenting Mr. Swaine himself, for he was often in evidence as a commander of the boat excursions. Indeed, Vancouver did write Swaine's name on the maps of the west coast, but not in the Puget Sound region.

Spelman Swaine joined the *Discovery* in 1791 as master's mate, giving his birthplace as Lynn and his age as twenty-two years. Frequent reference is made to him in the journal, and in August, 1792, at Nootka, he was promoted to be master of the *Chatham* and in the following month when Lieutenant Mudge was sent to England with despatches necessitating several promotions, Swaine was made third lieutenant of the *Discovery*. On returning to England, in 1795, he was lieutenant in the *Spitfire* and the *Princess Charlotte*. He was promoted to the rank of commander, and in the *Raven* sloop on the Mediterranean in October, 1803, he led Lord Nelson's fleet through the Straits of Bonnifacio. He was wrecked off the coast of Sicily in 1804. In 1814 he commanded the *Satira* and was again wrecked on an unknown rock off Cuba. He was posted or given captain's rank on July 13, 1815, and in 1846 was promoted a rear-admiral on the retired list. On the death of Colonel Watson, in 1836, Swaine was appointed by the Bishop of Ely to the ancient and honorable office of Chief Bailiff of the Isle of Ely in Cambridgeshire, which he held to the time of his death on January 14, 1848, at the age of seventy-nine years. The Annual Register for 1848 has an appreciative sketch of his career. His father was Spelman Swaine of Liverington, Cambridgeshire.

In that word "Cambridgeshire" is found a solution of the enigma referred to above. Philip Yorke was returned as member of Parliament from Cambridgeshire first on September 14, 1780, and continuously thereafter until his succession to the peerage on the death of his uncle on May 16, 1790, when he became the third Earl of Hardwicke. The new earl would probably be interested in a son of one of his constituents starting on such a voyage, and

EARL OF HARDWICKE.

From the engraving by W. Giller after the painting by Sir Thomas Lawrence. Photograph copyrighted by Walker & Cockrell. Rights secured for this work in England and America.

straits our course was now bent to the southward, trusting we should find a passage into them to the westward of point Mudge.

Little remains further to add respecting the station we had just quitted, but to state the general satisfaction that prevailed on leaving a region so truly desolate and inhospitable. During our stay at that gloomy place, I was enabled to take only ten sets of lunar distances; which, with six sets taken at our anchorage near the entrance of the sound, gave a mean result for the longitude 235° 5′ 30″. Kendal's chronometer, by ten sets of altitudes taken on different days, shewed the mean result, allowing the Birch bay rate, to be 235° 21′. This I considered to be nearer the truth than that deduced from the few lunar observations above mentioned, and have accordingly adopted it as the longitude of Desolation sound, whose latitude by six meridional altitudes of the sun was found to be 50° 11′. The mean result of eighteen sets of azimuths taken on board, differing from 17° 45′ to 23°, gave 19° 16′ easterly variation; seventeen sets taken on shore differed from 14° 26′ to 19° 30′, gave a mean result of 16° variation in the same direction. The irregularity of the tides was such that no correct inferences could well be drawn. They appeared to be principally influenced by local or inci-

---

it is certain that the sailor boy would be interested in the member of Parliament from his home who had so recently become an earl.

Philip Yorke was the son of Lord Chancellor Yorke and was born on May 31, 1757. He was educated at Queen's College, Cambridge, and in 1806 was elected high steward of that university. He was for six years, 1801 to 1806, Lord-Lieutenant of Ireland. He did much to allay the irritation over the union of Ireland and Great Britain, and became a strong convert to Catholic emancipation, to which cause he adhered until its triumph in 1829. He also supported the Parliamentary Reform Bill in 1831.

Hardwicke was a Knight of the Garter, receiving the insignia at Dublin in 1805. He was also a Fellow of the Royal Society, Fellow of the Society of Antiquaries, a Trustee of the British Museum, and from 1790 Lord-Lieutenant of Cambridgeshire.

He died on November 18, 1834.

The portrait used for this work is taken from an engraving by W. Gillar from the fine painting by Sir Thomas Lawrence.

dental causes; possibly by the operation of both. They were greatly affected by the direction or force of the winds, which seemed as equally to act on the rise and fall, as on the current when there was any. This, however, was not always the case; as in the course of some days there would not be the least perceptible stream; and in others a very rapid one, that generally continued in the same direction twenty four hours, and sometimes longer. The time of high water was equally vague and undefinable; this I attributed to its insular situation, nearly at the extremity of the influence of two tides flowing from directly opposite points, causing their divided streams to act, according to the incidental circumstances that might operate upon them.

In this route we passed through the assemblage of islands and rocks lying at some distance before the entrance into Desolation sound; some of which presented an appearance infinitely more grateful than that of the interior country. These were mostly of a moderate height from the sea, tolerably well wooded, and the shores not wholly composed of rugged rocks, afforded some small bays bounded by sandy beaches. The wind continued light from the northern quarter, and the weather being serene and pleasant, made a most agreeable change. Numberless whales enjoying the season, were playing about the ship in every direction; as were also several seals; the latter had been seen in great abundance during our residence in Desolation sound, and in all the remote excursions of our boats, but they were so extremely watchful and shy, that not one could be taken. These animals seemed to have had the exclusive possession of the gloomy region we had just quitted; but the scene now before us was more congenial to our minds, not only from the different aspect of the shores, but from the attention of the friendly Indians, who, as we were crossing the gulf, visited us in several canoes, with young birds, mostly sea fowl, fish, and some berries, to barter for our trinkets and other commodities. Soon after mid-day we anchored about half a mile to the northward of point Mudge, in 37 fathoms water, on a bottom of black sand and mud. A very strong *flood tide* came from the northward, and although nearly convinced that our conjectures were right, the launch and cutter with lieutenant Puget and Mr. Whidbey, were immediately dispatched to examine the channel as to its communication with Johnstone's straights; that in the event of there being any obstructions where such rapid tides were running, we might have sufficient notice, and be prepared to avoid them.

From the village situated on point Mudge, we were visited by several of the natives, who brought fish and the wild fruits of the country, which they exchanged for our European articles, in a very fair and honest manner.

After dinner, accompanied by Mr. Menzies and some of the officers, I went on shore to return the visit of our friends, and to indulge our curiosity. On landing at the village which is situated a little to the N. W. within the promontory, and nearly at the summit of a steep sandy cliff, we were received by a man who appeared to be chief of the party. He approached us alone, seemingly with a degree of formality, though with the utmost confidence of his own security, whilst the rest of the society, apparently numerous, were arranged and seated in the most peaceable manner before their houses. I made him such presents as seemed not only to please him excessively, but to confirm him in the good opinion with which he was prepossessed; and he immediately conducted us up to the village by a very narrow path winding diagonally up the cliff, estimated by us to be about an hundred feet in height, and within a few degrees of being perpendicular. Close to the edge of this precipice stood the village, the houses of which were built after the fashion of Nootka, though smaller, not exceeding ten or twelve feet in height, nearly close together in rows, separated by a narrow passage sufficiently wide only for one person. On the beach, at the foot of the cliff, were about seventy canoes of small dimensions, though amongst them were some that would carry at least fifteen persons with great convenience. On a computation, therefore, deduced from these and other circumstances, we were led to consider that this village, though occupying a very small space, could not contain less than three hundred persons.

The spot where it was erected appeared to be well chosen to insure its protection; the steep loose sandy precipice secured it in front, and its rear was defended by a deep chasm in the rocks; beyond these was a thick and nearly impenetrable forest: so that the only means of access was by the narrow path we had ascended, which could be easily maintained against very superior numbers. Having gratified our curiosity, and, in return for the cordial attention of these friendly people, made our acknowledgements by presents of such trivial articles as we had about us, we took our leave of the village for the purpose of indulging ourselves before dark, with a refreshing walk, on a low margin of land extending from the more elevated woodland country, some distance along the water-side to the northward; a luxury we had not for some time experienced. In this excursion, which was extremely grateful and pleasant, we saw two sepulchres built with plank about five feet in height, seven in length, and four in breadth. These boards were curiously perforated at the ends and sides, and the tops covered with loose pieces of plank, as if for the purpose of admitting as great a circulation of air as possible to the human bones they enclosed, which were evidently the relics of many different bodies. A few of the Indians attended us in our walk, picking the berries from the trees as we passed, and with much civility presenting them to us on green leaves. The evening approaching obliged us to return on board, against a very strong ebb tide.

The *Chatham* having been detained some hours in Desolation sound after we had sailed, had now arrived and anchored near us. She had been stopped by her anchor when nearly half up, hooking a rock; every means that could be devised had been resorted to without effect, until the moment when they were about to cut it away, it cleared itself, which fortunately saved the anchor and cable.

With a fresh breeze from the N. W. and a continuation of pleasant weather, at high water about three o'clock on the morning of Saturday the 14th, we were under sail, and with the assistance of the ebb tide, turned about four leagues up the inlet towards a commodious anchoring place, that had been discovered by our boats, and was the appointed rendezvous on the return of the launch and cutter. About six o'clock we arrived and anchored in 24 fathoms water, sandy bottom. In this situation each side of the arm formed a bay affording commodious anchorage; and that on the western side being the most extensive was preferred. Nearly in the center is a shallow bank of sand, with a navigable passage all around it. The ships were stationed between this bank and the north side of the bay, near a small Indian village, whose inhabitants had little to dispose of, though they were very civil and freindly. Whilst turning up in the ship, many of the natives came off; but the swiftness of our motion prevented their coming on board.

The clearness of the sky and atmosphere enabled me to procure some observations, by which our latitude was ascertained to be 50° 7' 30". Ten sets of lunar distances, with those made in Desolation sound, amounting in all to twenty-six sets taken on different sides of the moon, brought forward by Kendal's chronometer and the protraction, agreeing extremely well together; gave the mean result of the longitude by the lunar distances 15' 15" to the westward of the watch. On such authority, however, I could not possibly determine that the chronometer erred so materially; yet had reason to believe, that it was not gaining at the rate we had allowed since our departure from Birch Bay. The *true longitude*, therefore, of the respective places hereafter mentioned, from Desolation sound to Nootka, will be deduced from such observations as I was enabled to make at the latter place for correcting the error of the chronometer; by which, according to the Birch bay rate, the longitude of our present rendezvous was 234° 57'; its true longitude, by the subsequent observations, 234° 52½'; the variation of the compass by three sets of azimuths, 18° 30' eastwardly.

From point Mudge to this bay the channel is nearly straight; the western shore is compact, the eastern one has some rocky islets and rocks lying near it; it is about half a league wide; in turning up we found not the smallest obstruction; and the shores are sufficiently bold for vessels to stand as close to them as inclination may direct. Immediately above this station the channel contracts to a short half mile, by the projecting land that forms the north sides of these two bays, and by an island on the eastern shore (navigable round for boats only) which projects so far as to reduce the channel to nearly one half its width. The tide, setting to the southward through this confined passage, rushes with such immense impetuosity as to produce the appearance of falls considerably high; though not the least obstruction of either rocks or sands, so far as we had an opportunity of examining it, appeared to exist. The returning tide to the north, though very rapid, does not run with such violence; this was estimated to move at the rate of about four or five miles; the other, at seven or eight miles per hour. They seemed regular in their quarterly change, but the visible rise and fall by the shore in this situation was so inconsiderable as to allow us merely to distinguish the ebb from the flood tide.

In the evening of the 14th our boats returned, having found the channel from these narrow parts gradually increasing its width to a mile, and half a league, and to communicate with Johnstone's straits in nearly the same N. N. W. direction, about four leagues further, without any visible obstruction or impediment to the navigation. The eastern shore, like that to the northward, was much broken; the western shore continued firm, and afforded some small bays in which there was good anchorage. As they proceeded, not any inhabitants were seen, but, on returning, they met twenty canoes filled with Indians, who, at first, were a little distant, but at length approached our party with confidence, and with every appearance of civility and friendship.

These were observed to be more variously painted than any of the natives our gentlemen had before seen. The faces of some were made entirely white, some red, black, or lead color; whilst others were adorned with several colors; and the generality had their hair decorated with the down of young sea-fowl. In these respects they evidently approached nearer to the character of the people of Nootka, than of any

SECOND EARL OF CHATHAM.
From the mezzotint by C. Turner after the painting by John Hoppner. Photograph copyrighted by Walker & Cockrell. Rights secured for this work in England and America.

other we had yet seen, either in the entrance of the strait of De Fuca, or in the gulf of Georgia.

The winds being too light and variable to command the ship against the influence of such rapid tides, we were under the necessity of waiting for the ebb in the afternoon of the following day, Sunday the 15th, when, with pleasant weather and a fresh breeze at N. W. we weighed about three o'clock, turned through the narrows, and, having gained about three leagues by the time it was nearly dark, we anchored on the western shore in a small bay, on a bottom of sand and mud, in 30 fathoms water, to wait the favorable return of tide. On Monday morning the 16th, with the assistance of a fresh N. W. wind, and the stream of ebb, we shortly reached Johnstone's straits; passing a point which, after our little consort, I named POINT CHATHAM, situated in latitude 53° 19½',

---

John Pitt, Second Earl of Chatham. — The important place of first Lord of the Admiralty was held by the Earl of Chatham from 1788 until 1794, when he was succeeded by Earl Spencer. This covered nearly the whole period of Vancouver's voyage. The armed tender that sailed as consort of the *Discovery* sloop bore his name. The name of this consort was given by Lieutenant Broughton to the island he discovered near New Zealand, and now we see it again bestowed to the point opposite the southern end of Thurlow's Island. The earl had signed the papers of the expedition, and the bestowal of the name Chatham was as much in compliment to him as to the little vessel.

It was said in his time that William Pitt, the younger, was not only a chip off the old block; he was the whole block itself. No such fine compliment was ever paid to his older brother John, who inherited the title as second Earl of Chatham. Wraxall said he resembled his father in face and person and in nothing else. His manners were such as to forbid approach and prohibit familiarity.

John Pitt was born on September 10, 1756, and succeeded to his father's title in 1778. He entered the army and in 1778 was appointed a lieutenant in the Thirty-ninth Foot. He served in the siege of Gibraltar in 1779-1783. It was in the cabinet of his younger brother that he served as first Lord of the Admiralty. He was admitted to the Privy Council on April 3, 1789, and was created a Knight of the Garter on December 15, 1790. On retiring from the position of first Lord of the Admiralty he remained in the cabinet as Lord Privy Seal and was transferred from that to the presidency of the council, which he held until his brother resigned as premier in July, 1801.

longitude 235° 45'. This point is rendered conspicuous by the confluence of three channels, two of which take their respective directions to the westward and south-eastwards towards the ocean, as also by a small bay on each side; by three rocky islets close to the south, and by some rocks, over which the sea breaks to the north.

Immediately on our entering these straits, we were affected by more swell than we had experienced in this inland navigation, indicating that the ocean, in a westerly direction was not quite so remote as, by Mr. Johnstone, it had been estimated.

In the bay, to the north-westward of point Chatham, was situated an Indian village, from whence some of the natives

---

He continued in the army all this time, receiving numerous promotions. In command of a brigade under the Duke of York on October 2, 1799, he relieved General Coote when hard pressed by the French in the battle of Bergen. He was wounded at the battle of Beverwyk. On returning home he was made master-general of ordnance on June 27, 1801, which position he held until February 8, 1806. He became lieutenant-general in 1802, governor of Plymouth on March 30, 1805, and governor of Jersey on September 22, 1807. He owed much of this advancement to the favor of George III, but on his own account, he was ambitious for military glory. He was greviously disappointed when, instead of himself, Wellington was sent to the peninsula in 1808. To soothe him he was given command of the land forces in the expedition to Walcheren, for the reduction or capture of Flushing and Antwerp. Successful at first, he did not press his advantage, and the expedition was a failure. He claimed in defence that he had not been properly supported by the naval forces under Admiral Strachan. This gave rise to the following:—

> "Great Chatham, with his sabre drawn
> Stood waiting for Sir Richard Strachan;
> Sir Richard, longing to be at 'em
> Stood waiting for the Earl of Chatham."

Friends of the admiral retorted against Chatham's charges and called him "the late" Earl of Chatham. An investigation produced revelations that deeply compromised the earl's reputation.

Notwithstanding all this he continued to receive further promotions. He was made a general in the army on January 1, 1812, and in 1820, on the death of the Duke of Kent, he was made governor of Gibraltar, which post he held until his death. He died at London on September 24, 1835.

The portrait for this work is from the mezzotint by C. Turner, after the painting by John Hoppner of the Royal Academy.

LORD THURLOW.

From the painting by T. Phillips, now in the National Portrait Gallery, London. Photograph copyrighted by Walker & Cockrell. Rights secured for this work in England and America.

attempted to give us their company; but the wind, blowing heavily in squalls, prevented their venturing alongside. After we had proceeded about ten miles from point Chatham, the tide made so powerfully against us as obliged us, about breakfast time, to become again stationary in a bay on the northern shore in 32 fathoms water. The land, under which we anchored, was a narrow island, which I distinguished by the name of THURLOW'S ISLAND, it is about eight leagues long,

---

Edward, First Baron Thurlow. This is a case of a very bad boy developing into a powerful, though not a great or good, man. He was born at Bracon Ash, Norfolk, on December 9, 1731. His father was Rev. Thomas Thurlow, who was unable to manage the boy at home and sent him to Rev. Joseph Brett, master of Seckars School, Scarning, Norfolk, who was a type of the severe disciplinarians. Years afterward this schoolmaster approached the great lawyer and claimed acquaintanceship, whereupon Thurlow blurted, "I am not bound to recognize every scoundrel that recognizes me." He had endured four years at Scarning when he was dismissed with the character of an incorrigible bad boy. He finally was prepared for Cambridge, but his conduct was such that he was removed without a degree in 1751. He was then put at the study of law and during that time met William Cowper, the poet, with whom he continued on friendly terms.

He distinguished himself at the bar and in Parliament, having been returned for Tamworth on December 23, 1765, and retaining the seat until raised to the peerage on June 3, 1778, as Baron Thurlow of Ashfield, Suffolk. Later in the House of Lords, the Duke of Grafton publicly taunted him with his plebeian origin and the recency of his patent. Thurlow rose splendidly to the occasion. He haughtily contrasted his own honorable exertions with "the accident of an accident," to which he ascribed Duke Grafton's seat. He "protested that he had not solicited but had been solicited by the peerage, and that both as chancellor and as man he was as respectable and as much respected as the proudest peer he then looked down upon." The House of Lords followed Thurlow after that.

He became Lord Chancellor or attained the wool-sack, as it was usually put, in July, 1778. In American affairs he always insisted upon the rights of the mother country and the duty of exerting her full might. While he was still Lord Chancellor, burglars broke into his house and stole the great seal. It was a political trick, but a new seal was hastily cast and the trick failed. The seal was never recovered, nor was there ever found a clew to the burglars.

He sided with the king in an effort to raise Warren Hastings to the peerage, but when the famous impeachment was begun, Thurlow maintained fully the reputation of British justice. In politics he was unstable, and in present-day language would be described as a rough sort of trimmer.

and was passed to the northward by Mr. Johnstone in going, and to the S. E. on his return. The bay was observed to be in latitude 50° 23′, longitude 234° 31′; three sets of azimuths gave the variation 19° eastwardly; it affords good anchorage; and wood and water may be easily procured. Our efforts with the seine, though unremitted, were ineffectual, not having afforded us the least supply since our departure from Birch bay; nor, with the hooks and lines, had we been more successful. About four in the afternoon, we again proceeded, but made little progress against a fresh westerly gale. In the evening we passed another village, when the inhabitants, more knowing than their neighbors, embraced the opportunity of the ship being at stays, of selling a few small fresh salmon. They had some with them ready cooked, and they seemed to have great pleasure in throwing them on board as we passed their canoes. We anchored again about nine in the evening, on the southern shore, nearly abreast of the west end of Thurlow's island, in 22 fathoms, sandy bottom; having gained, this tide, little more [than] three leagues.

The wind blew strong from the westward, with squalls, during the night; and when we weighed, at three in the morning of Tuesday the 17th, we were obliged to ply, under double-reefed topsails, to windward, with little prospect of making

---

He retired from office on May 21, 1792, and as a mark of favor received a patent, dated June 11, 1792, changing his title to Baron Thurlow of Thurlow, Suffolk, and allowing this title to descend to his nephew. He continued to take part in the judicial business of the House of Lords and to cultivate his tastes as a scholar. He died at Brighton on September 12, 1806.

Fox is credited with this: "No man ever was so wise as Thurlow looks."

Thurlow is described as "tall, well built, and singularly majestic in appearance. His features, though stern, were regular, and a swarthy complexion matched well with his keen black sparkling eyes and bushy eyebrows. He was fond of the company of men of letters, and even Dr. Johnson respected his conversational powers."

He never married, but by his mistress, Mrs. Hervey, to whom he was much attached, he had several children for whom he provided.

The portrait for this work is by T. Phillips of the Royal Academy. The original painting is in the National Portrait Gallery, Number 249. It was painted in 1805, a year before the baron's death.

much progress, until we had passed Thurlow's and Hardwick's islands.

The meeting of these channels added great velocity to the tides; and, as the day advanced, the weather became fair and pleasant, which enabled us to spread all our canvass; yet we were very apprehensive of losing, by the adverse tide, all we had gained by the favorable stream; not having been able to reach the bottom with 100 fathoms of line, although repeated trials had been made, on traversing within a ship's length of each shore. At last, about eleven, in a small bay on the southern side, soundings were gained at the depth of fifty fathoms, where we instantly anchored, about half a cable's length from the rocks, to wait the return of the favorable current, not knowing by what name to call it. That which came from the eastward we had stiled the ebb; but, on going on shore to observe the latitude, the stream that came rapidly from the westward, appeared to be the reflux, as the water on the shore, during the afternoon, had evidently retired, though to no very great distance.

Our station here was nearly opposite the first opening on the northern shore, passed by unexamined by Mr. Johnstone; who had also declined visiting two others, apparently on the continent, further to the westward. Lieutenant Puget and Mr. Whidbey, were dispatched in the launch and cutter, in order to explore the former, lying from us N. 50 E.; about a league distant, with instructions to join me, in the ship, either in the third unexplored opening on the north side of the straits, or at the village where *Maquinna* was stated to be; it being my intention, that the *Chatham* should pursue the second opening, whilst I proceeded in order to procure an interview with *Maquinna*, through whom I might be able to inform Señor Quadra of the time he might expect to see us, and forward Señor Galiano's letter.

In the afternoon we were visited by two canoes, having a musket, with all the necessary appurtenances in each. These were the first firearms we had seen from the ships, but, from the number Mr. Johnstone had seen in his late excursion, it would appear, that the inhabitants of this particular part are amply provided with these formidable weapons.

Having the tide in our favor, at four o'clock we quitted this station, the latitude of which was found to be in 50° 27', longitude 235° 53'. At this time, it appeared to be low tide, the water having fallen, since my landing in the forenoon, nearly five feet; the stream was in our favor, though running at a very gentle rate, and the wind from the N. W. being very light, we advanced so slowly, that, by ten at night, we had only gained three leagues, where another small bay, or cove, was seen on the southern shore, with low land extending some distance from the mountains. Here I was in hopes of finding a commodious resting place, but was obliged to stand very near to the shore before soundings could be gained; at length, with forty fathoms of line, the bottom was reached, and on wearing, which the ship did very briskly, in order to anchor in a less depth of water, our next cast was ten fathoms, when the anchor was instantly let go; yet, before we had veered a third of the cable, the ship grounded abaft; but, on heaving in a few fathoms of the cable she very easily swung off the bank. The *Chatham* grounded also, and was likewise got off with little difficulty.

At this station, it was again low water about four on Wednesday morning, or nearly so, as the inner part of the bank on which we had grounded, and at that time was covered with water, was dry at no great distance from us. We again proceeded, with the current in our favor, to the westward; and on passing two small villages of the natives, a few of the inhabitants, from each, paid us their respects. At this time we were nearly abreast of the second opening, passed by unexamined by Mr. Johnstone. It appeared infinitely more capacious than the other, which, agreeably to my former intentions, Mr. Broughton was directed to pursue, appointing the same rendezvous with him, that had been fixed for the boats.

We remained under sail the whole day, but made so little way, that by nine at night, we had advanced about five leagues only. Then, in a small bay, close to the rocks on the southern shore, we again anchored, in forty-five fathoms water, sandy bottom.

Light variable winds prevented our sailing until eight in the morning of Thursday the 19th, when, with a gentle breeze from the eastward, we weighed; and, what was not a little extraordinary, without heaving the least strain on the cable, on fishing the anchor, its lower arm was discovered to be broken off close to the crown, and to have been left at the bottom. On further examination, it proved to have been just welded round the surface, so as barely to hold the parts together, within which the bars, composing the internal mass, preserved their original unaltered shape, distinctly separate from each other; and, in the spaces remained the blacksmith's coal, without any appearance of their having undergone the action of fire.

Whilst we remained inactive the fore part of the morning, our time was not unprofitably employed, in receiving the welcome visits of some hospitable friends from the shore; who brought us such an abundant supply of fresh salmon, that we purchased a sufficient number to serve the crew as long as they would keep good; which was a great relief from our salted provisions, being a luxury we had not lately experienced.

We had not long been under sail, when the officers, who had been dispatched in the boats on the 17th, arrived on board. From these gentlemen I became acquainted, that they had examined the inlet to which they had been directed. Off its western point lies a small island; its entrance is about half a mile wide, but with no more than four fathoms water in mid-channel; from whence it extends about eight miles, in a direction N. 75 E.; this depth however increased as they advanced, to five, six, and seven fathoms, affording good anchorage about two thirds of the way up: beyond which limits, like all the channels of this kind that we had explored, it terminated in shallow water. The country bore a more pleasing aspect than that seen from Johnstone's straits; and the soil, where they landed, at the upper part, was composed of black mould and sand, producing pine-trees of large dimensions. They saw one run of water at the head; but the shoal stretching from thence, prevented their ascertaining its qualities; yet as a deserted village was observed half way up on the northern shore, in all probability this place is not destitute of wholesome water, the only undiscovered requisite to constitute it a very snug and commodious port; to which I gave the name of PORT NEVILLE.

The weather was serene and pleasant, but the wind so light and variable, that, although we were not more than four leagues from the village where we expected to meet *Maquinna;* it was not until past ten at night that we reached that station, when we anchored just without the sandy island, in seven fathoms water.

The next morning showed the village in our neighborhood to be large; and, from the number of our visitors, it appeared to be very populous. These brought us the skins of the sea-otter, of an excellent quality, in great abundance, which were bartered for sheet-copper, and blue cloth; those articles being in the highest estimation amongst them. Most of these people understood the language of Nootka, though it did not appear to be generally spoken.

The *Ty-eie,* or chief of the village, paid us an early visit, and received from me some presents which highly delighted him. I understood his name to be *Cheslakees.* He acknowledged *Maquinna* to be a greater chief; as he also did *Wicananish;* but, so far as I could learn, he did not consider himself to be under the authority of either.

On inquiring if *Maquinna* was at the village, he answered in the negative, saying they seldom visited; and that it was a journey of four days across the land to Nootka sound, which from hence towards the S. S. W. is about twenty leagues distant.

Accompanied by some of the officers, Mr. Menzies, and our new guest *Cheslakees,* I repaired to the village, and found it pleasantly situated on a sloping hill, above the banks of a fine fresh water rivulet, discharging itself into a small creek or cove. It was exposed to a southern aspect, whilst higher hills beyond, covered with lofty pines, sheltered it

CHESLAKEE'S VILLAGE IN JOHNSTONE'S STRAITS.

From the steel engraving by J. Landseer in Vancouver's Journal. Drawn by W. Alexander from a sketch on the spot by J. Sykes.

completely from the northern winds. The houses, in number thirty-four, were arranged in regular streets; the larger ones were the habitations of the principal people, who had them decorated with paintings and other ornaments, forming various figures, apparently the rude designs of fancy; though it is by no means improbable, they might annex some meaning to the figures they described, too remote, or hieroglyphical, for our comprehension. The house of our leader *Cheslakees* was distinguished by three rafters of stout timber raised above the roof, according to the architecture of Nootka, though much inferior to those I had there seen in point of size; the whole, from the opposite side of the creek, presented a very picturesque appearance.

On our landing, three or four of the inhabitants, only, came down to receive us at the beach; the rest quietly remained near their houses. These, *Cheslakees* informed me, were his near relations, who consequently received, in the shape of presents, compliments from me, with which they seemed greatly pleased.

The houses were constructed after the manner at Nootka, but appeared rather less filthy, and the inhabitants were undoubtedly of the same nation, differing little in their dress, or general deportment. Several families lived under the same roof; but their sleeping apartments were separated, and more decency seemed to be observed in their domestic economy, than I recollected to be the practice at Nootka. The women, who in proportion appeared numerous, were variously employed; some in their different household affairs, others in the manufacture of their garments from bark and other materials; though no one was engaged in making their woolen apparel, which I much regretted. The fabrication of mats for a variety of purposes, and a kind of basket, wrought so curiously close, as to contain water like an earthen vessel without the least leakage or drip, comprehended the general employment of the women, who were not less industrious than ingenious.

As inquiries into the laudable ingenuity of others are not to be satisfied in the civilized world without some expence, so investigations of the like nature amongst the uncultivated regions were not to be had in this society without due acknowledgments, which were solicited by these female artizans in every house we entered; and so abundant were their demands, that although I considered myself amply provided for the occasion with beads, hawk's bells, and other trinkets, my box, as well as my pockets, and those of the gentlemen who were of the party, were soon nearly emptied. At the conclusion of this visit we were entertained at the house of an elderly chief, to whom *Cheslakees*, and every other person paid much respect, with a song by no means unmelodious, though the performance of it was rendered excessively savage, by the uncouth gestures, and rude actions accompanying it, similar to the representations I had before seen at Nootka. The song being finished, we were each presented with a strip of sea-otter skin; the distributions of which occupied some time. After this ceremony a song from the ladies was expected; and during this interval, I observed in the hands of the numerous tribe that now surrounded us, many spears pointed with iron, clubs, large knives, and other weapons with which they were not furnished on our first approach to the village. I was not altogether satisfied with this change in their appearance, though I had every reason to believe their intentions were of the most inoffensive nature, and that it was most probable they had thus produced their arms to shew their wealth, and impress us with an idea of their consequence: I deemed it, however, most adviseable to withdraw; and having distributed the few remaining articles we had reserved, *Cheslakees* was informed I was about to return; on which he, with his relations who had attended us through the village, accompanied us to the sandy island, whither I went to observe its latitude.

Some few others of the Indians attended us on this occasion, whose behavior being orderly and civil, they were permitted to assemble round me whilst observing. They were excessively amused with the effect of the sun's rays through the reading glass; and the extraordinary quality of the quicksilver used for the purpose of an artificial horizon, afforded them the greatest entertainment, until our business was ended, when they in a very friendly manner took leave, and confirmed me in the opinion, that the martial appearance they had assumed, was purely the effect of ostentation.

In most of the houses were two or three muskets, which, by their locks and mounting, appeared to be Spanish. *Cheslakees* had no less than eight in his house, all kept in excellent order: these, together with a great variety of other European commodities, I presumed, were procured immediately from Nootka, as, on pointing to many of them, they gave us to understand they had come from thence, and in their commercial concerns with us, frequently explained that their skins would fetch more at Nootka than we chose to offer. Their total number we estimated at about five hundred. They were well versed in the principles of trade, and carried it on in a very fair and honorable manner. Sea-otter skins were the chief objects of our people's traffic, who purchased nearly two hundred in the course of the day. Mr. Menzies informed me, that these had been procured at least an hundred per cent dearer than when he visited the coast on a former occasion, which manifestly proved, that either a surplus quantity of European commodities had been since imported into this country, or more probably, that the avidity shown by the rival adventurers in this commerce, and the eagerness of an unrestrained throng of purchasers from different nations, had brought European commodities into low estimation. Iron was become a mere drug; and when we refused them fire arms and ammunition, which humanity, prudence, and policy directed to be with-held, nothing but large sheets of copper, and blue woollen cloth engaged their attention in a commercial way; beads and other trinkets they accepted as presents, but they returned nothing in exchange.

These were the principal circumstances that occurred to me on our short visit to this station. The further and more general observations, that fell under my notice respecting the very extraordinary region we had lately passed through, and which were not noticed in the narratives of the several parties [who] were employed in exploring it, I shall now briefly state, with such reflections as were consequent thereon.

The length of coast from point Mudge to this station, about thirty-two leagues, forms a channel which, though narrow, is fair and navigable; manifested by the adverse winds obliging us to beat to windward every foot of the channel, and to perform a complete traverse from shore to shore through its whole extent, without meeting the least obstruction from rocks or shoals. The great depth of water not only here, but that which is generally found washing the shores of this very broken and divided country, must ever be considered as a very peculiar circumstance, and a great inconvenience to its navigation. We however found a sufficient number of stopping places to answer all our purposes, and, in general, without going far out of our way. In coming from the westward, through Johnstone's straits, the best channel into the gulf of Georgia in thick weather might, though not easily, be mistaken. Such error however may be avoided, by keeping the southern shore close on board, which is compact, and so steep that it may be passed within a few yards in the greatest safety; indeed I have every reason to believe the whole of the passage to be equally void of dangers that do not evidently shew themselves. The height of the land that composes these shores and the interior country, has been already stated to decrease as we proceeded westward. The land on the southern side, which is an extensive island, appeared to be the most elevated, composed of very lofty mountains, whose summits, not very irregular, were still in some places covered with snow. The northern side, for a considerable distance, seemed less elevated, and the intire forest that covered its surface, might have favored the belief of great fertility, had we not known that pine trees innumerable are produced from the fissures and chasms of the most barren rocks, of which, we had great reason to suppose, the whole of the country before us was composed. Its low appearance may possibly be occasioned by its being much divided by water, as we evidently saw, through an opening, about four miles only to the westward of that appointed for our rendezvous, a much greater space so occupied, than that which comprehended these straits. Our general view to the northward, was, however, bounded by a mountainous country, irregular in the height of its eminences, and some of them capped with snow. The retired hills of the most eastern part of the straits, were, as we passed, so obscured by the high steep rocky cliffs of the shores, that we were unable to describe them with any precision. As the elevation of the northern shore decreased, I was in expectation of seeing a continuation of that lofty and connected range of snowy mountains, which I have repeatedly had reason to consider, as the insurmountable barrier to any extensive inland navigation. Herein I was disappointed, as this lofty structure either decreases in its vast degree of elevation, or it extends in a more inland direction.

The residence of all the natives we had seen, since our departure from point Mudge, was uniformly on the shores of this extensive island, forming the southern side of Johnstone's straits, which seems not only to be as well inhabited as could be expected in this uncultivated country, but infinitely more so, than, we had reason to believe, the southern parts of New Georgia were. This fact established, it must be considered as singularly remarkable, that, on the coast of the opposite or continental shore, we did not discover even a vestige of human existence, excepting the deserted villages! This circumstance, though it countenances the idea of the original inhabitants of the interior country having migrated, fallen by conquest, or been destroyed by disease; still leaves us unable to adduce any particular reason as the cause of this evident depopulation. The width of the passage scarcely anywhere exceeding two miles, can hardly have induced the inhabitants of the northern side, to quit their dwellings for a residence on the opposite shore, merely for the purpose of being that small distance nearer to the commerce of the sea-coast. On regarding the aspect of the two situations, and on reflecting that the winter season under this parallel must be severe and inclement, it appears reasonable to suppose, that any human beings, not restrained in fixing their abode, would not hesitate to choose the very opposite side to that which is here preferred, where, in general, their habitations front a bleak northern aspect, with mountains rising so perpendicularly behind them, that, if they do not totally, they must in a great measure, exclude the cheering rays of the sun for some months of the year. The northern side labors not under this disadvantage, and enjoying the genial warmth denied to the other, at certain seasons, most probably, possesses the requisites necessary to their present mode of life, at least in an equal degree; especially, as this country has, in no instance, received the advantages of cultivation. This would appear to be the situation of choice, the other of necessity; for the same source of subsistence, which is evidently the sea, affords equal supplies to the inhabitants of either shore. And that there was a time, when they resided on both, is clearly proved, by their deserted habitations, yet in existence, on the northern shore.

As neither *Maquinna*, nor any of his people, were at this village, I intrusted to the brother of a man named *Kaowitee*, who seemed next of importance to *Cheslakees*, the letter I received from Señor Galiano, as also one from myself, to be forwarded to Señor Quadra at Nootka, which this man undertook to deliver, on the promise of being handsomely rewarded for his service.

The sandy island, by my observations, is situated in latitude 50° 35½′, longitude 232° 57′; the variation of the compass here being 20° 45′ eastwardly.

CHAPTER XI

THE VESSELS IN DANGER ON THE ROCKS IN QUEEN CHARLOTTE SOUND

[July, 1792.] [Original Journal, Pages 279-280, Book II, Chapter IX.]

HAVING replaced our broken anchor with a new one from out of the hold, which had employed the whole of the preceding day, about ten in the forenoon of Saturday the 21st we proceeded with a favorable breeze from the westward, to the appointed rendezvous, that lies from the sandy island N. 89 E. at the distance of about fourteen miles, where, at three in the afternoon, we anchored in twenty fathoms water, sandy bottom, about a cable's length from the shore, of a similar nature to those already described.

Wishing to acquire some idea of the probable extent of this opening, I left the ship after dinner, and was not a little surprized to find it communicate with the extensive space of water, to the north of the channel or straits already mentioned, making the land under which we were at anchor, an island about a league and a half long, nearly in a direction N. 70 W. with many rocky islets and rocks lying about its western extremity, some along its north side, and others off the east end. Northward of this island, and a chain of others which lie to the westward of it, an arm of the sea, not less than four or five leagues across, stretched westward towards the ocean, where the horizon, in that direction, appeared to be intercepted only by a few small islands; the eastern and northern shores seemed wholly composed of rocky islands and rocks, and presented in their examination a very laborious task, to ascertain the continental boundary. But as this important line had been already determined to the entrance of an opening, not more than three leagues to the eastward of our present station, now under the survey of Mr. Broughton in the *Chatham*, and as a branch of this opening to the eastward of us took a direction that way through a multitude of islands, any investigation of this broken country was rendered unnecessary, until I should understand how far the *Chatham* had been able to succeed in fixing the continuation of the continental shore.

Our very inactive, unpleasant situation, whilst we anxiously waited the arrival of our consort, was somewhat relieved by the visits of a few Indians from the southern shore of the straits, who brought us a small supply of fish, very acceptable, being unable to obtain any by our own efforts. Among the number of our visitors we were honored with the company of *Cheslakees*, with those importunities for various articles I had with pleasure complied. He remained on board most part of the day; and as he sat at my elbow whilst writing, saw me frequently advert to a small memorandum book, which he managed to take away in the most dexterous manner, unperceived. Having occasion for its use, and knowing no other person had been near me, the purloiner could not be mistaken. A Sandwich island mat which I had given him, he had contrived to fold up in a very small compass, and in the center of it was the missing book. He appeared somewhat ashamed at the detection, but more mortified at my taking away the presents he had received; these were however, about two hours afterwards restored, on his contrition, and penitential application. Stealing a book, incapable of being in the least degree serviceable to him, or useful to any other person than the owner, strongly marked that natural inordinate propensity to thieving, which, with few exceptions, influences the whole of the uncivilized world, as if impelled by mere instinct, and destitute of reason, they were unable to restrain such inclinations.

Without any occurrence of an interesting nature, we remained uncomfortably idle until the arrival of Mr. Broughton in the afternoon of Friday the 27th, who came on board in his cutter, the *Chatham* having been obliged, by adverse winds, to anchor the preceding evening three leagues to the westward of our rendezvous.

OF PUGET SOUND

Mr. Broughton informed me, that after he had entered the opening he had been sent to examine, the eastern point of which is situated in latitude 50° 32', longitude 233° 32', he found it take an irregular course towards the N. E. passing a narrow branch leading to the westward. This opening, about a mile in width, occupied their attention until sunset, when they anchored at its head in 35 fathoms water, and found it to terminate like the many others already described, in latitude 50° 42½', longitude 234° 3½': which, after Sir John Call, was named CALL'S CHANNEL. On the evening of the next day they reached the narrow branch leading to the westward, which lies from their last place of anchorage S. 68 W. about four leagues distant. Here the *Chatham* stopped for the night in 17 fathoms water, near a small village of the natives, who brought them an abundance of fresh salmon. Mr. Broughton examined this narrow branch, and found it communicating with an arm of the sea in latitude 50° 43', longitude 233° 33', just navigable for the *Chatham;* and with the assistance of a strong flood tide, and their boats, they passed it the next morning, through a channel that continued for about half a league, not a hundred

---

Sir John Call. The name of Call's Channel has been changed on the British Columbia maps to Call's Creek. It lies south of Knight Inlet.

John Call was the son of John Call of Launcells, Cornwall, and was born at Fenny Park, near Tiverton, in 1732. When about seventeen he was taken as secretary by Benjamin Robins, the celebrated mathematician who was appointed chief-engineer and captain-general of artillery in the East India Company's settlements. They arrived in India in 1750. Robins died in 1751. War broke out and Call was rapidly advanced in the work of engineering under Clive, becoming engineer-in-chief. He became a member of the governor's council and was recommended by Clive for the governorship of Madras. On receiving news of his father's death he returned home against the advice of Clive. In 1771 he served as high sheriff of Cornwall. In 1782 Lord Shelburne, Prime Minister, employed him on a commission to inquire into the state of the crown lands, woods, and forests. Moving to London, he desired to become a member of Parliament, and in 1784 was unanimously returned for Callington, near his country residence. He was created a baronet on July 28, 1790. He was a Fellow of the Royal Society and of the Society of Antiquaries. He became totally blind in 1795 and died of apoplexy in London on March 1, 1801.

yards wide. The shallowest water, from three fathoms, gradually increased to seven fathoms, as they approached the arm of the sea, which is about two miles wide, and extends in an east and west direction. Here the *Chatham* anchored, and Mr. Broughton pursued its eastern course in his boat along the continental shore, leaving a branch leading to the northward, near the entrance of which are two islands and some rocks. This arm of the sea continued a little to the northward of east, six leagues, to the latitude of 50° 45′, where its width increased to near a league, taking an irregular northerly direction to its final termination in latitude 51° 1′, longitude 234° 13′. To this, after Captain Knight of the navy, Mr. Broughton gave the name of KNIGHT'S CHANNEL. The shores of it, like most of those

---

Sir John Knight. Lieutenant Broughton honored his friend, Captain Knight, on this occasion. He also honored the same man by naming after him an island he discovered southeast of New Zealand. This is not strange when the history of the two men is studied. Sixteen years before, Broughton was a midshipman and Knight was second Lieutenant on the *Falcon* sloop. This sloop was one of the vessels that covered the attack on Bunker's Hill. In the early part of 1776, while attempting to destroy a schooner which had been driven ashore in Cape Ann Harbor, Knight and Broughton were made prisoners. Here is the bond that endeared these two men to each other.

John Knight was born at Dundee about 1748. He entered the navy in 1758 in the Tartar frigate commanded by his father and was in the expedition against St. Malo and Cherbourg under Lord Howe. After the peace of 1763 he served in the *Romney*, carrying the flag of Lord Colville on the North American coast. He was promoted to be lieutenant on May 25, 1770. He was exchanged from the American prison and was appointed by Howe to command the *Harlem*, hired ship, against the American coasting trade. He returned to England in 1778 and two years later went with Hood to the West Indies, where he received post rank on September 21, 1781. He served under Hood and then under Mann as captain of the *Barfleur* in the years 1793, 1794, and 1795. In the *Montagu* he had an unpleasant experience during the mutiny at Nore. The crew took the surgeon, tarred and feathered him, and then rowed him through the fleet and put him on shore with other obnoxious officers. After the mutiny the *Montagu* took a prominent part in the battle of Camperdown. His next service was on the coast of Ireland in 1798 and in the blockade of Brest in 1799–1800.

On January 1, 1801, he was promoted to the rank of Rear-Admiral and in 1805 he succeeded Sir Richard Brickerton at Gibraltar. He became Vice-

ADMIRAL JOHN KNIGHT.
From an engraving by Ridley after the painting by Smart. From the collection of Augustin Rischgitz, London.

lately surveyed, are formed by high stupendous mountains rising almost perpendicularly from the water's edge. The dissolving snow on their summits produced many cataracts that fell with great impetuosity down their barren rugged sides. The fresh water that thus descended gave a pale white hue to the channel, rendering its contents intirely fresh at the head, and drinkable for twenty miles below it. This dreary region was not, however, destitute of inhabitants, as a village was discovered a few miles from its upper extremity, which seemed constructed like that described in Desolation sound, for defence; the inhabitants were civil and friendly. Near this place Mr. Broughton joined the *Chatham* on the morning of the 23d, and proceeded in her towards the branch above mentioned, leading to the northward. This in the evening he reached, and anchored for the night in 75 fathoms water. The next morning its course was pursued about three leagues towards the N. E. where this direction terminated in latitude 50° 51½′, longitude 233° 49′, from whence it irregularly stretched to the N. W. and westward. Inhabitants were still found on these inhospitable shores, who brought fish and skins of the sea-otter to sell, demanding in return blue great coats. A passage through this channel was accomplished on the 25th, notwithstanding the wind was very fickle and blew hard in squalls, attended with much lightning, thunder, and rain: the night was nearly calm, gloomy, and dark; and not being able to gain soundings, although within thirty yards of the rocky shores, they were driven about as the current of the tides directed, and happily escaped, though surrounded on all sides by innumerable rocks and rocky islets. On the 26th, the boundary of the continent was determined to a point, which, from its appearance and situation, obtained the name of DEEP SEA BLUFF, in latitude 50° 52′, longitude 232° 29′. This station Mr. Broughton judged to be as far to the westward as the

---

Admiral on November 9, 1805, and Admiral on December 4, 1813. He was made a Knight-Commander of the Bath on January 2, 1815. He died on June 16, 1831.

appointed rendezvous; and for the purpose of repairing thither, directed his course to the south-westward, through a channel that bore every appearance of leading to the sea, as had been understood from the natives. With the assistance of a fresh gale from the N. E. he shortly arrived at its southern entrance, which presented the opening I had seen on the day we arrived at this station. Across it his course was directed to the southward, leaving between his present track and the route he had pursued to the northward, an extensive cluster of islands, rocky islets, and rocks. These, in commemoration of his discovery, I distinguished by the name of BROUGHTON'S ARCHIPELAGO.

William Robert Broughton. An experience of Broughton while midshipman on the *Falcon* has already been related in the sketch of Sir John Knight, with whom he was made a prisoner in the American Revolution. His commission as lieutenant is signed by Chatham, Arden, Hood, and A. Gardner. On December 28, 1790, he was given the following document, signed by Richard Hopkins, Arden, and Hood of the Board of Admiralty:—
"Whereas we think fit that you shall command His Majesty's Armed Tender the *Chatham* at Deptford, you are hereby required and directed to repair forthwith on board the said Tender and take upon you the charge and command of her accordingly, her officers and company being hereby strictly required to observe and follow your orders; and you are strictly required to observe and execute the General Printed Instructions and such orders and directions as you shall at any time receive from us or any other your superior officer of His Majesty's Service. For which this shall be your Warrant."

After the expedition had explored Puget Sound and vicinity, Broughton, in the *Chatham*, explored the Columbia River, discovered and named by the American, Robert Gray, earlier in the same year, 1792. On reaching Monterey, Vancouver decided to send Broughton to England with dispatches. Señor Quadra agreed to help him on his way. He made the trip from San Blas to Vera Cruz overland and sailed thence to England. He was then made commander of the *Providence* and sent back into the North Pacific. Finding Vancouver gone, he crossed the ocean and explored the Asiatic coast. In 1804 he published the results of his work, a summary of which is given in the title as follows: "Voyage of Discovery to the North Pacific Ocean, in which the coast of Asia from the latitude of 35° N. to the latitude of 52° N., the island of Insu (commonly known under the name of the land of Jesso), the north, south, and east coasts of Japan, the Lieuxchieux and the adjacent isles, as well as the coast of Corea, have been examined and surveyed, performed in H. M. sloop *Providence* and her tender in the years 1795–6–7–8."

OF PUGET SOUND

[July, 1792.]

Whilst at this station, I had an opportunity of observing the latitude by five meridional altitudes of the sun to be 50°

In recognition of this important work and while it was in progress, on January 28, 1797, he was advanced to the rank of Captain. On May 16, 1797, the *Providence* was wrecked on a coral reef off the coast of Formosa. The crew was saved and the work was continued in the tender. In May, 1798, he was discharged at Trincomalee for passage to England, where he arrived in February, 1799.

In 1809 he commanded the *Illustrious* under Lord Gambier. In 1810 in the same ship he went out to the East Indies and was present at the reduction of the *Mauritius* in December of that year. He was in charge of the squadron that assembled at Malacca on June 11, 1811, to move against Java. Broughton is thought to have been too cautious. It was the beginning of August before troops were landed, and on August 9 Rear-Admiral Stopford arrived to take command of the squadron. Broughton did not like this and applied for a court-martial on the rear-admiral "for behaving in a cruel, oppressive, and fraudulent manner, unbecoming the character of an officer, in depriving me of the command of the squadron."

At the same time Lord Minto wrote in his private letters, "The little commodore's brief hour of authority came to an end, to the great relief of all in the fleet and army."

The Admiralty did not grant Broughton's request for a court-martial. He returned to England in 1812. He was made a Commander of the Bath.

The last years of his life were spent at Florence, Italy, where he died suddenly on March 12, 1821. The following entry is made in the Burial Register of the Old British Burial Ground, Leghorn, "Captain Broughton of the R.N. died in Florence on the 13th of March, 1821, and was buried on the 14th next following in the English Burial Ground at Leghorn by me Thomas Hall."

Over that grave has been erected a tombstone, a photograph of which was secured through the British Vice-Consul. Under the sculptured tiller and anchor crossed is the following comprehensive inscription: —

"Sacred to the memory of William Robert Broughton, Esq., Captain in the Royal Navy of England and Colonel of Marines. His professional career was honorable to himself and beneficial to his country, in two voyages of discovery he traversed the Pacific Ocean with the perseverance, intrepidity, and skill of a British seaman. On the intricate coast of Java, as commander in chief of the English squadron he steered the fleet to victory and secured that valuable island to his sovereign. After having braved and overcome danger for forty-seven years in the service of his country, on the 12th of March 1821 in the 59th year of his age, he died suddenly at Florence in the bosom of his family, to whom he was endeared by those qualities which ameliorate the evils and enliven the joys of domestic life. It is now the consolation, as it was the happiness of his afflicted widow and children, that to

35', its longitude 233° 19'. The variation of the compass, differing in eight sets of azimuths from 18° 30' to 23° 53', shewed a mean result of 20° 5', eastwardly variation. The tides were irregular, on some days being very rapid, on others scarcely perceptible; the rise and fall, the time of high water, and other fluctuations and irregularities, I attributed, as already stated, to the influence of the winds, and the operation of other local causes on this insulated region.

With a fresh breeze from the E. N. E. we directed our course to the westward, on the morning of Saturday the 28th, in order to proceed to the northward round the west end of this island. The channel through which we passed, though very unpleasant on account of the many rocks in it, is infinitely less dangerous than that to the eastward of the island, which is by no means advisable for ships to attempt.

We had not been long under weigh before we were joined by the *Chatham*, and steered to the northward for the channel leading to Deep Sea bluff, which I called FIFE'S PASSAGE. As we crossed the main arm the squally hazy weather permitted our seeing, but very imperfectly, the several islands and rocks that it contains. About two o'clock in the afternoon, we entered Fife's passage, and found its eastern point (named by me, after Captain Duff of the royal navy, POINT DUFF) situated in latitude 50° 48', longitude 233° 10'. A small rocky island lies off point Duff, covered with shrubs; and off the west point of this passage, named POINT GORDON, bearing N. 83 W. from point Duff,

---

the character of a brave and gallant officer was united in the object of their sorrow, that of a good Christian."

Broughton's Archipelago of the Vancouver chart has disappeared on the British Columbia map. The largest island in the group, however, retains the name of Broughton.

Fife's Passage, Point Duff, and Point Gordon. Here are three names which Vancouver gave to the headlands and the passage between them leading past the present Broughton Island into the waterway, part of which he had named Knight's Canal. All three of the names have disappeared from the recent British Columbia maps, unless the Gordon Group of Islands to the north and west are intended as a substitute for the old Point Gordon. It seems certain in selecting the names and placing them as he did Vancouver intended to

GRAVE OF CAPTAIN BROUGHTON.
In the English burial grounds at Leghorn, Italy.

are several white flat barren rocks lying at a little distance from the shore. Although the tide appeared to be in our favor, we made so little progress in this inlet, that we were compelled to anchor at five in the afternoon not more than two miles within the entrance, in 20 fathoms water, on the northern shore, near some small rocky islets. The shores that now surrounded us were not very high, composed of rugged rocks steep to the sea, in the chasms and chinks of which a great number of stunted or dwarf pine trees were produced. Some few of the natives favored us with their company, but brought little to dispose of; these were not quite so much painted as the Indians of *Cheslakee's* village, nor did they seem in the least acquainted with the Nootka language.

On Sunday morning the 29th, about nine, we were under sail, with a light favorable breeze, sufficient to have carried us at the rate of near a league per hour; yet the ship remained stationary and ungovernable, not answering to her helm in any direction. In this very unpleasant and disagreeable situation, attributed by us to a kind of under tow, or counter tide, we continued until near dark, when a most powerful breeze springing up, we reached Deep Sea bluff, and anchored about eleven at night in a small opening on its

---

honor old families of English nobility which had interlocked by marriage. He makes the point that the name of Duff was given in honor of Captain Duff of the Royal Navy. That simplifies one case and helps to solve the others. Vice-Admiral Duff died in that rank in 1787 before Vancouver sailed, so he could not have been the captain referred to in 1792. But he had married, in 1764, Helen, the daughter of his cousin, the Earl of Fife. The present Duke of Fife says he is without information concerning his gallant ancestor. It is known that Admiral Duff had numerous children, and one of them must have caused the names of Duff and Fife to appear on the chart of Vancouver. There is a swarm of Gordons in English history, and in trying to pick the one honored by Vancouver the effort becomes largely a matter of conjecture. In support of the above theory there is found such a name as Sir Alexander Cornewall Duff-Gordon and his famous wife, Lady Duff-Gordon. There is a long line of Scotch marquises and dukes by the name of Gordon, and it is possible that Alexander, fourth Duke of Gordon, who was living in Vancouver's day, was the man honored.

western side in 70 fathoms water; having passed a more extensive one to the south of this, which took its direction to the N. W. On the next day, Monday the 30th, this appeared a very small branch of the sea; and as it was now manifest there was no certainty in confiding in appearances, directions were given that both vessels should be removed higher up near to a convenient spot for recruiting our wood and water; whilst, in the yawl, I proceeded to examine whither this arm was likely to lead. It continued about four miles from Deep Sea bluff to the north-eastward, then stretched to the westward, and terminated behind the hill under which the vessels were at anchor, about two miles to the westward of them, forming a narrow isthmus, over which we walked, and had a distinct view of the opening before mentioned, extending to the westward. Being perfectly satisfied on this head, I returned, and found the vessels at the appointed station, riding in 30 fathoms water near the western shore, conveniently situated for procuring the only supplies this dreary region seemed likely to afford. But, as tolerably secure anchorage was not on all occasions to be found, I determined the vessels should remain stationary here, whilst the boats explored the broken country before us; which promised to furnish other passages, into the great western channel we had quitted, and bore every appearance of leading to the Pacific Ocean.

The *Discovery's* yawl, launch and cutter, were ordered to be equipped, and in readiness to depart at day-light the next morning. Mr. Broughton accompanied me, attended by lieutenant Puget in the launch, and Mr. Whidbey in the cutter. On Tuesday the 31st, at sunrise, our little squadron put off with intention of following up the continental shore, until we might find a more western passage leading to the sea; there to appoint a rendezvous for the launch and cutter, which were to continue the examination of the continental boundary, whilst we returned to conduct the vessels to the appointed station.

From Deep Sea bluff, the shore of the main, across this small opening, took a direction N. 50 W. for about four miles; then extended N. N. E. about a league to a point, where the arm took a more easterly course, passing an island, and several rocky islets, forming passages for boats only; whilst, to the westward of the island, the main channel was a mile in width, and no doubt was entertained of our there finding a greater depth of water than we required for the vessels. We were however obliged to quit the direction of that which appeared, and afterwards proved to be the main channel, to pursue the continental line along this, which apparently led to the N. E. and eastward. In this route, a poor unfortunate deer, that seemed to have eluded the pursuers, had found an asylum in a small recess on the rocky precipice forming the shore, about twenty yards in a direction almost perpendicular to the water, from whence he could only escape by the way he had come. In this very exposed situation, the two headmost boats passed him unnoticed; but, on the third making the discovery, a platoon of muskets was discharged at the defenceless animal by the whole party without effect. On this a seaman landed, and, with a boat-hook, dragged him from the rocks by the neck, and secured to us this valuable acquisition. Upwards of twenty muskets on this occasion were fired, seven of which hit him, but no one mortally; or wounded him in such a manner as to have prevented his escaping, had not the overhanging precipices of the rocks rendered it impossible. Venison had long with us been a scarce commodity; our buck proved excellent, and afforded us all one or two excellent fresh meals.

We pursued the examination of this arm to its head in latitude $51°$, longitude $233° \ 46'$; where it terminated in a similar way to the many before described. Its shores, about a mile apart, were composed of high steep craggy mountains, whose summits were capped with snow; the lower cliffs, though apparently destitute of soil, produced many pine trees, that seemed to draw all their nourishment out of the solid rock. The water, near four leagues from its upper end, was of a very light chalky color, and nearly fresh. From its shores two small branches extended, one winding about four miles to the S. E. and S. W. the other about a league to the N. N. W. The examination of this branch employed us until noon the next day, Wednesday the 1st of August, when we pursued that which appeared to be the main channel leading to the westward, having several rocky islets and rocks off its north point of entrance. This I called POINT PHILIP, lying N. 56 W. from Deep Sea bluff, at the distance of not more than eight miles. So tardy was our progress in fixing the boundary of this broken continental shore, which we traced from point Philip, about two leagues in the direction of N. 78 W. when it again became divided into various

---

Sir Philip Stevens. The names of Point Philip and Mount Stephens, after Sir Philip Stevens, seem among the most appropriate of the honors conferred by Vancouver. Stephens was comparatively humble, but he was an exceedingly useful man and one, also, whom the officers of the navy of that day must have held in high esteem. His record of thirty-two years, from June 18, 1763, to March 3, 1795, as secretary of the Board of Admiralty, has never been equalled. During those years he must have become acquainted with every officer in the Royal Navy.

He came from a family settled for many generations at Eastington in Gloucestershire. His father was Nathaniel Stephens, Rector of Alphamstone in Essex, and there the youngest son, Philip, was born in 1725. The boy was educated at the free school at Harwich, and while still a lad he got a position as clerk in the navy victualling office as his older brother had done before him.

Rear-Admiral (afterward Lord) Anson, on returning from his voyage around the world was attracted to young Stephens and had him moved to the Admiralty. He also had him for a time as his own secretary. While devoting his life to the Admiralty in a secretary's place he received some honors.

He was elected a Fellow of the Royal Society on June 6, 1771, and from 1768 to 1806 he represented Sandwich in Parliament. In 1795, when he applied for permission to resign from his position with the Admiralty, he was on March 17 created a baronet and was also appointed one of the Lords of the Admiralty. By a special recommendation on October 15, 1806, at the age of eighty-one, he was granted a pension of £1500, which he enjoyed till his death on November 20, 1809. His heirs died before him, and the baronetcy thus became extinct.

The portrait used for this work has under it, in the original engraving, this legend: "Painted by W. Beechey R.A. Painter to Her Majesty. Published as the Act directs 5th April 1798 by Captain James Colnett R.N. Engraved by J. Collyer A.R.A. Engraver to Her Majesty."

SIR PHILIP STEPHENS.

From the engraving by J. Collyer after the painting by Sir William Beechey. Photograph from the collection of Augustin Rischgitz, London.

channels. The most spacious one, leading to the southwestward, presented an appearance of communicating with the sea. The shores, on all sides, were high, steep and rocky; though they seemed tolerably well clothed with pines of different sorts.

We kept the continental shore on board through a very intricate narrow branch that took a direction E. by N. for near two leagues, and then terminated as usual at the base of a remarkable mountain, conspicuous for its irregular form, and its elevation above the rest of the hills in its neighborhood. This I have distinguished in my chart by the name of MOUNT STEPHENS, in honor of Sir Philip Stephens of the Admiralty. It is situated in latitude 51° 1′, longitude 233° 20′, and may serve as an excellent guide to the entrance of the various channels with which this country abounds.

As we prosecuted our researches, we visited a small Indian village situated on a rocky islet. The whole of it was nearly occupied, well constructed for its protection, and rendered almost inaccessible by platforms similar to that before described though not so strong, nor so ingeniously designed. The inhabitants did not exceed thirty or forty persons, who exactly corresponded with those seen to the southward of Deep Sea bluff, and from whom we met with, as usual, a very cordial reception. A few indifferent seaotter skins, for which they demanded more iron than we were inclined to give, comprehended all their stock in trade; they had a distant knowledge of a few words of the Nootka language, but did not always seem properly to apply them. The narrow passage by which we had entered, is a channel admissible for boats only; and thence, to the foot of mount Stephens, was merely a chasm in the mountains, caused, probably, by some violent efforts of nature. This idea originated in its differing materially in one particular from all the channels we had hitherto examined; namely, in its having regular soundings, not exceeded the depth of 13 fathoms, although its shores, like all those of the channels which had no bottom within the reach of line, were formed by perpendicular cliffs, from their snowy summits to the water's edge.

The stupendous mountains on each side of this narrow chasm, prevented a due circulation of air below, by excluding the rays of the sun; whilst the exhalations from the surface of the water and the humid shores wanting rarefaction, were, in a great measure, detained, like steam in a condensed state; the evaporation thus produced a degree of cold and chillness which rendered our night's lodging very unpleasant.

We quitted this unwholesome situation, at the dawning of the next day, Thursday the 2d, and directed our course through another passage, which, from the northern shore, led about a league to the westward, and then turned to the south. This channel is excessively dangerous, owing to the number of rocky islets, sunken rocks, and, by the tides setting through it with great rapidity and irregularity. By breakfast time we reached the opening leading to the south-westward, about half a league from the village we had visited the preceding day. Here I intended to conclude my excursion as soon as a place of rendezvous for the vessels and boats should be found; in quest of which we proceeded down the opening leading to the south-westward; which I called WELLS's PASSAGE; this now seemed, on a certainty, to communicate with the great channel, which we supposed to lead to sea. But another branch soon appearing, that stretched a little to the south-westward of west, I was in

---

Wells's Passage. The name still appears on the recent British Columbia maps as Wells Pass, extending between Broughton Island and the mainland. No such name appears on the muster books of the *Discovery* or the *Chatham.* Vancouver is silent as to the source of the name. When he left England there was living in London a doctor, William Charles Wells (1757-1817), who was born in South Carolina of Scotch parents, but who had returned to Great Britain at the outbreak of the American Revolution. He was a noted student and observer, receiving the Rumford medal of the Royal Society for his explanation of the phenomena of dew. There was also a William Frederick Wells (1762-1836), a native water-color artist. It is possible that one of these was the man complimented by Vancouver.

[August, 1792.]

hopes my object would have been further attained, by finding some more westerly station for our rendezvous than the end of Wells's passage. In this hope we continued our examination about two leagues, leaving some part of the shore to the north of us, not fully explored. On landing to dine about the time of high water, we soon perceived a rapid ebb tide coming from the westward. This rendered a communication with the ocean in that direction, if not impossible, at least very improbable; and as the time its examination was likely to engage from its apparent extent, might render my design ineffectual, I determined to return, leaving the launch and cutter to carry on the survey. Our future meeting I appointed near the west point of Wells's passage; this, after Captain Boyles of the navy, I named POINT BOYLES; it is situated in latitude 50° 51′, and in longitude 232° 52′.

About one o'clock the next day, Friday the 3d, we arrived on board, and immediately proceeded with the vessels toward the rendezvous, but so slowly that it was not till the evening of Saturday the 4th, that we arrived within two leagues to the S. E. of it. There the boats joined us, and the want of wind obliged us to anchor in 60 fathoms water, on the S. W. side of a low island, about half a league from its shores, bearing by compass from N. 42 E. to N. 38 W.; point Duff N. 87 E.; the land of the southern shore from S. 50 to S. 22 W.; a high island appearing to lie nearly in mid-channel, from S. 55 W. to S. 64 W.; and point Boyles N. 84 W.; having many rocky islets and rocks in view, too numerous to be here noticed.

I now became acquainted, that the officers had returned, as directed, to the examination of the continental shore from the place where I had quitted it, and on pursuing it to the southward, they had found it indented with small bays, that afforded, like the narrow arm before mentioned, snug and

---

Captain Boyles, R.N. This captain evidently did not attain high rank or fame, as his name does not appear in the usual biographical collections. No trace of his career has thus far been found.

convenient anchorage; but the passages into them were intricate and dangerous, owing to the strong currents, and the many rocky islets, and sunken rocks, in their neighborhood. The arm, leading to the westward, that I had been in, was traced to the latitude of 50° 59′, longitude 232° 36′. In it were many rocky islands and sunken rocks; which, with the velocity of the tide, rendered it dangerous, even for the navigation of boats. Near its termination, they pursued a very narrow opening on its northern shore, winding towards the E. N. E. replete with overfalls and sunken rocks, and ending by a cascade similar to several that had before been observed. These are perfectly salt, and seem to owe their origin to the tidal waters, which, in general, rise seventeen feet, and, at high water, render these falls imperceptible, as the bar of obstruction, at that time, lies from four to six feet beneath the surface of the sea, and consequently at low water causes a fall of ten or twelve feet; some of which are twenty yards in width. One of these Mr. Whidbey ascended nearly at low water, and found the internal reservoir to be a small lake, or rather a large pond, seemingly of deep water, divided into several branches, winding some distance through a low, swampy, woodland country. These salt-water cascades may probably be occasioned by the great rapidity of the tides, after they have risen above these obstructions, (acting with considerable pressure) and rushing forward in those inland narrow channels, where they soon overflow the plain, and, finding an extensive field for their expansion, a sufficient quantity of water, with the addition of the drains and springs of the country, is thus collected, to replenish these reservoirs every twelve hours, and to cause a constant fall during the reflux of the tide. Within a few yards of one of these cascades was discovered a considerable stream of *warm* fresh water.

By this expedition, the continental shore was traced to the westernmost land in sight. We had now only to proceed along it, as soon as the wind and weather would permit our moving. This, however, a thick fog and a calm prevented, until the afternoon of Sunday the 5th, when a light breeze between S. W. and west enabled us, by sunset, to advance about two leagues to the westward of point Boyles, which, by compass, bore from us S. 85 W.; an island, previously considered to lie in mid-channel, but now discovered to be divided into four or more islets, S. 38 E.; the most distant part of the opposite shore south, four or five leagues off; and the nearest taken by us to be an island, W. S. W. about a league. These positions are not, however, to be received as correct, because the fog, still continuing, alternately obscured place after place, in the southern quarters, so as to render it impracticable either to acquire the true position, or even gain a distant view of those shores. The northern, or continental side, was not in the like manner obscured; its nearest part bore by compass north about half a league from us; and its western extremity, N. 78 W. Between this point and a cluster of islands, bearing west, a channel appeared to lead along the coast of the main land, in which were some small islets and rocks; south of the cluster, the haze and fog rendered it impossible to determine of what that region principally consisted, though the imperfect view we obtained, gave it the appearance of being much broken. In this situation, we had 60 and 70 fathoms, muddy bottom; but as we had sufficient space to pass the night in under sail, I preferred so doing, that we might be ready to pursue the above-mentioned channel in the morning.

The wind continuing light in the S. W. quarter, we plied until day-break of Monday 6th, when the breeze was succeeded by a calm, and a very thick fog that obscured every surrounding object until noon, without our being able to gain soundings; so that we were left to the mercy of the currents, in a situation that could not fail to occasion the most anxious solicitude. The fog had no sooner dispersed, than we found ourselves in the channel for which I had intended to steer, interspersed with numerous rocky islets and rocks, extending from the above cluster of islands towards the shore of the continent. The region to the S. W. still remained obscured by the fog and haze; at intervals, however, something of it might be discerned, serving only to shew there was

VANCOUVER'S DISCOVERY

no great probability of our finding a less intricate passage to navigate, than that immediately before us along the continental shore; which must either be now traced by the ship, or by the boats on a future occasion. This made me determine on the former mode, although there was reason to apprehend it would engage our utmost attention, even in fair weather to preserve us from latent dangers. The dispersion of the fog was attended by a light breeze from the N. N. W., and as we stood to windward, we suddenly grounded on a bed of sunken rocks about four in the afternoon. A signal indicating our situation was immediately made to the *Chatham*, she instantly anchored in fifty fathoms water, about a cable and half distant from us, and we immediately received all her boats to our assistance. The stream anchor was carried out, and an attempt made to heave the ship off, but to no effect. The tide fell very rapidly; and the force with which the ship had grounded, had occasioned her sewing considerably forward. On heaving, the anchor came home, so that we had no resource left but that of getting down our topmasts, yards, etc., etc. shearing up the vessel with spars and spare topmasts, and lightening her as much as possible, by starting the water, throwing overboard our fuel and part of the ballast we had taken on board in the spring. Soon after the ship was aground, the tide took her on the starboard quarter; and as she was afloat abaft it caused her to take a sudden swing, and made her heel so very considerably on the starboard side, which was from the rocks, that her situation, for a few seconds, was alarming in the highest degree. The shoars were got over with all possible dispatch, but notwithstanding this, by the time it was low water, the starboard main chains were within three inches of the surface of the sea. Happily, at this time, there was not the smallest swell or agitation, although we were in the immediate vicinity of the ocean. This must ever be regarded as a very providential circumstance, and was highly favorable to our very irksome and perilous situation, in which, under the persuasion of the tide falling as low as had been lately observed in our several boat expeditions, nothing short of immediate

SLOOP *DISCOVERY* ON THE ROCKS IN QUEEN CHARLOTTE SOUND.

From the steel engraving by B. T. Pouncy in Vancouver's Journal. Drawn by W. Alexander from a sketch on the spot by Zachary Mudge.

and inevitable destruction presented itself, until towards the latter part of the ebb tide, when more than one half of the ship was supported by such a sufficient body of water, as, in a great measure, to relieve us from the painful anxiety that so distressing a circumstance necessarily occasioned. When the tide was at the lowest, about nine at night, the ship's fore foot was only in about three and a half feet water, whilst her stern was in four fathoms.

In this melancholy situation, we remained, expecting relief from the returning flood, which to our inexpressible joy was at length announced by the floating of the shoars, a happy indication of the ship righting. Our exertions to lighten her were, however, unabated, until about two in the morning of Tuesday the 7th; when the ship becoming nearly upright, we hove on the stern cable, and, without any particular efforts, or much strain, had the inexpressible satisfaction of feeling her again float, without having received the least apparent injury. We brought up in 35 fathoms water, about a quarter of a mile from the bed of rocks from whence we had so providentially escaped. After about three hours rest, all hands were employed in the re-equipment of the ship. The main top-gallant top-rope unluckily broke, and by this accident, John Turner, a seaman, had his arm fractured. By noon, the hold was restowed, and the ship, in every respect, ready again to proceed.

A light breeze springing up from the S. W. about one o'clock, we were again under sail, and knowing of no safer channel, we directed our course through that before us, along the continental shore. This was a narrow passage, and as we advanced, became more intricate by an increased number of rocky islets and rocks, as well beneath, as above the surface of the water; the former being ascertained by the surf breaking with some violence upon them. This dangerous navigation seemed to continue as far as was discernible towards the ocean, between the shore of the continent and the land forming the opposite side of the channel, which appeared to be an extensive range of islands.

Having so recently been preserved from the dangers of a

most perilous situation, the scene before us, in presenting a prospect of many such snares, was extremely discouraging. We had, however, not the least hope of finding a less difficult way for the execution of the adventurous service in which we were engaged; nor any alternative but to proceed with all the circumspection and caution that the nature of our situation would permit, through a channel not more than half a mile wide, bounded on one side by islands, rocks, and breakers, which in some places appeared almost to meet the continental shore on the other. However intricate, this was apparently the only navigable channel in the neighborhood. About five in the afternoon we had fortunately escaped through its narrowest part; the wind now became light and baffling; the ebb tide sat us towards the ocean, where we had a view of the distant horizon, although intercepted by the same rocky region that surrounded us in every direction. About six o'clock some of its hidden dangers arrested the progress of the *Chatham*. We instantly anchored in seventy fathoms water, and sent our boats to her assistance. Thus, before we had recovered from the fatiguing exertions and anxious solicitude of our distressing night, the endurance of a similar calamity was our portion for the next.

I had less reason at first to hope for the preservation of the *Chatham* under the circumstances of her disaster, than I had the preceding night for that of the *Discovery;* as the oceanic swell was here very perceptible, and caused a considerable surf on the shore. On the return of our small boat, I became acquainted that, in consequence of its having fallen calm, she had been driven by the tide on a ledge of sunken rocks, but had the consolation of hearing, that although she had frequently struck when lifted by the surge, it had not been violently; that no damage had yet been sustained; and that her present very uncomfortable situation could not be of long duration, as it was nearly half ebb when she grounded.

Our present anchorage bore by compass from the rocks, on which the *Discovery* had struck, though intercepted by various others, S. 42 E. five miles, and from the ledge of rocks on which the *Chatham* was then lying, S. 6 E. three miles distant. Our estimated latitude was 51° 2', longitude 232° 25'. Since the commencement of the month of August, the foggy weather had totally precluded our making any celestial observations; the situation therefore of the islands, coasts, rocks, etc., westward from Deep Sea bluff, could only be ascertained by an estimated protraction, which may be liable to errors we had no means to detect; hence this portion of intricate navigation is not to be implicitly depended upon in this particular, as exhibited by the chart; but the continued direction of the continental shore, (the nearest part now bearing by compass N. E. at the distance of about half a league) was positively ascertained to this station; and I trust, its latitude and longitude will not be found to deviate many miles from the truth.

The rocks between our present anchorage and the ocean having the appearance of being almost impenetrable, Mr. Whidbey was dispatched to discover the most safe channel for us to pursue. The day-light just served him to execute his commission; and on his return at night he informed me, that there were three passages; one nearly through the center of the rocks; another about midway between the continental shore, and a very broken country to the southward of us; and a third between the nearest cluster of rocks and the continent. This for a small distance seemed to be clear; but further to the north-westward a labyrinth of rocks appeared to stretch from the continent towards land, forming like two islands. These rocks nearly joined to the north-easternmost about nine miles from us, bearing by compass N. 50 W. the westernmost at about the same distance, N. 64 W.

The nearest cluster of rocks, whose southern part was almost in a line with the easternmost island, not quite a league from us, we were to pass to the south of; between them and other rocks and rocky islets, to the westward and S. W. forming a channel about two miles wide, in which no visible obstruction had been discovered by Mr. Whidbey. These rocks and rocky islets presented an appearance of being as nearly connected with the southern broken shore, as those further north did with the continent, giving us little to expect but a very intricate and hazardous navigation.

An extremely thick fog ushering in the morning of the 8th, precluded our seeing or knowing anything of the *Chatham's* situation; and obliged us to remain in the most painful state of suspense until about nine in the forenoon, when the fog in some measure dispersing, we had the satisfaction of seeing our consort approaching us under sail; and having a light southerly breeze, with the ebb tide in our favor, we immediately weighed in order to proceed together through the channel before mentioned between the rocks.

On the return of the boats, Lieutenant Baker, who had been with our people assisting the *Chatham* during the night, informed me that latterly she had struck so hard, as intirely to disable both the spare topmasts, which had been used for shoars: but that about half past one they succeeded in heaving her off, without the appearance of her having sustained any very material damage. Our sails were scarcely set when the wind became variable; and soon after mid-day partial fogs and a clear atmosphere succeeded each other in every direction. These by one o'clock obliged us again to anchor in fifty-five fathoms water, as did the *Chatham* about two miles to the northward of our former station, and within a quarter of a mile of the continued shore. Here we were detained until nine the following morning of Thursday the 9th, when with a light eastwardly breeze, and clear weather, we directed our course as before stated. On passing near the rocks on the eastern side of the channel, we had soundings at the depth of twenty-eight fathoms, rocky bottom; but immediately afterwards gained no ground with sixty and seventy fathoms of line. As it was my intention to seek a channel between the two islands, the *Chatham's* signal was made to lead. The wind being light we advanced slowly, passing some very dangerous rocks, whose situation was only to be known by the breakers upon them at low tide, lying about two miles to the S. E. of the north-easternmost island.

Though clear immediately overhead, the horizon was encumbered with partial fogs in every direction. This rendered the view of surrounding objects not less limited than undefined, and prevented such observations being made, as were necessary for ascertaining our positive situation. About noon we were becalmed between these islands, whose shores are about two miles and a half asunder; soundings were obtained at the depth of seventy fathoms, rocky bottom. They lie from each other about north and south; the southernmost is about a league in circuit, with a small island lying off its eastern extremity. The northernmost, instead of being one island, as had been supposed, was now found to comprehend eight or nine small islets, lying in a direction about N. 50 W. and occupying in that line an extent of four miles; their breadth about half, or perhaps three quarters of a mile. With the assistance of the boats a-head, we passed through this channel about one o'clock. At this time a light breeze springing up from the northwestward, we stood towards the southern shore; it was not however, as was usual with the north-westerly winds, attended with clear and pleasant weather, but with a remarkably thick fog; and having no soundings we were obliged to ply to windward under an easy sail until about five o'clock, when we gained bottom, and anchored in fifty-five fathoms water. The fog soon after cleared away, and discovered our situation to be near the southern shore, before a small opening at the distance of about a mile. This by compass bore S. 7 W.; a channel that appeared to stretch to the S. E. through the range of islands to the southward of that we had navigated, bore S. 80 E. and seemed tolerably clear of those dangers and impediments with which we had lately contended. The southernmost of the islands we had passed at noon bore by compass N. 7 E. at the distance of about a league; and the north-westernmost of the islets, N. 8 W. distant about two leagues; a low point of land forming the south point of an opening on the continental shore N. 14 W. a high distant mountain being the northernmost land in sight N. 30 W. and the westernmost land on the southern shore S. 55 W. Between these latter directions the oceanic horizon seemed perfectly clear and uninterrupted.

VANCOUVER'S DISCOVERY

[Original Journal, Page 308.]

[August, 1792.]

We now appeared to have reached the part of the coast that had been visited and named by several of the traders from Europe and India. The *Experiment*, commanded by Mr. S. Wedgborough, in August, 1786, honored the inlet through which we had lately passed, with the name of "QUEEN CHARLOTTE'S SOUND;" the opening on the con-

---

Queen Charlotte. Vancouver here states that the name of Queen Charlotte Sound was conferred by Mr. S. Wedgborough, commanding the *Experiment* in August, 1786. In Bancroft's Works, Volume XXVII, page 177, it is stated that the *Experiment* was commanded in 1786 by Captain Guise. Her companion was the ship *Captain Cook*, commanded by Captain Lowrie. Both ships were under the supervision of James Strange. He had brought the ships from India, where they were fitted for the fur trade by the merchants at Bombay. It was this expedition which left John McKey among the Indians. It was at his own request, but he was glad to sail away with Captain Barclay the next year. It was he who had learned from the Indians that Nootka was on a large island. To the north of Queen Charlotte Sound lie the Queen Charlotte Islands. They were discovered but not named by the Spaniard Juan Perez, in 1774. He named the northern point, now called North Point, Point Santa Margarita. In July, 1787, Captain George Dixon in the ship *Queen Charlotte*, the companion of Captain Nathaniel Portlock in the ship *King George*, rounded Cape St. James and sailed northward. He named the islands after his ship, and he called the waterway Dixon's Straits after himself. This, in brief, explains how the name of Queen Charlotte came so prominently into our northwestern geography.

Charlotte Sophia (1744–1818) was the youngest daughter of Charles Lewis, brother of Frederic, third Duke of Mecklenburg-Strelitz. It is supposed that the first attention drawn to her on the part of the English was on account of a letter she wrote to the king of Prussia, asking him to restrain his troops from despoiling the lands of her kinsman. Search was being made for a suitable bride for the young King George III. She accepted the proposal and journeyed to England. She saw the king for the first time on September 8, 1761, and later declared that from that hour until the king's first illness she never knew real sorrow. They were married late on that same day of the first meeting.

Horace Walpole describes her appearance at that time in this fashion: "She is not tall nor a beauty. Pale and very thin; but looks sensible and genteel. Her hair is darkish and fine; her forehead low, her nose very well, except the nostrils spreading too wide. The mouth has the same fault, but her teeth are good. She talks a great deal, and French tolerably."

She was domestic in life and tastes. She never discussed affairs of state even with her husband, the king. Scandal could only say of her that she was somewhat mean in money matters. In 1788, when the king became ill,

QUEEN CHARLOTTE.

From the painting by Allan Ramsay, now in the National Portrait Gallery, London. Engraving made in England for this work.

tinental shore was discovered, and called "SMITH'S INLET," by Mr. James Hanna, the same year; the high distant mountain that appeared to be separated from the main land, formed part of a cluster named by Mr. Duncan "CALVERT'S ISLANDS;" and the channel between them and the main land, was by Mr. Hanna called "FITZHUGH'S SOUND." These being the names given, as far as I could learn, by the first discoverers of this part of the coast, will be continued by me, and adopted in my charts and journal.

Destitute of any other authority, our estimated latitude in this situation was 51° 4' longitude 232° 8'. In the evening I visited the shores, and found the opening take a winding southerly direction, dividing the land most probably into two or more islands. Westward of the opening a sandy beach stretched along the coast, and afforded tolerably good shelter, with anchorage from six to twenty fathoms depth of water. Some detached rocks were observed to lie at a little distance from these shores.

Having a fine breeze from the eastward on the morning of Friday the 10th, we weighed at seven, and stood across Queen Charlotte's sound for the entrance of Smith's inlet. The *Chatham* being ordered to lead, at half past ten made the signal for soundings, at the depth of ten to eighteen fathoms. In this situation the island, near which the *Chatham* had grounded, bore S. 43 E. distant about six or seven leagues; and the labyrinth of rocks that before had appeared to extend along the continental shore, now seemed to exist no further than a low sandy point bearing by compass E. S. E. at the distance of about two leagues. The shores of the main from this point seemed free from rocks, and possessed some small sandy bays to the south point of entrance into Smith's inlet, which bore by compass N. 18 W. about a league

---

the care of his person and the household were placed in her hands, as was the case in 1810 when he became permanently insane. She bore the king fifteen children. She died at Kew on November 17, 1818, and was buried in St. George's Chapel, Windsor.

The portrait here used has already been referred to in the sketch of George III. It is by Ramsay and is in the National Portrait Gallery.

distant; where detached rocks were again seen to encumber the shore.

The weather, less unfavorable to our pursuits than for some time past, permitted our having a tolerably distinct view of the surrounding country. The opening before us, Fitzhugh's sound, appeared to be extensive in a northerly direction. At noon we found our observed latitude to be 51° 21', longitude 232° 4'. In this situation, the south point of Calvert's island bore by compass N. 29 W. its westernmost part in sight N. 60 W. two clusters of rocks S. 73 W. and N. 70 W. these were discovered by Mr. Hanna, who named the former "VIRGIN," the latter "PEARL ROCKS," both which being low, and at some distance from the shore, are dangerously situated. The south point of Smith's inlet terminating the continental shore in a north-westwardly direction, bore by compass S. 40 E. from which the Virgin rocks, about thirteen miles distant, lie N. 75 W. and the Pearl rocks N. 38 W. distant about eight miles.

Intending to continue the investigation of the continental shore up Smith's inlet, the *Chatham* was directed that way; but as we advanced, the great number of rocky islets and rocks, as well beneath as above the surface of the sea, and the irregularity of the soundings, induced me to abandon this design, and to steer along the eastern side of Calvert's island, forming a steep and bold shore, in quest of "Port Safety," laid down in Mr. Duncan's chart, or of any other convenient anchorage we might find; and from thence to dispatch two parties in the boats, one to prosecute the examination of the broken shores to the south-eastward of us, the other to explore the main branch of Fitzhugh's sound leading to the northward. In consequence of this determination, the necessary signal was made to the *Chatham* for quitting her pursuit; and we made all sail to the northward.

On passing that which we had considered as the south point of Calvert's island, it proved to be two small islets lying near it; and from the southernmost of them, the Virgin and Pearl rocks in a line lie S. 68 W. the former eleven, and the latter four miles distant.

OF PUGET SOUND

[August, 1792.]

As we proceeded up this sound, the eastern shore still continued to be much divided by water; towards the sea it was of moderate height, though the interior country was considerably elevated; the whole was apparently one intire forest of pine trees produced from the chasms in the rugged rocks of which the country is formed. The western, or shore of Calvert's islands is firm, and rose abruptly from the sea to a very great height, seemingly composed of the same rocky materials, and like the eastern shore, intirely covered with pine trees. About four in the afternoon of Saturday the eleventh, a small cove was discovered on the western shore, bearing some resemblance to Mr. Duncan's port Safety, but differing in its latitude according to our run since noon. Appearing however likely to answer all our purposes, we hauled in for it; the shores we found to be bold, steep on either side, and soundings at the entrance were from twenty-three to thirty fathoms, soft bottom. We anchored about six in the evening in seventeen fathoms on the south side of the cove, as did the *Chatham* on the opposite shore, steadying the vessels with hawsers to the trees. My first object after the ship was secured, was to examine the cove. It terminated in a small beach, near which was a stream of excellent water and an abundance of wood: of these necessaries we now required a considerable supply; and as the field of employment for our boats would be extensive, there was little doubt of our remaining here a sufficient time to replenish these stores. Being tolerably well sheltered in this cove, I was willing to hope the *Chatham* might with security, and without much difficulty, be laid on shore to examine if she had sustained any damage whilst striking on the rocks.

After giving directions for the execution of these services, I ordered the yawl, launch, and two cutters belonging to the *Discovery*, and the *Chatham's* cutter to be equipped, supplied with a week's provisions, and to be in readiness to depart early the next morning. The boats being prepared and supplied, agreeably to my wishes, we departed about five o'clock; and having proceeded together nearly into the middle of the sound, I directed Lieutenant Puget and Mr.

Whidbey, in the *Discovery's* launch and large cutter, to examine the coast we had left unexplored to the south-eastward, from the termination of the continent in its N. W. direction, to a certain point on the eastern shore, where Mr. Johnstone, in the *Chatham's* cutter, attended by Mr. Humphreys in the *Discovery's* small cutter, would commence his inquiry. Conceiving the northern survey would be infinitely more extensive than that to the south, I joined Mr. Johnstone's party, in order to fix on a rendezvous where, agreeably to my proposed plan, he would on his return find the vessels, or they would be on their way from the cove to the place so appointed.

Our separation had scarcely taken place, when our southerly breeze freshened to a brisk gale, attended by a torrent of rain. The wind however having favored our pursuit, we reached the eastern shore about five miles to the northward of the cove where the ships rode. It was low but compact, with one small opening only, impassable for our boats by breakers extending across it. On the westernside two conspicuous openings had been observed; the southernmost had the appearance of being a very fine harbor; the other, about two leagues further north, formed a passage to sea, in which were several rocky islets. About noon we arrived at the point where Mr. Johnstone's researches were to commence, nearly in the direction of north from the ships, and at the distance of about sixteen miles. From this point, the north point of the passage leading to the sea, lies S. 39 W. four miles distant; but the thick rainy weather prevented our seeing any objects that were to the northward. Increased torrents of rain, and thick stormy weather from the S. E. obliged us to take shelter in the first safe place we could discover, which presented itself in a small cove, about a mile from the point above mentioned, where we were very unpleasantly detained until near noon the following day, Sunday the 12th, when the wind having moderated, and the rain in some degree abated, we resumed our examination along the starboard or continental shore, extending from the above point about a league and a half in a north direction. Here the inlet divided into two capacious branches; that which appeared to be the principal one still continued its northerly course, the other stretched E. N. E. and was in general about a mile wide. In order to prosecute the survey of the continental shore, which I presumed this to be, the latter became the first object of our examination, for which we quitted the former, whose width we estimated at a league. The intermission of the rain was for a short time only; at three in the afternoon it again returned with such squally and unpleasant weather, that we were necessitated, at six, to take up our abode for the night on a long sandy beach, about eight miles within the entrance of this eastern branch. In the S. E. corner of this beach was the largest brook of fresh water we had yet seen on the coast. It bore a very high color, and emptied itself into the sea with considerable velocity. Here the mountains, which appeared to be a continuation of the snowy barrier from mount Stephens, retired a small distance from the beach, and the low land, occupying the intermediate space, produced pine trees of inferior growth, from a bed of moss and decayed vegetables in the state of turf, nearly as inflammable as the wood which it produced. A continuation of the unpleasant weather confined us to this uncomfortable spot until the afternoon of Monday the 13th; when, about four, we again proceeded up the branch, which, from the beach, took a direction N. by E.; the furthest point seen in that line was at the distance of about three leagues; this, after passing an extensive cove on the starboard side, we reached about nine at night. Excepting this cove, and that we had just before left, no other was seen; the sides of this channel were composed of compact, stupendous mountains, and nearly perpendicular, rocky cliffs, producing pine trees to a considerable height above the shores, and then nearly barren to their lofty summits, which were mostly covered with snow.

During the night we had much rain; the next morning, Tuesday the 14th, the weather was cloudy, with some passing showers, which at intervals enabled us to obtain a tolerably distinct view of the region before us; and for the first time, since the commencement of this expedition, it shewed the branch we were navigating to be about two miles wide, extending in a N. E. by E. direction, several leagues ahead. I had been in continual expectation of finding that the larboard shore would prove to be an island, in which case, on the return of the launch and cutter, the vessels should have been removed to its northern extremity, and by that means the return of the boats that were still to proceed, would be materially shortened; but, seeing little reason to indulge this hope any longer, I appointed a rendezvous with Mr. Johnstone, a little to the south of the entrance into this arm; where, on his return, he would find the vessels, or they would be on their way thither; and, after bidding him farewell, returned on my way towards the ships.

By noon we had reached the entrance of this branch of the inlet, where, on a small islet near its south point, I observed the latitude to be $51° 52'$, making the station at which I had parted with Mr. Johnstone, and which I had concluded to be the continental shore, in latitude $52° 3'$, longitude $232° 19'$. This rendezvous was about 37 miles from the station of the vessels, in as desolate inhospitable a country as the most melancholy creature could be desirous of inhabiting. The eagle, crow, and raven, that occasionally had borne us company in our lonely researches, visited not these dreary shores. The common shell-fish, such as muscles, clams, and cockles, and the nettle samphire, and other coarse vegetables, that had been so highly essential to our health and maintenance in all our former excursions, were scarcely found to exist here; and the ruins of one miserable hut, near where we had lodged the preceding night, was the only indication we saw that human beings ever resorted to the country before us, which appeared to be devoted intirely to the amphibious race; seals and sea-otters, particularly the latter, were seen in great numbers.

Having dined, and dedicated a short interval of sunshine to the drying of our wet clothes, we made the best of our way towards the ships; where, about midnight, we arrived, most excessively fatigued; the inclemency of the weather having, on this occasion, been more severely felt than in any of our former expeditions.

[August, 1792.]

The same very disagreeable weather had prevailed during our absence, attended with much more wind than we had experienced. From the S. W. the gale had blown particularly hard, which caused the most grateful reflections for our having providentially reached so comfortable a place of shelter, from the dangers that must necessarily have awaited our navigating, in such tempestuous weather, the intricate and unexplored region we had so recently quitted.

During our absence, a sufficient quantity of salmon had been taken, for every person on board the vessel; the necessary supplies of wood and water were nearly completed; but the rise and fall of the tide had not been equal to our wishes for the purpose of grounding the *Chatham*, without landing the greater part of her stores and provisions; and, as the bottom at low tide was found to be soft mud, unfavorable to such an operation, that business was necessarily deferred.

The weather, though clear at intervals for a short time, continuing very boisterous, filled our minds with much solicitude for the welfare of our friends in the boats; particularly those detached to the S. E. who were greatly exposed not only to its inclemency, but to the violence of the sea, which, from an uninterrupted ocean, broke with great fury on the southern shores. One consolation, however, always attended my anxious concern on these perilous occasions, that, in the exposure of my people to such fatiguing and hazardous service, I could ever depend on their cheerful and ready obedience to the prudent and judicious directions of the officers who were intrusted with the command of these adventurous expeditions.

Friday, the 17th. Whilst we thus remained under much concern for the safety of our detached parties, we were suddenly surprised by the arrival of a brig off the entrance of the cove, under English colors. A sight so uncommon, created a variety of opinions as to the cause that would induce any vessel in a commercial pursuit, (for so she appeared to be employed) to visit a region so desolate and inhospitable. Our suspense, however, was at an end on the return of Lieutenant Baker, who informed me she was the *Venus* belonging to Bengal, of 110 tons burthen, commanded by Mr. Shepherd, last from Nootka, and bound on a trading voyage along these shores; that having found the price of skins so exorbitant on the seacoast, he had been induced to try this inland navigation, in the hope of procuring them at a less extravagant price. By him we received the pleasant tidings of the arrival of the *Dædalus* store-ship, laden with a supply of provisions and stores for our use; and he acquainted Mr. Baker that Señor Quadra was waiting with the greatest impatience to deliver up the settlement and territories at Nootka. But, as fortune too frequently combines disastrous circumstances with grateful intelligence, Mr. Shepherd had brought with him a letter from Mr. Thomas New, master of the *Dædalus*, informing me of a most distressing and melancholy event. Lieutenant Hergest the commander, Mr. William Gooch the astronomer, with one of the seamen belonging to the *Dædalus*, had been murdered by the inhabitants of Woahoo, whilst on shore procuring water at that island. A circumstance so much to be deplored, and so little to be expected, was sincerely lamented by us all, and sincerely felt by myself, as Mr. Hergest had, for many years, been my most intimate friend; he was a most valuable character; and I had ever esteemed him as a man not less deserving my respect than intitled to my regard. The loss of Mr. Gooch, though I had not the pleasure of his acquaintance, would unavoidably be materially felt in the service we had to execute during the ensuing part of our voyage.

For although Mr. Whidbey, with the assistance of some of our young gentlemen, relieved me of considerable labor, by attending to nautical astronomy; yet, for the purpose of expediting this arduous service on which we were employed, the absence both of Mr. Whidbey and myself frequently became necessary, whilst the ships remained stationary for some days, in situations where many opportunities might occur of making various astronomical observations on shore. Although we were compelled to appropriate such time to those pursuits as were indispensibly requisite to determine the position of different points, promontories and stations, yet we had little leisure for making such miscellaneous observations as would be very acceptable to the curious, or tend to the improvement of astronomy.

The weather was less disagreeable and boisterous the next morning, Saturday the 18th, when, to our great satisfaction, the launch and cutter returned, without having met with any accident, although infinitely fatigued by the severity of the weather, with which they had so long contended.

The entrance into Smith's inlet was nearly closed by rocky islets, some producing shrubs and small trees, others none; with innumerable rocks as well beneath as above the surface of the sea, rendering it a very intricate and dangerous navigation for shipping. Within the islets and rocks the northern shore appeared the clearest; but the opposite side could not be approached without some difficulty, not only from the numerous rocks, but from a great oceanic swell occasioned by the prevailing tempestuous weather. From the entrance into the inlet, whose north point lies from its south point N. 20 E. about a league distant, they found it extend, nearly in an east direction, about six leagues; here it took a turn to the northeastward, and terminated in latitude 51° 24′, longitude 232° 47½′. About three leagues within the entrance, the rocks and islets ceased to exist, and the inlet contracted to a general width of about half a mile; though, in particular places, it was nearly twice that distance from shore to shore; both of which were formed by high rocky precipices covered with wood.

About half way up the channel a village of the natives was discovered, which our gentlemen supposed might contain two hundred or two hundred and fifty persons. It was built upon a detached rock, connected to the main land by a platform, and, like those before mentioned, constructed for defence. A great number of its inhabitants, in about thirty canoes, visited our party, and used every endeavor they thought likely to prevail on them to visit their habitations. They offered the skins of the sea-otter and other animals to barter; and beside promises of refreshment, made signs too unequivocal to be misunderstood, that the female part of

VANCOUVER'S DISCOVERY

[Original Journal, Pages 323-324.]

[August, 1792.]

their society would be very happy in the pleasure of their company. Having no leisure to comply with these repeated solicitations, the civil offers of the Indians were declined; and the party continued their route back, keeping the northern or continental shore on board. On the 16th they entered another opening, about a league to the north of the north point of Smith's inlet. The entrance into this seemed less dangerous than the former; it had, however, on its southern side, many rocky islets and rocks; but they discovered no one below the surface of the water, nor any danger that could not easily be avoided; and, by keeping on the north side of the entrance, which is about half a league across, a fair navigable passage was found about half a mile wide, between the north shore and the rocky islets that lie off its southern side. Along this the continent was traced about a league, in an east direction, where the opening took its course N. 15 E. about 16 miles, and terminated in latitude 51° 42', longitude 232° 22'. About a league and a half south of this station, a small branch extends about four miles to the W. N. W.; and, half a league further south, another stretches about the same distance to the N. E.

In this inlet, which I have distinguished by the name of RIVERS'S CHANNEL, the land continued of a more moderate

---

George Pitt, First Baron Rivers. This nobleman became more famous because of the beauty of his wife than for any achievement of his own. Horace Walpole says that Rivers himself was a very handsome man who, when young, was a great favorite with Lady Mary Wortley Montagu. But Walpole celebrated the charms of Lady Rivers in "The Beauties, an Epistle to Mr. Eckardt the Painter." He never tires of praising the "lovely wife, all loveliness within and without," while he refers to Rivers as "her brutal and half-mad husband."

George Pitt was the eldest son of George Pitt of Stratfieldsaye, Hampshire. He was born about 1722. He graduated from Magdalen College, Oxford, M.A., in 1739, and D.C.L. in 1745. In 1742 he was returned to the House of Commons for Shaftesbury. From 1761 to 1771 he was in the diplomatic service. He was created Baron Rivers of Stratfieldsaye in the county of Southampton on May 20, 1776. He held several positions, such as one of the Lords of the Bedchamber and Lord-Lieutenant of Dorset. He published a number of political essays with elaborate titles. He died on May 7, 1802.

PENELOPE PITT, LADY RIVERS.
From the portrait by R. Houston. Photograph copyrighted by Walker & Cockrell.
Rights secured for this work in England and America.

height, further up, than had generally been found to be the case: but where it branched off in the above directions towards its head, the shores were composed of high steep rocky mountains, and, like Smith's inlet, and many other channels of this kind that we had examined, afforded no soundings in the middle with 80 fathoms of line; though in the bays, found in most of them, anchorage may, in all probability, be procured. Having finally examined these branches, they returned, by a very narrow intricate passage on the northern shore, leading through an immensity of rocky islets and rocks, until they reached POINT ADDENBROOKE, and again arrived on the eastern shore of Fitzhugh's sound; making the land they had passed, in going up this last inlet, on their larboard side, an island about six or seven miles long. The continental shore, abreast of this station, having been so far ascertained, their supply of provisions being exhausted, and being greatly fatigued by the inclement weather, they returned on board without proceeding agreeably to my original design to the northern extremity allotted to their examination. The further labour, however, of this party, I deemed unnecessary, having become perfectly satisfied as to the intermediate space. Every thing was therefore directed to be taken from the shore, that we might

---

He was married on January 4, 1746, to Penelope, daughter of Sir Henry Atkins. The only son George died unmarried, and the barony became extinct in 1828.

The portrait of Penelope Pitt, Lady Rivers, used in this work is by R. Houston.

Point Addenbrooke. This name is retained on all recent maps for the point of the mainland opposite the southern end of Calvert Island. It has not yet been learned who it was that Vancouver had in mind at the time. The " Dictionary of National Biography " has but one entry of that name, — Dr. John Addenbrooke (1680–1719), — who founded the Addenbrooke Hospital at Cambridge. The little hospital has been of great service to the university. He was the author of a well-known essay on freethinking, which included this: "Two things are essential to true freethinking — absence of prejudice and the full exertions of abilities of thought. The understanding may be distempered, and is so more often than the body. Hence no man can determine the guilt of another in having erroneous opinions."

sail in the morning towards the rendezvous I had appointed with Mr. Johnstone.

Since my return from the last boat expedition, I had fortunately obtained, during the few short intervals of fair weather that had occurred, some tolerably good observations for the latitude and longitude of this station. The former, by three meridional altitudes of the sun, appeared to be 51° 32', the latter, 232° 3' 15": the variation of the compass, 17° 7' eastwardly. This cove is at its entrance, the points of which lie from each other N. 30 W. and S. 30 E., about a quarter of a mile wide; and from thence, to its head, in a direction S. 68 W., about a mile. A small rock and two rocky islets lie off its north point of entrance. It undoubtedly bore some resemblance at first to Mr. Duncan's port Safety; but on reference to particulars, differed very materially. Mr. Duncan places port Safety in latitude 51° 41'; and in his sketch takes no notice of the above-mentioned islets and rocks. By him port Safety is recommended as a very proper place for cleaning and refitting vessels; and he says, that the opposite shore is not more than six or seven miles distant. We however found the opposite shore within a league of us; and at the entrance of the cove, instead of 100 fathoms, as stated by Mr. Duncan, we had only 30 fathoms water; decreasing gradually to its head, the whole a soft muddy bottom, and consequently very improper for the operations of cleaning or repairing vessels. Notwithstanding this manifest disagreement, there were those amongst us, who having heard Mr. Duncan's discourse on this subject, insisted upon the certainty of its being his port Safety. In this opinion, however, I could not concur, for the obvious reasons above stated, and was more inclined to suppose, that the opening I had seen when in the boats on this shore, to the south of that which led to sea, was Mr. Duncan's port Safety, as that corresponded nearer in point of latitude, and had more the appearance of a *port* than this small cove: it however is the first place that affords safe and convenient anchorage on the western shore, within the south entrance into Fitzhugh's sound, and proved a comfortable retreat to us from the dangerous situations to which

ARCHIBALD MENZIES.
From the painting by Eddis, now in possession of the Linnean Society of London, who gave special permission for this photograph to be made.

[August, 1792.]

we had so recently been exposed. Hence I have distinguished it by the name of SAFETY COVE; and have only further to add, that the rise and fall of the tide was about ten feet, and that it is high water at the time the moon passes the meridian. The same circumstances respecting the tides were observed by those employed in the boat excursions from this station.

In the morning of Sunday the 19th, we sailed out of Safety cove, having for the first time since the commencement of the present month, a pleasant breeze from the S. E. with serene and cheerful weather. About eleven o'clock we had the gratification of being joined by our other boat party; and from Mr. Johnstone I learned, that about four miles to the N. E. of the spot where I had quitted them, they pursued a narrow branch of the inlet winding to the south and southwestward, to the latitude of 50° 57′, due south of the place of our separation. The inclemency of the weather detained them in this situation until the 16th, when they pursued the main branch of the inlet, which is from one to two miles broad, in a north-easterly direction, to a point which I called by the name of POINT MENZIES, after Mr. Menzies who had

---

Safety Cove. This name still stands on all recent maps. The cove is on the eastern shore of Calvert Island.

Archibald Menzies. To many readers this will prove the most attractive and interesting member of the entire expedition. He was the naturalist. At the present time students, especially of botany, in the western portion of America are familiar with his name, though few of them have taken the trouble to learn about the man. How many men, women, and children have admired the Madrona tree of the western forests! Bret Harte has sung its beauties in a poem concluding with this stanza: —

> "Where, oh, where shall he begin
> Who would paint thee, Harlequin?
> With thy waxen burnished leaf,
> With thy branches' red relief,
> With thy polytinted fruit, —
> In thy spring or autumn suit, —
> Where begin, and oh, where end,
> Thou whose charms all art transcend?"

Ask a botanist the name of this beautiful tree, and he will tell you it is Arbutus menziesii, and then, if he loves the work, his face will lighten up as he adds, "That name is in honor of Archibald Menzies, the naturalist

accompanied me, and afterwards Mr. Johnstone, in this excursion; here the inlet divides into three branches, each

---

of the Vancouver expedition, who discovered this and many other plants on our western shores."

Menzies was born at Weims, Perthshire, on March 15, 1754. His elder brother William got him a place with him as a gardener in the Edinburgh Botanical Garden. Dr. John Hope, professor of botany, helped the young man get the training for a surgeon at the university. He made a botanical tour through the Highlands and the Hebrides in 1778, and then became assistant to a surgeon at Carnarvon. He entered the navy as assistant surgeon on the *Nonsuch* under Captain Truscott and was present with Rodney's fleet at the victory over the Comte de Grasse on April 12, 1782. He was serving on the Halifax station after the peace until 1786 when he was engaged as surgeon on board the *Prince of Wales* under Lieutenant Colnett, on a fur-trading voyage of discovery to the northwest coast of America. He returned to England from China in 1789. He was then mustered in on board the *Discovery* among the "supernumaries" as botanist. Of this fact Vancouver writes as follows in the introduction to his Voyage: —

"Botany, however, was an object of scientific inquiry with which no one of us was much acquainted; but as, in expeditions of a similar nature, the most valuable opportunities had been afforded for adding to the general stock of botanical information, Mr. Archibald Menzies, a surgeon in the royal navy, who had before visited the Pacific Ocean in one of the vessels employed in the fur-trade, was appointed for the specific purpose of making such researches; and had, doubtless, given sufficient proof of his abilities, to qualify him for the station it was intended he should fill. For the purpose of preserving such new or uncommon plants as he might deem worthy of a place amongst His Majesty's very valuable collection of exotics at Kew, a glazed frame was erected on the after part of the quarter-deck, for the reception of those he might have an opportunity of collecting."

There are many entries in the journal showing the activities of this naturalist. Surgeon Cranstoun of the *Discovery* had been ill and was released on September 8, 1792, to go home from Nootka. Menzies had been doing the work while the surgeon was ill, and he was then appointed to the vacancy. Vancouver afterwards complimented him by showing that no one life had been lost by sickness during the entire voyage.

Menzies made great collections of plants and other objects of natural history. In the Sandwich Islands he ascended Wha-ra-rai and Mauna Loa, an active volcano over thirteen thousand feet high. He measured their heights with the barometer.

The botanists who contributed the two fine large volumes of botany in the Geological Survey of California authorized in 1860 pay a tribute to Menzies, saying: "He visited California on three successive years, each time coming

[August, 1792.]

nearly as wide as that they had navigated. The first led to the N. W. the second to the northward, and the other to the south. Several leagues to the S. W. of point Menzies, the

---

to the American coast from the Sandwich Islands in the spring, spending the summer northward, and passing south in the autumn. In November and December, 1792, he visited Bodega, San Francisco Bay, Santa Clara, and Monterey. In May, 1793, he was at Trinidad Bay, and from October to December of the same year at various places, from Bodega to San Diego, including the islands below Santa Barbara. Again, in November and December, 1794, he touched at several places along the coast from Santa Cruz southward. A set of his collections is in the British Museum, another at Kew, and a portion of his earlier collections, particularly the cryptogams, are in the herbarium of the Botanical Society of Edinburgh."

The new species of the plants discovered by Menzies were described by Sir J. E. Smith, Robert Brown, and Sir W. J. Hooker. Menzies himself, published an account of the voyage in Loudon's "Magazine of Natural History," Volumes I and II.

Menzies served on board the *Sanspariel* in the West Indies under Lord Hugh Seymour but on returning to London resigned and took up the practice of his profession. He died in Ladbroke Terrace, Notting Hill, on February 15, 1842, and was buried at Kensal Green Cemetery, London, N.W. His grave is number 706. It may become interesting as a point to visit by American botanists while in London.

Menzies left no family, and his wife died some five years before his own decease.

He had been elected a fellow of the Linnean Society in 1790, and on the death of A. B. Lambert on January 10, 1842, he became the father of the Society for the one month of life that remained for him. A fine painting of this dear old naturalist hangs on the walls of the Linnean Society's Burlington House, London, W. The council of the Society gave special permission for a photograph to be made of the portrait for this work. On a table at the right, almost hidden in the shadow, stands a vase holding one of his loved plants. The painting is by Eddis, and the photograph by F. W. Reader, Aldenham Road, Watford.

The Royal Society's Catalogue, Volume IV, page 345, gives four papers published by Menzies as follows: (1) Descriptions of three new animals found in the Pacific Ocean (*Echeneis lineata, Fasciola clavata,* and *Hirudo branchiata*), "Linnean Transactions," 1791. (2) A new arrangement of the genus *Polytrichum,* in the same publication for 1798. (3) *Polytrichum rubellum* and *Polytrichum subulatum,* in the same publication for 1798. (4) Account of an ascent and barometrical measurement of Wha-ra-rai, a mountain in Owhyhee, "Magazine of Natural History," for 1829, Volume I, pages 201-208; volume II, pages 435-442.

water had assumed a pale white color, and was not very salt, which had encouraged them to push forward in constant expectation of finding its termination; but on reaching the above station, all hopes intirely vanished of carrying their researches further into execution, having extended their excursion beyond the time I had prescribed, and the period for which they had been supplied with provisions. These on the morning of the 17th, being nearly expended, Mr. Johnstone considered it most prudent to decline any further investigation, and to return to the ships. These they reached two days afterwards, almost exhausted with hunger and fatigue.

The country they had visited differed in no one respect from the general appearance we had long been accustomed to, nor did anything occur to vary the continual sameness, or chequer the dreary melancholy scene before them, if we except their finding near the conclusion of their examination, a canoe about forty feet long, hauled up by the side of a miserable hut, near which was the remains of a fire still burning; indicating the vicinity of some human beings, for whom they left in the canoe some copper, nails, and other trifles; these on their return were found in the same state, without any appearance of the canoes or hut having been visited in their absence; but concluding the natives could not be far removed, they added a few more articles to their former donation. The soil in this place was principally composed of roots, leaves, and other decayed vegetable matter, and the fire that had been kindled, had caught this substance, and made considerable progress on the surface.

Had Mr. Johnstone found a termination to the inlet under his examination, I should have proceeded up the main arm of this sound to the northward along the shore of the continent, in quest of a more northerly passage to sea; but as that had not been effected, I pursued that which I had seen from the boats leading to the westward through Calvert's islands; being now resolved, in consequence of the intelligence I had received from Nootka, to abandon the northern survey of the continental shore for the present season. This I had otherwise intended to have continued at least a month longer;

[August, 1792.]

but as the distressing event of Mr. Hergest's death necessarily demanded my presence in the execution of His Majesty's commands at Nootka, I determined to repair thither immediately. This determination favored also another design I much wished to execute, namely, that of extending the examination of the coast this autumn, southward from cape Mendocino, to the southernmost point of our intended investigations in this hemisphere. Having the greatest reason to be satisfied with the result of our summer's employment, as it had by the concurrence of the most fortunate circumstances enabled us finally to trace and determine the western continental shore of North America, with all its various turnings, windings, numerous arms, inlets, creeks, bays, etc., etc. from the latitude of 39° 5', longitude 236° 36', to point Menzies, in latitude 52° 18', longitude 232° 55'; we took our leave of these northern solitary regions, whose broken appearance presented a prospect of abundant employment for the ensuing season, and directed our route through the passage above-mentioned, in order to make the best of our way towards Nootka.

CHAPTER XII

MEETING WITH QUADRA AT NOOTKA — NEGOTIATIONS OVER THE TRANSFER OF SOVEREIGNTY

[Original Journal, Pages 331-332, Book II, Chapter X.] [August, 1792.]

HAVING on Sunday the 19th directed our course towards a passage, which appeared to lead to the ocean as stated in the last chapter, its N. E. point of entrance was found to be situated in latitude 51° 45', longitude 232° 1'; south of this point lies a sunken rock, which though near the shore is dangerous, being visible at low tide only by the surf that breaks upon it. In turning into the channel we must have passed twice very near it, but did not discover it until we were some distance beyond it; and had not light baffling winds retarded our progress, it would have escaped our notice. From the point above-mentioned the passage extends S. 60 W. about seven miles; its northern shore is composed of rocky islets and rocks, with some scattered rocks lying off its southern shore: between these and the rocky islets is the passage, generally from one to two miles wide, without any apparent obstruction, yet it is rendered unpleasant by the want of soundings, as within 50 and 100 yards of the shore, on either side, no bottom could be obtained, with 150 fathoms line. In this very disagreeable situation we were detained by faint unsteady winds until eleven at night, when, by the assistance of a light breeze from the S. E. we reached the ocean, and stood to the south-westward.

The next morning, Monday the 20th, was very unpleasant; fresh squalls from the S. E. attended with thick rainy weather, continued until noon the following day, Tuesday the 21st, when it cleared up, and we saw Scot's islands, bearing S. 22 E. about seven leagues distant. The wind during the day was light and variable, though attended with fair weather; in the evening it seemed fixed at S. S. W. when, not being able to pass to the windward of Scot's islands, our course was directed to the north of them, towards cape Scot, having soundings and a soft muddy bottom at the depth of eighty and ninety fathoms, until about nine in the evening, when the water suddenly shoaled from sixty to seventeen fathoms, and the bottom became rocky. On this we instantly stood back to the westward, lest we should approach some danger, but we did not perceive either breakers or shoals, although the night was still and clear. These soundings were from the westernmost of Scot's islands N. 18 E. about five leagues; from this circumstance, and from the distant rocks and shoals we saw extending from the shores of Calvert's islands, it is highly necessary that the space between Calvert's and Scot's islands should be navigated with great caution.

We were detained about Scot's islands by light variable winds until Friday the 24th, when we passed to the south of them, and continued to the eastward along their southern shores.

The westernmost of them is situated in latitude 50° 52', longitude 231° 2'. The group consists of three small and almost barren islands, with many small rocks and breakers about them. West from the westernmost of them, a ledge of rocks extends about two miles, and south of it is another about a league distant. The easternmost of Scot's islands being much larger than the rest, may probably be the same to which Mr. Hanna gave the name of "Cox's island;" by others of the traders it has been represented as a part of the main; this is certainly wrong, and as Mr. Hanna's chart is very erroneous, even in point of latitude, no certain conclusion can be drawn.

The wind, which was from the westward, was so light, that it was not until the forenoon of Saturday the 25th, that we passed the N. W. point of the large island, which forms the south and western shores of the gulf of Georgia and Queen Charlotte's sound. This point (called by former visitors "Cape Scott") is situated in latitude 50° 48', longitude 231°

40′, and with the easternmost of Scot's islands, forms a passage which appears to be about four miles wide. About cape Scot the land is composed of hills of moderate height, though to the south-eastward it soon becomes very mountainous, and at the distance of three or four leagues appeared to be much broken and to form many inlets, coves, and harbours, all the way to Woody point, which we passed in the afternoon within the distance of about two miles; it is situated in latitude 50° 6′, longitude 232° 17′. West from it lies a small rocky islet about half a league distant, and another larger one lying N. 28 W. about a league from the north part of the point, which is an extensive and projecting promontory.

From Woody point as we sailed along the shore to the eastward, we saw several openings in the land, which was about three or four miles from us, that appeared like coves and harbours. Innumerable rocky islets and rocks lined the shores, which as we advanced became low, but the country behind swelled into hills of considerable height divided by many valleys; beyond these it rose to mountains so elevated, that even at this season of the year many patches of snow were yet undissolved.

As I intended to ascertain the outline of the coast from hence down to Nootka; at dark we brought to, about six leagues to the eastward of Woody point, in expectation of accomplishing this design the following day, but in this I was disappointed; the N. W. wind was succeeded by light winds, which continued until the afternoon of Tuesday the 28th, and prevented in the present instance my acquiring such authority as I deemed necessary for delineating this part of the coast.

Foggy weather during the forenoon precluded us the advantage of steering for Nootka with the favorable wind that prevailed from the N. W. but on its clearing away about two we steered for that port. On reaching its entrance we were visited by a Spanish officer, who brought a pilot to conduct the vessel to anchorage in Friendly cove, where we found riding his Catholic Majesty's brig the *Active*, bearing the broad pendant of Señor Don Juan Francisco de la Bodega y Quadra, commandant of the marine establishment of St. Blas and California.

The *Chatham*, by the partial clearing of the fog, had found her way in some time before us: the *Dædalus* store ship, and a small merchant brig called the *Three Brothers* of London, commanded by Lieutenant Alder of the navy, were also there at anchor.

As Señor Quadra resided on shore, I sent Mr. Puget to acquaint him with our arrival, and to say, that I would salute the Spanish flag, if he would return an equal number of guns. On receiving a very polite answer in the affirmative, we saluted with thirteen guns, which were returned, and on my going on shore accompanied by some of the officers, we had the honor of being received with the greatest cordiality and attention from the commandant, who informed me he would return our visit the next morning.

Agreeably to his engagement, Señor Quadra with several of his officers came on board the *Discovery*, on Wednesday the 29th, where they breakfasted, and were saluted with thirteen guns on their arrival and departure: the day was afterwards spent in ceremonious offices of civility, with much harmony and festivity. As many officers as could be spared from the vessels with myself dined with Señor Quadra, and were gratified with a repast we had lately been little accustomed to, or had the most distant idea of meeting with at this place. A dinner of five courses, consisting of a superfluity of the best provisions, was served with great elegance; a royal salute was fired on drinking health to the sovereigns of England and Spain, and a salute of seventeen guns to the success of the service in which the *Discovery* and *Chatham* were engaged.

Maquinna, who was present on this occasion, had early in the morning, from being unknown to us, been prevented coming on board the *Discovery* by the centinels and the officer on deck, as there was not in his appearance the smallest indication of his superior rank. Of this indignity he had complained in a most angry manner to Señor Quadra, who very obligingly found means to sooth him; and after receiving some presents of blue cloth, copper, etc., at breakfast time he appeared satisfied of our friendly intentions: but no sooner had he drank a few glasses of wine, than he renewed the subject, regretted the Spaniards were about to quit the place, and asserted that we should presently give it up to some other nation; by which means himself and his people would be constantly disturbed and harassed by new masters. Señor Quadra took much pains to explain that it was our ignorance of his person which had occasioned the mistake, and that himself and subjects would be as kindly treated by the English as they had been by the Spaniards. He seemed at length convinced by Señor Quadra's arguments, and became reconciled by his assurances that his fears were groundless. On this occasion I could not help observing with a mixture of surprise and pleasure, how much the Spaniards had succeeded in gaining the good opinion and confidence of these people; together with the very orderly behavior, so conspicuously evident in their conduct towards the Spaniards on all occasions.

The tents, observatory, chronometers, instruments, etc., were sent on shore the following day, Thursday the 30th, and all hands were busily employed on the several necessary duties of the ship, such as caulking, overhauling the rigging and sails, cleaning the hold and bread-room for the reception of stores and provisions. The boats, in consequence of the services they had performed during the summer, were in want of much repair, and were hauled on shore for that purpose.

From the unfortunate death of Lieutenant Richard Hergest, late agent to the *Dædalus*, I considered it expedient that an officer should be appointed to that store-ship, and I therefore nominated Lieutenant James Hanson of the *Chatham* to that office; Mr. James Johnstone, master of the *Chatham*, I appointed to the vacant lieutenancy; and Mr. Spelman Swaine, one of my mates, to be master in the *Chatham*.

In the forenoon I received an official letter from Señor Quadra respecting the restitution of this place, with several copies of a correspondence resulting from the inquiries he had made during his residence here, respecting the English establishments on the coast, at the time the British vessels were captured, and the Spaniards effected an establishment at Nootka. On this occasion I considered myself very fortunate in finding a young gentleman (Mr. Dobson) on board the store-ship, who spoke and translated the Spanish language very accurately, and who politely offered me his services.

The *Chatham* was hauled on shore the next day to examine her bottom, and to repair the damage she had sustained by getting a-ground. A part of the gripe, a piece of the forefoot with part of the main, and false keels, were broken off, and some of the copper was torn away in different places.

Señor Galiano and Valdes arrived the following day, Saturday, September the 1st, from the gulf of Georgia; they had pursued a route through Queen Charlotte's sound to the southward of that which we had navigated, and obligingly favored me with a copy of their survey of it.

Mr. Dobson having translated Señor Quadra's letter and the documents accompanying it, it appeared that Señor Quadra had, after his arrival at Nootka in April, 1792, commissioned all the vessels under his command to inspect the coast; in order that the proper limits to be proposed in the restitution of these territories might be ascertained, and that the several commanders might inform themselves of all the matters and circumstances that preceded the capture of the *Argonaut* and *Princess Royal* merchantmen in the year 1789.

Señor Quadra stated, that the court of Spain had expended large sums in sustaining the department of St. Blas, with the sole view of its being an auxiliary to other establishments which were then in contemplation of being formed. That Nootka was seen in the year 1774, and in 1775 possession was taken 2° to the south, and 6° to the north of it; and as in this space Don Estevan Joseph Martinez found no kind of establishment whatever, that therefore no one should take it ill that he (Martinez) should dispute his prior right to the port. Under the orders of the viceroy of New Spain, Martinez entered Nootka, and took possession the 5th of May, 1789, with visible demonstrations of joy in the Indians;

and afterwards fortified the place, without any objection being made on the part of a Portuguese commander of a trading brig called the *Ephigenia*, then in the cove. On the arrival of the *Columbia* and *Washington*, American vessels, he examined their papers and passports, as he had before done those of the Portuguese; and disapproving some expressions contained in those of the *Columbia*, she was detained until an explanation took place, when she was released. The English schooner *North West America*, and sloop *Princess Royal* arrived soon afterwards, and were permitted to depart, after receiving the most friendly attention. Captain Colnett, commanding the English vessel *Argonaut*, fearing to enter, the Spaniards visited him, and his fears vanished; but as Captain Colnett did not confine his views to the commerce of the country, but wished to fortify himself, and to establish an English factory, Martinez arrested him and sent him to St. Blas. The like conduct was observed towards Thomas Hudson, who commanded the *Princess Royal*, on his return to Nootka. The vessels of both were detained.

This was the real situation of things, says Señor Quadra, who offers to demonstrate in the most unequivocal manner that the injuries, prejudices, and usurpations, as represented by Captain Meares, were chimerical: that Martinez had no orders to make prize of any vessels, nor did he break the treaty of peace, or violate the laws of hospitality: that the natives will affirm, and that the documents accompanying his letter will prove, that Mr. Meares had no other habitation on the shores of Nootka than a small hut, which he abandoned when he left the place, and which did not exist on the arrival of Martinez: that he bought no land of the chiefs of the adjacent villages; that the *Ephigenia* did not belong to the English; that Martinez did not take or detain the least part of her cargo; and that Mr. Colnett was treated with the greatest distinction at St. Blas, and his officers and crew received the wages of the Spanish navy for the time of their detention: that the vessel and cargo were restored, and that Mr. Colnett obtained a great number of skins on his return to Nootka.

OF PUGET SOUND

[September, 1792.]

These circumstances duly considered, adds Señor Quadra, it is evident that Spain has nothing to deliver up, nor damage to make good; but that as he was desirous of removing every obstacle to the establishment of a solid and permanent peace, he was ready, *without prejudice to the legitimate right of Spain,* to cede to England the houses, offices, and gardens, that had with so much labor been erected and cultivated, and that himself would retire to Fuca:* observing at the same time,

* Meaning an establishment they had in the entrance of De Fuca's Straits.

Neah Bay. This little harbor, at the very entrance to the Puget Sound region, lies about five miles to the eastward of Cape Flattery. On account of its location and on account of the virility of the Makah Indians living there, Neah Bay has had an interesting history. Excepting Nootka, it is the only port of the Northwest actually occupied by the Spaniards. The place was discovered by Quimper on August 1, 1790. He named it Nuñez Gaona. In Zerolo's monumental work, "Diccionario Enciclopedico de la Lengua Castellana," the word "gaon" is given as a term of honor or glory, used in the olden times in referring to men learned in Biblical knowledge. "Gaona" would be the feminine form, and that is accounted for by the word "Bahia." The full Spanish name of the place was Bahia de Nuñez Gaona. The man whom Quimper sought to honor was undoubtedly Alonso Nuñez de Haro y Peralta, who was born in Villagarcia, October 31, 1729, and died in Mexico, May 26, 1800. He was a distinguished Spanish prelate, was archbishop of Mexico from 1772, and viceroy from May 8 to August 16, 1787.

Apparently the Spaniards could not believe that they were going to lose sovereignty of the northern coasts as the result of the treaty with England of October 28, 1790, for in March, 1792, the authorities in Mexico, besides sending Quadra to Nootka to meet Vancouver, despatched Lieutenant Salvador Fidalgo to Nuñez Gaona to fortify and hold the port for Spain. He arrived there in May and at the present time there is occasionally found a fragment of old Spanish brick from the foundation of the little fort he started to build there. In September of the same year, Quadra ordered the fort abandoned and moved Fidalgo and all the property to Nootka, where the lieutenant would command until further instructions were received from the governments of Spain and Great Britain.

Vancouver sailed past the bay one month before Fidalgo had arrived to occupy it. The bay is indicated on Vancouver's chart, but he did not attempt to explore or name it. The fur-traders who followed these explorers called the place Poverty Cove, and the United States Exploring Expedition under Captain Charles Wilkes in 1841 named it Scarborough Harbor. The Indian village there was a part of the Makah tribe. That village was called by the

that Nootka ought to be the last or most northwardly Spanish settlement, that there the dividing point should be fixed, and that from thence to the northward should be free for entrance, use and commerce to both parties, conformably with the fifth article of the convention; that establishments should not be formed without permission of the respective courts, and that the English should not pass to the south of Fuca.

After enumerating these particulars, Señor Quadra concludes his letter by expressing, That if I should find any difficulty in reconciling what he had proposed, or if I should have any other honourable medium to offer that might be the means of terminating this negociation, and secure the desired peace, he begged I would communicate it to him.

The documents accompanying this letter were copies of a correspondence between Señor Quadra and Don Francisco Joseph De Viana, the commander of the *Ephigenia;* Mr. Robert Gray and Mr. Joseph Ingraham, commanders of the *Columbia* and *Washington;* from all of whom Señor Quadra appears to have solicited every information respecting the transactions at Nootka, previously to his arrival, and the reasons which induced Mr. Meares to represent things to the prejudice of Don Estevan Joseph Martinez. The Portuguese captain briefly sets forth, that his vessel was seized, and that he was made prisoner by Don Martinez; during his captivity he was very well treated, and on his being liberated, his vessel and cargo were completely restored, and he was furnished with whatever provisions and supplies he required. He also states, that when Don Martinez entered Nootka, there was not the least remains of a house belonging to the English.

Señor Quadra had addressed Mr. Gray and Mr. Ingraham jointly, and consequently they both replied to him in the same way. These gentlemen state, that on the arrival of Don Estevan Joseph Martinez, in Friendly cove, the 5th of

---

Indians "Deeah," or "Neeah," and gradually that Indian name has persisted above all the others, and the bay remains to-day on all charts and maps as Neah Bay.

May, 1789, he found there the *Ephigenia* only; the *Columbia* being at that time six miles up the sound at Mahwinna; the *Washington* and *North West America* being then on a cruize. Martinez demanded the papers of each vessel, and their reasons why they were at anchor in Nootka sound, alledging that it belonged to his Catholic Majesty. Captain Viana, of the Portuguese vessel, answered, that he had put in there in distress to wait the arrival of Captain Meares from Macao, who was daily expected with supplies, and that on his receiving them he should depart; that Captain Meares had sailed from Nootka in 1788, under the colors of Portugal, had a Portuguese captain with him on board, and was expected to return with him in the same vessel, which, with the *Ephigenia*, belonged to a merchant at Macao. The *Ephigenia* wanting provisions and stores, the same were supplied by Martinez, who seeming satisfied with the answers which he had received from the several commanders, not the least misunderstanding was suspected. On the 10th of May arrived the *Carlos* Spanish ship, Captain Arro, and on the following day Martinez captured the *Ephigenia*, and his reason assigned for so doing, *as these gentlemen understood*, was, that in the Portuguese instructions, they (the Portuguese) were ordered to capture any English, Spanish, or Russian vessel they might meet on the N. W. coast of America, and could take. This was afterwards said to have been a mistake, originating in a want of due knowledge in reading the Portuguese language. The vessel and cargo were liberated, and Martinez supplied the *Ephigenia's* wants from the *Princessa*, enabling her, by so doing, to prosecute her voyage, without waiting for the return of Mr. Meares. They then proceeded to state that, on the arrival of the *Columbia* in the year 1788, there was a house, or rather a hut, made by the Indians, consisting of rough posts covered with boards; this was pulled down the same year, the boards were taken on board the *Ephigenia*, and the roof was given to Captain Kendrick, so that on the arrival of Martinez in May, 1789, there was no vestige of any house remaining. That Mr. Meares had no house, and as to land, they had never heard, although they had remained nine months amongst the natives, that he had ever purchased any in Nootka sound. From *Maquinna* and other chiefs they had understood, that Mr. Kendrick was the only person to whom they had ever sold any land.

These gentlemen stated, that the *North West America* arrived the 8th of June, and that on the following day the Spaniards took possession of her; ten days afterwards came the *Princess Royal*, commanded by Mr. Hudson from Macao, who brought the news of the failure of the merchant at Macao, to whom the *Ephigenia* and other vessels belonged. That Martinez assigned this as a reason for his capturing the *North West America*, (although she was seized before the arrival of the *Princess Royal*) that he had detained her as an indemnification for the bills of exchange, drawn on her owner in favor of his Catholic Majesty. That Captain Hudson, after having been treated with the kindest attention by the commodore and his officers, sailed with the *Princess Royal* from Nootka, the 2d of July; and that the same evening arrived the *Argonaut*, Captain Colnett.

Mr. Gray and Mr. Ingraham state also, that they heard Mr. Colnett inform Don Martinez that he had come to hoist the British flag, and to take formal possession of Nootka; and that, in conjunction with Mr. Meares and some other English gentlemen at Macao, he had concluded to erect a fort, and settle a colony. To this the Spanish commodore replied, That he had taken possession already in the name of his Catholic Majesty. Captain Colnett then asked, if he should be prevented from building a house in the port? The commodore replied, That he was at liberty to erect a tent, to wood and to water, after which he would be at liberty to depart when he pleased. Captain Colnett said that was not what he wanted, that his object was to build a block-house, erect a fort, and settle a colony for the crown of Great Britain. To this Don Martinez answered, No; that in his acceding to such a proposal he should violate the orders of his king, relinquish the Spaniards' claim to the coast, and risk the losing of his commission. Beside which the commodore stated, that Mr. Colnett's vessel did not belong to the King of Great Britain, nor was Mr. Colnett invested with powers to transact any such public business. Captain Colnett replied, That he was a king's officer; but Don Martinez observed, That his being on half-pay, and in the merchants' service, rendered his commission as a lieutenant in the British navy of no consequence in the present business. In conversation afterwards on this subject, as we were informed, (say these gentlemen) for we were not present during this transaction, some dispute arose in the *Princessa's* cabin; on which Don Martinez ordered the *Argonaut* to be seized. Soon after this the *Princess Royal* returned, and, as belonging to the same company, the commodore took possession of her also. With respect to their treatment whilst prisoners, these gentlemen say, That although they have not read Mr. Meares's publication, they think it impossible that the officers and crew of the *Argonaut* can be backward in confessing, that Señor Don Estevan Martinez always treated them kindly, and consistently with the character of gentlemen.* They further state, That the captain, officers and crew of the *North West America* were carried by them to China, with one hundred sea-otter skins, valued at four thousand eight hundred and seventy-five dollars, which were delivered to Mr. Meares as his property.

To Señor Quadra's letter of the 29th of August, I replied to the following effect: That I did not consider myself authorized to enter into a retrospective discussion on the respective rights and pretensions of the court of Spain or England, touching the western coasts of America, and islands adjacent, to the northward of California. That subject having undergone a full investigation, and having been mutually agreed upon and settled by the ministers of the respective courts, as appeared by the convention of the 28th of October, 1790, and Count Florida Blanca's letter of the 12th of May, 1791, I considered any interference, on my part, to be incompatable with my commission, being invested with powers

---

* Some circumstances in contradiction to the whole of these evidences, which afterward came to my knowledge, will appear in a future chapter.

only to receive the territories which, according to the first article of the convention, Señor Quadra was authorized to restore and to put me in possession of, viz. ("*the buildings and districts, or parcels of land which were occupied by the subjects of his Britannic Majesty in April,* 1789, *as well in the port of Nootka or of St. Lawrence, as in the other, said to be called Port Cox, and to be situated about* 16 *leagues distant from the former to the southward.*") That agreeably to the express words of the fifth article in the said convention, ("*It is agreed, That, as well in the places that are to be restored to the British subjects by virtue of the first article, as in all other parts of the north-western coast of North America, or of the islands adjacent, situated to the north of the parts of the said coast already occupied by Spain, wherever the subjects of either of the two powers shall have made settlements since the month of April,* 1789, *or shall hereafter make, any of the subjects of the other shall have free access, and shall carry on their trade without any disturbance or molestation.*") I considered the Spanish settlement in the entrance of the straits of De Fuca, which I had reason to believe was formed no longer ago than May, 1792, to come within the meaning of a "*port of free access,*" *as well as all other establishments that have been, or that may hereafter be, formed from thence southward to port St. Francisco*, conceiving port St. Francisco to be the northernmost settlement occupied by the subjects of His Catholic Majesty, in April, 1789.

In my way to the observatory, on Sunday, I waited upon Señor Quadra, who informed me, that Mr. Dobson had translated my letter to him; and he was pleased to say, That he derived the greatest satisfaction from finding a person of my character, with whom he was to transact the business of delivering up Nootka; that he should accept the civil offers contained in my letter, and remain on shore until the carpenters had finished some additional accommodation to his apartments on board his little brig; which being completed, he would either wait my departure, to accompany us in our researches to the southward, and to conduct us to any of the Spanish ports I might wish to visit; or he would sail, and wait my arrival at any place I should think proper to appoint, recommending St. Francisco or Monterey for that purpose.

Señor Quadra requested to know who I intended to leave in possession of these territories; and being informed that it would be Mr. Broughton in the *Chatham*, in whose charge the remaining cargo of the *Dædalus* would be deposited, he gave directions that the store houses should be immediately cleared, and begged I would walk with him round the premises, that I might be the better able to judge how to appropriate the several buildings; which for the most part appeared sufficiently secure, and more extensive than our occasions required. A large new oven had been lately built expressly for our service, and had not hitherto been permitted to be used. The houses had been all repaired, and the gardeners were busily employed in putting the gardens in order. The poultry, consisting of fowls and turkies, was in excellent condition, and in abundance, as were the black cattle and swine: of these Señor Quadra said he should take only a sufficient quantity for his passage to the southward, leaving the rest, with a large assortment of garden seeds, for Mr. Broughton. Señors Galiano and Valdes added all they had in their power to spare, amongst which were three excellent goats; I had likewise both hogs and goats to leave with him; so that there was a prospect of Mr. Broughton passing the winter, with the assistance of the natural productions of the country, not very uncomfortably.

The orders under which I was to receive these territories, on the part of His Britannic Majesty, were intirely silent as to the measures I was to adopt for retaining them afterwards. Presuming, however, that the principal object which His Majesty had in view, by directing this expedition to be undertaken, was that of facilitating the commercial advantages of Great Britain in this part of the world; and for that purpose it might not be impossible, that a settlement was in contemplation to be made at this important station, which had become the general rendezvous for the traders of almost all nations; I had determined, on leaving this port, to commit it to the charge and direction of Mr. Broughton, who would retain the possession of it, and whose presence might restrain such improper conduct as had already been manifested on the part of several traders; whilst I should proceed to execute the remaining part of His Majesty's commands, until I should be furnished with further instructions for my future government.

Having satisfactorily arranged these matters, I gave directions for clearing the store ship, which was set about accordingly.

The politeness, hospitality, and friendship, shewn on all occasions by Señor Quadra, induced Mr. Broughton and myself, with several of the officers and gentlemen of both vessels, to dine at his table almost every day, which was not less pleasant than salubrious, as it was constantly furnished with a variety of refreshments to most of which we had long been intire strangers.

Señor Galiano informed me, that he intended to take advantage of the present serene weather, which without interruption had prevailed since our arrival, and sail for the Spanish ports to the southward, either in the course of the night, or early the next morning; and obligingly undertook to forward a short letter to the Lords of the Admiralty, containing a brief abstract of transactions since our departure from the Cape of Good Hope.

I had the honor of Señor Quadra's company on the morning of Monday the 3d at breakfast. He omitted no opportunity of impressing on the minds of the natives the highest and most favorable opinion of our little squadron; and the more effectually to insure a good understanding in future, he proposed a visit of ceremony to *Maquinna;* to him it would be grateful, and on my part he recommended it as essentially requisite. It was agreed we should set out the next morning for his royal residence, which was about seven leagues up the sound, at a place called Tahsheis.

In the evening I received from Señor Quadra a letter in reply to mine of the 1st of September.

Agreeably to appointment, about eight in the morning of

[September, 1792.]

Tuesday the 4th, Señor Quadra accompanied me in the *Discovery's* yawl, which, with our own and a Spanish launch, and the *Chatham's* cutter, containing as many Spanish and English officers as could be taken, we departed for Tahsheis; a message having been sent the preceding day to announce our intended visit.

The weather though cloudy was very pleasant, and having a favorable breeze, we reached Tahsheis about two in the afternoon: *Maquinna* received us with great pleasure and approbation, and it was evident that his pride was not a little indulged by our shewing him this attention. He conducted us through the village, where we appeared to be welcome guests, in consequence perhaps of the presents that were distributed amongst the inhabitants, who all conducted themselves in the most civil and orderly manner. After visiting most of the houses, we arrived at *Maquinna's* residence, which was one of the largest, though it was not intirely covered in; here we found seated in some kind of form, *Maquinna's* daughter, who not long before had been publicly and with great ceremony proclaimed sole heiress to all his property, power, and dominion. Near her were seated three of his wives, and a numerous tribe of relations. The young princess was of low stature, very plump, with a round face, and small features; her skin was clean, and being nearly white, her person altogether, though without any pretensions to beauty, could not be considered as disagreeable. To her and to her father I made presents suitable to the occasion, which were received with the greatest approbation by themselves and the throng which had assembled; as were also those I made to his wives, brothers, and other relations. These ceremonies being ended, a most excellent dinner was served, which Señor Quadra had provided, at which we had the company of *Maquinna* and the princess, who was seated at the head of the table, and conducted herself with much propriety and decorum.

After dinner *Maquinna* entertained us with a representation of their warlike achievements. A dozen men first appeared, armed with muskets, and equipped with all their appendages, who took their post in a very orderly manner within the entrance of the house, where they remained stationary, and were followed by eighteen very stout men, each bearing a spear or lance sixteen or eighteen feet in length, proportionably strong, and pointed with a long flat piece of iron, which seemed to be sharp on both edges, and was highly polished; the whole however appeared to form but an awkward and unwieldy weapon. These men made several movements in imitation of attack and defence, singing at the same time several war songs, in which they were joined by those with the muskets. Their different evolutions being concluded, I was presented with two small sea-otter skins, and the warriors having laid by their arms, performed a mask dance, which was ridiculously laughable, particularly on the part of *Maquinna*, who took a considerable share in the representation. We were not backward in contributing to the amusements of the day, some songs were sung which the natives seemed much to admire, and being provided with drums and fifes, our sailors concluded the afternoon's diversion with reels and country dances.

In the evening we took leave of *Maquinna*, who was scarcely able to express the satisfaction he had experienced in the honour we had done him, saying, that neither *Wacananish*, nor any other chief, had ever received such a mark of respect and attention from any visitors, and that he would in a few days return us the compliment; on which he was given to understand, he should be entertained in the European fashion.

From Tahsheis we proceeded a few miles in our way home, when, arriving at a convenient little cove, we pitched our encampment for the night, and passed a very pleasant evening.

After breakfast the following morning, Wednesday the 5th, we embarked and directed our route towards Friendly cove; the weather was pleasant though the wind was unfavorable; this occasioned our dining by the way on the rocks, for which however Señor Quadra was amply provided. About five we reached the cove, where I landed Señor Quadra and returned to the ship.

[September, 1792.]

In our conversation whilst on this little excursion, Señor Quadra had very earnestly requested that I would name some port or island after us both, to commemorate our meeting and the very friendly intercourse that had taken place and subsisted between us. Conceiving no spot so proper for this denomination as the place where we had first met, which was nearly in the center of a tract of land that had first been circumnavigated by us, forming the south-western sides of the gulf of Georgia, and the southern sides of Johnstone's straits and Queen Charlotte's sound, I named that country the island of QUADRA and VANCOUVER; with which compliment he seemed highly pleased.

During my absence the *Chatham* had hauled off from the shore, but in consequence of the inconsiderable rise of the tide her damages had not been repaired; it was therefore necessary that she should remain light until the next spring tides; this however, under our present arrangements, was a matter of little importance.

Thursday 6th, *Maquinna* with his two wives and some of his relations returned our visit. They had not been long on board when I had great reason to consider my royal party as the most consummate beggars I had ever seen; a disposition which seemed generally to prevail with the whole of this tribe of Indians, and which probably may have been fostered by the indulgences shewn them by the Spaniards. They demanded everything which struck their fancy, as being either useful, curious, or ornamental, though an article with which it might be impossible for us to gratify them; and if not immediately presented they would affect to be greatly offended, and would remain sulky for two or three days.

I was however particularly fortunate in having at hand

Quadra and Vancouver's Island. The reason for giving this name is fully set forth in the journal, and the lives of the two men have been fully discussed. It remains, however, to add that in the collections of the present writer is a copy of Mitchell's School Atlas, published by Thomas, Cowperthwait & Co., of Philadelphia, in 1851, in which the maps show the names of the two explorers still linked in partnership on that great island where they met in 1792.

everything requisite to satisfy the demands of *Maquinna* and his party. The liberality I had so recently shewn to himself and family when at Tahsheis, was perhaps not yet quite forgotten; they nevertheless made a profitable visit, as what their modesty precluded their asking of me, I was afterwards informed was amply made up by their begging from the officers and others on board.

The exhibition of fire-works which I had promised the party, was anxiously waited for; towards the evening their impatience was almost unrestrainable, as they could not, or would not understand that darkness was necessary to their entertainment, and accused us of a breach of promise and telling falsities. Señor Quadra however, after much persuasion, prevailed upon them to stay the night, by which they were convinced that our assurances were not to be discredited. The night being favorable to our operations, they succeeded extremely well. The rockets, balloons, and other fireworks, were in a high state of preservation, and were regarded by the Indian spectators with wonder and admiration, mixed with a considerable share of apprehension; for it was not without great difficulty that I prevailed on *Maquinna* and his brother to fire a few sky rockets, a performance that produced the greatest exultation. The Europeans present were not less entertained with the exhibition, than surprized that the several fire works should have remained so long on board in such excellent condition.

Saturday 8th, the *Aransasu*, a Spanish armed ship, commanded by Señor Caamano, arrived from a surveying expedition on the exterior coast to the north of Nootka, towards Biccareli, of the charts of which I was promised a copy, as soon as they should be properly arranged.

Mr. Cranstoun, the surgeon of the *Discovery*, having been rendered incapable of his duty by a general debilitated state of health since our departure from the cape of Good Hope, requested permission to proceed to port Jackson in the *Dædalus*, from whence he might soon procure a passage to England; he was consequently discharged, and Mr. Archibald Menzies, a surgeon in the navy, who had embarked

OF PUGET SOUND

in pursuit of botanical information, having cheerfully rendered his services during Mr. Cranstoun's indisposition, and finding that such attention had not interfered with the other objects of his pursuit, I considered him the most proper person to be appointed in the room of Mr. Cranstoun. The boatswain of the *Discovery*, Mr. William House, a careful, sober, and attentive officer, having labored under a violent rheumatic complaint, since our departure from New Zealand, which had precluded his attention to any part of his duty, was on his application in like manner discharged; Mr. John Noot, boatswain of the *Chatham*, was appointed in his room, and Mr. George Philliskirk was appointed boatswain of the *Chatham*.

Monday the 10th, I deemed it expedient, that their Lordships directions, prohibiting charts, journals, drawings, or any other sort of intelligence respecting our proceedings being made known or communicated, should be publicly read to the officers and persons under my command, and to urge every injunction in my power to enforce a due obedience to those orders.

The letter I received the 2d of this month from Señor Quadra, not having been translated till this day, in consequence of Mr. Dobson's indisposition, I was not a little surprized to find it differ so much from what I had reason to expect.

In this letter Señor Quadra informs me, that in conformity to the first article of the convention, and the royal order under which he is to act, he can only restore to His Britannic Majesty the edifices, districts, or portions of land which in April, 1789, were taken from his subjects; that he was in possession of full proof that the small hut the English had was not in existence on the arrival of Martinez, and that the then establishment of the Spaniards was not in the place where the British subjects had theirs. That if I did not think myself authorized to subscribe to the tenor of his commission and instructions, he would recommend that each should lay before his respective court all the circumstances of the pending negociation, and wait for further instructions; in the mean time Señor Quadra offered to *leave me* in possession of what Mr. Meares had occupied, and *at my command* the houses, gardens, and offices then occupied by the Spaniards, whilst he retired until the decision of the two courts should be known.

To this letter I immediately replied, that as, like his former one, it contained a retrospective view of matters which I had no authority to take cognizance of, I should accede to his proposal, and make a just and fair representation of all our proceedings to the court of Great Britain, and wait for further instructions. This letter I concluded by again repeating, that I was still ready to receive from Señor Quadra the territories in question, agreeably to the first article of the convention, and the letter of Count Florida Blanca.

In the course of the night arrived here the brig *Hope*, belonging to Boston in America, commanded by Mr. Joseph Ingraham, the person who jointly with Mr. Gray had given Señor Quadra a statement of the conduct of Don Martinez, and of the transactions at this port in the year 1789.

About noon the next day, Wednesday the 12th, I received from Señor Quadra a letter dated the 11th of September, in answer to my last, expressive of his confidence that I should make a faithful and true representation of the proceedings that had taken place respecting the points in question; and repeating the offer contained in his former letter, of relinquishing the territories on the terms and conditions therein expressed. To this letter I immediately replied, that I was ready whenever it suited Señor Quadra's convenience, to be put into possession of the territories on the N. W. coast of America, or islands adjacent, agreeably to the first article of the convention, and the letter of the Count Florida Blanca.

Having this day dined with Señor Quadra, on rising from table he requested, as no final determination had yet taken place respecting the restitution of these territories, to have some personal conversation on the subject, in hopes by that means of drawing the business to a more speedy conclusion. Besides ourselves there were present Señor Mozino and Mr. Broughton; so that with the assistance of Mr. Dobson, and these gentlemen who spoke French extremely well, we had a prospect of coming to so perfect an explanation as to render any further epistolary altercation totally unnecessary. Señor Quadra vindicated the conduct of Martinez, and laid considerable stress on the concession of *Maquinna*, who had put them into complete possession of the lands they then occupied; on this circumstance, and on the information he had obtained since his arrival at Nootka, certain parts of which he had by letter communicated to me, he seemed principally to establish the claims of the Spanish crown. The small spot on which Mr. Meares's house had been built, which did not then appear to be occupied by the Spaniards, Señor Quadra said I was at liberty to take possession of for His Britannic Majesty, whenever I should think proper. This offer being totally foreign to my expectations, and a repetition only of that which had taken place in our correspondence, Señor Quadra was made acquainted, that under such circumstances I did not feel myself justified in entering into any further discussion. The propriety of this determination being admitted, it was mutually agreed that we should each represent our objections and proceedings to our respective courts, and wait their decision on the important questions which had arisen in the negociation. In the mean time Señor Quadra proposed to leave me in possession of these territories, the instant his vessel was fitted for his reception. On his departure the Spanish flag was to be struck, and the British flag hoisted in its place, which Señor Quadra consented to salute, on my agreeing to return an equal number of guns. Thus did matters appear to be perfectly arranged, agreeably to the wishes of all parties, and the business brought to an amicable and pleasant conclusion, when to my great surprize I received on the morning of Thursday the 13th a letter from Señor Quadra, setting forth that he was ready to deliver up to me, conformably to the first article of the convention, the territory which was occupied by British subjects in April, 1789, and to leave the Spanish settlement at Nootka until the decision of the courts of England and Spain were obtained; which was proceeding, he said, as far as his powers extended.

This very unexpected letter produced an immediate reply from me, wherein I stated, that the territories of which the subjects of His Britannic Majesty were dispossessed in April, 1789, and which by the first article of the convention were now to be restored, I understood to be this place (meaning Nootka) *in toto*, and port Cox. These I was still ready to receive, but could not entertain an idea of hoisting the British flag on the spot of land pointed out by Señor Quadra, not extending more than an hundred yards in any direction. I concluded by observing, that the offer made in Señor Quadra's two last letters differed materially from that contained in his first letter to me on this subject.

On the morning of Saturday the 15th, a young lad, who for about two days had been missing from Señor Quadra's vessel, was found in a cove not far from the ships, most inhumanly murdered. The calves of his legs were cut out, his head nearly severed from his body, and he had received several barbarous wounds in other parts. Doubts arose whether this horrid act had been perpetrated by the natives, or by a black man of most infamous character, who had deserted from the Spanish vessel about the time the boy was first missed. The prevailing opinion seemed to criminate the former, and on Señor Quadra demanding of *Maquinna* that the murderer should be given up, the immediate departure of all the inhabitants of the sound from our neighborhood became a strong presumptive proof of their delinquency.

Señor Quadra gave an immediate answer to my letter of the 13th, but as he therein did not depart from the terms of his late offer of *leaving me in possession only, not formally restoring* the territory of Nootka to the King of Great Britain; it became necessary on my part to demand a categorical and definite answer from Señor Quadra, whether he would or would not restore to me for His Britannic Majesty the territories in question, of which the subjects of that realm had been dispossessed in April, 1789. These were Nootka and Clayoquot, or port Cox; the former is the place which was then occupied by the British subjects, from thence their vessels were sent as prizes, and themselves as prisoners to New Spain; this is the place that was forcibly wrested from them, and fortified and occupied by the officers of the Spanish crown; this place therefore, with Clayoquot or port Cox, were comprehended under the first article of the convention, and were by that treaty to be restored without any reservation whatsoever: on these terms, and on these only, could I receive the restitution of them. Señor Quadra having also laid some stress upon Mr. Meares's vessels being under Portuguese colours, I took this opportunity of signifying, that I considered that circumstance equally foreign and unimportant, it having been set forth in Mr. Meares's original petition to the Parliament of Great Britain, and of course must have come under the consideration of the Spanish and English ministers. Unless our negociation could be brought to a conclusion on the terms pointed out in this as well as in my former letters, I begged leave to acquaint Señor Quadra that I must positively decline any further correspondence on this subject.

It was a matter of no small satisfaction, that although on this subject such manifest difference arose in our opinions, it had not the least effect on our personal intercourse with each other, or on the advantages we derived from our mutual good offices; we continued to visit as usual, and this day Señors Quadra and Caamano, with most of the Spanish officers, honored me with their company at dinner.

On Monday morning the 17th, a Portuguese brig arrived here called the *Fenis and St. Joseph*, commanded by John de Barros Andrede, on board of which was a Mr. Duffin as supercargo. In the evening I had Señor Quadra's final determination; which resting on the same point where it had originated, I considered any further correspondence totally unnecessary; and, instead of writing, I requested in conversation the next day to be informed, if he was positively resolved to adhere, in the restitution of this country, to the principles contained in his last letter? and on receiving from him an answer in the affirmative, I acquainted him that I should consider Nootka as *a Spanish port*, and requested *his permission* to carry on our necessary employments on shore, which he very politely gave, with the most friendly assurance of every service and kind office in his power to grant.

On Tuesday the 18th, our negociation being brought by these means to a conclusion, Señor Quadra informed me, that Señor Caamano would be left in charge of the port, until the arrival of the *Princessa*, commanded by Señor Fidalgo; with whom the government of the port of Nootka would be left, and from whom the English might be certain of receiving every accommodation.

Señor Quadra was now making arrangements on board the *Active* for his departure, which he intended should take place in the course of a day or two. Agreeably to a former promise I had made him, he requested a copy of my charts for the service of His Catholic Majesty; but as our longitude of the several parts of the coast differed in many instances from that laid down by Captain Cook, I wished to embrace every future opportunity of making further observations whilst we might remain in this port, before a copy should be disposed of; but Señor Quadra wishing to make certain of such information as we had acquired, and conceiving the further corrections we might be enabled to make of little importance, solicited such a copy as I was then able to furnish; which, with a formal reply to his last letter, I transmitted to him on the evening of Thursday the 20th. In this letter I stated the impossibility of my receiving the cession of the territories in question on the conditions proposed by Señor Quadra, and that in consequence of the existing differences in our opinions on this subject, I should immediately refer the whole of the negociation to the court of London, and wait the determination thereof, for the regulation of my future conduct. The next day, Friday, the 21st, Señor Quadra acknowledged the receipt of my last letter, with the charts of this coast, etc. which concluded our correspondence.

As Señor Quadra intended to sail the next day, accompanied by most of the Spanish officers, he did me the honor of partaking of a farewell dinner, and was on this occasion received with the customary marks of ceremony and respect due to his rank, and the situation he here filled. The day passed with the utmost cheerfulness and hilarity: Monterrey was appointed as the rendezvous where next we should meet.

Having understood that Mr. Robert Duffin, the supercargo on board the Portuguese vessel that had arrived on the 17th, had accompanied Mr. Meares in the year 1788, and was with him on his first arrival in Nootka sound, I requested he would furnish me with all the particulars he could recollect of the transactions which took place on that occasion. This he very obligingly did, and at the same time voluntarily made oath to the truth of his assertions. The substance of which was, that towards the close of the year 1787, two vessels were equipped for the fur trade on the N. W. coast of America, by John Henry Cox & Co. merchants at Canton. That the command and conduct of the expedition was given to John Meares, Esq. who was a joint proprietor also; that for the purpose of avoiding certain heavy dues, the vessels sailed under Portuguese colours, and in the name and under the firm of John Cavallo, Esq. a Portuguese merchant at Macao, but who had not any property either in the vessels or their cargoes, which were intirely British property, and were wholly navigated by the subjects of His Britannic Majesty: That Mr. Duffin accompanied Mr. Meares in one of these vessels to Nootka, where they arrived in May, 1788, when Mr. Meares, attended by himself and Mr. Robert Funter, on the 17th or 18th of the same month, went on shore, and bought of the two chiefs, *Maquilla* and *Calicum*, the whole of the land that forms Friendly cove, Nootka sound, in His Britannic Majesty's name, for eight or ten sheets of copper, and some trifling articles: That the natives were perfectly satisfied, and, with the chiefs, did homage to Mr. Meares as their sovereign, according to the custom of their country: That the British flag, and not the Portuguese flag, was displayed on shore, whilst these formalities took place between the parties: That Mr. Meares caused a house to be erected on the spot which was then occupied by the *Chatham's* tent, as being the most convenient place: That the chiefs and the people offered to quit their residence and to retire to Tahsheis, that consequently the English were not confined to that particular spot, but could have erected houses, had they been so inclined, in any other part of the cove: That Mr. Meares appointed Mr. Robert Funter to reside in the house, which consisted of three bed-chambers, with a mess-room for the officers, and proper apartments for the men; these were elevated about five feet from the ground, the under part serving as warehouses: That, exclusive of this house, there were several out-houses and sheds, built for the convenience of the artificers to work in: That Mr. Meares left the houses in good repair, and enjoined *Maquilla* to take care of them, until he, or some of his associates, should return: That he, Robert Duffin, was not at Nootka when Don Martinez arrived there; that he understood no vestige of the house remained at that time, but that on his return thither in July, 1789, he found the cove occupied by the subjects of His Catholic Majesty: That he then saw no remains of Mr. Meares's house; and that on the spot on which it had stood were the tents and houses of some of the people belonging to the *Columbia*, commanded by Mr. John Kendrick, under the flag and protection of the United States of America: That His Catholic Majesty's ships, *Princessa* and *San Carlos*, were at this time anchored in Friendly cove, with the *Columbia* and *Washington* American traders: That the second day after their arrival they were captured by Don Martinez, and that the Americans were suffered to carry on their commerce with the natives unmolested.

Señor Quadra, at my request, very obligingly undertook to forward, by the earliest and safest conveyance, a short narrative of our principal transactions at this port, for the information of the Lords of the Admiralty.

On Saturday morning the 22d, he sailed from Friendly cove, and having saluted us with thirteen guns, I returned the compliment with an equal number.

Our attention had been most particularly directed to the re-loading of the store-ship, and the re-equipment of the *Chatham*, whose hold had been intirely cleared for the purpose of repairing the damages she had sustained. The *Discovery* being in all respects ready for sea, all hands were employed in the execution of these services, which were materially retarded by the very bad condition of the provision casks on board the *Dædalus*, most of which required a thorough repair, and to be recruited with pickle. A very material loss was also sustained in the spirits and wine; large quantities of the slop-clothing were intirely destroyed, and many others, with some of the sails, were materially damaged. Circumstanced as we were, these deficiencies and damages were objects of the most serious concern, and appeared to have been intirely occasioned by the very improper way in which the cargo had been stowed.

The circumstances already related, with the correspondence at large between Señor Quadra and myself, though comprehending the substance of the negociation which took place respecting the cession of these territories, may yet require some further explanation; and when the very important commerce of this country shall be properly appreciated, I trust the circumspection with which I acted will not be found liable to censure.

Our transactions here have been related with the greatest fidelity, and precisely in the order in which they occurred. Being unprovided with any instructions but such as were contained in the *convention*, and the very general orders I had received, it appeared totally incompatable with the intention of the British court, with the spirit and words of the said convention, or with those of the letter of Count Florida Blanca, that the identical space only on which Mr. Meares's house and breast-work had been situated in the northern corner of this small cove, and forming nearly an equilateral triangle not extending an hundred yards on any one side, bounded in front by the sea, and on the other two sides by high craggy rocks, which continued some distance down the beach, and, excepting at low tide, completely separated this triangular space from that occupied by the Spaniards' houses and gardens, could possibly be considered as the object of a restitution expressed by the terms "*tracts of land*," according to the first article of the convention; the "*districts or parcels of land,*" mentioned in the letter of Count Florida Blanca; or the "*tracts of land, or parcels or districts of land,*" *pointed out to me*, and repeated in their Lordships' instructions communicated to me on that subject.

On due consideration, therefore, I concluded, that the cession proposed by Señor Quadra could never have been that intended: that, at least, the whole port of Nootka, of which His Majesty's subjects had been forcibly dispossessed, and at which themselves, their vessels and cargoes had been captured, must have been the proposed object of restitution.

Under these impressions, I felt that if I had acceded to the proposals of Señor Quadra, I should have betrayed the trust with which I was honored, and should have acted in direct opposition to my duty and allegiance, by receiving, without any authority, a territory for His Britannic Majesty, under the dominion of a foreign state.

These principles uniformly governed the whole of my conduct throughout this negociation, in which I acted to the best of my judgment; should I be so unfortunate, however, as to incur any censure, I must rely on the candour of my country, to do me the justice of attributing whatever improprieties I may appear to have committed, to the true and only cause; to a want of sufficient diplomatic skill, which a life wholly devoted to my profession had denied me the opportunity of acquiring.

After having so uniformly persisted in my determination of strictly adhering to the line of my duty, by an implicit obedience to the instructions I had received, in opposition to the judgment and opinion of Señor Quadra, and the evidences which he had proposed; I could not but consider the unexpected arrival of a gentleman, who had personally attended Mr. Meares on his forming the establishment at Nootka, and who it seems had been present on most occasions when differences had arisen between Señor Martinez and Captain Colnett, as a very fortunate circumstance, since his report and affidavit cleared up every point of which, from other testimonies, I could entertain any doubt, and confirmed me in the opinion, that the conduct I had pursued had not been incompatible with the trust committed to my charge and execution. On comparing his representation with that which had been communicated to me on the same subject by Señor Quadra, a very material difference appeared, which most probably operated to direct Señor Quadra's conduct, in refusing me possession of the country agreeably to the terms of my instructions.

The vessels employed in commercial pursuits this season on the north-west coast of America, have I believe found their adventures to answer their expectations: many were contented with the cargo of furs they had collected in the course of the summer; whilst others who had prolonged their voyage, either passed the winter at the Sandwich islands, or on the coast, where they completed small vessels which they brought out in frame. An English and an American shallop were at this time on the stocks in the cove, and when finished were to be employed in the inland navigation, in collecting the skins of the sea-otter and other furs; beside these, a French ship was then engaged in the same pursuit, and the following vessels in the service of His Catholic Majesty: the *Gertrudes* and *Conception* of thirty-six guns each, the *Active* brig of twelve guns, *Princessa*, *Aransasu*, and *St. Carlos*, armed ships, with the vessels of Señor Galiano and Valdes. Both these gentlemen had been, and were still employed, not only in geographical researches, but in acquiring every possible information respecting the commerce of the country; this circumstance, together with the guarded conduct observed by Señor Quadra, in his endeavours to retain the whole, or at any event to preserve a right in Nootka, evidently manifested the degree of jealousy with which the court of Spain regards the commercial intercourse that is likely to be established on this side of the world.

Considering it an indispensable duty, that the Lords of the Admiralty should, from under my own hand, become acquainted with the whole of my negociation at this port by the safest and most expeditious conveyance, a passage was procured for my first lieutenant Mr. Mudge on board the *Fenis* and *St. Joseph*, bound to China, from whence he was to proceed with all dispatch to England. To this gentleman I intrusted extracts from the most important parts of my journal, with a copy of our survey of this coast; and I had every reason to indulge the hopes of his speedy return, with further instructions for the government of my conduct in these regions.

On this occasion, I appointed Lieutenant Puget and Baker to be first and second lieutenants, as also Mr. Spelman Swaine to be third lieutenant of the *Discovery;* and Mr. Thomas Manby to be master of the *Chatham*.

Señor Quadra having used no rigorous measures to detect and bring to justice the murderer of the young Spaniard, the alarm of the natives soon subsided, and in a day or two they visited us as usual. *Maquinna* and the other chiefs were not, however, so cordially received at the Spanish habitations as they had been in Señor Quadra's time; at which they expressed much dislike to all the Spaniards, excepting Señor Quadra, and particularly to Martinez; who, *Maquinna* asserted, went on shore with a number of armed people, and obliged him by threats to make cession of Nootka to the king of Spain. He lamented also the prospect of our speedy departure, saying, that his people would always be harassed and ill-treated by newcomers, and intreated that I would leave some persons behind for their protection. Very little dependance, however, is to be placed in the truth or sincerity of such declarations; since these people, unlettered as they are, possess no small share of policy and address, and spare no pains to ingratiate themselves, by the help of a little flattery (a commodity with whose value they seem perfectly acquainted) with strangers, to whom they represent their actions as resulting from the most sincere friendship; by which means they frequently procure very valuable presents, without making any return.

From the time of Señor Quadra's departure until Wednesday the 26th, my time had been mostly employed in preparing my dispatches for England; they were now completed, and Mr. Mudge would have sailed this day, had not a hard gale of wind from the S. E. attended with a heavy rain, prevented his departure, and retarded our operations in the equipment of the *Chatham* and *Dædalus*. This boisterous unpleasant weather continued until the 30th in the afternoon, when the wind shifting to the N. W. brought fair weather, with which the *Fenis and St. Joseph* sailed for China.

On Tuesday, October the 2d, the *Hope* brig, which had sailed on the 20th of last month, and the Spanish armed ship *Princessa*, arrived here from the establishment before mentioned, that the Spaniards had formed near the southern entrance of the straits of De Fuca; which was the same open bay we had passed in the afternoon of the 29th of April last; but it having been found much exposed, and the anchorage very bad, owing to a rocky bottom, the Spaniards, I was given to understand, had been induced intirely to evacuate it; and it appeared also that Señor Fidalgo had brought with him to this place all the live stock that had been destined for its establishment.

Our new suit of sails, after soaking some hours in the sea, were bent on Saturday the 6th. The observatory, with the instruments and chronometers, were on that day also taken on board, as well as those supplied me by the Navy Board, as those intrusted by the Board of Longitude to the care of the late Mr. William Gooch the astronomer, intended for this expedition.

The very unsettled state of the weather much retarded our re-equipment, and the appearance of winter having already commenced, indicated the whole year to be divided here into two seasons only. The month of September had been delightfully pleasant, and the same sort of weather, with little interruption, had prevailed ever since the arrival of Señor Quadra in the spring; during which period of settled weather, the day was always attended with a refreshing gale from the ocean, and a gentle breeze prevailed through the night from the land; which not only renders the climate of this country extremely pleasant, but the access and egress to and from its ports very easy and commodious.

As my attention, during our continuance in this port, had

VANCOUVER'S DISCOVERY

[Original Journal, Pages 381-383.] [October, 1792.]

been principally engrossed by the negociation already adverted to, I had little leisure to prosecute other inquiries; I shall therefore conclude this chapter by the insertion of such observations as were made on shore at the observatory.

The observations commenced on the 30th of August, at which time Kendall's chronometer, according to the Birch-bay rate gave the longitude..................................233° 58′ 15″
By the Portsmouth rate...............................231° 16′ 30″
Arnold's watch, on board the *Chatham*, by the Birch-bay rate..232° 47′ 45″
1792. Longitude of the observatory.
Sept. 7, Myself, two sets of distances, moon and sun.......233° 22′ 30″
— Mr. Whidbey, two do. do........................ 19′
8, ditto, eight ditto ditto............................. 44′ 20″
— Myself, eight ditto ditto......................... 38′ 41″
9, ditto, eight ditto ditto............................. 31′ 30″
— Mr. Whidbey, eight do. do..................... 37′ 17″
12, ditto, eight ditto ditto............................ 32′ 32″
— Myself, six ditto ditto............................ 27′ 5″
23, ditto, eight ditto ditto............................ 26′ 34″
— Mr. Whidbey, eight do. do..................... 13′ 9″
23, ditto, eight ditto ditto............................ 12′ 34″
— Myself, eight ditto ditto......................... 12′ 50″
Oct. 1, Mr. Whidbey, six ditto moon and aquila.......... 35′ 25″
Aug. 22, Five sets per ☽ a ☉, taken by myself at sea, and reduced at this place by the chronometer, according to its rate of going found here................... 49′ 9″
— Five sets, taken by Mr. Whidbey, ditto............ 36′ 5″
24, Four sets by myself, ditto........................ 36′ 49″
— Four sets by Mr. Whidbey, ditto.................. 34′ 45″
The mean of the whole, *collectively* taken; being forty-nine sets by myself; and fifty-seven by Mr. Whidbey; amounting in all to one hundred and six sets of lunar distances gave the longitude..233° 31′ 30″

By which our observations place Nootka sound about 20′ 30″ to the eastward of the longitude assigned to it by Captain Cook, and about 10′ to the eastward of Señor Malaspina's observations; whence it should seem to appear, that our instruments for the longitude were erring on the eastern side.

Although I should have been very happy to subscribe to

OF PUGET SOUND

the longitude as settled by astronomers of superior abilities, yet, on the present occasion, such a concession would have been attended with a very material inconvenience, in deranging the position of the different parts of the coast that have already been surveyed, and laid down by our own observations. For this essential reason, I have been induced to retain the meridian of Nootka, as ascertained by our own observations, which shewed Kendall's chronometer, on our arrival, to be 26′ 45″ to the eastward of what I have considered as the true longitude; and as I had reason to believe this error commenced about the time of our departure from Desolation sound, and that it had been regularly increasing since that period, the longitude has been corrected both in my journals and charts from that station.

On this authority, the errors of the chronometers have been found, which, on the 5th of October at noon, were as follow: (viz.)

Kendall fast of mean time at Greenwich..............1h 13′ 43″ 41‴
And gaining per day, on mean time, deduced from thirty-six sets of corresponding altitudes, at the rate of............ 11″ 15‴
Arnold's No. 82, on board the *Chatham*, fast of mean time at Greenwich...4h 3′ 35″ 41‴
And gaining, per day, on mean time, at the rate of......... 28″ 7‴
Arnold's No. 14, from the *Dædalus*, fast of mean time at Greenwich.. 42′ 4″ 41‴
And gaining per day, on mean time, at the rate of......... 14″ 45‴
Arnold's No. 176, fast of mean time at Greenwich.........2h 16′ 38″ 41‴
And gaining per day, on mean time, at the rate of......... 32″ 27‴
Earnshaw's pocket watch, fast of mean time at Greenwich..1h 7′ 39″ 41‴
And gaining, per day, on mean time, at the rate of......... 5″ 30″

The calculations by the Portsmouth rate of Kendall's chronometer have hitherto been noticed, in order to shew the degree of accuracy with which it had gone, according to its then ascertained motion, in encountering the various climates it had passed through since our departure from that port; but as I have no similar documents, or the least information, respecting the three chronometers I received from the

VANCOUVER'S DISCOVERY

[Original Journal, Page 385.] [October, 1792.]

Dædalus, to compare with the going of Kendall's, those calculations from hence will cease to attract our attention.

The latitude of the observatory, by thirty meridional altitudes of the sun..49° 34′ 20″
The variation of the compass, by thirty sets of azimuths, taken by three different compasses, varying from 16° to 21°, gave the mean result..18° 22′ east

The vertical inclination of the magnetic needle.

Marked end, North face East.........................	74°	0′
Ditto,	West.........................	73° 47′
Marked end, South face East.........................	73°	7′
Ditto,	West.........................	74° 52′

Mean inclination of the marine dipping needle.........73° 56′

Departure from Nootka. On Friday, October 12, 1792, Captain Vancouver, with his fleet of three vessels,—*Discovery, Chatham*, and *Dædalus*,—sailed out of Nootka and headed for the Spanish ports in California. On the way the *Dædalus* was to stop and survey Gray's Harbor and the *Chatham* was to do a similar service in the Columbia River. Vancouver allowed his denial of such river and arm of the sea to remain in his written journal even after he had learned of the American's discoveries while negotiating with Quadra at Nootka. This candor is another evidence of Vancouver's perfect honesty as an explorer.

APPENDIX

Muster Tables

The following muster tables are copied from the originals among the Admiralty Records in the Public Record Office, London. The Muster Book of His Majesty's Sloop *Discovery* from 24 December, 1790, to 31 October, 1795, is number 11310, Series I.

Most of the abbreviations in the column of "Qualities" will be readily understood. "A. B." means "able-bodied seaman"; the others are too plainly indicated to need explanation.

MUSTER TABLE OF HIS MAJESTIES SLOOP THE *DISCOVERY* BETWEEN 1ST APRIL AND THE 31ST MAY, 1791

COMPLEMENT 100

Men's Names	Qualities	Place and County Were Born	Age
Geo. Vancouver	Capt.		
Rich'd Richard	Boat's		
Rich'd Collett	Gunner		
Henry Phillips	Carpenter		
James Gransell	Cook		
Widow's Man	A. B.		
Robert Stephens	Mid.	London	19
Edw'd Williamson	A. B.	Southwark	31
Chas. Mason	A. B.	Wales	24
W. M. Waller	A. B.	Gilling, York	24
Geo. Hart	Qtr. Mr.	Bermudas	24
Philip Butcher	A. B.	London	23
Jn'o Lucas	A. B.	Pinsford	35
James Hitchcock	A. B.	Prittlewell	18
Geo. Simpson 1 April '91	A. B. } Corp'l	Isleworth	18

APPENDIX

Men's Names	Qualities	Place and County Were Born	Age
E. C. Harris.	A. B.	London	19
Arthur Crews	Mid.	Lostwethel	22
Jn'o Noot	Bo. M'te	Newton Bushel	29
Geo. Philliskirk	Bo. M'te	Whitly	23
James Drummond	A. B.	Edinburgh	37
Jno. Davidson	A. B.	Carmarthen	21
Jno. Evans	A. B.	Carmarthen	19
Jno. Thomas	A. B.	Carmarthen	19
Lewis Jones	A. B.	Cardiganshire	22
And'w Gibson	2'd M'r	Scotland	27
James Wilkinson	A. B.	Northcumberland	21
Walter Dillon	A. B.	Ireland	27
Jos. Whidbey	Master		
Jno. Campbell	A. B.	America	20
Jno. Carter	A. B.	Mitcham	22
Jno. Nicholas	Mid.	London	19
Jno. Barrymore	A. B.	Greenby Crook	22
And'w Macready	A. B.	Glasgow	20
Fras. Brown	A. B.	Baltimore	27
Jno. McAlpine	A. B.	Deptford	22
Wm. Patterson 8 May '91	Sailmakers M'te } A. B.	Cumberland	29
Jno. Cummings	A. B.	Newry	21
Corn's Downey	Carp't Crew	Ireland	18
Jno. McKinley	A. B.	Londonderry	19
Jno. Allen	A. B.	Norfolk	19
Rich'd Henley	A. B.	Dublin	30
Edw'd Berry	Gun'r Mte.	Cork	23
Isaac Wooden	A. B.	Chatham	23
Jno. Blake	A. B.	Portsmouth	18
Thos. Laithwood	Carp'rs Mate	Lancaster	26
Wm. Guy	A. B.	Jamaica	27
Alex. Foord	Carp't Crew	Liverpool	19
Jno. Gobourn	Carp't Crew	Warwick	23
Geo. McKenzie	Mid.	Edinburgh	16
Spelman Swaine	Mr's Mte.	Lynn	22
Henry Humphreys	Mid.	America	18
Jno. Sykes 1 Feb. '91	Mid. } Mr's Mte.	London	19
Stephen Man	A. B.	Nottingham	25
James Green	Carp. Mte.	Leeds	22
Rod'k Betton	A. B.	Glasgow	25

APPENDIX

Men's Names	Qualities	Place and County Were Born	Age
Jno. Mitchell	A. B.	Kent	25
Thos. Brown	A. B.	Glasgow	26
Jos. Baker	3rd Lt.		
Wm. Wooderson	A. B.	Hants	19
Jos. Morgan	A. B.	London	23
Jno. Rogers	A. B.	Kent	20
Geo. Evans	A. B.	Surry	25
James Harris	A. B.	America	28
Jno. King	A. B.	Essex	23
Jos. Murgatroyd	Carp'r Mate	Woolwich	38
Jn'o Davies	A. B.	Chatham	27
Rich'd Bown	A. B.	London	19
Jno. Willis	A. B.	Norfolk	25
Donald McNeal	A. B.	Scotland	20
Thos. Spearer	Q'r M'r	Newhaven	26
Jno. Cook	A. B.	Liverpool	21
Robert Barrie	Mid.	America	19
Wm. Milne	A. B.	Aberdeen	27
A. P. Cranstoun	Surg'n		
Thos. Clarke 1 Feb. 91	A. B. } Mid. }	London	18
Thos. Manley	Mr's Mte.	Norfolk	21
Humphrey Evans	Q'r M'r	Wales	30
Henry Hankins	A. B.	Denham Bucks	23
Adam Mill	Surgeons 1, Mate	Scotland	25.
Alex. Bell	A. B.	Leith	24
Wm. Underwood	A. B.	Suffolk	21
Peter Puget	2nd Lieut.		
Zac. Mudge	{ 2nd Lieut. 15 Dec. '90 { 1st Lieut. 3 Jan.'91		
James Bailey	A. B.	London	23
Thomas Taylor	A. B.	Glasgow	25
Sam. Manning 4 Mar. '91	A. B. } Bo. Mte. }	Norfolk	23
Thos. Keld	Q'r M'r	Hull	29
Jno. Brown	Q. M'r	Dundee	28
James Englehart	Sailmaker	Waterford	20
Alex. Norval	Cook's Mte.	Aberdeen	20
Jno. Aisley Browne	A. B.	London	17
Robt. Pigot	Mid.	Dulwich	16
H. M. Orchard	Clk.	Cornwall	31
Jno. Stewart	A. B.	Galloway	17

APPENDIX

Men's Names	Qualities	Place and County Were Born	Age
G. C. Hewitt	Surg. 1st Mate		
Jos. Mears	Surg. 2nd Mate		
Ben Reeve	A. B.	Warwickshire	26
Thos. Keld	Boat'n		
Jno. Monroe	Q'r M'r	Scotland	28
Edw'd Roberts	A. B.	London	18
Nath. Ridley	Cook		
Jno. Roome	A. B.	Cork	26
James Butters	Gun'r Mate	Scotland	38
V. V. Ballard	A. B.	Ludlow	19
Fras. Griffin	A. B.	Antigua	24
Jno. Ash	A. B. }	Topsham	30
3 Mar. '91	Armourer		
Jno. Willcocks	Corp'l Mast'r at Arms	Tavistock	27
Thos. Townshend	A. B.		
Honble C. Stuart	A. B.	London	16
Honble Thos. Pitt	A. B.	Cornwall	16
Geo. Fox	A. B.	Bristol	30
Thos. Young	A. B.	Bristol	19

(Signed) Geo. Vancouver, *Captain*
J. Whidbey, *Master*
Thos. Keld, *Boatswain*.

Marines borne as part of the Complement: —

Sergt. Edw'd Flynn; Corp'l Williams; Drummer Jno. Barnes
Privates Geo. Bull   Thos. Millward   Thos. Green   Jno. McCardell
        Jno. Glasspole Hugh Kelty   Wm. Pender   Jno. Withers
        Jno. Godfray   Sam'l Scott   Neil Coyle   Jno. Simpson
        Wm. Bonchin   Peter Faris

(Signed) Geo. Vancouver, *Captain*
J. Whidbey, *Master*
Thos. Keld, *Boatswain*

Supernumaries for Victuals only: —

Towereroo p. Admiralty or'd for a passage to the Sandwich Islands
Arch'd Menzies — Botanist   Revenue officers (4): —
Jno. Jane   Wm. Weakam   Wm. Udell   Mich'l Tewry.
Jno. Ewins — Botanist's L't

(Signed) Geo. Vancouver, *Captain*
J. Whidbey, *Master*
Thos. Keld, *Boatswain*

APPENDIX

These are to certify the Principal officers and Commissioners of His Majesty's Navy that the Articles of war and abstract of the Act of Parliament for the encouragement of seamen etc were read on board His Majestys Sloop *Discovery* between the 1st of April 1791 and the date hereof as prescribed by the said Act.

Dated on board His Majestys said Sloop at sea the 31st May 1791

(Signed) Geo. Vancouver, *Capt.*
J. Whidbey, *Master*
Thos. Keld, *Boatswain*

MUSTER TABLE OF HIS MAJESTY'S SHIP THE *CHATHAM* ARMED TENDER BETWEEN THE 1ST DAY OF MAY AND THE 30TH DAY OF JUNE 1791 INCLUSIVE

COMPLEMENT 45 MEN

Men's Names	Qualities	Place and County Were Born	Age
Wm. Robt. Broughton	Lieut. & Commander		
James Hanson	2nd Lieut.		
James Johnstone	Master		
Wm. Wager	Q'R Mt'r	Hull	23
David Dorman	A. B.	Whitchaven	21
Adam Brown	A. B.	London	17
Charles Maskill	A. B. afterwards Q'nd M'r Mate	Newbury Bucks	25
John Messingham	A. B.	Lynn Norfolk	22
William Gamble	A. B.	Lynn Norfolk	22
John Wilkinson	Q'r M'tr Mate	Mansfield	26
Edward Bell	Clk.	Dublin	20
Sandford Martin	Carp'r		
Wm. Gifford	Gunner		
Wm. Walker 2nd,	Surgeon		
John Rycraft	A. B.	Yarmouth	24
Thos. Heddington	Mid.	Chatham	15
Chas. Guthrie	Bo. Mte.	Edinborough	23
Thos. Miller	Q'r M'tr	London	45
Wm. House	Boats'n		
Wm. Howard	Gun'r Mate	London	29
John Rogers	Q'r M'tr Mate	Waterford Ireland	35
James Beckett	Carp. Mate	Eastbourne	30

APPENDIX

Men's Names	Qualities	Place and County Were Born	Age
James Webster	Bo. M'te	Dundee	35
Hawkins Lloyd	A. B.	Sunderland	22
James Robinson	A. B.	London	21
Thomas Deacon	A. B.	Sheffield	19
David Munro	A. B.	Gosport	18
Geo. Rosewell	A. B.	Salisbury	18
Wm. Bennett	A. B.	Workshop Nottingham	22
John Best	Cook		
James Bray	Carp'r		
William Nicholl	Surgeon Mate		
John Sheriff	Master's Mate		
James Wood Scott	Mid.		
John Miller Garnier	Mid.		
Wm. Le Meswier	M'r Mte. to 31 Mar. '91 then A. B.		
Henry Barfleur	A. B.		
Thomas Young	A. B.	London	20
James Etchinson	A. B.	Arnech, Northum'ld	34
Edward Williams	A. B.	Carnarvon	27
Thomas Townsend	Q'r M'r after Sailmaker	Sunderland	27
William Willson	Q'r M'r Mate	Rotherhithe	25
Aug's Boyd Grant	Mid.	Dublin	18
Edmund Atkinson	M'r Mate	Carlisle	22
James Coote	A. B.	Queen's County Ireland	18

These are to certify the Principal Officers and Commissioners of His Majesty's Navy that the Articles of War and the Abstract of the Act of Parliament were read to the Ship's Company agreeable to the general printed instructions.

(Signed) W. R. Broughton, *Lieut. & Commander*
J. Johnstone, *Master*
William House, *Boatswain*

Marines borne as part of the Complement p Admiralty Order: —

Sergt John Fellbrook; privates John Rose, Peter Farris, James Landon, John Langley, Wm. Clark, Richard Stephens, Arthur Botting, John Reyners, Josh Potten.

(Signed) W. R. Broughton, *Lieut. & Comm'd*
J. Johnstone, *Master*
William House, *Boatswain*

INDEX

Admirals, degrees and grades of, 3.
Admiralty Inlet named, 166.
Adventurer, schooner built at Clayoquot by Americans, 34.
Agricultural possibilities of the country, 120.
Alaska, discovery of, 22.
Alava, General, 39.
Alberni Canal, 26.
Alberni Document, 36.
Alleviation Island named, 235.
American captains appear on the coast, 32.
Anian, fabled Straits of, 1.
Anvil Island named, 191.
Appendix: Muster tables of *Discovery* and *Chatham*, 335.
Arriago, 38.
Arrival of Vancouver at Nootka, 302.
Artists with Vancouver, 47.
Asiatic origin of Indians, 4.
"Astoria," 47.
Australia, 12.

Baker, Joseph, biography of, 82.
Barclay, Captain, 26.
Barclay Sound, 26.
Barrington, Daines, "Miscellanies," 4.
Bellingham Bay named, 209.
Bellingham, Sir William, biography of, 209.
Bering, Vitus, 22.
Biography of Bodega y Quadra, 50.
Biography of Vancouver, 7.
Birch Bay named, 210.
Bodega y Quadra, 4, 23, 50.
"Boston-man," 46.
Boston owners of first American ships in the Pacific, 34.
Brabant, Rev. Father A. J., 44.
Brig *Venus* met, 289.
British ships and crews seized by Spaniards at Nootka, 32.
Broughton's Archipelago named, 264.

Broughton, William Robert, 13, 52; biography of, 264.
Burial customs of the Indians, 124.
Burial-place of Vancouver, 20.
Burrard Inlet named, 188.
Burrard, Sir Harry, biography of, 188.
Bute, John Stuart, Third Earl of, biography of, 223.
Bute's Canal named, 223.

Caamano, Lieutenant Jacinto, 38.
Call, Sir John, biography of, 261.
Call's Channel named, 261.
Calvert's Islands, 283.
Camelford, Lord, remarkable record of, 15.
Canal de Haro, 2.
Cape Disappointment, 62.
Cape Flattery, 73.
Cavalho, of Macao, 27.
Chatham, armed tender, 12.
Chatham, muster table, 339.
Chatham, Second Earl of, biography of, 245.
Cheslakees, Indian Chief, 252, 255, 258, 267.
China, 11.
Chinese laborers at Nootka, 28.
Chinook Jargon, birthplace of, 44.
Clayoquot Sound, 28, 71.
Colnett, Captain, 26.
Columbia River, discovery of, 35; Vancouver denies its existence, 84.
Commerce at Nootka, 329.
Cook, Captain James, 9, 23, 24.
Cook Inlet examined, 13.
Coolidge, Captain R. D., 35.
Cranstoun, Surgeon, discharged, 318.
Cypress Island named, 177.

Dædalus, storeship, 290.
Davidson, Professor George, tribute to Vancouver, 21, 69, 81.
Deception Bay, 62.

INDEX

Deception Passage named, 178.
Deep Sea Bluff named, 263.
De Fuca, Juan, Strait of, 27, 29, 67.
Departure from Nootka, 334.
Desolation Sound named, 229.
Destruction Island, 65.
Discipline, Vancouver criticised for, 15.
Discovery, muster table, 335; sloop of war, 3; sloop on the rocks, 276.
Dixon, George, 26.
Douglas, William, 27.
Drake, Sir Francis, 22.
Duffin, Robert, testimony at Nootka, 325.
Duncan, Captain, 26.
Duncan Rock, 74.
Dungeness, New, 79.

Early sovereignty, relative claims, 5.
Elisa, Lieutenant Francisco, 36.
Exploring expedition, complete list of party, Appendix, 335.

Fidalgo, Lieutenant Salvador, 36.
Fife's Passage named, 266.
Fireworks displayed, 318.
First picture made of Mount Rainier, 138.
Fitzhugh Sound, 26, 283.
Flags lowered at Nootka, 39.
Foulweather Bluff named, 102.
Friend Penn, 165.
Fur hunters begin harvest, 25.

Gallians, Dionisio, 38.
Gardner, Sir Alan, 10, 11; biography of, 169.
Geographic names, summary of, 5.
George III, 2; biography of, 167.
Georgia, Gulf of, 2.
Gosnell, R. E., 37, 51.
Gower, Sir Erasmus, biography of, 196.
Gray, Captain Robert, 32, 69.
Gray's crew escape massacre, 72.
Gray's Harbor, discovery of, 35.
Grenville, Lord, biography of, 64.
Grey, Captain George, biography of, 185.
Gulf of Georgia named, 167.
Guyraldo, 38.

Hanna, James, 25.

Hardwicke, Third Earl of, biography of, 238.
Hardwicke's Island named, 238.
Harwood, Edward, 214.
Harwood's Island named, 214.
Haswell, Robert, 34.
Hazel Point named, 105.
Hood, Lord, 2; biography of, 109.
Hood's Canal named, 109.
Howe, Admiral Earl, 2; biography of, 193.
Howe's Sound named, 193.

Indian children offered for sale, 92.
Indians, observations of, 4, 85, 124, 131, 139, 147, 162, 186, 198, 221, 233, 257.
Ingraham, Captain Joseph, 35, 320.
Iron and copper among Indians, 38.

Jervis, Admiral Sir John, biography of, 202.
Jervis's Canal named, 202.
Jesup Expedition, 4.
Jewitt, John R., enslaved by Nootka Indians, 41.
Jewitt's Journal read at Nootka one hundred years later, 47.
Johnstone, James, biography of, 237.
Johnstone's Straits named, 237.
Juan de Fuca, Straits of, 26.

Kendrick, Captain John, 33.
"King George-man," 46.
Knight, Sir John, biography of, 262.
Knight's Channel named, 262.

Loughborough, First Baron, biography of, 230.
Loughborough's Channel named, 230.

McGee, Captain James, 35.
McKey, with Nootka Indians, 26.
Maquinna, Chief of Nootka Indians, 28, 41, 233, 236, 249, 252, 258, 303, 314.
Marrowstone Point named, 99.
Marshall, William, biography of, 213.
Meares, John, 26, 27.
Meeting between American and British captains, 69.
Menzies, Archibald, 70; biography of, 295; promoted to surgeon's place, 319.

342

INDEX

Monroe Doctrine, beginning of, 10.
"Most lovely country," 128.
Mount Baker, 82.
Mount Chatham, 3.
Mount Olympus named, 29.
Mount Rainier named, 99.
Mount Stephens named, 271.
Mudge, Zachary, biography of, 226; sent home with despatches, 330.
Murder of Spanish boy at Nootka, 322.
Mysterious poles erected by Indians, 85.

Neab Bay, name of, 307.
Neale, Sir Harry Burrard, 188.
Negotiations of diplomacy between Quadra and Vancouver, 304.
New Albion, 70, 114.
New Dungeness, 79.
New Georgia, 2; name conferred, 168.
New Hanover, 2.
New Holland, 12.
New Zealand, 13.
"No Body Knows What," 12.
Nootka Controversy, 32.
Nootka Convention, 10.
Nootka Monument, 46.
Nootka Sound, 11, 22.
Northwest America, first vessel built on this coast, 30.

Oak Cove named, 102.
Observatory work at Birch Bay, 211.
Observatory work at Nootka, 332.
Observatory work at Port Discovery, 115.
Official list of the members of the Vancouver expedition, 335.
Orchard, H. M., biography of, 135.

Passage Island named, 191.
Pearl Rocks, 284.
Penn's Cove named, 165.
Perez, Juan, 23.
Pierce, Lieutenant Thomas, 39.
Point Addenbrooke named, 293.
Point Atkinson named, 190.
Point Boyles named, 273.
Point Chatham named, 245.
Point Duff named, 266.
Point Gordon named, 266.
Point Gower named, 196.
Point Grenville, 64.

Point Grey named, 185.
Point Marshall named, 213.
Point Mary named, 219.
Point Menzies named, 295.
Point Mudge named, 226.
Point Partridge named, 173.
Point Philip named, 270.
Point Roberts named, 182.
Point Sarah named, 219.
Point Upwood named, 205.
Point Wilson named, 174.
Poles at New Dungeness, 85.
Port Cox, 28.
Port Discovery, 3; named, 89.
Port Gardner named, 169.
Portlock, Nathaniel, 26.
Port Neville named, 252.
Port Orchard named, 135.
Portraits of Vancouver, 19.
Port Susan named, 169.
Port Townshend named, 95.
Potlatch, meaning of, 44.
Promotion of officers, 330.
Prophecy of future greatness of the country, 4.
Protection Island, 89.
Puget, Peter, 2, 70; biography of, 148.
Puget Sound, 1; name conferred, 147.

Quadra and Vancouver Island, 51; partnership name conferred, 317.
Quadra, Bodega y, 4, 23, 50.
Queen Charlotte, biography of, 282.
Queen Charlotte Islands, 71.
Queen Charlotte Sound, 282.
Quimper, Ensign Manuel, 36.

Rainier, Rear-Admiral, biography of, 99.
Restoration Point named, 156.
Rivers, First Baron, biography of, 292.
Rivers's Channel named, 292.
Roberts, Captain Henry, 10, 11; biography of, 182.
Rosario Strait, 2, 38.
Royal Academy of History at Madrid aids in working up life of Quadra, 55.

Safety Cove, 295.
St. Patrick's Bay, 26.
Salter, Captain John, massacre of his crew at Nootka, 40.

INDEX

Sandwich Islands ceded to Great Britain through Vancouver, 14.
San Juan County, 3.
San Lorenzo, former name of Nootka Sound, 23.
Santa Rosalia, former name of Mount Olympus, 29.
Savary's Island named, 215.
Scotch-Fir Point named, 202.
Scot's Island, 301.
Sea Otter Harbor, 26.
Shoalwater Bay discovered, 29.
Smith Inlet, 26, 283.
"Some Body Knows What," 13.
Spaniards met by Vancouver, 206.
Spaniards seize British ships and crews at Nootka, 32.
Spanish Armament, the, 10.
Spanish names, temporary, 38.
Spanish occupation of Nootka, 36.
Stephens, Sir Philip, biography of, 270.
Stewart, John, extracts from the sailor's log, 15.
Straits of Juan de Fuca, 67.
Strange, James, 26.
Strawberry Bay named, 174.
Sturgeon Bank named, 208.

Tatootch, Chief, 29.
Texada Island, 206.
Thompson, John, enslaved by Indians at Nootka, 42.

Thurlow, First Baron, biography of, 247.
Thurlow's Island named, 247.
Tonquin, destruction of, by Indians, 48.
Townshend, Marquis, biography of, 95.
Tragedy on ship *Boston*, 40.
Trees observed, 118.

United States Coast Survey, 2, 3.

Valdes, Cayetano, 38.
Vancouver, Captain George, 1, 2, 3, biography of, 7, 25.
Vancouver, John, 7.
Vashon, Captain James, biography of, 145.
Vashon Island named, 145.
Virgin Rocks, 284.
Visit to Maquinna at Tahsheis, 314.

Warm Spring discovered, 274.
Washington, George, 2, 10.
Washington Sound, 2, 3.
Washington, Territory of, 2.
Wells's Passage named, 272.
Whidbey, Joseph, 86; biography of, 178.
Whidbey's Island named, 178.
White slaves among the Indians, 29.
Willapa Harbor, new name of Shoalwater Bay, 29.
Wilson, George, biography of, 174.

Yankee bargain with the Indians, 34.

OTHER BOOKS BY VERTVOLTA PRESS

PIONEER DAYS ON PUGET SOUND, by Arthur A. Denny

978-1-60944-051-0, $11.00

D'ORCY'S AIRSHIP MANUAL: *An International Register of Airships With A Compendium of the Airship's Elementary Mechanics*, by Baron Ladislas D'Orcy

978-1-60944-126-5, $19.95

ANARCHISM AND OTHER ESSAYS, by EMMA GOLDMAN

978-1-60944-113-5, $14.00

THE GROWING DISCONTENT OF THE MASSES: *Three Essays on the Social Condition*, by EMMA GOLDMAN

978-1-60944-139-5, $7.99

CONTRADICTIONS & CONTRACEPTION: *Essays on Feminism and Social Justice*, by EMMA GOLDMAN

978-1-60944-163-0, $13.99

BE AS IRRITABLE AND QUARRELSOME AS POSSIBLE: *The Simple Sabotage Field Manual in the 21st Century*, by OFFICE OF STRETEGIC SERVICES

978-1-60944-167-8, $9.00

FRANKENSTEIN: OR, THE MODERN PROMETHEUS. 1818 EDITION (BOOKSELLERS' PREFERRED EDITION), by MARY SHELLEY

978-1-60944-124-1, $14.99

WHITE NIGHTS, by FYODOR DOSTOEVSKY

978-1-60944-168-5, $10.99

THE KING IN YELLOW: *and Other Stories*, by ROBERT W. CHAMBERS

978-1-60944-096-1, $15.00

ASHENDEN: *or, The British Agent*, by W. SOMERSET MAUGHAM

978-1-60944-096-1, $14.99

THE MERCURIAN: *Three Tales of Eric John Stark*, by LEIGH BRACKETT

978-1-60944-138-8, $13.99

www.ingramcontent.com/pod-product-compliance
Lightning Source LLC
Chambersburg PA
CBHW030441090526
44586CB00044B/449